Competence
in the Learning Society

E D I T E D   B Y

John Raven & John Stephenson

PETER LANG
New York • Washington, D.C./Baltimore • Bern
Frankfurt am Main • Berlin • Brussels • Vienna • Oxford

Library of Congress Cataloging-in-Publication Data

Competence in the learning society / edited
by John Raven and John Stephenson.
p. cm. — (Counterpoints; vol. 166)
Includes bibliographical references.
1. Organizational learning. 2. Knowledge management. I. Raven, John. II.
Stephenson, John. III. Counterpoints (New York, N.Y.); vol. 166.
HD58.82 .C65   658.4'038—dc21   2001029030
ISBN 0-8204-5164-9
ISSN 1058-1634

Die Deutsche Bibliothek-CIP-Einheitsaufnahme

Competence in the learning society / ed. by: John Raven and John Stephenson.
–New York; Washington, D.C./Baltimore; Bern;
Frankfurt am Main; Berlin; Brussels; Vienna; Oxford: Lang.
(Counterpoints; Vol. 166)
ISBN 0-8204-5164-9

Cover design by Joni Holst

The paper in this book meets the guidelines for permanence and durability
of the Committee on Production Guidelines for Book Longevity
of the Council of Library Resources.

Printed in the United States of America

Contents

Foreword

John Stephenson
John Raven

This book has been produced in an effort to, on the one hand, contribute a Capability perspective to the worldwide Competency-Based Education movement and, on the other, rescue considerable achievements of the latter that are in danger of being submerged.

The competence-based education (CBE) movement is a response to the widespread recognition that the educational system rarely delivers the benefits that most people hope for and expect. Those who advocate CBE argue that teachers and lecturers need to focus on helping pupils and students develop the competencies they need to carry out various kinds of activity instead of filling their heads with information.

Unfortunately, despite recent worldwide work on competencies variously described as key skills, core skills, enterprise skills, life skills, and personal transferable skills, the competencies that are to be nurtured, the ways in which they are to be nurtured, and the ways in which they are to be assessed remain unclear. Perhaps worse, even the *way* to make explicit—that is, the way to conceptualise—the competencies that are to be fostered so that they *can* be nurtured remains unclear.

Insofar as attempts are made to engage with these problems, the chosen route—via the decrees of authorities (often administrators) and the deliberations of working groups and committees—is, as is powerfully illustrated in this book and, perhaps more fully, in its companion (O'Reilly, Cunningham, & Lester, 1999), inappropriate.[1] Fundamental and adventurous empirical research is required.

Most of the committees of enquiry which have been set up have produced long lists of fragmented knowledge, which, it is argued, may possibly one day be useful to the incumbents of the occupational groups concerned. The fact that these bits of knowledge do not meet students' needs to learn how to *do* (rather than to regurgitate information) is justified on the grounds that such knowledge "underpins high-level competence." And the assessment procedures prescribed by these working groups and administrators generally consist of tests of knowledge or demonstration of low-level skills.

This suggests that at least one sector of those who have advocated CBE have failed to articulate both the nature of the problem that the educational system needs to address and the kind of response that is required.

This absence of an adequate conceptual base has left the movement open to a pincer-like attack which will, we believe, undermine its credibility unless steps are taken to redress the situation.

On the one flank, the movement is open to attack by academics—like Barrett and Depinet (1991)—who are, on the one hand, fundamentally correct when they argue that those who advocated CBE and alternative assessments in the early 1960s have not delivered on their promises, but who, on the other, fail to understand:

(1) the practical problems recognition of which has fuelled the movement,
(2) the deficiencies in (a) the image of science and (b) both the specific psychometric model and the wider concepts of validation with which they themselves are working—and hence the impossibility of researchers working in the area meeting the criteria they think they have a right to expect, and
(3) the paradigm shift that is required to do better.

On the other flank, what has become a huge multibillion-dollar international CBE movement contains—as Alison Wolf so clearly demonstrates below—more than the seeds of its own destruction. This immense programme simply does not deliver in terms of solving the problems that led to its introduction. Its courses and assessments, despite their introductory rhetoric, are mainly comprised of the very kinds of knowledge with which the general public has become so uncomfortable and which the movement's political spokespersons have so widely attacked.

It emerges that the mainstream CBE programme, like other prescriptions stemming from central institutions, mainly operates to create a false impression that the problem is understood and being vigorously attacked.

Governments must be seen to be doing *something*. It is not a serious attempt to identify and introduce the developments that are so badly needed.

A somewhat separated response to the malaise of the educational system are the formulations of *Education for Capability* network. This was initiated in 1980 by the Royal Society for the Encouragement of Arts, Manufactures, and Commerce (RSA). The movement approached the promotion of competence by working within schools, colleges, and universities. Since 1988, Higher Education for Capability (HEC) has promoted debate about the nature of capability and ways of nurturing it within the university sector. The notion of capability has attracted academics who reject a narrowly defined notion of competence and who seek to embrace qualities such as commitment, values, creativity, courage, and intuition—all of which are perceived to be both essential to effective performance and missing from the fragmented, narrowly focused, vocational skills that mainstream variants of CBE seem to be promoting. Moreover, in the higher education context, capability is interwoven within specialist knowledge, both in its development and in its application.

Two aspects of capability are proving particularly attractive to higher education. The first is that capability is acknowledged to be an all-around human quality, an integration of skills, knowledge, understanding, and personal qualities. The second is the emphasis on the development of personal commitment by giving students experience of being responsible and accountable for managing and demonstrating their own learning and development. The capacity for autonomous learning and development meets the interests of two very different groups: (1) the research communities (the traditional destination of "the best" students) and (2) employers faced with managing rapid change without the supervisory role of middle managers.

In curriculum development terms, a capability approach differs dramatically from those CBE approaches which predetermine learning outcomes and test their achievement. A capability curriculum encourages learners to (1) engage in explorations of their own needs and the needs of the field they wish to enter, (2) negotiate approval for particular outcomes and their plans for achieving those outcomes, and (3) propose ways in which they might demonstrate their achievement to appropriate bodies. This approach, particularly the obligation to negotiate both the content and the means of demonstrating achievement with relevant authorities, not only helps students to achieve *specific* competence relevant to their chosen field but also helps students develop a range of "soft"—generic or personal—skills and qualities such as problem-formulation, courage, creativity, decision-making, interaction, and negotiation skills. In a higher education context, this approach also takes students into deeper levels of learning and to higher levels of conceptual capability.

The capability movement is beginning to identify the kinds of high-level skills that another part of the other tradition—the high-level competency movement—is also seeking to identify. Part of the problem of communication between the two groups is the use of language. Even the word "competence" causes concern amongst many academics because of the dominance of the low-level, minimal-competence, sector within the competence movement. Proponents of CBE have failed to communicate (or academics have failed to understand) that competence can and does embrace the holistic integration of human qualities, skills, and knowledge that the capability group admires. Both groups can come together on a common commitment to the promotion of autonomous learning and development.

Although about 20% of those working within the competency movement are concerned with high-level generic competencies, and despite the outstanding contributions made by those who have worked in what may be called the "McClelland tradition" over the past 35 years—especially Lyle and Signe Spencer, Murray Dalziel, George Klemp, Richard Boyatzis, Sheila Huff, and David Kolb (all of whose work is represented in this book)—there is still an urgent need to reconceptualise competence and the way in which high-level competencies interact with organisational, institutional, and cultural variables to produce different kinds of effect.

The absence of appropriate assessment procedures is of particular importance because what happens in educational institutions is primarily determined by what is assessed. Unless students can get credit for having developed high-level competencies, both lecturers and students tend to be unwilling to spend time on relevant activities.

We find these observations particularly distressing because, so far as we can see, the key insights required to reconceptualise competence and psychometrics were embedded in work carried out and published by McClelland and his colleagues more than 40 years ago.

The primary aim of this book is, therefore, to draw on the experiences of the different groups represented within it to achieve greater conceptual and methodological clarity about the nature of competence and/or capability and its assessment so that educators, policy makers, and employers can work more effectively together on its delivery and, perhaps even more important, to promote wider recognition of the *need* for a major programme of research and development in the area.

But, alongside these major aims, another has grown up. In the course of the conferences HEC has organised to encourage practitioners working in the area to share their experiences and learn from each other, it has become clear that a great deal needs to be done to disseminate what is actually already known about the nature, development, and assessment of competence; the barriers to effective work in the area; and the kinds of action research, evaluation, and programme development that are required. A secondary aim of this book—which strongly supports the first— is, therefore, to disseminate some of this information. But we hope that one of the strongest impressions to emerge will be that, while previous research has indeed been too limited in quantity and creativity, one of the most serious problems has been that very little has been targeted at understanding the systems processes that result in the perpetuation of the current social and economic system despite almost universal recognition of its faults and awareness of what ought to be happening. In this way, the material that will be presented raises serious questions about the competencies of academics and, to make the point in terms more suited to a capability perspective, their levels of capability—the levels of vision, efficacy, and responsibility that are required to get together with others to gain control over the institutional constraints on their work.

In fact, the book will start and finish by looking at these wider constraints. It will begin by exploring what is meant by a "learning society," the developments that such a learning society most urgently needs to bring about, and the implications for the competencies to be nurtured in the educational system. We hope this will provide readers with a vantage point from which to view what follows. Thereafter, having reviewed material on goals, competencies, possible activities, and potential assessments, we come back to the question of the systemic barriers to change in education and the developments needed to overcome them. In this way, the educational system will itself be used as a case study to underline the importance of the very topics with which the book is most centrally concerned.

Note

1. It was initially intended to produce a single book of papers arising out of the
    conferences organised by Higher Education for Capability, but there were too
    many. A loose division was therefore made between those that focussed on the
    conceptualisation, development, and assessment of competence and those that
    shared working experience. Nevertheless it became clear that both books would
    be incomplete without certain papers. These chapters therefore appear both here
    and in O'Reilly, Cunningham, and Lester (1999).

References

Barrett, G. V., & Depinet, R. L. (1991). A reconsideration of testing for competence rather than intelligence. *American Psychologist, 46* (10), 1012–1024.

O'Reilly, D., Cunningham, L., & Lester, S. (Eds.). (1999). *Developing the Capable Professional*. London, UK: Kogan Page.

Preface

This book has deep roots in the past. Both editors have been associated with competency oriented education since the 1960s. We watched with concern as, it seemed to us, the competency-based education movement focussed on minutia and lost sight of the wider problems of education and their potential solution. At the heart of this, we felt, lay a failure to develop an adequate framework for thinking about, and discussing, high-level competencies.

In the UK, our concerns were articulated in a *Capability Manifesto,* generated by a pressure group—"Education for Capability"—set up under the auspices of the Royal Society for Arts. One of us—John Stephenson— became Director of *Higher Education for Capability* (HEC). HEC generated most of its income by running workshops for the many people who had become involved in various government-supported competency-oriented initiatives. Most of those initiatives, it seemed to us, were unduly narrow and the proposed and prescribed forms of assessment unfortunate.

We therefore sought to mount a small seminar on *The Conceptualisation of Competence.* We invited as many as possible of those whose reputations for work in this area we respected to attend at their own expense. Somewhat to our surprise, many did so. But, for us, the conference was disappointing. As far as we could see, most of those who attended did not share our perspective on the nature of the problem and the way forward.

At the same time, many of the participants in the HEC workshops seemed unaware of, or unable to use, some of the knowledge that was available. Many of those who had attended the invitational seminar—as well as others—were therefore invited to address the HEC workshops.

Acknowledgments

With the following exceptions, the copyright of the individual chapters
rests with their authors.

Incompetence: An Unspoken Consensus by *Irene Ilott*. Partially reproduced from a longer version which appeared as Chapter 2 in *Success and Failure in Professional Education: Assessing the Evidence* edited by I. Ilott and R. Murphy. © Whurr Publishers, Ltd.,
1999.

Professional Capability—Requirements and Accreditation in the Legal
Profession by *Diana Tribe*. Reproduced from Chapter 11 in *Devel-
oping the Capable Professional, Professional Capability through
Higher Education* edited by D. O'Reilly, L. Cunningham, and S.
Lester. © Kogan Page, 1999.

The Crisis of Professional Knowledge and the Pursuit of an Epistemology
of Practice by *Donald Schön*. Reprinted by permission of Harvard
Business School Press. From *Teaching and the Case Method, Instruction Guide* by Louis Barnes, C. Roland Christensen with Abby
J. Hansen, Boston, MA, 1987, pp. 241–254. Copyright © 1984
by the President and Fellows of Harvard College, all rights reserved.

Essentials of Action Learning by *Reg Revans* edited by *David Botham* ©
Reg Revans. Previously published in *Link Up with Action Learning*, Vol. 1, No. 2, August–October, 1997, pp. 2-4.

Inputs and Outcomes: The Experience of Independent Study at North
East London Polytechnic by *John Stephenson*. Partially reproduced
from Chapter 20: "Creating the Conditions for Capability" by John
Stephenson and Mantz Yorke, in *Capability and Quality in Higher
Education* edited by J. Stephenson and M. Yorke. © Kogan Page,
1998.

Assessing the Self-Managing Learner: A Contradiction in Terms? by *Stan Lester*. Reproduced from Chapter 9 in *Developing the Capable Professional, Professional Capability through Higher Education* edited by D. O'Reilly, L. Cunningham, and S. Lester. © Kogan Page, 1999.

Beyond Competences: Lessons from Management Learning by *Ian Cunningham*. Reproduced with minor alterations from Chapter 17 in *Developing the Capable Professional, Professional Capability through Higher Education* edited by D. O'Reilly, L. Cunningham, and S. Lester. © Kogan Page, 1999.

Where Do We Stand on Assessing Competencies? by *David McClelland* is a heavily edited version of a much longer manuscript with the same title which was handed to the editors for consideration for inclusion in this book. It is © 2000 by Hay Acquisition Company I, Inc. and is printed here with their agreement. All rights reserved.

The Summary of Generic Competencies, and the summary of the scoring systems for "Developing Others" and "Impact and Influence" reproduced in Chapter 9, as well as the summaries of the scoring systems for "Achievement Orientation," "Analytical Thinking," and "Conceptual Thinking" in Chapter 15—all from McBer's *Scaled Competency Dictionary 1996*—are printed here by permission of the Hay Group and are © 1996 of Hay Acquisition Company I, Inc. All rights reserved.

The extracts from *A Brief Scoring Manual for Achievement Motivation* by D. C. McClelland and G. Litwin, (1967) reproduced in Chapter 15 are © Hay Acquisition Company I, Inc. They are printed here with permission from the Hay Group. All rights reserved.

The quotations from Rosabeth Moss Kanter in the chapter by Lynne Cunningham, come from *The Change Masters,* London, Unwin (1984) are © (1983) by Rosabeth Moss Kanter. They are reprinted here with the permission of Simon & Schuster.

PART I

SOCIETAL LEARNING
AND COMPETENCE

Chapter 1

Learning Societies, Learning Organisations, and Learning: Their Implications for Competence, Its Development, and Its Assessment

John Raven

In a sense, the aim of this chapter is to provide a foretaste of what is to come. One of the fundamental problems of the competence-based education movement is that, even when discussions of the competencies that are to be nurtured are grounded in empirical studies (itself a rare enough accomplishment), those studies have been backward looking. Most have been studies of the qualities required to perform narrowly defined aspects of current jobs effectively. They thereby ignore the qualities required to perform those aspects of current jobs that will contribute to future development and those required in future jobs. Moreover, it is surely vitally important to set any discussion of competence or capability in the context of an understanding of the competencies needed to establish, and function effectively in, learning organisations and a learning society.

One aim of this chapter is, therefore, to consider what is meant by the terms "learning society," "learning organisation," and "learning" with a view toward underlining the importance of high-level competencies or capabilities in modern society. In this way it is hoped to highlight the need for new thinking about the nature of such competencies, the means to be used to promote the development of many varieties and components of competence, and the assessment of competence.

That, in itself, sounds innocuous. But the implications are profound. It means that the objective here must be none other than to summarise what can be discerned about the problems of modern society, their causes, the institutional arrangements that are required to run society more effectively, and the competencies that are required to both introduce these developments and run the new society more effectively. This is a huge agenda. Condensing into one chapter what we have learned about the topic over the past 30 years has had the effect that the material comes across as cataclysmic on the one hand and unattainable on the other. The cataclysmic part is now beyond dispute. The particular institutional arrangements proposed as a way forward are debatable. But such a statement only underlines our main point—which is that we, as a society, need, through our educational system and elsewhere, to nurture the competencies—capabilities—that will lead to the rapid evolution of radically improved societal learning and management arrangements.

The Nature of a Learning Society

Our attempt to clarify key features of a learning society (and hence the competencies required to introduce and run such a society) may be begun by noting something to which Adam Smith and Fred Hayek drew attention. This is that any society that claims to be a "learning society" must have a *societal information-handling and management **system** which is capable of learning and managing **itself***.

The quintessence of the market mechanism as proposed by Smith was precisely this. No individual or group within the system had to know anything very much. As Hayek put it:

> "The peculiar character of the problem of rational economic order is determined precisely by the fact that the knowledge of which we must make use never exists in concentrated or integrated form but solely in the dispersed bits of incomplete and frequently contradictory knowledge which all the separate individuals possess.

> "Practically every individual has some advantage over all others because he possesses unique information of which beneficial use might be made, but of which use can only be made if the decisions depending on it are left to him or are made with his active co-operation.

> "If we can agree that the economic problem of society is mainly one of rapid adaptation to changes in the particular circumstances of time and place, it would seem to follow that the ultimate decisions must be left to the people who are familiar with those circumstances, who know directly of the relevant changes and of the resources immediately available to meet them. We cannot expect that this problem will be solved by first communicating all this knowledge to a central board which, after integrating all knowledge, issues its orders. We must solve it by some form of decentralisation."

The *system* proposed by Smith and Hayek to handle this problem would *itself* stimulate experimentation, evaluate those experiments, learn, and promote evolution and development. This would come about as people voted with their pennies independently on a myriad of issues. People did not have to articulate the reasons for their behaviour: they could vote on the basis of their feelings. They could buy products and invest in enterprises. Those who thought they knew better than others what their fellows needed could experiment, both individually and collectively. If other people liked what they did—perhaps because it enabled them to satisfy their needs more fully or more efficiently—the innovation would prosper. As developments built on each other, previously unimaginable developments would come about. There were endless possible connections and feedback loops. Numerous experiments would be initiated and fail. But the information available from "failed" experiments would not be lost. It would be picked up and used by others.

In sum, the proposal was for a messy, inefficient, organic, interconnected, and evolutionary learning and management system. Quintessentially, what was proposed was a means of empowering and handling *information*.

Nothing could differ more sharply from the kind of arrangements with which bureaucrats tend to feel comfortable. The preference of bureaucrats is usually for tidy, efficient, systems. They want to know beforehand what is to be achieved and how it is to be achieved. They design tidy systems for translating the prescriptions of "authorities"—who are often arrogant, power-hungry, self-styled "wise men" (politicians)—into reality. Because the outcomes of any action as it interacts with the effects of other people's actions are inherently unknowable, such individuals—or committees of wise men or women—are necessarily ignorant of most of the information which should be taken into account when coming to decisions. In practice, most authorities ignore most relevant existing information, are rarely much concerned about the long-term public welfare, and are typically uninterested in finding out whether their prescriptions work—still less in seeking to understand the *ways* in which they work (or do not work) and changing those prescriptions as a result.

Deficiencies of the Market Mechanism

Unfortunately, as documented at some length in my *New Wealth of Nations* (1995), it has now become clear that there are major problems with the market mechanism as a societal learning and management system.

These problems cannot be reviewed here in any detail, but a few examples must be given in order to underline the importance of developing an alternative. Problems with the market-based societal management include:

- Market behaviour is not easily influenced by a great deal of important information—especially information about the long-term societal consequences of actions that are in the short-term interests of many individuals. (Many examples of this "tragedy of the commons"[1] spring to mind, but perhaps the most striking is the way in which the world is pursuing the "American dream" of material prosperity despite the fact that, as Wackernagel and Rees (1996) have shown, for all the world to live as we live it would be necessary to have five backup planets doing nothing but generating agricultural produce.)
- Major costs—such as those involved in dealing with pollution, acid rain, and the destruction of the soils, the seas, and the atmosphere— are not counted when prices are being established in the marketplace. The costs are externalised to the environment, the future, or the Third World.
- The market does not, and cannot, deliver the most important ingredients in a high quality of life. This follows from the fact that such ingredients cannot be commoditised and bought and sold. Examples of such components include high-quality working life (i.e., a working life which offers opportunities to feel that one has made a difference and opportunities to develop and use one's talents), networks of friends who provide security against misfortune of a kind unavailable through commercial insurance, love, and companionship.
- The market drives down quality of life. For example, the quest to do things quickly and cheaply degrades the quality of working life. Concern to keep costs down results in a demand for lower taxes that in turn destroys the livability of cities, the standard of health care, the adequacy of transportation systems, and the quality of economic and physical planning systems.
- The market, somewhat surprisingly, does not reward the most important contributions to the generation of either financial wealth or a high quality of life. It does not, for example, reward wives for looking after husbands and children, providing therapy for stressed and sick workers, soothing family relationships, and creating a warm family atmosphere. It does not reward the most important contri-

butions to innovation, for these come from people who are long since dead, from people whose businesses went bankrupt, and from those who work in public research and development laboratories.

Besides these fundamental problems with the theory there are major practical problems. These include:

- Money—the "ball bearings" on which the system depends—has become unbelievably flaky. Within countries, banks lend nine times their assets and deposits. This lent "money," when deposited in another bank, is used to justify a further round of lending. Loans to governments, especially in the Third World, do not require *any* such security: All the "money" supposedly "lent" is fictional, that is, it has not had to be withdrawn from any other potentially productive activity. This process has resulted in money to the value of more than 30 times the total annual world product circulating round the globe to manage one-thirtieth of itself. The banks' demand for a lien on real estate as security for these "loans" has resulted in a process whereby the banks either have a lien on, or own outright, virtually everything. We do not live in a property-owning democracy but in a nation in hock. Individual attempts to manage one's financial affairs soundly are fruitless: One finds that one's government has mortgaged one's assets on one's behalf. One result of these processes is that money does not "circulate," as classical economists believed and required, but is sucked, at an ever-increasing rate, into the coffers of the banks.
- Although neither Smith nor Hayek claimed that the market mechanism was efficient in the bureaucratic sense, and notwithstanding more recent claims for its efficiency, it has become almost unbelievably *inefficient*: between 65 and 98% of the sales price of most goods and services delivered through the marketplace pays for distribution and advertising.
- Prices do not, as Smith and Hayek claimed, reflect true costs. The greatest costs are externalised to the future and the Third World. Nominal costs depend not on the costs of land, labour, and capital but mainly on the decisions of public servants about which costs to spread over the entire community, which to load onto producers, which to load onto the future, and which to externalise to the environment. One of the best-known examples of this concerns the costs of cleaning up pollution. When a nation decides to make the

polluter pay, the result is that that country's goods become uncompetitive in the international marketplace. But, as shown in *The New Wealth of Nations*, even the apparent efficiency of centralised production depends entirely on failing to make the producer pay the costs of highway construction, transportation, damage to the environment from the emissions of transportation, the costs of treating the injuries arising from accidents on the way to work, and so on.

- Public servants—not management or workers—mainly determine prices. They do this:
  a) Via the administrative arrangements they make. It is public servants, for example, who organise most of the research on which our agricultural production depends, disseminate the results of that research, make arrangements to stabilise prices so that farmers are not at the mercy of the elements, and set up marketing arrangements. It is public servants who organise or carry out (via defence budgets, MITI[2] etc.) most of the research on which our aeroplanes and computers depend.
  b) By deciding which costs to load onto manufacturers and distributors and which to spread over the whole community.
  c) By determining tax and grant systems. Taxes are raised in many different ways, and the balance of these methods and which taxes are deductible from the price of exports has a dramatic effect on the apparent competitiveness of that country's products.

More fundamentally, as previously indicated, since quality of life depends primarily on public provision (e.g., the livability of our cities, levels of crime, quality of water and sewerage systems, economic planning, agricultural policy, and publicly funded research and development), and since these things are organised by public servants, contrary to the impression given by Smith and Hayek, *public servants create wealth*.

In fact, the importance of doing the things that public servants do has had the result that the spending of some 75% of the Gross National Product is, in some sense, under government control.[3]

This has a number of serious implications:

- We do *not* live in market economies.
- There is enormous government overload: It is impossible for any small group of elected representatives to effectively supervise so much activity.

- The role of money in the economy has been reversed. Instead of money providing, via the marketplace, a means of establishing goals and orchestrating their achievement, control of cash flows is now used to bring about the achievement of goals set through the political and bureaucratic process.
- "Customers" are typically government departments, QUANGOS,[4] the TNCs,[5] or people complying with government directives. They are rarely individuals using their pennies to express their personal preferences. They are therefore much less cost and benefit conscious than classical economic theory requires.
- Since it is government agents who let most of the contracts for goods and services, privatisation does not, as is so often suggested, give more control to the public. It results in central governments having *more* control over what happens because they can prescribe all sorts of actions that the public service would not previously have been prepared to endorse and dismiss contractors who do not do what they want as "inefficient." Those contractors are even less easily influenced than are public servants by the clients the policies are supposed to serve because those clients are not their paymasters and because they are not pervaded by any public service ethic. (When the costs of tendering, accounting, and checking on whether contractors have delivered the services they contracted to provide are counted, the costs of such privatised services are typically *very much greater* than the costs of an unashamedly public service system, and one also gets a different—and typically inferior—product or service[6].)

So it seems that the market mechanism does *not* do what its proposers hoped it would do and what it is often claimed that it does do.

Latent Functions of the Market Mechanism
Clearly, we need an alternative. But, if we are to develop one, it behoves us to try to understand why it is so hard to dislodge whatever it is that we have that is typically misdescribed as a "market mechanism". What *does* it do? What are its latent functions?

I have argued in *The New Wealth of Nations* that one of the most important functions of the processes that are typically described as "the market mechanism" is to *manufacture* work for the hands which would otherwise have become idle as we have moved toward energy-negative, fossil-fuel-intensive, agriculture. Contrary to the claims that are made for it, the marketplace is the least efficient way of doing anything. It amounts to a huge job-creation programme. This will be illustrated by considering the effects of privatising insurance.

Insurance should be a simple matter of transferring resources from those who have them to those who do not. State provision is reasonably efficient in doing this, although the maze of means-tested benefits that has grown up over the past 50 years has led to an army of handbook-writers, accountants, administrators, assessors, advisors, lawyers, and appeals-procedure administrators—with the result that it could be rationalised in such a way as to become a great deal *more* efficient. Privatisation of the insurance industry creates middle-class jobs for people generating insurance packages, selling those packages, collecting and keeping account of small sums of money, assessing entitlement, pursuing legal wrangles, assessing the profitability of companies in which it might be suitable for an insurance company to invest, monitoring their profitability, and intervening in those companies to maximise the return to their investors or "owners". These "owners" actually turn out to include the pension schemes of post office workers, miners, and dockers—that is, much the same public that "owns" state insurance schemes. These owners and beneficiaries get much the same benefits as before. But it costs society vastly more to provide them. Not only does privatisation of the insurance industry create jobs within itself, it also creates jobs for a host of individual pension plan managers, researchers to conduct consumer surveys to determine which insurance company is offering the "best buy," and personal accountants and advisors to advise individuals on which plan is best for them and make appropriate tax arrangements. The privatised system transfers money from the less fortunate to the more fortunate: Those who are already unlucky enough to have been forced to change their employer in the course of their lives get miserable pensions so that the pensions of those who have already had secure employment can be maintained. And it externalises many of the costs to Third World countries (whose own companies are required by their new transnational insurance company owners to become more "profitable") and to future generations (because our children will have to pay more for their goods and services so that the companies concerned can make the profits that our insurance companies will require to pay the pensions of those of our generation that are lucky enough to get them).

Nor is this the end of the job-creation programme. The use of the market to provide pensions is one of the strongest factors driving the whole privatisation programme: Privatisation of post office workers' and miners' pension schemes created a demand for investment opportunities. This created a demand for the privatisation of other nationalised industries as well as a demand for their increased profitability and thus to pressures to downsize and hive off work to small private firms in which the insurance companies would *not* invest and which could therefore be exploited and forced to exploit their employees by evading social security (including pensions) legislation. This in turn created even greater demands for "education" to get into "good" jobs and for insurance against job losses.

The market mechanism also creates differentials that have the effect of impelling people to participate in the system in order to avoid the consequences of not doing so. Likewise, it induces them to engage in unethical behaviour—such as to misrepresent the social value of what they are doing in order to retain their jobs. It generates more of the "double-talk" that perpetuates the system. It thus induces acquiescence in behaviour which is not in the long-term public interest—that is, in immoral behaviour.

Market rhetoric also obscures: Claims about "economic realities," "privatisation," and so forth dominate discussion and thus prevent people noticing what is really going on.

In conclusion, then, not only does the market mechanism not perform the information-handling, learning, and societal management functions it was proposed as a means of carrying out—that is, not only does it not create a society which can learn and manage itself without anyone having to know more than a fraction of what needs to be known—market rhetoric also contributes to the perpetuation and maintenance of a series of sociological functions that help to perpetuate our destructive social system.

The Effectiveness of Public Management

We may turn now to the problems which have been experienced with current forms of public management in the hope of learning something about what we need to do to develop a societal learning and management system which will in fact meet the need so clearly identified by Smith and Hayek.

Our current arrangements for managing the public service are inadequate. One problem is that, as the market so clearly recognises, there is, in *every* area—education, health care, housing, transportation, and so on—not *one* public but numerous publics who have different needs and priorities. Yet a pervasive assumption in public policy is that all should be offered very nearly the same thing. This is nowhere more apparent than in the educational system, where the central prescription of what is to be learned, how it is to be learned, and how whether it has been learned is to be assessed has become an almost worldwide obsession.

Another pervasive problem has been the absence of effective evaluation procedures—never mind procedures that examine the relative merits of different products for different populations and seek to improve them in the way in which the market first responds to financial feedback and then stimulates research to evaluate and improve products.

The sums invested in market research and product development (though small in comparison with the sums spent on marketing existing products) in connection with relatively trivial goods and services supplied through the marketplace are huge in comparison with public investment in such research and development. Yet public-sector provisions are generally of very much greater importance than those offered through the marketplace.

Compared with the needs that market processes typically engage with and satisfy, the problems, provisions, and policies the public service is expected to handle are extremely complex. They include education, crime control, and ecologically oriented environmental management. Not only are the problems complex and difficult, the procedures and arrangements through which public servants are expected to tackle them are also dysfunctionally compartmentalised. For example, the first steps toward the improvement of health should really involve the redesign of living and working arrangements and changes in agricultural policy. Yet the links between the ministries of health, agriculture, and urban planning are both weak and inappropriate.

Recognition of the need for *systems* intervention has generally been interpreted as evidence of the need for systemwide intervention, although, as we shall see, the two are very different. The perceived need for systemwide intervention has led to an emphasis on centralised planning, and this in turn has led to a demand for larger and larger units—such as the European Community and the United Nations—although, as Smith and Hayek correctly observed—these cannot work.

The role of democratic institutions in the management of public provision has been fundamentally misunderstood. The observation of Aristotle and Mill that the function of democratic assemblies is not to govern ("a task for which they are eminently unsuited") but to "compel full justification of every act and make apparent to everyone who did everything," has been almost completely lost sight of. Governments clearly believe they have a right to command the public service, to determine what different sectors of the population will get, and to require the public service to conceal information that does not suit their purposes.

More seriously still, public management, like the marketplace, frequently functions in ways that actually run *counter* to the public interest. For example, public services often:

- Promote war and the development of nuclear, chemical, and biological weapons.
- Destroy societies by imposing "conditions in which the market can work." For example, there was no shortage of food in Ireland at the time of the Irish famine. The problem was that the British government ordered the food that there was to be shipped out of the country under armed guard "because it would be wrong to intervene in market processes." The same was true in the more recent Ethiopian famine: Huge quantities of grain were shipped out of Ethiopia to feed Europe's cattle. These examples are far from atypical. Market processes failed from the beginning to commend themselves to those they were supposed to benefit and were imposed by military force orchestrated by the "public service" for the benefit of those who controlled the organisations that benefited from the arrangements.
- Run "aid" programmes that suck money and educated personnel out of poor countries and communities. This is achieved by both demanding "interest" on loans of fictional money and "matching" funds "to demonstrate serious interest" from those communities. Both the "loan" and the matching funds are then typically spent in the West.
- Generate legislation that benefits the transnational corporations while presenting that legislation as benefiting the consumer.
- Promote "educational" systems whose main effect, as we shall see, is to perpetuate the social order.

Clearly, then, our most urgent need is to invent an alternative societal learning, information-handling, and management system to replace both the market mechanism and the kind of centralised bureaucratic management that we have. Where should we look for guidance on how to do this?

Learning Organisations

One place we might look is in the literature dealing with learning *organisations*. But here we come up against a problem. Most of those who have written about learning organisations—such as Senge (1990)—have not got beyond recognising the importance of systems analysis. Without in any way wishing to minimise the importance of systems thinking, one has to say that their writings are dominated by an authoritarian mindset. They assume that some*one*—some authority, some manager—will be able to know all and make good decisions about what to do. If any one thing should have become clear so far in this chapter, it is that this is naïve. No one person, or small group of people, can be in possession of more than a fraction of the relevant information.

Having learned from Smith and Hayek something about what to look for, let us therefore briefly comment on Kanter's *Change Masters*, although we will come back to this later. Kanter, like Klemp, Munger, and Spencer (1977) and Schön in *Beyond the Stable State* (1971), noted the importance of creating climates of innovation; of managers releasing the energies of others; of creating a messy, organic, ferment of innovation; of avoiding seeking to prescribe in advance what the outcome of activity directed toward innovation would be; of network working, of non-hierarchical working; of avoiding the attempt to prescribe in advance who is to perform various roles in working groups but instead allowing leaders, ideas persons, and so forth to *emerge* (and change) as the activities being carried out require; and of allowing the networks for learning and innovation to dissolve as their task is completed.

Kanter described this cluster of activities as "Parallel Organisation Activity Concerned with Innovation." She chose the term to highlight the fact that these activities, for which time and resources had to be set aside, went on *in parallel with* the day-to-day operation of the organisation. The *same people* created the innovations as carried out the day-to-day activities of the organisation, because *they*—as Hayek noted—knew the deficiencies in their methods, saw new possibilities, knew the organisational barriers, knew the reactions of customers, saw the potentialities of developments they stumbled across, and so on. But in the course of their "parallel organisation activities," they worked in a different relationship with each other, used different talents, and contributed in different ways.

What we have here is an account of organisational arrangements that make it possible for an organisation to monitor and learn from its environment—and enact the conclusions—in all sorts of different ways; to learn from the responses of customers, clients, and the wider environment and invent better ways of meeting their needs; to learn from "mere" operatives who have noted better ways of doing things and new things to do; to learn from those who have noted the possibility of running the organisation more effectively; to better utilise the idiosyncratic talents of its people; to create conditions in which its staff can *learn* to do new things—to lead, to invent, to put others at ease, to communicate, to . . . In essence, what we have is a description of arrangements which make it possible for an organisation *to learn in ways which go far beyond the learning of individuals*. No one, but no one, has to know more than a fraction of what the organisation as a whole knows and acts upon.

In effect then, we, looking at the work of Schön, Kanter, and Klemp et al. through the spectacles of Smith and Hayek, have seen something that these authors themselves do not appear to have seen. This may help to explain why, as is implied by these authors and as has been more recently demonstrated by Hogan (1990) and underlined by Lester in a later chapter, most organisations *don't* learn and, in due course, collapse.

Implications

It would seem, therefore, that two central questions to be addressed in the remainder of this chapter, and in this book as a whole, must be "What are we currently able to discern about the nature of the arrangements required for a learning society?" and "What competencies will people need to develop if they are to further clarify, introduce, and run such a society?"

It would seem that those who are to clarify and introduce an appropriate societal learning and management system need, above all, to be able to articulate the purposes of their activity—where they are trying to get to, in a sense their *values*—and be able to understand and influence social and political processes, legal systems, and cultural concerns, thoughtways, and assumptions. As I have shown in *Competence in Modern Society* (1984), these cultural values and assumptions and social and political processes are the main determinants of behaviour. Lees (1996) has made the point more succinctly in Diagram 1.1. Most attempts to introduce societal change through the development and deployment of competence—human resource management—have focussed on introducing changes in the processes at the centre of Lees' diagram. But it is obvious that if behaviour is mainly determined by the peripheral constraints, it is the competence to influence cultural values, economic assumptions, legal frameworks, and social and political processes that is most important. Put another way, the greatest source of incompetence in modern society

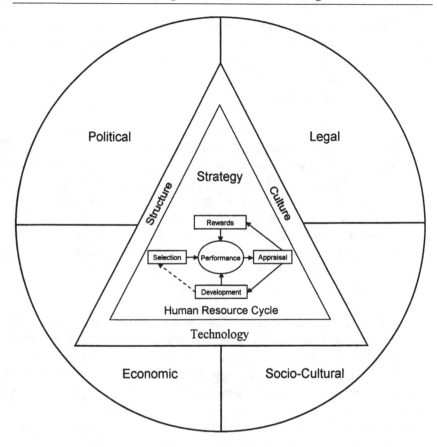

Diagram 1.1 The Context of Human Resource Management Practice. Reproduced, with permission, from Lees (1996)

is the unwillingness and inability to influence these wider social and political processes. It is what people do *outside* their jobs (as jobs are traditionally defined) that is most important.

A similar point has been made by Weaver (1994) and those who drew up the *Capability Manifesto*. However, unlike them, I am arguing that competence in modern society *inherently includes* the competence to influence the "external" constraints that otherwise undermine one's capability. It encompasses and requires the ability to consider the long-term societal (i.e., "moral") consequences of one's actions, the commitment to get together with others to act in the public interest, and the willingness and ability to clarify how society works and then change it in the public interest. As Lees' diagram emphasises, unless we recognise the need for people to engage in these activities, the framework within which we seek to build up our model of competence will be altogether too narrow and we will continue to wonder why individuals who appear to be competent continue to be incapable of carrying out vital activities.

Learning

Having explored some of the meanings and implications of the words "learning society" and "learning organisation," we turn now to the word "learning" itself. With the exception of its use to denote learning to read, to write, and to count, the word "learning" is generally used by educators to refer to learning *content*: to memorising a smattering of scientific truths and formulae, to learning the names of cities and the products for which they are famous, to memorising dates and famous battles, and to learning to decline irregular French verbs. The word is rarely used to refer to such things as learning to make one's own observations; learning to lead; learning to work with others; learning to clarify one's values; learning to invent; learning to initiate action, monitor its effects, and take corrective action; learning how to discover how organisations work; or learning how to influence them. One can learn to persuade, to put others at ease, to influence those above one, to control others, to gain preferment, to win affection, and so on. The list is almost endless.

Having noted that societies and organisations can learn and develop without anyone having to *know* anything very much, one is forced to ponder whether people can learn and behave competently without knowing very much. And, of course, as Schön and others have demonstrated—and again emphasise in the chapters that follow—they both can and do. Indeed, very little competent behaviour depends on formal *knowledge*.

The questions—to which we will come back in later chapters of this book—are: "What really are the competencies our pupils, students, superiors, subordinates, and fellow citizens need to develop?" "How can we most fruitfully think about these qualities?" "How *do* people learn to do these things?" "Why is it that our schools and universities so rarely promote such development and learning?" "What are the most important things for more people to learn to do if they are to influence the institutional constraints that prevent our educational establishments from nurturing these competencies?" "What are the talents which it is most important for more people to develop if we are to introduce a sustainable society? (For the introduction of such a society is dependent on the introduction of a learning society.)"

Part II
Why the Urgency?

Although we are now able to discern some of the features to be possessed by a genuine learning society and something about the competencies required to introduce and run it, and while we will shortly summarise the results of our research into the management of the educational system with a view toward further clarifying the nature of the developments needed in society and the educational system more narrowly if more high-level competencies are to be developed and utilised, it is worth stopping to ask why it is that so many people are now so anxious to create a more effective learning society.

The answer is that it has become widely apparent that public policy does not work as well as it should. This is nowhere more evident than in relation to social division and "economic development" on the one hand and conservation, protection of the environment, and sustainability on the other.

Fears about our economic survival have somehow coalesced with severe doubts about the actual viability and sustainability of our economic system to produce widespread feelings of malaise and recognition of an urgent need to dramatically change our way of life if there is to *be* a future—any future—for our planet in anything approaching its present form.

If we are to overcome these interrelated problems and survive as a species, we must develop a societal learning and management system that will, as a matter of course, initiate the collection of information relating to the long-term *societal* consequences of alternative courses of action, sift it for good ideas, and then initiate, and comprehensively evaluate, numerous experiments. No authoritarian system can meet the need.

Effective (societal) management depends on making new arrangements to initiate a host of innovative actions or experiments in every nook and cranny of society, on motivating individual action, and on obtaining and acting on information about the effectiveness of those actions considered both singly and in combination with actions initiated by others.

Arrangements that provide for comprehensive, continuous feedback are required because one cannot know in advance what the effects of individual actions are going to be—in part because the effects of what any one person or group does always depend on what others do.

In order to further underline the urgency of nurturing the competencies required to clarify the nature of, introduce, and run a learning society and contribute to dramatic societal change, let us look briefly at some of the problems which confront us.

Just to stop the destruction of the soils, the seas, and the atmosphere, it will be necessary to:

- Largely disband our centralised production and distribution arrangements (which means getting rid of about 25% of the economy as we know it).
- Dramatically reduce our CO_2 emissions (which means getting rid of most of our cars and the industries associated with them—including the hospital, legal, and insurance systems, the need for which our cars are so largely responsible for creating—that is, another 25% of our economy).
- Dismantle our so-called "defence"—that is, our industrial-military—system (which means another 25%).
- Replace our energy-intensive agricultural arrangements by much more human-resource–intensive, sustainable ways of doing things. (This will at least provide an opportunity to re-involve more people in productive activity.)
- Redesign our cities and working and living arrangements. (Doing this will also, in some ways fortunately, involve the creation of numerous new jobs.)

As if awareness of the need for all these reforms were not enough to make us quake at the enormity and urgency of the problem, the imminent collapse of our financial system means that it will be necessary to develop alternative means of stimulating and rewarding effort and providing such things as security in the face of disaster.

Put bluntly, we urgently need to rebuild our society on very different lines.

Given the daunting nature of this task, it is not surprising that so many people recognise the need but fail to take relevant action because they cannot see where to begin. More specifically, many people can see that they could recycle their beer cans or make less use of their cars, but most also recognise that the first is trivial and that the second will result in huge personal problems unless there are general systems changes that reduce the "need" for cars and that it will, in any case, fail to confer the desired benefits unless everyone else does the same.

Similar thoughts pass through their minds when they consider giving up jobs that contribute little to their own or other people's quality of life—

even those that they can see contribute dramatically to the destruction of the planet—or escaping from the non-developmental "education"[7] in which they find themselves trapped.

To assist in our quest for insights into the kinds of development that are needed, some of the results of our research on the educational system will now be briefly summarised. Unfortunately, as has been said, the attempt to condense what has been learned into a few pages—so that it can be built on later in this book—will, in the absence of the arguments on which the conclusions are based, necessarily give the impression of being utopian. However, if that is indeed the case, it only reinforces our more basic claim that there is an urgent need to clarify and nurture the capabilities that will quickly lead to the development of a workable alternative.

Managing the Educational System Effectively

When asked—and the results of numerous surveys are summarised in my *Managing Education for Effective Schooling* (1994)—most people say that the main goals of education include nurturing the confidence and initiative required to introduce change; helping people to identify, develop, and get recognition for their particular talents; and developing the talents needed to create a sustainable society.

Yet they realise that, not only do our educational institutions generally fail to nurture these qualities, most of what happens in most schools and universities is a waste of time. In seeking to handle the dissatisfaction that these observations cause, politicians of all political parties have little recourse to research. Like the wise men of Adam Smith's day, they *know* what should be done. Secure in the faith that they alone have the answers and that implementing them will result in changes that will secure votes in the next election, they use their power to prescribe what schools and universities should be doing, how it should be done, and how to determine whether it has been done. Feeling that it is necessary to exude confidence, and, in any case, not wishing to run the risk of collecting information that might be used against them, they usually fail to make arrangements to monitor the effects of the changes that are introduced in such a way that it would be possible to learn from what happens and do better in the future.

The result is the mess we all know about.

Actually, as we have studied why the educational system fails and what needs to be done to improve it, we have uncovered more and more barriers to its effective operation. These barriers, which are summarised in my

Managing Education, point to the need for some very surprising actions, almost endless interrelated developments, and much evaluated experimentation.

For a start, it has become clear that there is very little formal understanding of the nature of high-level competence, how its components are to be nurtured, or how the these competencies are to be assessed. The absence of appropriate assessment procedures is particularly important because teachers and lecturers teach, and pupils and students work, toward the goals that are assessed, particularly when those assessments control entry to further and higher education and jobs.

But there are more serious problems. Qualities such as the ability to make one's own observations, the ability to understand and intervene in society, and initiative are all heavily value-laden. As a result, as soon as a teacher, for example, even encourages children to ask questions and make their own observations, he or she is confronted by parents who angrily insist that their children should be taught to sit still, do as they are told, and pass their examinations.

One way of handling this problem would be to create a variety of distinctly different educational programmes, document the consequences of each, and feed that information to pupils and parents so that they could make informed choices between them.

But inventing ways of meeting clients' needs, generating variety and choice, and ensuring that each option is comprehensively evaluated requires public servants and teachers to do things they are not used to doing. So does feeding the information to the public and debating the value of options. More seriously, it bypasses traditional forms of bureaucratic accountability and the perceived (and self-perceived) role of politicians.

Our investigations into the reasons why the educational system fails to achieve its goals have revealed still more barriers of this sort. In the end they have led us to the surprising conclusion that if we are to move forward, it will be necessary to:

- Involve all teachers, in one way or another, in creating a general ferment of innovation to find ways of improving the curriculum, the assessment procedures that are available, and the interface between schools and the public. This means that one of the priorities is to set aside the time needed for teachers to become involved in "parallel organisation activity" in order to experiment and innovate in these areas. Another is to find ways of giving them credit for engaging in the difficult, demanding, frustrating, and often fruitless activities that are involved.

- Encourage public servants to create a variety of very different types of educational programme, demonstrate that each is of high quality, document the consequences of each, and feed that information outward to the public (so that parents and pupils can make meaningful choices between the options), not upward in a bureaucratic hierarchy to elected representatives who are expected to take decisions binding on all.

Implications for the Design of a Learning Society

It would seem to follow from these observations that if we are to manage public provision more effectively, we will need:

1. To change our expectations of public servants, to introduce very different job definitions for them, and to introduce staff-appraisal and organisational-appraisal procedures that will induce them to behave in very different ways.
2. New arrangements to promote a flow of information between the public service and the public.
3. New arrangements to ensure that public servants act on information in the long-term public interest. (Such arrangements will include exposing their behaviour more effectively to the public gaze.)
4. New arrangements to enable the public to influence what is going on, both directly and by exercising choice between a range of options that have been carefully developed to meet the needs of a cross-section of the population.
5. Arrangements for involving most people in a hive of monitored, systems-oriented, experimentation that will enable and induce them to contribute in one way or another to the difficult, demanding, and pervasive range of innovations that are required and give them credit for so doing.

It therefore emerges that the most fundamental and most important developments that are required will involve explicit experimentation and information collection on the one hand and new forms of bureaucracy and democracy on the other.

Among the things we most urgently require is a new understanding of the institutional arrangements and staff- and organisational-appraisal systems which are required to run a society characterised by messy, organic, evaluated, experimentation of the kind that Smith and Hayek sought to promote. In other words we need much more adventurous, fundamental but applied, social research.

Note the implications for the role of public servants. It emerges that their job is, above all, to introduce and manage an organic, societal, learning and management system that, like Smith's market mechanism, learns about, and acts appropriately on, its internal and external environment without more than a fraction of the necessary information having to be present in any one person's mind. It is *not* to introduce and run a managerial system based on "experts" and central control.

This means releasing, comprehensively evaluating, and learning from, experiments and thereafter taking appropriate action on the basis of the results.

Doing these things will involve:

1. Leading people to study and experiment with ways of tackling systems problems.
2. Arranging for *comprehensive* evaluations that will enable us to learn from the effects of action—and especially to learn about hidden systems processes and how to intervene in them. Comprehensive evaluation is required because most activities have effects which are undesired and undesirable as well as effects which are desired and desirable. But one can only move toward something which, in retrospect, can be recognised as a more (rather than a less) comprehensive evaluation if one studies outcomes which few people previously thought it was important to examine. This means that we must support the work of people who are regarded as cranks, heretics, and mavericks.
3. Ensuring that the results are disseminated and acted upon: This means disseminating the results through public debate to people who are held accountable for acting on information in the long-term public interest.

Creating a climate of innovation and experiment also means making arrangements for "parallel organisation activity," setting up network-based working arrangements, and linking such networks to appropriately managed policy research units.

All of this means changing current beliefs about the way public policy is to be administered and the way research is to be organised. This means changing our images of bureaucracy, democracy, and science.

As far as we can see, getting people to act on information in the public interest means that we need to introduce new staff appraisal criteria and expose more of their behaviour to the public gaze through professionally developed evaluation procedures in such a way as to induce them to be more likely to act in the public interest.

How are we to hold public servants accountable for:

- creating variety?
- arranging for comprehensive evaluation of each of the options?
- feeding this information to the public so that they can take better individual and collective decisions?
- drawing attention to factors that have been overlooked?
- taking genuine, discretionary, and often unpopular managerial decisions that are in the long-term public interest?
- making arrangements to monitor the effects of those decisions?
- changing their decisions in the light of experience?

If we are to encourage them to do these things, we will have to ask not whether specific decisions are correct—because that would discourage innovation and experiment—but whether those concerned have followed *procedures* that are likely to result in decisions that are *likely* to be in the long-term public interest. That is, we will have to focus on their *procedural* rather than their substantive rationality.

What *are* the procedures they should have followed? How are they to be held accountable for having followed them? As we have seen, we already know a fair amount from the work of Schön, Klemp et al., and Kanter about the procedures that are likely to lead to innovation, to the evaluation of decisions, and to the correction of mistakes. In principle, therefore, it should not be too difficult to find out whether they have followed these procedures.

To whom is information on whether our public servants do these things to be fed? How are we going to get them to *do* these things? It is obvious that it would be impossible for all this information about everyone who is responsible for creating a climate of innovation—from street-sweepers to senior public servants—to be monitored by any small centralised group of public representatives.

Instead, it will be necessary for all citizens to become involved in participative forms of democracy—in a network of monitoring groups having overlapping responsibilities and memberships to oversee the work of the public service. As previously mentioned, the function of the demos is not to govern, but to make apparent to everyone who did everything and in this way induce action in the public interest.

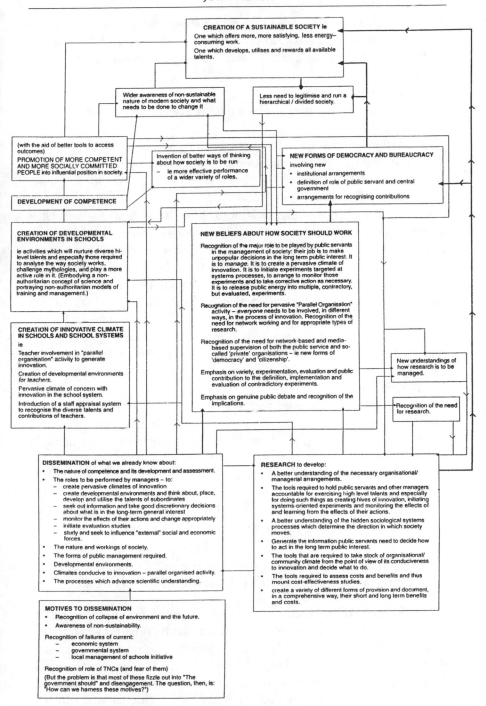

Diagram 1.2 The New Societal Management Arrangements.

The functions of citizen-network-based supervision of the public service are to expose, to assist, to promote a two-way flow of information and ideas, and to promote public debate. When we have a system which:

- generates information,
- leads to the invention of a better societal learning and management system,
- identifies problems and shows how they can be tackled,
- halts the dominators (the Stalins, Bushes, Amins, and Thatchers of this world),

we will at last have a workable system. More than that, we will have something of worldwide interest. The knowledge of how to run a sustainable society will flow across international boundaries. We will at last have means of intervening (as we must, if we are to survive as a species) in Europe more generally, in America, in China, and in the Third World: We will be able to show why certain activities should be stopped and others done; how these things are to be done, including how to intervene effectively in the doings of transnational corporations (including armaments manufacturers), and how to redeploy personnel without them suffering the huge economic consequences that would currently follow from the loss of their jobs.

The kinds of development that are required can again be illustrated from our work on education. They are portrayed in Diagram 1.2.

It would not be appropriate here to review the contents of this diagram in any detail. We will return to it in a later chapter. Attention may, however, be drawn to the fact that the two largest boxes are those dealing with research on the one hand and new beliefs about how society should work on the other. It may also be noted that the heaviest feedback lines are those running up the right-hand side of the diagram.

Implications for Our Understanding of "Competence" and the Questions To Be Teased Out in This Book

One purpose of this chapter has been to create a frame for the rest of the book. If we are to think effectively about the nature of the competencies required in modern society, it is essential that we start by considering the nature of the society and organisations in which we live and work, the developments that are needed in that society and those organisations, the nature of the competencies that are required to introduce and run that new society and those organisations, the way in which those competencies are to be nurtured, and the developments that are required in the educational system and its management if those competencies are to be nurtured and utilised. We have said something about all of these issues. They remain topics to be taken up at greater length in later chapters.

Notes

1   Historically, the "Tragedy of the Commons" refers to the process whereby it is in the individual interests of all who graze stock on common land to put out more stock although the collective result is ruination of the pasture and thus to the disbenefit of all. Hardin (1968) has generalised this idea to all collectively held wealth—including not only such things as the seas and the atmosphere but also the livability of the built environment.

2   (Japanese) Ministry of International Trade and Industry.

3   See Raven (1995) for details of how this figure is arrived at.

4   Quasi Autonomous National Government Organisations (sometimes Non Governmental Organisations).

5   Trans National Corporations.

6   See Raven (1995).

7   The word "education" comes from the Latin root "to draw out" (the talents of students). Yet, as will be shown in some detail in later chapters, the current "educational" system rarely draws out, or nurtures, the potentialities of those involved. A summary of the evidence will be found in Raven (1994), but striking American evidence comes from Flanagan's (1976) follow up of students involved in "Project Talent".

References

Flanagan, J. C. (1976). *Implications for Improving Education from a Study of the Lives of 10,000 30-Year-Olds*. Palo Alto, CA: American Institutes for Research.

Hardin, G. (1968). The tragedy of the commons. *Science, 162*, 1243–1248.

Hogan, R. (1990). Unmasking incompetent managers. *Insight* (21 May), 42–44.

Kanter, R. M. (1985). *The Change Masters: Corporate Entrepreneurs at Work*. Hemel Hempstead: Unwin Paperbacks.

Klemp, G. O., Munger, M. T., & Spencer, L. M. (1977). *An Analysis of Leadership and Management Competencies of Commissioned and Non-Commissioned Naval Officers in the Pacific and Atlantic Fleets*. Boston: McBer.

Lees, S. (1996). *Strategic Human Resource Management in Transition Economies*. Proceedings of Conference: Human Resource Management: Strategy and Practice. Alma Atat, Khazaksthan: Alma Atat Management School.

Raven, J. (1984/1997). *Competence in Modern Society: Its Identification, Development and Release*. Unionville, New York: Royal Fireworks Press (1997); Oxford, England: Oxford Psychologists Press (1984).

Raven, J. (1994). *Managing Education for Effective Schooling: The Most Important Problem is to Come to Terms with Values*. Unionville, New York: Trillium Press; Oxford, England: Oxford Psychologists Press.

Raven, J. (1995). *The New Wealth of Nations: A New Enquiry into the Nature and Origins of the Wealth of Nations and the Societal Learning Arrangements Needed for a Sustainable Society*. New York: Royal Fireworks Press; Sudbury, Suffolk: Bloomfield Books.

Schön, D. (1971). *Beyond the Stable State*. London: Penguin.

Senge, P. M. (1990). *The Fifth Discipline*. New York: Doubleday.

Wackernagel, M., & Rees, W. E. (1996). *Our Ecological Footprint: Reducing Human Impact on the Earth*. Philadelphia: New Society Publishers.

Weaver, T. (1994). Knowledge alone gets you nowhere. *Capability, 1*, 6–12.

Chapter 2

Beyond Competence through Parallel Organization Activity: Applying the Principles of Rosabeth Moss Kanter's Concept of Parallel Organizations to Learning Organizations and the Learning Society

Lynne Cunningham

Context

A current preoccupation in the "post-competence" learning society debate is how to generate the kind of all-round personal capability that generates positive and often unanticipated outcomes for organizations. Variations on the original theme of standards of competence have evolved (see other chapters in this book). Some companies have researched and developed company-specific high-level competencies, concentrating on person/role matching and behavioral skills applied to both recruitment and staff development. Much of the U.S. literature linking competence to the learning organization focuses on the development and impact of high-level competencies in high-flying individuals. Published case studies celebrate successful, heroic endeavors by extraordinary enterprises and managers. In contrast, Kanter's (1983) work promotes the realization that both ordinary and extraordinary competences are present in everyone, including ordinary players at all levels in organizations. She suggests ways in which corporate bodies may harness this "extra-ordinariness" to their advantage through the recognition of two dimensions of organization that operate in parallel.

Creating the Conditions for Change

In *The Change Masters* (1983) Kanter builds on themes first developed in one of her earlier studies of North American corporations (*Men and Women of the Corporation,* 1977), which revealed that:

> "there are cycles of disadvantage around opportunity and power. Low opportunity breeds low motivation, low ambition and low commitment, which reinforces low opportunity; and low power breeds overcontrol, rules focus rather than results focus, and low morale, which in turn keeps power low. But the positive cycles of advantage involve upward spirals: opportunity producing higher motivation producing more opportunity, and power producing better management behavior producing more power" (Kanter, 1983, p. 406).

The application of these findings to subsequent organizational studies produced insights into the impact of formal and informal dimensions of organization on a corporation's capacity for innate organizational dynamism and innovation and the proactive management of change. Such insights are important because they have implications for corporate survival strategies in the current climate of accelerated economic change. Equally important, they pose questions about the opportunity and capacity of individuals to exercise power and contribute to society at large, questions that are ineluctably linked to the meaning and achievability of a "learning society."

The Concept of the Parallel Organization

Kanter identified two kinds of involvement by individuals in organizations—through the "routine hierarchy" for everyday maintenance activity; and through a "parallel organization" concerned with change. She describes organizational hierarchy as

> "the maintenance-oriented structure for routine operations: it defines job titles, pay grades, a set of relatively fixed reporting relationships, and related formal tasks . . . Power flows from the contacts and resources inherent in a defined position" (Kanter, 1983, p. 204).

An alternative organization alongside the larger whole may also exist in a much more flexible way—for example, for such ad hoc purposes as a specific multifunctional task force, a standing working group, a lateral team with some overarching purpose such as quality control ("quality circles"), or any temporary grouping for problem-solving tasks "not lim-

Maintenance Organization	Parallel Organization
• routine operation—low uncertainty	• problem-solving—high uncertainty
• primary focus on "production"	• focused primarily on "organization"
• limited "opportunities" (e.g., promotion)	• expandable "opportunities" (e.g., participation in a task force)
• fixed job assignments	• flexible, rotational assignments
• competency established before assignment	• developmental assignments
• long chain of command	• short chain of command
• objectives usually come from the top down	• objectives also come from the bottom up
• rewards: pay/benefits	• rewards: learning, recognition/ visibility, different contribution, bonus possibility, new contacts
• functionally specialized	• diagonal slices—mixed functions
• leadership a function of level	• leadership drawn from any level

Figure 2.1 Maintenance and Parallel Organizations. Source: R. M. Kanter (1983). *The Change Masters*. London: Unwin (p. 407).

ited by position in the hierarchy." In such examples, a different set of decision-making channels and "reporting relationships" is in operation, and "the organization as a whole is flexible and flat."

Kanter highlights the fact that

"in this parallel, more fluid, structure, opportunity and power can be expanded far beyond what is available in the regular hierarchical organization. The main task of the parallel organization is the continued re-examination of routines, exploration of new options; and the development of new tools, procedures, and approaches—that is, the institutionalization of change" (Kanter, 1983, pp. 204–205).

Implications for Structured Organizations

Kanter observed that parallel organization activity within organizations is successful in fostering individual creativity, releasing untapped potential, and generating the challenges of teamwork. New competences thus acquired can then be applied to the maintenance organization, maximizing its corporate expertise and its potential for the effective management of change. Of significant benefit to the organization is the transfer into the mainstream of the skills, enthusiasm, energy, creativity . . . manifest in "ordinary" individuals, who thereby become *extra*ordinary without changing their role or their place in the routine hierarchy. Unlike the standards-of-competence model, which is based on extant knowledge and predetermined organizational needs, this model acknowledges that all employees are active contributors to the organization (as opposed to mere "human resources"), capable of contributing in an *extra*ordinary way through participation in important activities outside their prescribed role. High-level competencies thus developed are not confined to the higher echelons of management or applied only to strategic decision-making, but can be released, without prior definition, anywhere in the organization.

Where this happens, a series of concentric cycles is generated, creating an upward spiral that includes:

- breaks from routine, revitalizing individual commitment and motivation
- interaction with others beyond the routine workplace, leading to reciprocal learning and new horizons and approaches
- high opportunity around valued contribution, leading to high self-esteem.

These outcomes stimulate confidence in individuals to acknowledge and learn from mistakes and to seek out and apply further learning that is not necessarily linked to their aspirations within the organization. A secondary impact on change may occur through a willingness to challenge the status quo and articulate concerns in parts of the organization that may once have seemed remote.

Application to the Learning Organization

Practical applications of Kanter's parallel organization model may be constrained by its cultural specificity. She has researched and written about large U.S. corporations characterized by relatively high structural rigidity and horizontal specialization. Nevertheless, despite the exhortations of management theorists and continuing experimentation with flat or matrix organizations, one could hypothesize that most large organizations in the private and public sectors still cling to hierarchical management structures with a high degree of technical horizontal specialization and increasing demands on individuals by the maintenance organization. This contrasts with evolving smaller high-tech enterprises, such as the new Internet companies, where the structure, or lack of it, is predicated on individual creativity and high entrepreneurial motivation as the key to survival.

Creative and interesting work in all industrial sectors still has to be supported by routine administrative tasks. New technology may automate and facilitate such tasks. However, even with e-commerce, information still has to be processed manually up to a point. Human intervention is necessary to organize the delivery of goods, to evaluate and evolve systems, to ensure compliance with statutory regulations, to maintain equipment, and to solve problems. In addition, standardization of processes resulting from new technology means there is less and less opportunity for individuals to put their personal stamp on the work they produce. In production processes, most of the remaining craft skills, and individual pride in them, have been replaced by automated systems in which quality is governed by the predetermined speed of the process—a situation of absolutely no power and minimal opportunity—hardly an advance from the Fordism of the first half of the century. The modern call-center, with its wired-up "battery hens" pressured to produce results in small coops for hours on end, under constant observation and autocratic rule, with minimal opportunity to realize their individuality, is probably the modern-day equivalent of the early production lines. In other words, technological advance may have changed working practices, but it has not liberated individual self-expression. The polite reiteration of a standard script to different callers all day long may constitute a competence, but it is severely self-limiting.

In other ways, new technology has actually limited individual creativity at lower levels in organizations where specialist human support skills, valued for themselves up to a decade ago, have been absorbed into the daily routine of other roles. Where support systems are dispersed in this way, it creates frustration and dissatisfaction at all levels of organizations, particularly because the loss of specialist expertise results in an unreasonable amount of low-level problem-solving involving the malfunction of equipment and electronic systems. "Opportunity" may be limited to cut-throat competition between employees for a small number of high-status, well-rewarded, but still highly regulated jobs. The successful management of change depends upon willing and cooperative responsiveness. In the face of external commercial threats, many Western industrial enterprises have, perhaps unwittingly, fostered competitive individualism focused on short-term extrinsic rewards. This may prove to be self-destructive in the face of the benefits to be gained from releasing the full potential of individuals through intrinsic satisfaction at work. This untapped potential is crucial to anticipating and facilitating change.

So although Kanter's model was conceived at the start of the 1980s, the impact of new technology and global economic change over the last two decades and their debilitating effect on many organizations could be said to make it even more relevant today. From her empirical research, Kanter was able to identify positive changes in the behavior, attitudes, and job-satisfaction levels in company employees operating in parallel organization mode, stating that

> "it appears that when it is in the interests of the people involved, and they are given genuine opportunity and power, they can be committed to finding time to contribute to solving organizational problems" (Kanter, 1983, p. 202).

One way of replicating the success stories she found is for organizations to adopt practices entailing interactions that cross routine functional and hierarchical boundaries, thus releasing the full capacity and potential of people operating at the lowest levels of power and opportunity.

For structured organizations of any size, Kanter's message is simple. She advocates:

> "a clear structure for routine operations overlaid with vehicles for participation . . . a predictable routine punctuated by episodes of high involvement in change efforts" (Kanter, 1983, p. 359).

Such an approach needs commitment, clear leadership, and participation by key decision-makers—those who head the maintenance organization must also demonstrate their "capacity to work together cooperatively regardless of field or level to tackle the unknown, the uncertain" (Kanter, 1983, p. 359).

In other words, the top manager must be prepared to cooperate towards given ends with the production or service worker, including accepting their leadership in relevant circumstances, to suit the purpose of each particular parallel organization activity. The "adaptive population" must be encouraged and participation positively steered, perhaps by a core group. Prerequisites, embodied in the provision of information, resources, and support, are identified as:

- educational support and team-building
- company data and funds
- access to high-level decision-makers and experts

Other important elements include:

- encouragement of a culture of pride
- highlighting of achievements
- enlarged access to the power tools for innovative problem-solving
- improvement of lateral communication
- reduction of unnecessary layers of hierarchy
- barriers removed and decisions pushed downwards
- reduced secretiveness—for example, early information about corporate plans
- genuine invitations to all to contribute to strategic decisions
- a willingness by top managers to share power

(summarized from Kanter, 1983, p. 361).

The larger and more entrenched the organization, the more problematic the change process. Previous experience may have rendered the workforce disillusioned and cynical, so it is vitally important to demonstrate the contrast between authentic parallel organization activity and "just another talking shop" through transparent mechanisms, such as structure, steering and monitoring, that avoid results and recommendations disappearing down institutional black holes. Pain and negative feelings may also arise in the relinquishing of power by the currently powerful. Openness which encourages challenge, question, and criticism can also be upsetting for some as it releases the potential of others. Consensus is not always possible. Disagreements may rankle. No one is perfect. Part of the process in moving on to a new plane is the mutual acceptance of imperfections—individual, institutional, and systemic—and their management to channel the energy of frustration into strengthening the organization.

Beyond Competence Through the Parallel Organization

At this point it is worth considering how the parallel organization (PO) model and methodology relate to and lead on from the notion of competence. Management developers will already be familiar with the guiding principles of experiential and collaborative learning. For instance, Adair's *Action-Centred Leadership* and Revan's *Action Learning* approach share aspects of the same philosophical plane. The latter incorporates experience of working for a period in a different organization and is still relevant after nearly half a century, despite being overshadowed by the "standards-of-competence" model. In this sense the idea of parallel organizations is not new, but it raises some relevant questions:

"What is Actually Happening in the PO?
What is it That Makes the Difference?"

After all, it is not the abstract notion of the PO that promotes change, but the motivation and behavior of the people who constitute it.

First, one can say that normal yardsticks and conventions of organizational behavior are abandoned in the PO model. Personal and occupational aspirations and demands blend. Individuals have the freedom to express their ideas and their contributions are accorded equal value, whatever their outcome. Creativity is promoted; idiosyncrasies are absorbed rather than marginalized. Power and control are shared. Mistakes are acknowledged as learning experiences. Constructive criticism slices through hierarchies. There is a common pursuit of achievements which are positive and measurable. The ultimate consequence—which comes as no surprise to motivational theorists—is that people feel better about themselves, which is reflected in all spheres of their lives. The elements that appear to make a difference are those of intrinsic reward, that is:

> self-esteem and freedom of expression linked to social interaction through cooperation with others and the achievement of identifiable results.

The competencies associated with these elements (not an exhaustive list) include the ability, humility, strength, confidence, and willingness:

- to trust and value others equally
- to participate on an equal basis
- to listen and synthesize
- to step back, receive, and test new ideas
- to collect and analyze data
- to initiate and contribute suggestions
- to articulate concerns
- to intervene on behalf of others
- to be self-critical and acknowledge mistakes
- to challenge and question
- to take risks
- to combine the expertise of others in unconventional ways
- to actively seek and share opportunities
- to share decision-making and rewards
- to secure results through interactions with others
- to value participation as well as achievement
- to learn from experience and apply this learning

These may be described as interactive competencies, combining practical with empathetic skills to achieve a positive focus and concrete results.

The parallel organization model approaches a plane beyond competence in that participating individuals are not tested for the presence of these skills and attributes before being admitted to a privileged elite. It is assumed that whatever their role is in the maintenance organization, they already possess the necessary potential to make a positive contribution and that their potential will be enhanced exponentially through the learning experience of parallel activity. Such potential must be translated into the required interactive competencies by or for participants at all levels, who will already evince some of them but will need to learn others.

It could be argued that where these interactive competencies are not present, participation in the parallel organization will kick-start them into existence, just as Kanter observed positive behavioral changes in the subjects of her research. However, as the decision to operate in this way must be taken by the most senior managers in the maintenance organization, they must first demonstrate their own capability in this sphere by exposing their own behavior to scrutiny, evaluation, and change. Methods applied to the recruitment, selection and development of managers, and subsequently of all employees, need to reflect and secure the interactive competencies that encompass this capability. This highlights the importance of the educational support identified by Kanter as a prerequisite of successful parallel activity.

It could be argued that any form of activity that generates this partial list of interactive competencies is likely to improve the capability of individuals to function in any sphere, in all aspects of their lives. This has implications not just for work organizations but for governance, personal and family life, and leisure, all of which already represent a source of prior learning. Above all, it should open doors for educators who are in the unique position of being able to underpin the social and work behaviors of future adults through collaborative and self-managed learning methodologies that replicate the key elements of the parallel organization. These elements are just as relevant to formal learning processes and educational institutions as they are to other work organizations.

From the Parallel Organization to the Learning Society

The underpinning principles of the parallel organization and the competencies contributing to and arising from it can be extended from work or other singular organizations to society as a whole, encompassing the role of citizens in local communities through:

- contribution by individuals within their local community
- interaction between organizations within local communities
- the operation of local democracy—local government, interest groups, media relations

One initiative that exemplifies the impact that the PO concept can have on society, beyond the confines of the work organization, is the Common Purpose program originally introduced in Britain by The Industrial Society.

Common Purpose

Common Purpose is a registered charity that provides one-year courses with a key objective of establishing networks of local decision-makers from three main sectors of society within a designated area:

- to exchange knowledge and expertise
- to address issues of local concern
- to work towards a shared vision

The statutory, voluntary, and corporate sectors are represented on each course. The statutory and corporate sectors pay their own fees and the corporate sector sponsors the voluntary sector. For instance, participants have included a senior housing manager, an assistant CEO of a National Health Service Trust, a director of a council for voluntary service, directors of larger local charities, store managers and a senior mail-delivery service manager.

Following a two-day induction program, which includes expert tuition in relevant skills as well as contextual briefing, the participants are then committed to one 12-hour day of intensive joint activity per month. This would usually follow a format of:

- a pre-course written briefing on the topics for discussion
- local keynote speakers on the selected topics—for example, crime prevention might include an address by a prison governor
- relevant visits—for example, to the prison in question
- a networking lunch

- workshop sessions linked to the day's activities
- intensive questioning by participants of an experienced panel (following training by journalists)

At the end of 12 months, the participants formally graduate from the program and may continue to take part in further "graduate" activities. The idea is to sustain the contacts and operate as a continuing network. Each Common Purpose course acts as a PO within a community alongside its democratically accountable bodies, its structured volunteering, and its industrial employers. It serves the purpose of enabling a select group of individuals from those sectors to enjoy the benefits of PO activity already outlined and to disseminate those benefits both within their own organizations and as contributors to the wider community—formally and informally.

Common Purpose has been criticized for establishing small, elite networks of people who are already extraordinary doing extraordinary things. In this respect it does not fulfill all Kanter's principles of POs enabling ordinary people in ordinary jobs to contribute to non-routine activities. Nevertheless, it is a model that could be extended to achieve this, transporting the Beyond Competence debate into the practicalities of the wider learning society.

Extending the Networks

A logical extension of this highly structured program would be for the "graduates" to initiate further interagency networks for specific purposes through POs. The public sector is already bursting with interagency multidisciplinary working groups. However, they usually function at similar hierarchical levels—service directors network with service directors, middle managers network with other middle managers, and the lower organizational strata get forgotten altogether. Also, although the public and voluntary sectors may cooperate regularly, tripartite formations including the corporate sector are less common and usually only operate at senior levels. Various local authority-led regional regeneration initiatives have sparked some local tripartite networks for public consultation, and these also represent parallel organizations of a kind but tend to lack the key elements of equal valuing of contributions and genuine bottom-up participation. A learning society may also benefit through reflecting in formal networks the individual talents from all sectors and levels that are already combined in voluntary and leisure activity.

Beyond Competence: The Parallel Approach
to Learning Organizations

Kanter has demonstrated that a learning organization achieved through parallel organizations is one that balances and maximizes the contributions and rewards of all its players. It actively provides and supports opportunities for learning through participation by removing internal fences and incorporates the consequent positive outcomes for corporations and individuals. It also acknowledges prior and external learning, valuing the experience imported from other aspects of contributors' lives and encouraging participation in other spheres. Through harnessing the expertise, energy, and power of individuals in this way, organizations may open more doors to the contextual awareness, alertness, and proactivity that they need to innovate, metamorphose, and survive. This goes beyond competence through institutionalizing the expectation of positive and unanticipated outcomes from any source as part of a continuing symbiotic learning process and not through the prior definition of organizational gates and the limited distribution of the associated access codes.

References

Adair, J. (1983). *Effective Leadership.* Aldershot: Gower.

Kanter, R. M. (1977). *Men and Women of the Corporation.* New York: Basic Books.

Kanter, R. M. (1983). *The Change Masters.* London: Unwin.

Revans, R. W. (1979). *Action Learning.* London: Blond & Briggs.

Chapter 3

Societal Learning and Competence: Commentary

John Raven

In Chapter 1 ("*Learning Societies*"), we saw that a distinctive feature of both learning organisations and learning societies is that they learn *without any of the individuals within them having to know more than a fraction of what needs to be known.* As Lynne Cunningham has now shown in greater detail, Kanter's work reveals that some "parallel organisation" teams start with a salesmen's observation of a way in which a specific product could be improved to better meet customers' needs, with the observation of customers' needs for a new product, or with an observation of how the working of the organisation itself could be improved. Other people—people who know how to promote a good idea—then become involved in disseminating awareness of the value of each of these observations. Still others work out how to develop the new product or introduce the desirable changes in the organisation, and so on. Doing each of these things calls for different kinds of learning about different things and for exercising different competencies—and developing higher levels of those competencies in the process. The end result is that the *group* has competencies—*emergent* competencies—that are not possessed by any of the individuals within it.

How does an organisation monitor its environment and its personnel and create a pervasive climate of experimentation and evaluation? It needs to better meet external needs, capitalise on ideas, and make internal changes. That is easily said. But the point is that to do so it needs to learn to do new things that no one person has noticed the need for or would initially know how to do.

To move forward, *cultural* change is required. How is this to be brought about? *Systemic*—but not authoritarian or centrally decreed—change is

required in every nook and cranny of the system. To get this, one thing
that would seem to be needed is classic academic research and development contributions from organisational psychologists. There seems to be
a need for an integrated framework for thinking about competence—its
assessment, its development, and its deployment—about what it actually
is that people occupying particular job designations need to do, about the
organisational arrangements required for different kinds of progress, and
about the range of consequences of the interaction of these components
that need to be studied. There seems to be a need for tools to assist in
organisational change—to help organisations think about the tasks to be
performed by their various employees and about their organisational arrangements, to assist in staff-appraisal and the development and deployment of human resources, to help to ensure that organisations release
and utilise the talents that are available to them, and to find ways of
inducing managers to act on information.

But at another level the observations we have made heavily underscore
Ian Cunningham's[1] call to transform many more—indeed virtually all—
workplaces into genuine learning organisations (both in the sense of becoming more developmental environments for those who work in them
and in the sense of becoming better at learning how to deal with their
environments and monitor and improve their internal working)—for it is
very difficult to see how the vital and diverse competencies of which we
have spoken could be nurtured in off-the-job training programmes and
still less how they could be credentialled through any of the assessment
processes with which we are familiar.

The question of how schools and colleges could become genuine learning environments then emerges as a still more important—but even more
daunting—question than we had previously thought.

Note

1. Cunningham, I. (1995). Developing organisations: The wisdom of strategic learning. *Capability, 1* (4), 11–14.

PART II

INCOMPETENCE

Much of the demand for competence-based education and testing is fuelled by the observation and fear of professional *incompetence*. The brief papers in this Part of our book reveal just how justified is this fear. But they also suggest that the way the problem is most commonly conceptualised and, even more important, the ways in which it is most commonly proposed to solve it (grounded, as they usually are, in the initial training and certification of practitioners), are wide of the mark.

In the end, the papers forcefully challenge conventional ways of thinking about competence and how its components are to be nurtured and assessed.

Chapter 4

The Incapable Professional

Tony Becher

This short account of professionals who are lacking in capability draws on the research I have been doing for the past years on how professionals cope with change. Although this study is not directly concerned with capability, it offers a fair amount of indirect evidence on the subject, deriving from some 190 in-depth interviews with practitioners in six professions: medicine, pharmacy, law, accountancy, architecture and structural engineering, together with an extensive search of the literature. A fuller discussion will be found in Becher (1999).

My choice of topic is based on the premise that one way of helping to throw light on a concept is by looking at its antithesis: more specifically that an understanding of competence may be helped by exploring its lack. It is of course important to distinguish incompetence—or if you prefer it, an inadequate level of capability—from other forms of professional malfunction. In particular, you can be a perfectly capable practitioner and yet be arraigned for unethical conduct (especially if you are a doctor) or fraud (especially if you are a lawyer or accountant). My concern in what follows will be exclusively with those aspects of misconduct that stem from a lack of capability in the technical aspects of a professional's work.

If one asks why the issue of professional incompetence is important, the answer is obvious in most professions, but there are different reasons for that answer. As might be expected, the problems loom largest in medicine—and to a lesser extent in pharmacy—where lives can be directly at risk. Accordingly, many of my examples will be drawn from medical practice. Incompetence assumes a different importance in the other four professions involved in the study. In law and accountancy, inadequate professional service is likely to lead to some form of financial or even criminal problem for the client. In architecture and structural engineering, the consequences may have a deleterious effect on the environment, or at worst cause fatal danger through structural failure.

The perceived political importance of professional capability is usefully brought out in relation to one of the many professions not included in my research. In early December 1995, the proposals announced by the New Left for improving educational standards sought to outdo those of the Old Right by undertaking to "sweep away the second-rate [teachers] and tackle head-on the half-baked and the ineffective." Like many political nostrums, this would seem more resonant in words than realisable in deeds. In particular, it notably begs the question of how to identify incompetence and how to prove its existence.

It is a widely remarked feature of current professional life that clients are far less subservient, more questioning, and more sophisticated than they used to be. It is not therefore surprising that many of the complaints about unsatisfactory levels of professional competence received by the relevant professional bodies come from members of the public rather than fellow members of the profession. As far as the latter are concerned, a number of professional associations—such as the Institute of Chartered Accountants—require, in their codes of ethics, that any member identifying a significant degree of incompetence in a colleague should report that colleague to the profession's disciplinary committee for further investigation. In its recent guidance to doctors on "good medical practice," the General Medical Council has for the first time explicitly laid it down that "you must protect patients when you believe that a colleague's conduct, performance or health is a threat to them . . . if necessary, you must tell someone from the employing authority or from a regulatory body." However, enforcing this requirement is easier said than done. All of us are aware of a deep cultural tradition in schools against "telling on" other pupils.

There are similarly strong informal sanctions against "blowing the whistle" on someone in hospital medicine. Among my interview data, there is a case of an anaesthetist who reported a leading consultant surgeon whose incompetence had caused several fatalities. The anaesthetist was sacked; the surgeon was allowed to go on killing people.

It is one thing to identify a lack of professional competence and quite another to establish it. But even supposing incompetence is proved, the question remains what can be done about it. In cases in which a professional's poor performance can be seen to be remediable, various kinds of training programme can be required, perhaps leading to recertification. In more serious cases, a professional may be persuaded to resign or retire early. Being relieved of one's appointment, though it occurs in larger professional organisations, can be subject to unfair dismissal procedures and tends to be shied away from. At the extreme, of course, one's name may be removed from the professional register, which makes it illegal in some professions to go on practising at all.

According to a television documentary, Nicholas Siddle, a well-regarded consultant, was able to go on unsuccessfully using a particular surgical technique for some years before being finally struck off. Even then, he clearly believed that he had been unfairly treated, and apparently found it difficult to accept the grounds for the General Medical Council's verdict. So the process of proving a seriously inadequate level of professional capability can be not only protracted but highly legalised and adversarial, leading to a clear view that prevention is better than prosecution.

It is a notable characteristic of the current scene that much is being done, mainly by professional bodies and national agencies, to safeguard against inadequate performance. As far as individuals, as opposed to professional organisations, are concerned, one can distinguish two main strategies. The first, quality assurance, concentrates on guaranteeing to the public at large that practitioners are suitably licensed, usually through some form of certification. The initial requirements before an individual can act professionally on his or her own are in general clearly defined: What is as yet less established are the proper prerequisites for more specialised activities, though the incidence of these is increasing. For example, practising laproscopic, or "keyhole," surgery now requires compulsory prior training, and accountants dealing with cases of insolvency are currently expected to earn an additional qualification in this specialism. One problem is, of course, that notions of capability change as the content and methods of the profession change, so that possession of a certificate is not an automatic guarantee of sound performance.

This is where the second strategy—quality control—comes in. Where assurance is passive, relying on the recognition of past achievement, control implies a more active and regular monitoring of current capability. One example is compulsory legislation, which is usually policed more or less effectively by some form of inspection. Another, adopted in some of the larger professional firms, is formal peer review or appraisal. Again, in all the six professions in my study, the relevant professional bodies lay down voluntary or semi-compulsory requirements for continuing professional development. These CPD policies do not, unfortunately, seem very effective in dealing with what the medical profession graphically calls the "rotten apples". In practice, monitoring them is usually far from easy and it is readily possible for those who are unmotivated merely to go through the motions of compliance.

Even the many strongly committed professionals in my interview sample commented on the burden of regulatory and other demands. As in other sectors affected by the quality industry, the problem is to prevent the whole apparatus from becoming too overelaborate, particularly as the best available estimates of those lacking adequate professional capability tend to come out at less than 5% of the population in question. As one medic in my sample, centrally concerned with maintaining quality, remarked:

> "There is an awful lot of wasted effort just to get a bit of benefit, so there are going to be a lot of perfectly competent doctors who do all the things like being re-assessed and re-accredited and getting resentful because of it. It's like getting in a long queue at the airport, going through a security check: you know it's right and proper but you know very well that you haven't got a bomb in your case, so why shouldn't you go through? Yes, of course it is desirable to prevent incompetence and bad practice, but you need to pay careful attention to making sure that it isn't heavy handed."

But despite all the difficulties in ensuring that incompetence is limited in its scope and that capability is promoted, the prospects for overall improvement seem good. Even if there will always be cases that are a cause for concern, their incidence is likely to be steadily reduced. I have already suggested that clients have become more vigilant and professional bodies have become more proactive than before. In addition, professional firms are more competitive, and professionals themselves are more conscious of the need to keep up to date with the best of current practice. The professions, in short, would seem a richer field for cultivation by the capability movement than they have ever been.

Reference

Becher, T. (1999). Quality in the professions. *Studies in Higher Education, 24,* (2), 225–236.

Chapter 5

Incompetence:
An Unspoken Consensus

Irene Ilott

Editorial Introduction

As we have seen, the observation of, and fear of, *incompetence* is a strong force driving the competence movement. This short chapter (consisting of excerpts from Chapter 2 of Ilott & Murphy, 1999, which dealt with the unspoken consensus relating to *competence* as well as incompetence), reports an interesting study of perceptions of incompetence. It graphically illustrates components of competence or capability that tend to be missing from studies in which no attempt is made to direct the attention of those whose views are canvassed to aspects of incompetence which would not normally spring to mind when the word "competence" is used. Not reproduced here are the sections of the original publication reporting results which suggest that most people believe that the solution to these problems is to be found through training and retraining. The chapter therefore raises issues to which we will return in our concluding comments to this section of our book.

Incompetence: An Important Construct

There is a plethora of literature presenting the philosophical or practical pros and cons about the different conceptualisations of competence. In contrast, there is little about incompetence, even though accusations and evidence of malpractice, negligence, or misconduct are costly for all parties. The cost may be measured in lives, distress, or monetary terms. The case of the nurse Beverly Allitt, convicted of murdering four children and harming nine others, is perhaps the most tragic. An editorial in *The Times* (1993) noted the similarity of career patterns between Allitt and a residential social worker, Frank Beck. He was convicted of abusing 200 children, both physically and sexually, over a 13-year period. The estimated cost of medical negligence claims—£52.3 million for England in 1990–1991 (Fenn et al., 1994)—almost pales into insignificance when compared with these extreme cases of abuse of power.

These cases and costs may have contributed to an increasing interest in incompetence in a range of professions. For example, the branding of 15,000 teachers as "incompetent" attracted much attention from the media, politicians, and policymakers. One headline proclaimed a "quarter of pupils have bad teachers" (Scott-Clark & Hymas, 1996). Another report describes how the funding system is "designed to . . . discourage keeping on students who seem unlikely to make good teachers, just to avoid losing associated funding" (Tysome, 1996).

Statutory and professional bodies responsible for "kite marking" (i.e. giving approval to standards of) education and practice are also interested in misconduct as part of their disciplinary responsibilities. Statutory bodies as the governing bodies of self-regulating professions have a "duty to protect the public against the genially incompetent as well as the deliberate wrongdoers" (Law Report, 1995). These include the General Medical Council (GMC), the United Kingdom Central Council for Nursing, Midwifery and Health Visiting (UKCC), and the discipline-specific boards of the Council for Professions Supplementary to Medicine (CPSM). Some 1,600 doctors are reported to the GMC annually with reference to their professional conduct. Donaldson describes his experience of dealing with problem doctors as "difficult, distasteful, time consuming, and acrimonious work. For these reasons the temptation to avert one's gaze . . . is at times very great . . . I have no doubt that many employers do look away when they should not" (1994, p. 1281). This statement highlights a tendency to avoid, rather than confront, incompetent, unsafe, or unscrupulous practitioners.

Method: Identifying a Criteria for Assigning a Fail Grade as a Baseline Definition of Incompetence

The research to identify the constituents of incompetence was part of a wider investigation into the assessors' perspectives on awarding a fail grade (Ilott, 1993). This element concentrated upon the margins of the competence-incompetence continuum. It drew upon the assumption that competence "is recognisable more by its absence than by readily measurable behaviours" (Burrows, 1989). Initially, the aim was to devise an instrument containing knowledge, skills, and attitudes considered to be unsatisfactory or inappropriate to complement existing assessments of "competence to practice." Positive evidence of both is necessary for good judgements. However, as the research progressed an unspoken consensus became apparent.

Information was collected from different sources using different methods for triangulation purposes. These included in-depth, focused, interviews with 25 academic and 5 work-based assessors; syndicate sessions with 398 health-care professionals as part of a training course about failure held in the UK and Sweden; and a literature review to analyse competence. All informants were responsible for judging "competence to practise" either in academic or work-based settings, primarily for occupational therapy but also physiotherapy, radiography, nursing, and social work. The interview questions focused on their criteria for failure, encompassing how they differentiated between a borderline and clear fail, differences in criteria between academic and practice settings, and the influence of attributions of effort, ability, and task difficulty. The syndicate groups, comprised of those with and without experience in assigning a fail grade, compiled a minimum standard or checklist of behaviours, skills, and attitudes to define student failure and differentiate between borderline and unsatisfactory performance (Ilott, 1995).

While acknowledging the limitations of each method and the self-selected samples, the results revealed a surprising degree of convergence about the constituents of incompetence and competence.

Constituents of Incompetence and Competence in Some "Caring Professions"

The criteria for failure consisted of an array of implicit and explicit assessment constructs. Professional behaviour and personal transferable skills, not profession-specific knowledge, were the most preferred criteria elicited during the focused interviews and syndicate groups. These results are summarised in Table 5.1 and a number of the main categories are discussed in more detail in the paragraphs which follow.

Professional Unsuitability
This is another intangible, elusive concept. Yet what does it mean? Some personal and professional qualities are embodied in codes of ethics and

Table 5.1 Constituents of Incompetence

Construct		Frequency	Percentage
Unprofessional Behaviour:	Lack of initiative, irresponsible, unprofessional, unreliable, misconduct, breaches of confidentiality, inappropriate appearance	144	23%
Skills Deficits:	Interpersonal, communication, general, clinical, practical	109	17%
Personality:	Too little or too much confidence, immaturity, lack of insight	58	9%
Knowledge:	Limited application, inadequate knowledge, poor understanding	55	9%
Inappropriate Attitudes:	General, toward clients, staff, and profession	47	7%
Unsafe:	General, Health and Safety, dangerous practice	41	7%
Response to Feedback:	Inability or unwillingness to learn and change	39	6%
Lack of Motivation:	Disinterest, low effort	38	6%
Self-Management:	Limited self-evaluation, poor time management	26	4%
Miscellaneous:	Feedback from MDT, intuition, stage of training	24	4%
Objectives Unmet:	General, departmental, school	23	4%
Personal Factors:	Personal problems, prejudice	20	3%
Implicit Assessment Construct:	Employ or accept treatment	7	1%

Source: Ilott (1993)

professional conduct and statements of professional misconduct or infamous conduct. The multifaceted criteria of unprofessional behaviour was the most frequently reported reason for assigning a fail grade by the syndicate groups. It consisted of lack of initiative (n=27), irresponsibility (n=20), unprofessionalism (n=19), unreliability (n=18), and misconduct, defined either as a general term (n=8) or specified as lack of punctuality, dishonesty, aggression, theft, fraud, abuse (including alcohol and cruelty) (n=19), breaches of confidentiality (n=16), inappropriate appearance (n=10), untrustworthiness (n=4), unethical behaviour (n=3), and passive or manipulative avoidance of situations (n=3).

Interestingly, these items mirror the two most frequent problems among senior hospital doctors cited by Donaldson (1994, p. 1279). These were poor attitude and disruptive or irresponsible behaviour (n=32) and lack of commitment to duties (n=21). Brandon & Davies (1979) defined unprofessional attitudes as lying, breaching confidentiality, causing unjustifiable offence to clients, lack of punctuality, and inadequate standards of attendance and record-keeping. Such "abstract moral traits" including loyalty, honesty, and reliability are consistently highly rated by employers (Hyland, 1991).

Poor Communication Skills

Deficits in communication, interpersonal, and, to a lesser extent, practical skills constituted the second most frequently mentioned category. The issue occurs and recurs in the inter-professional international literature. Deficiencies in communication and interpersonal skills were the largest categories for Holmes et al. (1990) and Battles et al. (1990). This is unsurprising, considering that what is traditionally termed "the bedside manner," or the equivalent, "therapeutic use of self," is the primary tool of many health care and social welfare professions.

Dangers: Unsafe Practices and Lack of Learning

The danger of overconfidence leading to practising beyond the limits of knowledge links the criteria of safety, knowledge, and personal factors. Hausman et al. (1990) revealed a significant relationship between overconfidence and lower examination scores in paediatric residents.

Although unsafe practices were infrequently reported by occupational therapists (seeming to be an implicit criteria) they were prominent in the medical, nursing, physiotherapy, and radiography professions. The issue is multifaceted, consisting of trust that was defined by a work-based supervisor as "Can you leave the student with the patients for 30 seconds?" It also includes respecting Health and Safety policies, the ability to recognise significant cues and act appropriately, and awareness of limitations to prevent practising beyond the level of knowledge or skills. This is one of the criteria for unsafe practice adopted by Darragh et al. (1986).

Interestingly, although profession-specific knowledge forms the checklist of "how to spot a bad teacher" (Scott-Clark & Hymas, 1996), it did not figure in this research. The focus was upon the process of learning that included evidence of improvement, application of knowledge, the ability to learn from mistakes, and a willingness to change to enable the integration of theory with practice. This is another constant criteria across time that is noted by Towle (1954), Wong (1979), and Ford & Jones (1987), for example.

Implicit Criterion

Implicit constructs ranged from the temptation to reward effort, interest, and hard work even though the threshold standards had not been achieved to a global definition of competence. This was encapsulated by two questions: "Would I employ him/her?" and "Would I want him/her to treat me or my family?" These simple questions epitomise "fitness for purpose" from the perspective of both employer and consumer. Although this criteria appears in the literature (Green, 1991) and has been used to validate assessment tools (Crocker et al., 1975) it seems to be an implicit rather than explicit assessment criteria.

Conclusion: Supporting the Unspoken Consensus

The consensus about the constituents of competence and incompetence between diverse professions was as fascinating as it was unexpected. It may be related to several factors, including working within public sector organisations, using person-centred partnership models of practice, and the requirement to abide by codes of ethical behaviour. Informants seemed to find it easier to articulate the criteria for assigning a fail grade—to identify the constituents of incompetence—than define competence. This approach avoids the semantic confusion and conflict between the different definitions of competence or capability.

Competence remains a vague, elusive concept. But perhaps this is appropriate because:

> "practice . . . depends on a subtle blend of values, attitudes, knowledge and skills; and on the capacity for making flexible responses to an infinite variety of situations, many of which cannot be anticipated" (Brandon & Davies, 1979).

This quotation mirrors the definition of higher-level National Vocational Qualifications (Mitchell, 1993) and Capability. Because this global definition has a sound foundation in the constants of professional and ethical behaviour, it allows flexibility for development, to ensure that these retain priority within the new health care and social welfare industries. It is also important to consider how these metadisciplinary concepts are integrated into earlier stages of the educational process, in the admission criteria and curriculum, for example.

A global conceptualisation may become a heretical suggestion as explicit standards and outcomes dominate the competency movement. Academic and work-based assessors *can* balance objective and subjective evidence of "intuitive and analytic thinking . . . to grasp the situation as a whole" (Blomquist, 1985). This ability may be grounded in an unspoken consensus about what constitutes incompetence. It is enhanced by clarifying and comparing criteria and reviewing the use and misuse of implicit or explicit constructs with intra- and inter-professional colleagues (Ilott, 1995). The reassurance gained from recognising similar criteria and threshold standards affirms their expert role by confirming both the validity and interrater reliability (Friedman & Mennin, 1991) of their judgements. Such preparation is important to enable all assessors fulfil their obligation to protect the public and minimise the number of "horror stories."

References

Battles, J. B., Dowell, D. L., Kirk, M. et al. (1990). The affective attributes of the ideal primary care specialist. In W. Bender et al. (Eds.), *Teaching and Assessing Clinical Competence*. Groningen: Boek Werk Publications.

Blomquist, K. B. (1985). Evaluation of students: Intuition is important. *Nurse Educator, 10* (8), 8–11.

Brandon, J., & Davies, M. (1979). The limits of competence in social work: The assessment of marginal students in social work education. *British Journal of Social Work, 9* (3), 295–347.

Burrows, E. (1989). Clinical practice: An approach to the assessment of clinical competencies. *British Journal of Occupational Therapy, 52* (6), 222–226.

Clothier, C., MacDonald, C. A., & Shaw, D. A. (1994). *The Allitt Inquiry*. London: Her Majesty's Stationery Office.

Crocker, L. M., Muthard, J. E., Slaymaker, J. E. et al. (1975). A performance rating scale for evaluating clinical competence of occupational therapy students. *American Journal of Occupational Therapy, 29* (2), 81–86.

Darragh, R., Jacobson, G., Sloan, B., & Sandquist, G. (1986). Unsafe student practice: Policy and procedures. *Nursing Outlook* 34 (4), 176–178.

Donaldson, L. J. (1994). Doctors with problems in an NHS workforce. *British Medical Journal, 308,* 1277–1282.

Editorial. (1993). Patients come first. *The Times,* 19 May, 17.

Fenn, P., Hermans, D., & Dingwall, R. (1994). Estimating the cost of compensating victims of medical negligence. *British Medical Journal, 309,* 389–391.

Ford, J. A., & Jones, A. (1987). *Student Supervision*. Houndmills: Macmillan Education Ltd.

Friedman, M., & Mennin, S. P. (1991). Rethinking critical issues in performance assessment. *Academic Medicine, 66* (7), 390–395.

Green, C. (1991). *Identification of the responsibilities and perceptions of the training task held by workforce supervisors of those training within the caring professions.* Project 551, prepared for the Further Education Unit, Anglia Polytechnic.

Hausman, C. I., Weiss, J. C., Lawrence, J. S. et al. (1990). Confidence weighted answer techniques in a group of paediatric residents. *Medical Teacher, 12* (2), 163–168.

Higher Education Quality Council. (1995). *Graduate Standards Programme. Interim Report, Executive Summary.* London: HEQC.

Holmes, B. D., Mann, K. V., & Hennen, B. K. E. (1990). Defining fitness and aptitude to practice medicine. *Medical Teacher, 12* (2), 181–191.

Hyland, T. (1991). Knowledge, performance and competence-based assessment. *EDUCA,* December, 7.

Ilott, I. (1993). *The process of failing occupational therapy students: A staff perspective.* Unpublished Ph.D. thesis, University of Nottingham.

Ilott, I. (1995). To fail or not to fail? A course for fieldwork educators. *American Journal of Occupational Therapy, 49* (3), 250–255.

Ilott, I., & Murphy, R. (Eds.) (1999). *Success and Failure in Professional Education: Assessing the Evidence.* London: Whurr Publishers Ltd.

Law Report (1995). Professional misconduct in negligent treatment. *The Times, 42,* 12 December.

Mitchell, L. (1993). NVQs/SVQs at higher levels: A discussion paper to the higher levels seminar. *Competence & Assessment,* Briefing Series No. 8.

Scott-Clark, C., & Hymas, C. (1996). Quarter of pupils have bad teachers. *The Sunday Times,* 28 January, 5.

Towle, C. (1954). *The learner in education for the professions: As seen in the education for social work.* Chicago, IL: University of Chicago Press.

Tysome, T. (1994). Cheating purge: Inspectors out. *The Times Higher Education Supplement,* 19 August, 1.

Tysome, T. (1996). Teaching courses set a price-list. *The Times Higher Education Supplement,* 22 March, 3.

United Kingdom Central Council for Nursing, Midwifery and Health Visiting. (1994). *Professional conduct—Occasional Report On Standards Of Nursing In Nursing Homes.* London: UKCC.

Wong, J. (1979). The inability to transfer classroom learning to clinical nursing practice. *Journal of Advanced Nursing, 4,* 161–168.

Chapter 6

Commentary: The Pernicious Effects of Incompetence on Society, Education, and Assessment

John Raven

The two papers in this Part of our book are of the greatest importance for at least the following reasons:

1. Although issues relating to *incompetence* were raised by a number of speakers at the Higher Education for Capability conferences that gave rise to this book, these papers are the only markers of this concern here.

2. *Incompetence* is indeed of the greatest importance. For example, Hogan (1990) has shown that the base rate for gross incompetence among American managers is about 50%: They destroy the competence of their subordinates, undermine their colleagues, and drive their organisations into the ground. Hope (1984), Day and Klein (1987), and Raven and Dolphin (1978) have published similar findings for public servants. Raven (1995) reviewed a much wider range of evidence demonstrating not only the inability of public servants to manage public provision in the long-term public interest but also their complicity in socially destructive acts. These studies, taken together with those of Becher and Ilott, raise the question of whether it is possible to draw a firm distinction between professional competence and the ethics ("incompetence" as judged from looking at the effects of behaviour on the wider organisation or society) of their behaviour. Indeed, one of Weaver's (1994) reasons for preferring the term "capability" to "competence" when promoting *Education for Capability* was precisely to underline the importance of these wider aspects of competence.

3. The observation and fear of *incompetence* is one of the most powerful motives contributing to the feeling (a) that all prospective entrants to all occupational groups should have certificates demonstrating that they are familiar with all knowledge which may one day be relevant to them, and (b) that, throughout their lives thereafter, they should enrol in courses to update that knowledge. The full report from which Ilott's chapter here is extracted documents this process. It reveals the way in which a concern with incompetence stemming from failure to exercise high-level competencies (i.e., sins of omission) gets translated into the prescription of low-level competencies to be mastered and demonstrated (usually in the course of training programmes). It would therefore seem to behove us to carefully examine the foundation and logic of this process.

4. Both papers forcefully raise the question of how incompetence is to be assessed and how such information is to be given teeth so that it will lead to appropriate action.

5. They raise the question of whether most *incompetence* stems from deficiencies in technical-rational competence or from an inability to, as Schön puts it, "deal with the swamp". They therefore raise questions about the focus of any competency-oriented educational programmes which may be required.

6. They raise the question of whether the obvious problems are to be overcome by focusing on continuously updating the technical-rational competence of those concerned or by making more appropriate arrangements to ensure that those concerned are encouraged to develop, and move into positions in which they can utilise, high-level competencies at work and by making more appropriate arrangements to oversee their work. If the latter is the case, the implication is that we need to pay more attention to the nature of the organisational arrangements required to lead people to develop and display high-level competencies, and thus to the competencies which are required by those who are to clarify, introduce, and run, more appropriate societal management arrangements. Adams and Burgess (1989), in a carefully researched radical publication that is generally assimilated back to the conventional,[1] are among the very few who have developed ways of surfacing and promoting practical discussion of such high level competencies and the organisational arrangements required if they are to be nurtured, recognised, and utilised.

7. The papers might have dwelt on aspects of incompetence that only become apparent if one considers the wider social (moral) consequences of action and sins of *omission*—such as the failure of teachers to band together to change the nature of educational assessment because of its effects. (As Raven, 1991, has shown, these effects include depriving most pupils of opportunities to develop and gain recognition for their talents, legitimising the consignment of many highly capable people to an occupational scrapheap, depriving society of many hugely important talents, and promoting into senior management positions in society a disproportionate number of those least able and willing to make acute observations about the workings of society and those least willing and able to act on their convictions in the long-term public interest.)

8. If it is true, as implied by 7, that the level of both competence and ethics that people can be said to display is determined by the extent to which they engage effectively with the wider social forces that otherwise push them toward incompetent and unethical behaviour, what are the perceptions and competencies which are required to understand, and intervene in, these social forces?

If *in*competence arises mainly from failure to deal adequately with Schön's "swamp"—i.e., from failure to deal with all the non-narrowly technical issues which plague one in the course of one's daily work—then serious questions must be asked about the focus of professional education. Perhaps more importantly, staff appraisal becomes problematic. Supposing, for a moment, that the most serious sources of incompetence among teachers might have to do with their failure to create opportunities for *most* of their pupils to develop, and get recognition for, their talents and depriving society of the talents it most importantly needs, what would be the implications? One implication would certainly be that society needs to establish policy research and development institutes that would raise and explore such questions and, in due course, develop the understandings and tools required if teachers are to run more broadly-based programmes. But whose responsibility is it to bring such developments into being? Do not teachers, given the professional responsibilities that society has entrusted to them, have a particular ethical responsibility, requiring very high levels of competence or capability, to raise and publicise such questions? In that case, what new expectations is it appropriate for society to have of the competence and behaviour of teachers? How are we to hold them accountable for performing these responsibilities? What organisational arrangements are required to enable them to carry out these tasks? How are we to ensure that they fulfil these and other responsibilities? Whose job is it to clarify these things? What organisational arrangements and competencies are required to do that?

These papers therefore indirectly call into question the whole way in which we think of incompetence, how incompetence is to be handled (certainly not mainly through initial technical training), whose responsibility it is to handle it (and thus what constitutes *incompetence* in *those* personnel—be they managers or citizens), what competencies are required to evolve the societal learning and management arrangements that are required to handle it, and what competencies are going to be required of those who man these new arrangements.

These issues are central to this book.

Note

1. Sales of Adams and Burgess's (1989) book were discontinued precisely because it was perceived as "yet another staff appraisal system". In fact, its basic message (essentially that it is vital to identify, develop, and utilise the superstar qualities of *everyone* in the organisation) was both radical and at loggerheads with the single-factor models of ability and hierarchy that dominate Western thought. We greatly regret being unable to include a chapter summarising this work here.

References

Adams, E., & Burgess, T. (1989). *Teachers' Own Records*. Windsor, England: NFER-Nelson.

Day, P., & Klein, R. (1987). *Accountabilities: Five Public Services*. London: Tavistock Publications.

Hogan, R. (1990). Unmasking incompetent managers. *Insight* (21 May), 42–44.

Hope, K. (1984). *As Others See Us: Schooling and Social Mobility in Scotland and the United States*. New York: Cambridge University Press.

Raven, J. (1991). *The Tragic Illusion: Educational Testing*. New York: Trillium Press; Oxford, England: Oxford Psychologists Press.

Raven, J. (1995). *The New Wealth of Nations: A New Enquiry into the Nature and Origins of the Wealth of Nations and the Societal Learning Arrangements Needed for a Sustainable Society*. New York: Royal Fireworks Press; Sudbury, Suffolk: Bloomfield Books.

Raven, J., & Dolphin, T. (1978). *The Consequences of Behaving: The Ability of Irish Organisations to Tap Know-How, Initiative, Leadership and Goodwill*. Edinburgh: Competency Motivation Project.

Weaver, T. (1994). Knowledge alone gets you nowhere. *Capability, 1*, 6–12.

PART III

STUDIES OF COMPETENCE

This book is about competence and capability. As illustrated in a later chapter by Alison Wolf, many committees have, by taking soundings from the great and the good, generated long lists of competencies allegedly required by the members of occupational groups and then gone on to set "standards" of competence to be displayed by prospective entrants to those occupations.

There has been much less empirical study of the qualities actually required—of what distinguishes high-level from low-level performance. Yet some of the first studies were conducted half a century ago by Flanagan and his co-workers[1] using "critical incident" methodology. People (superiors, colleagues, subordinates) were asked to describe actual incidents of behaviour that they regarded as effective and ineffective in a job role. These were then sorted into groups. The incidents in each group had something in common with others in the same group but differed from those in other groups.

The results have been more than a little surprising. For example, the effective machine operatives studied by Flanagan in the research just mentioned did such things as work out how the organisation worked and their role in it. They then used this information to take initiative *without having to be given instructions to do so*. In a remarkable study by Klemp, Munger, and Spencer,[2] effective naval officers were found to do such things as reconsider and redefine goals without waiting for orders. They were also more likely than others to develop the competence of their subordinates by having them help them do *their* jobs. This gave the officers an opportunity to make visible to their subordinates, and lead them to practice, the normally private psychological processes that make for competence.

Many of these studies were brought together in *Competence in Modern Society* (Raven, 1984/1997) and *Competence at Work* (Spencer & Spencer, 1993).

But researchers were not the only people to underline the importance of high-level competencies. They were also emphasised by the Manpower Services Commission[3] and Education for Capability[4] in Britain and the Secretary's Commission on Achieving Necessary Skills[5] in the United States.

But how many such competencies are there? Are they infinite? Even if infinite, can they be analysed and systematised in a manner analogous to the way in which we systematise chemical compounds? What's more, how do they knit together? Just as copper sulphate has emergent properties that cannot be predicted by adding together the properties of copper, sulphur, and oxygen (but nevertheless remain consistent), do consistent properties emerge from putting certain types of people together? What is more, how do their properties change as the environment changes—that is, in the sense in which copper is transformed by being placed in the environment of sulphuric acid? These questions—questions about the *conceptualisation* of competence—are topics we will return to in the next part of our book.

Here our objective is simply to illustrate what comes to light if one sets about studying occupational competence in the way just outlined. For space reasons, we have had to limit ourselves to five studies. We would very much have liked to have included at least two more. One would have consisted of a summary of the studies brought together in Donald Schön's *Reflective Practitioner*. Unfortunately, no such summary could be found. The other would have been by Vanessa Druskat on the *Emergent Competencies in Self-Managing Work Groups*. In this case publication was precluded by the logistics of academic publication.

The last chapter in this Part of our book discusses the conclusions that can and cannot be drawn from these studies and others like them. The papers in the Part that follow will take this discussion forward.

But, in pursuit of the theme developed in the chapter with which our book opened, there is one more question to be raised here. The thinking of most of the researchers who have conducted most of the competency studies that have been reported has been permeated by culturally limited notions of "ability," "hierarchy," and "power" and by very limited—non-ecological—concepts of "efficiency" grounded in a reductionist science that neglects (and in which there is almost an injunction to neglect) most of the inputs to, and outcomes of, the process being studied. Given that common observation points to the importance of *diversity,* one is forced to ask what drives this pre-occupation with single-factor concepts of "ability," and with monocultures in human affairs and agriculture. What perpetuates our blind faith in centralised, hierarchical, planning?[6] As we read the chapters which follow, we need to ponder the question of how the importance of the competence to seek to understand, and influence, such vital systems processes could possibly have emerged from them.

Notes

1. Flanagan & Burns (1955).

2. Klemp, Munger, & Spencer (1977).

3. Coopers & Lybrand (1985).

4. Royal Society of Arts (1980).

5. Secretary's Commission on Achieving Necessary Skills (1991).

6. We are indebted to Vandana Shiva (1993, 1998) for crystallising these issues.

References

Coopers & Lybrand (1985). *A Challenge to Complacency: Changing Attitudes to Training.* (A report prepared with, and for, MSC and NEDO). Sheffield: Manpower Services Commission.

Flanagan, J. C., & Burns, R. K. (1955). The employee performance record. *Harvard Business Review, 33,* 95–102.

Klemp, G. O., Munger, M. T., & Spencer, L. M. (1977). *An Analysis of Leadership and Management Competencies of Commissioned and Non-Commissioned Naval Officers in the Pacific and Atlantic Fleets.* Boston: McBer.

Raven, J. (1984/1997). *Competence in Modern Society: Its Identification, Development and Release.* Unionville, New York: Royal Fireworks Press (1997); Oxford, England: Oxford Psychologists Press (1984).

Royal Society of Arts (1980). *Capability Manifesto.* London: RSA.

Secretary's Commission on Achieving Necessary Skills (SCANS). (1991). *Skills and Tasks for Jobs: A SCANS Report for America 2000.* Washington, DC: U.S. Department of Labor.

Shiva, V. (1993). *Monocultures of the Mind: Perspectives on Biodiversity and Biotechnology.* London: Zed Books.

Shiva, V. (1998). *Biopiracy: The Plunder of Nature and Knowledge.* London: Green Books.

Spencer, L. M., & Spencer, S. M. (1993). *Competence at Work.* New York: Wiley.

Chapter 7

Leadership Competencies: A Study of Leaders at Every Level in an Organization[1]

Darlene Russ-Eft
Karen Brennan

The Need

Leadership has always been essential to human society. No human organization can survive long without it. In every culture and every historical period, leadership has played a vital role in the coherence and survival of the group. This universal need for leadership derives from the uncertainties and dangers inherent in the human condition. Day by day, moment by moment, all people experience the need to know what to think, feel, and do. In familiar situations, decisions are easy. But when conditions become confusing, uncertain, or dangerous, the choices are less clear. People instinctively look to leaders for help. Leaders provide models for how to act, think, and react. They can help group members uncover new possibilities within a situation and untapped resources within themselves.

In corporations across North America, real leadership has traditionally been confined to the upper echelons of the organization. The roots of this practice lie in the theories of Frederick S. Taylor (1911), an American engineer and efficiency expert. Taylor sought to optimize industrial efficiency by performing time-and-motion analyses on each industrial task. Each task was broken down into discrete actions and then reconfigured so. that workers could perform those tasks in the fastest and most efficient way possible. By mechanizing human labor—having each worker on the assembly line perform only a few specialized actions—Taylor sought to compensate for the overall lack of skills in the labor force. Along with this mechanization of labor came a sort of mechanization of management: an extensive management structure to organize and supervise employees. The idea was to minimize individual responsibility in order to maintain an efficient and uniform manufacturing process.

In an economic environment increasingly shaped by the globalization of competition, deregulation, the maturation of markets, and breathtaking rate of technological development, this kind of structure has proven unwieldy. Bending to the need to introduce new, high-quality products and services quickly, many corporations have moved toward flatter organizational structures that emphasize participative management and teamwork on the part of multiskilled employees. Individual contributors in team-based environments are taking on more and more responsibility for improving processes and products. As executives and managers find themselves sharing more of the decision-making authority with individual contributors, an emerging consensus highlights a need for leadership at all levels of the organization.

Popular books on management and business claim that effective leadership throughout an organization is now essential. Kotter (1988) stresses "the need for effective leadership at the lower levels of the hierarchy." Champy (1995) points out that the trend towards the re-engineering and flattening of organizations requires all employees of an organization to participate in leadership. Comments made in focus groups conducted by AchieveGlobal[2] in 1994 representing different types and sizes of organizations also support this view.

While there is growing consensus on the need for everyone to exercise leadership, there is still little agreement on what, precisely, leadership is. Block (1993) proposes replacing the "command-and-control" hierarchies with collaborative leadership arrangements in which both decision-making power and accountability are shared between managers and individual contributors. His concept of leadership rejects common notions of defining purpose for others, controlling others, or taking care of others. Champy seeks to recast the traditional manager as a "liberation leader," a leader who can "let go," who enables employees to get work done by providing support, removing obstacles, and challenging their imaginations. Carnevale (1990) describes leadership as a "delicately sculpted image" built upon attributes such as reliability, goal orientation, vision, and the ability to cultivate the respect of peers. To be effective, a leader must couple these skills with what Carnevale calls "organizational effectiveness," an understanding of the goals, value, and cultures of organizations and how to operate within them.

If the need for leadership is great, the need to identify and articulate the skills and attributes that make up effective leadership is also great. We undertook a review of the research literature on leadership and leader competencies in hopes of discovering a set of characteristics common to the competing models and definitions.

Analysis of Leadership Models

Researchers at AchieveGlobal analyzed over 100 leadership studies conducted during the 1980s and early 1990s in an attempt to identify the common attributes of good leadership. The only characteristic found to be universal in these reports was "vision." Effective leaders help to establish a vision, set standards for performance, and create a focus and a direction for organizational efforts.

Three other characteristics appeared repeatedly:

- Ability to communicate a vision effectively (often through the use of symbols and symbolic actions).
- Commitment to and passion for the organization and the ability to communicate that to others.
- Ability to inspire trust and build relationships.

Beyond these four characteristics, the consensus breaks down. Each study provides a long list of attributes associated with effective risk-taking (e.g., flexibility, self-confidence, interpersonal skills, task competence, intelligence, decisiveness, understanding followers, courage, and so on) but none of these attributes are identified by more than two of the studies.

General Competency Studies

In addition to leadership surveys, we also reviewed general competency studies—studies aimed at determining the basic skills and competencies employers look for in employees. From 1984 through 1991, five major studies of workforce skills were commissioned by the Secretary of the U.S. Department of Labor (SCANS, 1991), the American Society of Training and Development (ASTD), the Michigan Employability Skills Task Force, the New York State Education Department, and the National Academy of Sciences (NAS). Three of these studies—those commissioned by SCANS, ASTD, and Michigan—identified leadership skills as an important category of interpersonal or teamwork skills.

Each of the three studies, however, defined leadership skills differently. SCANS emphasized persuasion, while the Michigan study emphasized the capacity to "know when to be a leader and when to be a follower." The ASTD study focused on "sharing leadership," which was closely associated with interpersonal skills, teamwork, and negotiation.

What Are the Fundamental Leadership Attributes?

While each of the previous studies has shed some badly needed light on issues surrounding leadership, as a group they display a surprising lack of consensus about which characteristics of leadership are fundamentally important. Each study defines leadership differently. Each model develops its own categories of leadership characteristics or competencies; only rarely do these overlap. Significantly, none of the studies has queried individual contributors—those outside traditional management roles. Most of these studies surveyed only senior management, while others concentrated on or included middle and line managers.

Consequently, none of these studies gives us a true picture of the leadership characteristics needed currently at all levels of an organization. What, for instance, are the leadership qualities an individual contributor or team member will need when co-workers look to him or her for guidance on a certain issue? Clearly, as organizations grow increasingly flatter and more streamlined, a different kind of leadership model is needed.

The AchieveGlobal Study

As the first step toward developing that model, we undertook a study of leadership in over 450 organizations (representing a nearly 50 percent response rate). The object was to survey both managers and non-managers, in more or less equal numbers, and to ask them to identify instances of leadership at different levels throughout the organization.

A variety of organizations were surveyed: heavy industrial, hi-tech, service industry, government, and education. The study included organizations ranging in size from less than 250 to over 10,000 employees from all of the major regions of the United States and Canada. These organizations all had one thing in common: all had seen above average growth in the number of employees over the three years before the study was done.

Researchers randomly selected two individuals from each organization—one manager or executive and one individual contributor—and asked them to recount recent instances of both good and poor leadership. They were asked to cite examples of leadership in both managers (supervisors, middle management, and senior executives) and non-managers (individual contributors, team members, project and program leaders):

> Think of a time within the past month when a person in your
>   organization showed good leadership:
> What did the person do that showed good leadership?
> What was the result of this behavior?
> What was the person's position in your organization?

Researchers asked similar questions about poor leadership.

By asking respondents to name instances of both good and poor leadership, researchers hoped to identify the full range of characteristics that make up leadership at all levels of an organization. The respondents described hundreds of instances. Researchers broke these events down into "critical incidents" of either "good" or "poor" leadership—some events contained more than one incident of leadership. Using the critical incidents methodology originally developed and described by Flanagan (1954) and used in thousands of studies over the past 50 years, researchers set up tentative categories and broader headings for the incident, then revised and refined these as they sorted and classified the incidents.

A Simplified Model

Russ-Eft (1995) suggests that competencies can be thought of as though they are embedded components of a molecular structure of human behavior. In such a model, the behavioral indicators called critical incidents constitute the "sub-atomic particles." These critical incidents can be classified into larger units called competencies, or "atoms." Such competencies can be classified into a larger set of competencies, or "elements." Finally, a set of competencies can be classified into an even larger set, or "molecules."

Thus a number of critical incidents, or behavioral indicators, or "sub-atomic particles," such as "got the staff connected to PC systems without being given step-by-step directions" and "single-handedly started recycling projects throughout the company," were grouped into a competency labeled "takes initiative to solve a problem." These, in turn, were placed, along with other "atoms" (competencies such as "implements good ideas," "works extra hours or unsupervised," and "helps others") under a broader competency or "element," such as "taking responsibility."

This methodology did not involve a statistical analysis of a representative sample. The object was not to identify the most frequently mentioned leadership attributes but rather to uncover the full range of critical attributes that make up leadership, regardless of organizational level.

Results

Fifty different competencies for universal leadership behaviors emerged. These competencies, in turn, were grouped under 17 larger competencies within *AchieveGlobal*'s proven CLIMB model. CLIMB addresses a leader's ability to:

Create a compelling future,
Let the customer drive the organization,
Involve every mind,
Manage work horizontally, and
Build personal credibility.

The 17 competencies, criteria for inclusion in each, and negative and positive examples in each competency are listed in Table 7.1.

Table 7.1 Criteria and Examples

Create a compelling future

Setting a vision	Positive: sets goals and vision; communicates vision; supports a vision; moves the organization/group in a new direction; does strategic planning
	Negative: provides no vision; does not articulate goals or plans; lets outsiders chart course; doesn't support the vision
Managing a change	Positive: reorganizes to improve the business; shares information about changes; involves others in change effort; supports those who have problems with the change
	Negative: does not support a change; does not share information about a change; does not plan for change; does not involve others in the change effort

Lets the customer drive the organization

Focusing on the customer	Positive: makes improvements; makes changes for the customer's benefit; solves problems for the customer; handles customer complaints; makes sure customers are satisfied; is ready and available to help customers; stands up for customers; consults or surveys customers; is customer driven

Table 7.1 (Continued)

	Negative: is inflexible; does not respond to customers; makes decisions without considering customers; places own convenience ahead of that of customers; ineptness affects the customer; complains to customers; upsets or angers customers
Involves every mind	
Dealing with individuals	Positive: supports; expresses confidence; empowers; listens; solicits ideas and feedback; handles conflicts; resolves disputes; coaches; counsels; trains; reviews performance; supports training efforts; rewards; recognizes; thanks; respects rights and feelings; attacks the problem, not the person; is considerate; clarifies direction, boundaries, and values
	Negative: bad attitude toward others; berates; belittles; degrades; criticizes destructively or in front of others; micro-manages; talks behind the backs of others
Supporting teams and groups	Positive: facilitates meetings (organizes, leads, diffuses disruptions); solicits ideas and feedback; consults with group members; reaches consensus; defends groups under fire; rewards and recognizes group work; empowers; shows confidence in others; delegates; manages the workload among the team members; clarifies direction and boundaries; coaches; encourages training; encourages team spirit
	Negative: hinders meetings, etc.; fails to do the positive
Sharing information	Positive: shares information that is needed; shares at the right time; provides correct information in an appropriate manner about changes
	Negative: opposite of above
Solving problems and making decisions	Positive: includes relevant stakeholders; pays attention to solicited input; makes efficient, timely decisions; overcomes obstacles; works out bugs
	Negative: avoids decisions; doesn't get enough information; reverses or overrides a decision; fails to solve a problem
Manage work horizontally	
Managing business processes	Positive: manages procedures or ongoing activities within and between groups; promotes consistency or efficiency between groups; improves processes; sets and enforces work standards and testing; removes barriers between groups (two managers); solves problems related to processes; improves procedures; follows procedures

Table 7.1 (Continued)

	Negative: opposite of above; does not cooperate/coordinate in inter-group activities; does not support or stick to procedures
Managing projects	Positive: manages the "non-people" aspects of a project; conceptualizes; secures human and material resources; completes an effort successfully (in terms of time and budgets); implements; guides; assists; follows up on details; revitalizes a flailing project; contributes to implementation of projects
	Negative: opposite of above; unrealistic planning; constant change in schedule; no commitment
Displaying technical skills	Positive: meets or exceeds technical standards; applies skill and knowledge to technical jobs; gives/gets training or consulting in technical areas; has a good attitude toward work; completes work successfully; does or insists on high-quality work; is thorough; is well prepared
	Negative: makes technical errors; takes an unprofessional approach; ignores proper procedures; has a bad attitude toward work; does not work competently; lacks knowledge or understanding; does poor-quality work; is not supportive of technical training
Managing time and resources	Positive: meets deadlines; uses good time management; allocates resources; uses resources wisely; plans for a person's departure or absence; creates a new plan, process, or form that saves time/money
	Negative: misses deadlines; wastes resources; doesn't plan for personnel changes; causes duplication of effort; does something that results in a waste of time and/or resources

Build personal credibility

Taking responsibility	Positive: demonstrates accountability; takes responsibility when things go wrong; stops the buck; bites the bullet; makes risky or tough decisions; questions authority; takes a tough stand; blows the whistle; follows through; covers for other's absence; defends the group; works without direction or support
	Negative: passes the buck; oversteps authority; is absent when needed ("goes fishing"); blames others; doesn't act when action is required; is reactive, not proactive; doesn't stand firm
Taking initiative beyond job requirements	Positive: takes initiative; goes beyond what is expected; pitches in; takes over when boss or co-worker is absent; puts more effort into the task than was required; offers help; volunteers new ideas

Table 7.1 (Continued)

	Negative: doesn't measure up to what was expected; doesn't offer help; won't do more than absolutely required
Handling emotions	Positive: Handles own emotions; remains calm; maintains composure; handles emotional situations; diffuses heated situations; recognizes potential emotional blowups; takes control; calms others down
	Negative: blows up; loses temper; falls apart under stress; loses control; fails to handle emotional situations
Displaying professional ethics	Positive: works professionally; observes ethical guidelines
	Negative: lies; cheats; shows unfairness or favoritism; takes illegal actions; abuses others verbally; harasses others; tells off-color jokes; threatens; discusses confidential information; talks behind the backs of others
Showing compassion	Positive: helps charitable causes (e.g., food drives); aids someone in crisis; counsels/guides someone with personal problems; acts of sympathy and compassion
	Negative: antagonizes someone under personal stress
Making credible presentations	Positive: Makes persuasive presentations; skillfully presents information; has a good presentation style
	Negative: does not speak persuasively; fails to convey important, correct information; does not prepare well

Managers vs. Individual Contributors

As one looks over these 17 competencies, it seems reasonable to expect the critical incidents under one competency to involve mostly managers and those under another heading to involve mostly non-managers. Similarly, one might expect many categories to contain manager-related incidents exclusively. Managers (and other designated leaders) usually face a different set of tasks and responsibilities than do individual contributors. Interestingly, critical incidents involving individual contributors as well as those involving managers are well represented under each competency and under almost all critical incident competencies.

Several competencies contain almost equal numbers of incidents to which both managers and individual contributor contribute in significant ways (e.g., "takes initiative to make decisions," "implements a good idea," and "takes initiative to do a task"). Of the 50 critical incident competencies identified, only three ("is fair," "makes tough decisions," and "involves all stakeholders") contain no incidents pertaining to individual contributors. Critical incidents involving managers are represented in all categories.

Leaders both inside and outside of managerial positions, then, display a common set of leadership behaviors. The same capacities for setting vision, sharing information, and supporting teams and groups (to name but a few) are displayed by leaders at all levels of the organization.

Leadership Partners

This display of common behavior points to an emerging collaborative leadership between individual contributors and those in managerial positions. Effective leaders in managerial positions might be expected to spend a great deal of time communicating with and developing their co-workers, to work well under stress and constant change, and to possess flexible, consensus-oriented leadership styles.

Leaders outside traditional managerial roles look beyond their prescribed duties to identify problems and take responsibility for finding solutions. They develop a sense of ownership and vision and partner with their supervisors and co-workers to move their team, department, and organization forward. They speak frankly to both their peers and superiors yet maintain an environment of mutual respect in which teamwork and cooperation can flourish. In short, to paraphrase Kotter, they concentrate less on doing their jobs and more on getting the work done.

As the new century dawns, organizations find themselves embarked upon a journey—sometimes heady, sometimes terrifying—through the uncharted waters of the global marketplace. As organizations restructure to meet the demands of this new environment, a new model of leadership is emerging. Increasingly, individuals outside of designated managerial positions are being called upon to lead—to take their teams, departments, work groups, and organizations in new and innovative directions. Increasingly, it is they who must identify the problems and opportunities and devise the means to deal with them. Those in managerial and executive roles must learn how to support this new kind of leader through mentoring, encouragement, consulting, training, and facilitation. As companies grow leaner and more flexible, effective leaders at every level of the organization, including individual contributors, are coming to share a basic set of leadership skills. It is not hard to imagine a time when distinctions between those in formal and those in informal leadership positions in an organization will become almost invisible to an outsider.

Notes

1. The research on which this paper is based is published in full in Bergmann, Hurson, & Russ-Eft (1999).

2. AchieveGlobal, Inc. represents a merger of three organizations: Kaset International, Learning International, and Zenger-Miller.

References

Bergmann, H., Hurson, K., & Russ-Eft, D. (1999). *Everyone a Leader: A Grassroots Model for the New Workplace.* New York: Wiley & Sons.

Blake, R., & Mouton, J. S. (1985). *Managerial Grid III.* Houston, TX: Gulf.

Block, P. (1993). *Stewardship.* San Francisco: Berrett-Koehler Publishers.

Bolman, L. G., & Deal, T. E. (1991). *Reframing Organizations.* San Francisco: Jossey-Bass.

Bridges, W. (1993). *Job Shift.* Reading, MA: Addison-Wesley.

Carnavale, A. P., Gainer, L. J., & Meltzer, A. S. (1990). *America in the New Economy.* San Francisco: Jossey-Bass.

Champy, J. (1995). *Reengineering Management.* New York: Harper Collins.

Flanagan, J. C. (1954). The critical incident technique. *Psychological Bulletin, 51*, 327–358.

Hersey, P. (1984). *The Situational Leader.* New York: Warner Books.

Hurson, K. (1996). *Measuring Executive Return on Influence.* Paper presented at the Assessment, Measurement, and Evaluation of Human Resources Performance Conference, Boston.

Kotter, J. P. (1988). *The Leadership Factor.* New York: Free Press.

Russ-Eft, D. (1995). Defining competencies. *Human Resource Development Quarterly, 6*, 329–335.

Secretary's Commission on Achieving Necessary Skills (SCANS). (1991). *Skills and Tasks for Jobs: A SCANS Report for America 2000.* Washington, DC: US Department of Labor.

Taylor, F. W. (1911). *The Principles of Scientific Management.* New York: Harper & Row.

Young, R. S. (1995). Executive ROI: Return on Influence—An Analysis of the CLIMB Survey. Unpublished Report. San Jose, CA: Zenger Miller.

Chapter 8

On the Leading Edge: Competencies of Outstanding Community College Presidents

Carolyn Desjardins
Sheila Huff

Editor's Note

Our reason for including this chapter is to illustrate the nature of high-level competencies as they emerge from an empirical study. Few of those involved in the preparation of job specifications would have guessed at the importance of these competencies. The insights provided into the psychological nature of these competencies are also outstanding. Yet the chapter also reveals the need for a way of summarising and systematising these insights. Unfortunately, the chapter originally prepared by Carolyn Desjardins and Sheila Huff was too long for inclusion here. An editorial scalpel has therefore been rather crudely wielded . . . and the surgery has been increasingly severe as the text progresses—by which time it is assumed that readers will have "got the idea." For the many whom, it is hoped, would liked to know more, full information on the study will be published in Carolyn and Sheila's book, *The Leading Edge: Competencies for Community College Leadership in the New Millennium*.

Introduction

First, some comments anticipating readers' questions and reactions.

The material to be summarised is described as a "competency model." How was the model developed?

The methods used are generally referred to as "critical incident studies." Top performers in a role are identified and interviewed. The interviews average two hours in length and are tape-recorded for later analysis. The interviewees are asked to stay within the time frame of the last year to year-and-a-half, so that details of their experiences can be recalled, and to select episodes which represent challenges they have faced. These episodes are probed in depth to understand the context, what the interviewees did, and their underlying thoughts and feelings. The tapes are then analysed for themes. The themes are organised by concepts or constructs referred to as "competencies." Each competency is defined by the list of its associated themes, or "indicators."

For this updated model, six presidents were interviewed. Carolyn Desjardins, of the National Institute for Leadership Development, collected the nominations. It is important to state that not all presidents nominated as outstanding were included in the sample. A sample size of six was deemed sufficient for re-investigation, since we had a database of 74 interviews from an earlier community college presidents' model we developed in 1988. Sheila Huff, who conducted the interviews and analysis, independently rated all six current participants as outstanding based on competency models for other leaders that she has developed over the past 20 years (which included high school principals; presidents of non-traditional colleges and community colleges; navy senior officers; and auto and high-tech industry executives). The final stage in completing the competency model was to submit it for review to the six current participants in the sample. The response of participants was that the model accurately reflects the competencies of their positions.

This model certainly is value-laden

Indeed, the model is value-laden. We believe that underlying values drive the development and application of competencies as strongly as other "social motives," such as the needs for achievement, affiliation, and power—the latter of which receive considerable attention in the competency models of David McClelland and his associates.

Clearly, this community college presidents' model reflects a philosophy of leadership and education based upon principles of democracy and empowerment as opposed to authoritarianism and matriarchal or patriarchal administration. Thus, many values follow from the democratic and empowerment axioms. Others follow from a passion for the vocation of education, and so on. Rejection of these values would render much of the model "not applicable." That is precisely why models cannot automatically be transferred across cultures without further validation.

Isn't there something that transcends the competencies that guides their application?

What the competency model does not reflect is the transcendent wisdom and common sense involved in applying the competencies selectively in any given situation. For example, while it is important that presidents champion change, change is not good in and of itself. Change can be foolhardy in certain circumstances, and priorities must always be set as to what to change and when. Creating cohesiveness, likewise, might situationally be set aside as an objective. For example, when debate does not reach consensus, people may "agree to disagree" and proceed experimentally on two paths to see what transpires.

What is a competency model's shelf life?

The question is often raised as to the shelf life of a competency model. Our answer is to explain that a model is a function of the interplay of the environment and the values, motives, and preparation of leading practitioners in the role. In the list of competencies which follows, the competencies have been grouped under headings identifying key environmental factors and challenges faced by today's community college presidents and how they relate to the competencies. The participants suggested revisiting the model in three to five years as experience accumulates on how best to lead and manage in a global society, in the information age, and in a climate of shrinking funds from traditional sources. As a general rule of thumb, we like to revisit models at least every five years to identify changes and to adequately reflect advances in the state of the art.

Help! The model is overwhelming!

What follows is the comprehensive *research* competency model for the role of community college presidents. The model is long and complex, reflecting the complexities of the role. This comprehensive research model can serve you as the foundation for building many applications to enhance the state of the practice in the field. The research model can be streamlined based on priorities that *you* set for particular applications. For example, you can develop a set of interview questions for candidates for president based on a limited set of the competencies that have been identified by your search committee as priorities. The best way to handle complexity is to set priorities, and as researchers we believe it is you practitioners who should make these important decisions situationally.

Sorry. No one is this good!

The competency model is an "ideal" paradigm, or "written role model" reflecting the competencies that some of America's most outstanding community college presidents have *in common*. That is, while each president in the sample possessed all the competencies, each competency was not equally strong. Some, for example, were more creative and skilful than others at fund-raising, others were more experimental in developing new processes, etc. In other words, one would want to apprentice with each one of the presidents in the sample in order fully to develop each competency. Practically speaking, the wise and fortunate leader finds a complement to his/her capabilities within the management team.

The Competencies

Leadership
1. High-Involvement Leadership
2. Creates a Shared Vision
3. Champions Change
4. Maintains Perspective
5. Maintains Equilibrium

Culture/Climate
6. Student-Centered
7. Community-Centered
8. Values Cultural Pluralism
9. Creates Cohesiveness
10. Prevents Crises
11. Empowers Others
12. Fosters Creativity and Innovation
13. Recognises and Rewards Excellence

Influence
14. Influences Strategically
15. Communicates Effectively
16. Effectively Manages Board Relations

Business Management
17. Maintains High Standards
18. Manages Finances Proactively
19. Invests in Staff Development
20. Strengthens Infrastructure
21. Enhances Productivity
22. Corrects Performance Problems

Examples of the actions grouped under some, but not all, of these competency headings are shown on the following pages, followed by a sample of relevant quotations from those interviewed. (As explained in the editorial introduction, many of the quotations and some of the expansions have been eliminated here but can be found in Desjardins and Huff's book.)

1. High-Involvement Leadership

- Institutes and/or enhances democratic structures and broad-based participatory processes of governance, planning, and decision-making.
- Stays connected and involved in the teaching and learning activities of the college; maintains identity as an educator as well as an administrator.
- Stays highly accessible to faculty, staff, students, the board, and peers in the district; gets to know as many people as possible on an individual level.
- Serves as an exemplar of the philosophy, ethics, and values he/she espouses.
- Seizes opportunities to shape public policy and otherwise influence the future of community colleges.
- Strikes an optimum balance between providing ample opportunity for dialogue and debate and moving ahead decisively.
- Builds respect for his/her professional skills, wisdom, and good will that leads others to support decisions made unilaterally during crises.
- Retains veto power in decisions of the college in keeping with his/ her accountabilities as president.

Quotations

I don't know if you know that line in scripture that says "To each is given gifts for the whole," but I love that. And I've always thought that as the CEO or president, the only job I have is to figure out ways that all those gifts can be drawn out and moved in the same direction.

How we make decisions is more important than what happens in my view . . . I was hired because of my strong reputation in shared governance—particularly in faculty relations . . . We abolished the numerous steering committees and restructured the college from a governance standpoint . . . instituted a thorough, wide, shared-governance model.

We've got a leadership team of a dozen people now and we make decisions together and not until we get input from people who will be affected . . . My approach has never been one to dictate what should be done from the top down but to try to get as much bottom-up input into the solution to problems as possible.

I was very public during that period. I became a very strong and pretty articulate spokesperson for the need for restoring public investment in higher education. I wrote articles in regional papers and spoke to a lot of associations about investing in our public colleges.

2. Creates a Shared Vision

- Incorporates broad-based input in drafting and revising the college's vision statement (e.g., one-on-one conversations; facilitated forums).
- Spearheads a process for all sectors of the college to articulate their values and agree upon a common set to which the institution will publicly commit.
- Inspires faith that what might heretofore have been thought to be impossible can be done through teamwork, creativity, and dedicated effort; overcomes negativity and scepticism.
- Uses the college's vision statement as a touchstone for discussing priorities of the college and evaluating results.
- Helps people see the connection between their everyday activities and the broader vision for the college.
- Keeps the vision, values, and general principles of the college alive and central in everyone's thinking.

Quotations

A mission statement from the legislature doesn't give a group of people a direction to move in. So the thinking with a vision statement was that as a very large institution, it's difficult to communicate on a regular basis unless we have some organising framework that helps us all pull in a common direction . . . The challenge was for people throughout the organisation to feel good about and own what we came up with in a way that did not rely on me beating them over the head with it. They would own it and it would take off on its own steam and we'd be reinforcing one another. And frankly, it's an accountability mechanism. I mean if I start veering off in some direction, I can be held accountable by the entire group—"Hey, how does this fit?" So it is kind of a mutual check.

They (external people) had obscured their vision from the empty hole for the building just as they had obscured their vision from the blight, poverty, and racism in that other town. So how do you recapture, re-envision, and create a dream? And it took several years before we were to a point where we were financially ready to do it and where we could begin to make that happen . . . The facility is unbelievable, and the night that we opened was not the dream deferred but the dream unfurled, and it was a phenomenal thing, and black and white sat there together in that community and realised this was their field of dreams. We had built it. They had come! And now it serves as a major cultural center for that whole part of the country. And it was a phenomenal story. It captured the community. It captured their hearts and it made them believe that all things were possible again.

3. Champions Change

- Has high energy for moving ideas forward; serves as a catalyst for and champion of change.
- Bases decisions about major changes on careful investigation into the merits and drawbacks of what is currently in place; involves the college in weighing the costs and benefits of options.
- Tailors change projects and problem solutions to the unique characteristics and needs of the college; refrains from imposing preconceived concepts and models.
- Manages change from a vantage point of insight into the perspective and interests of the various stakeholders.
- Times change in accordance with windows of opportunity and people's receptivity (e.g., makes any major changes to the organisational structure early in his/her tenure when people expect such changes to occur).

- Selects priorities for change carefully, taking care not to exhaust people or detract resources from the central mission and priorities of the college.
- Satisfies people's need for more immediate, visible improvements while working on longer-term, less visible changes.

Quotations

In order to make changes like that, you have to know very well why the change is necessary and you have to be able to communicate that effectively to others or you won't get anywhere. Weak leadership or scattered leadership has never brought about change.

The president has a bully pulpit, too, and communicating effectively and leading people is critical, because a president who follows the old model of a few ceremonial functions but letting them teach and simply building buildings—that's not going to bring about change in an institution, and institutions need to change.

Big, arduous decisions have to be made early in your administration. I think if I were coming up with this now, it would be very difficult . . . People don't cut you as much slack as they do a brand-new president, so you need to take full advantage of the honeymoon period as long as you have full buy-in from the people.

I've found it very useful to focus on large themes in one's opening years rather than try to have a scattered chaotic agenda. Context is everything. What might work at one institution will not work at another.

It was important to me, while working on sort of invisible things in the area of governance infrastructure, to show dramatic progress in highly visible things. And of course there's nothing more visible than the physical plant.

4. Seeks Out Broad Context

- Maintains a broad perspective on the college; resists getting so involved with details that one loses sight of the big picture.
- Accumulates insight and understanding of what a healthy college looks like and is quick to spot departures from the ideal.
- Works quickly, on taking office, to become familiar with all aspects of the college's operations.
- Studies the history of how things came to be as they are at the college in order to put deliberations about change into historical perspective.

- Continually reflects upon own leadership experience and that of others to identify concepts and ideas of relevance to his/her practice.
- Stays abreast of social, economic, demographic, and other trends at the local, national, and global level, and considers what they could mean for the college.
- Engages in activities to expand his/her perspective on the college and community.
- Keeps the long-term good of the institution always in mind; does not sacrifice long-term good for short-term gain.

Quotations

Leadership is not a lot of statistics and detail . . . I think you should know the detail, but a good leader stays at the broad-brush level and keeps things moving.

To survive and become effective, the president has to be a creature of the institution. It can't be simply a distant presence. It has to be a functioning leader within the institution who knows that institution.

The guest lectures I gave were to help me just get a sense of who the students were, what the style was of teaching. You learn a lot about faculty members from doing that, and then teaching my own class was like a crash course in the college itself.

I also taught twice when I was there. Two years ago I taught a freshman class at 8:00 a.m. because I wanted to see what our students were like.

This is my (XX) year of being a college president, and there are things you pick up along the way and if you listen carefully and read and draw parallels and relationships between events elsewhere, you can do a lot . . .

I can "gestalt" a situation pretty well and quite quickly. Some of that is because I worked at the staff level and did a lot of campus visits and have been an evaluator for an accreditation group and I've been in a lot of different situations myself, so I have a pretty clear vision of what a healthy college ought to look like.

I keep trying to look at things and think, "Now what have I learned in the past to deal with this in the best way possible?"

I have personally found it more instructive to read about the Clinton administration, what went wrong in the Carter administration, etc., because they are far more analogous to what I'm doing than some of the trade books. Even to read about Alexander the Great and leaders from the past like Cleopatra and look for common themes away from one's business, as it were.

In years past, we would prepare students for jobs in a specific locale and it was very unlikely that they would move very far from that specific locale. Now we're preparing jobs for a global workforce or at least for jobs that have global requirements in terms of the skills needed for that workforce entry. So yes, the globalisation of the economy and the globalisation of the workforce has direct implications for what we do and the training we provide.

5. Maintains Equilibrium

- Carefully matches own career choices to his/her skill set, interests, and longer-term developmental and career goals.
- Makes the huge job of the presidency manageable by identifying people in the organisation to whom he/she can reliably delegate.
- Balances work and obligations with activities that sustain and refresh the spirit (e.g., hobbies, nonjob-related organizational memberships, intellectual interests).
- Cultivates a sense of humour and an ability to keep life's ups and downs in perspective.
- Reaches (judiciously) out to trusted others for comfort and advice in troubling situations.
- Makes the difficult decision of changing venue when necessary to restore his/her vitality.

Quotations

You can't give that passionately or deeply for so long and not find yourself void sometimes.

Part of knowing one's own humanity is being in touch with some of the absurdities of being a human being—that we are pretty laughable and that we don't confuse our serious work with taking ourselves too seriously—so being able to see the difference, laughing at ourselves as we go about this serious work and actually putting that fun to work within an organisation. Consciously doing that. We actually at one point had it as one of our objectives for the institution to be able to laugh and play and put fun to work.

I really do try to meditate in the morning, at night, and as many chances as I get during the day to recognise that these things that I'm doing are the work that I am intended to do at this moment in time and that this is it! Right now! This is heaven, which is not to say that I don't believe in an afterlife. I do. But if I am fully present to the now, that's what it's going to be like. And I truly do find deep joy in that, and at a very practical level, I find that I have a real tailwind and save fuel when I can stay connected with the presence of that spiritual life.

7. Community-Centered

- Ensures that the college serves as a model institution for the community in its values, processes, and achievements.
- Becomes a visible, connected presence in the community, participating in activities and organisations that match his/her skills and interests.
- Coordinates his/her community involvement with the faculty and staff in an effort to gain as broad coverage as possible of all sectors of the community.
- Maintains high presence for the college at community ceremonies.
- Grounds curriculum planning and development firmly in community needs assessment (e.g., interviews, focus groups).
- Kindles cooperative, mutually beneficial organisational relationships with citizen groups and community organisations.
- Inspires allegiance in the business community by drawing clear links between the college's and business's values, commitments, and aspirations.
- Creates pride and ownership by engaging community members in planning the future of the college.
- Helps people in the communities the college serves to take on leadership roles for the betterment of the community.

Quotations
I have an almost messianic belief that education can make an incredible difference and we were the hope of the future for so many individuals within that area.

The community college to me is the very essence of the community . . . The college becomes a model of institutional change for the community.

If we were to make a difference, we had to put away all those biases and listen to those (community) women—most of them were women—tell us what their needs were and completely energise the system to look differently at how we serve that population.

My role with the community became really involved. Almost anything that went on in the county people would think of me as being one of the people to be involved directly or have somebody from our college involved. That was one of the things that surprised me becoming a president. My whole background has been in teaching and academic administration. I didn't realize how much of my time would be spent in public, external arenas and working with people in the community. Also with the legislature. And I enjoy that. I think it is interesting. But you have still to stay enough involved internally so you can speak authentically about what is going on.

8. Values Cultural Pluralism

- Views cultural pluralism as invigorating and exposure to diverse cultures as a vital component of a good education.
- Promotes cultural pluralism, from the board through the faculty and student body, as a priority of the college, soliciting ideas and supporting initiatives to that end.
- Uses the demographics of the communities served by the college as a benchmark for setting diversity goals.
- Ensures that recruiting practices and personnel policies and procedures support diversity goals.
- Recognises that various cultural/ethnic/social groups are not necessarily monolithic and homogeneous; attends to the differences and disagreements that exist beyond common bonds (e.g., Hispanics are not a single culture but rather, many cultures with diverse interests).

10. Prevents Crises

- Creates a culture where people debate, disagree, and air grievances in a manner that shows respect for each other's intelligence and humanity.
- Lets angry people voice their feelings; does not react defensively or punitively.
- Takes care never to shoot the messenger who bears bad news; asks to be the first to know about a serious problem.
- Sets a tone of concern and responsiveness when any group becomes upset about an issue.
- Stays alert for portents of adversity.

- Stays highly visible and accessible in tense situations; maintains personal connection with the people and events.
- Mitigates fear, rumours, and discord in difficult times for the college by broad-based dialogue, full disclosure of information, and timely status updates.
- Understands the interests, values, and affections of the various sectors of the college community sufficiently to predict their general responses to adverse developments.
- Publicly and energetically advocates on behalf of the college and its students when forces threaten its existence or integrity.
- Organises and prepares faculty and staff, in advance of potential crises, to deal with the situation effectively.
- Helps people think about concrete, positive steps they can take to deal with crises when they occur despite efforts to prevent them.
- Works cooperatively with the union(s) to clear up old grievances and prevent new ones from arising in the future.

Quotations

I was very public during that period (of financial crisis). I became a very strong and pretty articulate spokesperson for the need for restoring public investments in higher education in X (region of state). I wrote articles in regional papers and spoke to a lot of associations about investing in our public colleges. They were talking about closing colleges and ours was on the list. So I had to go and talk to all the legislators and people in the governor's office and newspapers about that, and they finally took our name off the list.

Whenever there was a serious problem, I always called an all-college meeting that was open to everybody so everybody could have a direct discussion of what I knew, and I used e-mail to keep people up to date. I think that broad, honest, and complete information about what was going on was critical in getting us through those times (large state budget cuts). It created a whole sense of trust, a sense of "we're all in this together," a sense that we had to work together to deal with these problems and that they could believe what I was saying.

My thinking was when in doubt, get everyone together and communicate, and it's got to be personal. You can't lead by memo in my book. Also, it's human nature for people to want to get together in a crisis, which is what this was.

Even though we didn't know the outcome, we had established an administrative command meeting for 7:30 the next morning in my office to talk about what we should do—for Wednesday morning. We had that ready to go. The second thing we had ready to go is that we have a voice mail system, and we pre-programmed it so that I could give a voice mail bulletin to everyone (faculty and staff). The bulletin was to simply let everyone know that this had passed, that it was complex, that they'd get lots of questions, but this is what they should say.

And the very first thing that happened was the X Student Organisation called me personally to come down where they had gathered to talk with them. They didn't hit the streets. They wanted me to come. Why? Because they knew me and wanted to discuss with me what should happen next. Now in a lot of other institutions, they just took to the streets. At X College, they were arrested. And last year at Y College, they were arrested. There's no need for these things to happen. If you have a personal, accessible relationship with students, they will turn to you.

The union leader asked me to go with her to discuss the situation with her union membership. She was in over her head. So I said, "Sure. This is *our* problem; we're not going to cut you off. You are in the circle. Your problems are our problems."

I was told that several men saw some of these women as strident feminists out to get them, so I proposed a meeting with the men who were expressing dissatisfaction, and they said they would love to do that. So I met with about twelve men, just them and me, and had about a three-hour discussion about what they were feeling and why this had become such an issue and what they were concerned about.

11. Empowers Others

- Encourages everyone in the college to take initiative and to provide leadership; does not view him/herself as "the leader" among followers.
- Gives people as much latitude as possible to determine how they will go about attaining agreed-upon goals and objectives; refrains from micro-managing.
- Takes steps to mitigate his/her positional power where it may interfere with the empowerment of others (e.g., suppresses his/her opinions when people are engaged in formative debate).
- Rejoices in others' optimism; takes care not to extinguish excitement or behave overprotectively.

- Empowers broadly (e.g., makes any adjustments to the governance structure required to achieve representation of all sectors of the college).
- Empowers in meaningful domains (e.g., includes faculty and staff in deliberations on how to downsize, how to operate the institution more efficiently, how to cut costs, etc.).
- Locates decision-making authority at the level where people are closest to the issues and in possession of the most reliable information.

Quotations

It's good for the institution to have a multitude of heroes within.

They came to me and I funded it, so it's not so much myself as the superstar, because this was a plan that was ten years old and was never done. They felt somehow that now, my being their president, allows them to make progress again.

The culture is different now—a more open environment and not paternalistic. I've told people "I can't take care of you but together we can take care of ourselves."

I had this whole idea (for getting broader participation) since I came here, but now the time is ripe. So we talked about it at some length. I more or less played the role of working with them to draw it out. That's something I worked hard to do because that achieves what I see as my ultimate end in leading a group and that is that they would become more self-reliant and develop more of an internal locus of control—that they would feel the satisfaction of having done something themselves and less reliant on formal leaders.

We have something we call a "town meeting," which is part of our strategic planning process. It is a way we have of engaging in corporate conversations. It is our way of deliberating. Instead of jumping right to a vote on something that is quite raw, pretty low level, underdeveloped and certainly not our best work, we deliberate on it together over a period of time . . .

That's where the role of CEO as cheerleader comes into play. I don't know how to write a specific technical grant proposal, but we have very capable people who do, and if I encourage them enough and motivate them enough and outline the need enough and cheer their efforts enough, I'm absolutely confident they will get where we need to be.

My role was setting the charge and letting people, again, do the creating. Although I could have done a lot of the work in the X area myself because that's my background and I had some strong feelings about that, it was sitting back because they came up with the best thinking that could possibly occur. They just did it! And they were willing to work out the bugs.

That was another part of my Management Assumptions (written document)—that decisions be made at the lowest possible level . . . like Committees would invite me in to share some of their thinking, and my comment to them was "Can I make a comment or two that you are not going to say is a mandate? Can I just talk to you?" Because sometimes when the president would say things, they'd listen to you when they really should tell you to shut up. So you have to be very cautious about everything you say.

Titles are just awful. They get people locked into all kinds of silly things. When people ask me about titles, I tell them, "I don't care. Call me Queen if you like. I don't care what you do, but this is what we have to get done! So let's get beyond this title thing."

She accepted the challenge provided she could revise her organisational structure, which I gave her total latitude to do.

We downsized and got a lot of people involved in the decisions. In fact, the first year I was here we had a large committee of people together and my instructions for them were to identify ways that we can effect savings at this institution without affecting the primary mission of the college, which is teaching and learning. They came up with a substantial amount of savings, and we implemented them, and some people didn't have their jobs as a result of what we did a few months later, but the people who lost their jobs were ancillary to the core of what we are all about . . .

I recall one person who had worked very diligently in industry. He was approached to develop a national curriculum in his speciality. The specifications of what they wanted were very complex. He was an excited young man and he told them, "Of course we can do that!" and he came to me and said, "Doc, I told him we can do it and we can deliver this in 13 weeks." Well, I bit my tongue and I thought "Oh, God, he's yet to meet the Curriculum Council. DON'T TELL HIM it will take 13 weeks just to get it on their agenda!" I realized that if I told him and set up all the barriers of how negative this is going to be, he'd leave here all deflated. So I said, "X, that sounds wonderful! Let me give you a few names of people you need to get to, starting this afternoon, and let's see how you are doing on this." I didn't set up any negatives. He bounced out and a couple weeks later he looked a bit deflated and said, "I just met with the

Curriculum Council and . . ." I said "Just don't let that discourage you." And wouldn't you know, at the end of 13 weeks it wasn't quite all done but he was darned close to completing the major tasks to be done!

This wonderful custodial services person came to me and said "This is what I'd like to do. I want to create this arboretum. We need to have wonderful plantings out here, and why don't we make this occur when there are births and deaths in the family, they can buy a tree here." Well we created a plan and you can't believe how lovely these places are, gorgeous places with plantings.

I knew what needed to happen all along, but they did it themselves and were proud of it.

12. Fosters Creativity and Innovation

- Creates an organizational culture that encourages people to experiment and take risks to solve problems and pursue opportunities.
- Appreciates the value of ambiguity; allows time for ideas to percolate.
- Encourages flexibility and imagination in finding ways to make the impossible happen.
- Experiments with techniques that unleash people's creativity.
- Generates and is receptive to unconventional ideas.
- Expands or modifies governance structures to incorporate innovative, creative thinkers.

Quotations

We had a lot of retreats and different things with faculty with all kinds of folks where we'd go and stay all night, two nights maybe, out on a YMCA camp on the edge of the lake and we would talk . . . We'd bring in people, like for our work on creating a new paradigm—some of that early work on paradigm. We did that years ago! It was cutting edge at that time.

I think it is also important to appreciate the value of ambiguity even as you seek clarity.

They knew that creativity was prized. Part of the values statement I put out, one of the things says "Prizing Creativity and Innovation," and the very next statement is "Everyone has the right to fail." And that is important too, because if you are going to have a creative atmosphere, you must permit failure to occur, and sometimes it will. And you have to let people know they won't be punished for that.

The program received recognition, and at the (national) conference podium he said, "I just want you to know that this was developed because I looked at her (pointing to me) and I knew she wasn't going to fire me if all did not go well because Item 14 on her list of management assumptions says 'Everyone has the right to fail!' " And he was serious.

13. Recognises and Rewards Excellence

- Knows how to say "thank you," and says it often.
- Takes care to acknowledge the contributions of everyone involved in the successes of the college.
- Makes certain people know that their efforts and achievements have been noticed by the president and are sincerely appreciated.
- Adds a special, personal touch in providing recognition (e.g., celebrates with people when they receive awards).

14. Influences Strategically

- Familiarizes him/herself with the political interests and agendas of the various individuals and groups within and related to the college—the board, the legislature, etc.
- Makes the investment of time and energy necessary to gain buy-in and support.
- Develops arguments that link to the perspective and appeal to the interests of those whom he/she wishes to convince (e.g., develops carefully constructed business cases to convince business-minded people of the merits and feasibility of proposals).
- Understands and capitalises upon the symbolic meaning of actions—the broader message being sent.
- Structures situations and the environment to convey messages and achieve particular objectives (e.g., president's office decor designed to put people at ease; round tables to signify equality).
- Advertises and "banks" successes; builds an outstanding reputation and network of supporters of the college.
- Thinks systematically about spheres of influence, taking care not to overlook people with non-official power.
- Develops team strategies and plans for complex lobbying efforts.
- Makes full use of his/her network and contacts to bring their influence to bear in matters important to the college.

Quotations

To get the kind of buy-in you want is a very slow, laborious, time-consuming process, but I'd rather go through that process to get understanding and ownership. I'd never swap that for some sort of dictum that might yield the same results short-term but not nearly the results long-term.

We have annual luncheons not only for the legislators but for their staff members, because . . . the legislators themselves are very busy people and oftentimes it is the staff members who can make or break a deal.

We went around and talked individually to the opponents and sat down, one on one, for a discussion . . . We spent time talking it through. Everyone who worked on this, and we did work as a team and almost lobbied these people, but we wanted to get somebody to talk with each one about their particular concern then to try to support their point of view but to bring them into understanding how this would be a positive thing for the college. And it did pass.

As you know, the official leader of any group gets to manage the language. So that (central governance concept) is one of the ways I managed the language. I just started talking about it in every possible way, and now I'm hearing everyone else use the language.

15. Effective Communications

- Has a genuine interest in what people have to say; listens attentively and with an open mind.
- Responds to incoming inquiries promptly; takes care not to slow down others' progress.
- Institutes and maintains routine communication vehicles targeted to all key sectors of the governance structure (e.g., sends monthly progress reports).
- Unclogs channels that prevent or inhibit direct communication with the president (e.g., invites e-mail; holds issue forums).
- Equips people with the information they need to take initiative and make wise choices.
- Emphasises to the college community the importance of communicating effectively and sharing information.
- Is meticulous about the details of key communications and presentations of the college; ensures a professional image and high impact.

- Uses the magic of language and the power of symbols to communicate memorably when the occasion demands.

Quotations

I use e-mail all the time because it's an easy way to flatten an organisation and to get the same information out to everybody and get responses. (In my new job) I'm encouraging people to use e-mail with me to dialogue back and forth. For them that's a whole new concept. I have people tell me it would never occur to them to think they would dare communicate directly with a president! So it is fun trying to change some of that.

When you spend time listening to someone—celebrating them—that's always a good time. That always feels good.

People are hungry for information and a chance to be included in a sense of what's happening and direction. You need to keep using multiple forums because it's a constant struggle to maintain openness in communications.

I spend a lot of money duplicating materials, but every member of the faculty gets a monthly packet showing enrollment changes, showing the impact of the various plans. It costs a little bit more to give everyone maybe a 20-page document once a month, but that's what we do. The board and district staff get it too.

The one-on-one communication with the leadership of these (college) organisations requires a lot of my time, and I think it's a wise investment of time because the leaders then go back and interpret decisions to their membership in more positive ways than would otherwise be possible.

When you are asking someone for a million-dollar gift, you give a million dollar presentation.

16. Effectively Manages Board Relations

- Invests time in educating board members about the operations of the college and providing background information to new board members.
- Makes time for casual contact to get to know board members as individuals.
- Attends to the dynamics of the board; invests time and effort in enhancing working relationships among board members.
- Maintains a high level of clear, trustworthy, and timely communications with the board.

- Keeps the faculty and staff well informed about important concerns and activities of the board. Builds ownership of decisions among board members by keeping them involved in key undertakings and decisions from the outset.
- Engages board members in sharing their knowledge, skills, and connections to help the college achieve its objectives.
- Encourages the Board to be active in professional associations and in touch with the state of the art in leadership and management practices.

Quotations

Even though I report indirectly to the board, I go to lunch regularly with the board members, some more than others. Usually at least once a month I have lunch with one or two of them. I make sure I have a semi-social relationship with each one of them. I just think it's important. My philosophy is that if you can draw upon personal good will, that's 90% of the struggle.

My approach here—and elsewhere too—has been to try to keep the leadership team as well informed as possible about everything that is going on with the board and, in turn, expect them to do the same with their staff members so that there is not a void of communication and so that there are no surprises whatever the issue might be.

I think every one of them called the board (with objections), but because the board had followed along and were kept well informed and knew me personally, they were able to respond to these people better than I could have.

When you get a new board member, you have a whole new set of dynamics working. Not only am I spending time making sure this new board member knows enough about the college to be an effective board member, but you're also spending time worrying about and working on the new dynamics created by even one new board member. That takes a good amount of time to do properly.

I ask board members who are well connected with the legislators to help make our case and convey our dilemmas—just one of a whole variety of vehicles to communicate and share the story of our need with legislators.

17. Maintains High Standards

- Conveys the philosophy that anything worth doing is worth doing well; stresses attention to quality in all aspects of the college's operations and endeavours.

- Recognises the limitations of solitary thinking; submits his/her ideas for review and critique and encourages others to do likewise.
- Appreciates what can be learned from professional consultants and employs their services to complement and enhance skill sets on campus.
- Ensures that sound processes are in place for finding the right person for each job in the college.
- Clearly contracts with people around values, standards, and expectations before hiring them.
- Hires strong people who are ethical and who will stand up for what they believe in.

Quotations

I wanted the legislators to see the college as an absolutely class act. That meant that everything we did had this incredible quality about it. It wasn't just slick presentation, but it was quality. And everybody felt so good about that. The centres and the college set a level of excellence for the community . . . And there was a level of expectation raised about how we delivered service, how we treated students, how we treated each other . . .

I have a list of management assumptions on how I will operate . . . There is a series of things that includes a whole belief in excellence, and everyone received that when they came to work for the college—whether they were the president of the faculty senate or the custodial staff. So that kind of level of expectation played itself out in everything that we did. And it was so inherently a part of who we were—part of the culture.

We have a group of very gifted people that we compensate fairly well, so why wouldn't we want them to share their ideas as often and as broadly as possible?

18. Manages Finances Proactively

- Thoroughly understands the fiscal foundations and status of the college (e.g., investment portfolio and rationale; historical funding patterns; cash flow; monthly reports).
- Knows what to examine or query to competently evaluate the college's financial situation.
- Brings the financial offices of the college into the governance mainstream (e.g., has financial officers demystify financial processes and reports, expand participation in budget preparation and allocation

decisions, and be open with faculty and staff about the financial condition of the college).

- Takes a proactive stance to develop new or expanded funding sources for the college.
- Augments the ideas and efforts of novices with expert assistance in developing sound strategic and tactical plans for fund raising.
- Opens doors and provides encouragement and backing for faculty engaged in fund-raising activities.
- Organises and spearheads lobbying campaigns and relationship-building activities targeted to legislators, government, and foundation programme officers and other funding sources.
- Partners with other colleges, joins consortia, etc., to increase the likelihood of successful proposal efforts and to provide opportunities and services the college could otherwise not afford.

Quotations

After about a year, when it became clear this (funding reduction) wasn't a one-time thing but a long systemic problem, at that point we really changed our whole approach. We realised we had to develop a plan for systematically living with a smaller budget or else developing new revenues, and we did both of those things. What we did was develop a policy approach to the whole thing which went around the college in several drafts and was eventually approved by our board of trustees. So there were no surprises in terms of the direction.

The successful president is the president who knows how to reallocate. Otherwise you simply watch everything slowly deteriorate.

Especially with the economic problems that the country has had in the last five years, the importance of dealing effectively and telling your story well with the legislature has just soared because we have to rely so heavily on them . . . We have legislators out here whenever we can and never let them leave without some little memento to remind them of us.

Working with the legislature is a year-round activity. People who think that you work exclusively with the legislature when it's in session couldn't be further from the truth, because it's a year-round challenge and responsibility.

We decided we would also pursue alternative sources of funding. I hired a grant developer who had been laid off from another college in their cut, which was interesting. He was very, very good and over three years we increased our grant activity dramatically. And there were several other things we did to raise money as well as to make cuts.

Ten million dollars doesn't come from a bake sale, so I sat down and worked with a couple of people and put together what we called "the hit list," if you will. I was trying to come up with what I considered the 50 real power brokers in the community. And I meant, as well, financial power brokers.

Finding the right people (for fund-raising) is part of what you do. You collaborate and you bring in the very best to do that . . . We did a very systematic job of looking at what we knew we could raise.

What I've found is that very few people call programme officers. I call them all the time, and they like to be called . . . because grant funding is personal as well, and if they like a certain group of faculty members, they go out of their way to be helpful.

19. Invests in Staff Development

- Evaluates the skill sets of the college against goals and objectives and develops plans to address discrepancies.
- Invests in formal education and training to increase the skills of the faculty and staff in their academic and speciality areas.
- Provides faculty and staff with opportunities to develop the skills they need to ready the college for the future.
- Provides education and training opportunities for people to enhance their leadership skills.
- Encourages and underwrites active participation in professional associations and attendance at conferences.
- Increases the value of training opportunities by sending people in groups and encouraging groups to convene afterwards to reinforce and apply learning on the job.
- Is generous in sharing his/her experience and expertise as coach or mentor.

Quotations

I still see so much of this old kind of thinking around an authoritarian approach to problem-solving, and midrange supervisors put into these positions and have no idea how to deal constructively with difficult human situations. We've done quite a bit of work on process improvement and getting work groups together and doing some experiential kinds of game-playing, then analyzing those things and looking at some quality improvement strategies and having the work groups take projects they're really dealing with and work on them over a period of a couple months—kinds of process improvement for work groups. That kind of thing is so critical. It's one thing to think about it for your top managers, but the real trick is trying to find ways to get that training and change approach to permeate the whole institution.

I also spend a lot of time one on one with the leadership, especially the leader of the college senate so that she feels she has total open access to me as the CEO of the organisation. That takes a lot of time, but it's great to see the "aha moment" when she sees the bigger picture, because faculty members have a limited job which is to teach and care for and nurture students. But within the parameters of the realities we deal with in trying to run an institution, there's a lot more involved to create a positive teaching and learning environment. The leader of a college senate, for example, can be very helpful as he or she understands some of the other challenges we face. So the one-on-one sessions with the leadership of these organisations requires a lot of my time, and I think it's a wise investment of time because the leaders then go back and interpret decisions to their membership in more positive ways than would otherwise be possible.

Acknowledgements

We wish heartily to thank the 74 community college presidents who participated in our earlier research beginning in 1986 and the six who participated in our 1995 update. Their encouragement, humanity, and candid sharing of experiences sustained us in the long hours of analysis.

Thanks to Nona Lyons and Jane Forbes Saltonstall for their insights and assistance in the beginning phase of the research and interviews in 1986 at Harvard University.

Thanks to the National Institute for Leadership Development family and to the American Association of Women in Community Colleges for their participation and support. Thanks also to the Maricopa Community College District for giving birth to the Institute, and especially to Phoenix College for providing a home for the Institute.

Great care was taken in the review and critique of this report by the six community college presidents in the 1995 update and by Sheila Huff's teammates: C. Ann Carver, Jeanne Douglass, Gary Villani, and Maureen

Webster. The assessment questionnaire that is available, based on the competencies in this report, was created primarily by C. Ann Carver, who has the prerequisite expertise and fortitude for such a daunting undertaking. We thank her immensely.

Reference

National Institute for Leadership Development (2000). *The Leading Edge: Competencies for Community College Leadership in the New Millennium* (Research by Dr. Carolyn Desjardins, presented by Sheila Huff). Phoenix, AZ.

Chapter 9

The McBer Competency Framework

John Raven

By the mid 1980s, some 350 studies of the kind illustrated in the chapters by Russ-Eft & Brennan and Desjardins & Huff had been carried out. These had placed the importance and operational accessibility of a whole range of high-level competencies that had previously eluded all but the most penetrating observers beyond reasonable doubt. At the same time, they called the assumed importance of a range of "motherhood" competencies of the kind dreamed up by committees of the great and the good—largely areas of *knowledge*—into serious question. As far as knowledge was involved, what was needed was unique combinations of up-to-date specialist—and largely tacit—knowledge, not general knowledge.

Unfortunately, the studies which had been carried out varied somewhat in methodology and considerably in the frameworks used to classify and discuss the results.

Building on a framework parts of which had previously been published by Dalziel, Boyatzis, and others, Lyle and Signe Spencer therefore set about trying to develop a common—or agreed-upon—framework of descriptors to use to describe the competencies noted in one study or another, the levels at which they were required or displayed, and to relate the competencies required or displayed to the nature of the work to be undertaken. This framework, together with extensive real-life illustrations of what was meant by the terms, was published in 1993 as *Competence at Work*.

It is important to note that the framework is entirely based on study of the thoughts, feelings, and overt behaviours associated with real actions—or "behavioural incidents." It is not based on the speculation of committee members and bureaucrats. Yet neither is it based solely—or even mainly—on external observation, or "ratings." It includes information from "inside the respondent's head"—information about his or her goals, thoughts, motives, feelings, strivings, and intentions.

The methodology used to elicit this information—*Behavioural Event Interviewing*—is fully described in *Competence at Work*. This is important not merely in its own right—as a contribution to the methodology required to assess competence. It is also vitally important because it demonstrates how radically these assessments differ from both external observers' *ratings* of observed behaviour and from "personality test" measures of what may at times be thought to be the same constructs. The latter are largely based on cumulating information that indicates how strongly people say they are predisposed to undertake one kind of activity as against another. Assessments derived from *Behavioural Event Interviewing* reveal the kinds of activity for which the individual concerned has in the past displayed a strong motivational predisposition to undertake and the *level* of competence displayed whilst performing those kinds of activity.

It is important to underline that what this research has shown is that what distinguishes more from less effective performance in a wide range of jobs has to do with the motivational predisposition to undertake certain kinds of activity and the *spontaneous tendency* to undertake those activities at a certain level of competence. While the ability to behave competently in one or other of these ways may or may not be teachable and learnable, it is the strength of the individual's spontaneous tendency to display high levels of competence in relation to certain activities in specific situations that determines his or her competence.

Further work by Spencer and his colleagues—as the number of competency studies grew to some 600—refined the competency by level dictionary published in *Competence at Work* and distilled it down to 18 generic competencies plus a number of competencies mainly of value in specific situations. This revised dictionary is available as McBer's *Scaled Competency Dictionary 1996*.

The list of generic competencies discussed in the *Scaled Competency Dictionary 1996* is shown in Table 9.1.

In order to illustrate how this works, the competency by level framework for two generic competencies—"developing others" and "impact and influence"—are given in Tables 9.2 and 9.3.

It must again be emphasised that this is not a framework for classifying observer's ratings. It is a framework for classifying the information obtained from interviews in which a carefully guided effort has been made to discover the kinds of activity people are strongly motivated to undertake and to elicit the respondent's thoughts and feelings while undertaking those activities.

Table 9.1 Generic Competencies: Summary

1. **Achievement Orientation (ACH)**
   Core: Does the person think about meeting and surpassing goals and taking calculated risks for measured gains?
2. **Analytical Thinking (AT)**
   Core: Does the person understand cause-and-effect chains and relationships?
3. **Conceptual Thinking (CT)**
   Core: Does the person match patterns? Assemble many pieces into a coherent whole? Create new ways to look at things?
4. **Customer Service Orientation (CSO)**
   Core: Does the person act on behalf of the person being served?
5. **Developing Others (DEV)**
   Core: Does the person work to develop the long-term characteristics (not just skills) of others?
6. **Directiveness (DIR)**
   Core: Does the person set firm standards for behavior and hold people accountable to them?
7. **Flexibility (FLX)**
   Core: Can the person change gears or drop the expected task when circumstances demand it?
8. **Impact and Influence (IMP)**
   Core: Does the person use deliberate influence strategies or tactics?
9. **Information Seeking (INF)**
   Core: Does the person go beyond the obvious and seek out information?
10. **Initiative (INT)**
    Core: Does the person think ahead of the present to act on future needs and opportunities?
11. **Integrity (ING)**
    Core: Does the person act in line with beliefs and values even when it is difficult to do so?
12. **Interpersonal Understanding (IU)**
    Core: Is the person aware of what others are feeling and thinking, but not saying?
13. **Organizational Awareness (OA)**
    Core: Is the person sensitive to the realities of organizational politics and structure?
14. **Organizational Commitment (OC)**
    Core: Does the person choose to act in accordance with authority, organizational standards, needs, and goals?
15. **Relationship Building (RB)**
    Core: Does the person take effort to build a personal relationship?
16. **Self-Confidence (SCF)**
    Core: Does the person take on risky tasks or conflicts with those in power over that person?
17. **Team Leadership (TL)**
    Core: Does the person lead groups of people to work effectively together?
18. **Teamwork and Cooperation (TW)**
    Core: Does the person act to facilitate the operation of a team of which he or she is a part?

Table 9.2 Summary of Scoring System for Generic Competencies: *Developing Others* (*DEV*)

Developing Others: Involves a genuine intent to foster the long-term learning or development of others with an appropriate level of need analysis and other thought or effort. Its focus is on the developmental intent and effect rather than on a formal role of training.

Core: Does the person work to develop the long-term characteristics (not just skills) of others?

Scoring Notes: The underlying intent to foster others' development must be clear. This is especially important for the lower levels of DEV which may otherwise be confused with lower levels of Directiveness (DIR). The *developmental intent* is the distinction between the two competencies.

Level	This Person:
1.	**Expresses Positive Expectations of Person:** Makes positive comments regarding others' developmental future: current and expected future abilities and/or potential to learn even in "difficult" cases. Believes others want to and can learn or improve their performance.
2.	**Gives How-To Directions:** Gives detailed instructions and/or on-the-job demonstrations, tells how to do the task, makes specific, helpful suggestions.
3.	**Gives Reasons, Other Support:** Gives directions or demonstrations with reasons or rationale as a training strategy. Gives practical support or assistance to make job easier for subordinate (i.e., volunteers additional resources, tools, information, expert advice, etc.). Asks questions, gives tests, or uses other methods to verify that others have understood explanation or directions.
4.	**Gives Feedback to Encourage:** Gives specific positive or mixed feedback for developmental purposes. Reassures others after a setback. Gives negative feedback in behavioral rather than personal terms, *and* expresses positive expectations for future performance or gives individualized suggestions for improvement.
5.	**Does Longer-Term Coaching or Training:** Arranges appropriate and helpful assignments, formal training, or other experiences for the purpose of fostering a person's learning and development. Has people work out answers to problems themselves so they really know how, rather than simply giving them the answer. This does not include formal training done simply to meet corporate requirements. May include identifying a training or developmental need and establishing new programs or materials to meet it.

Table 9.3 Summary of Scoring System for Generic Competencies: *Impact and Influence (IMP)*

Impact and Influence: Implies an intention to persuade, convince, influence, or impress others, in order to get them to go along with or to support the speaker's agenda. It is based on the desire to have a specific impact or effect on others where the person has his or her *own agenda,* a specific type of impression to make, or a course of action that he or she wants the others to adopt.

Core: Does the person use deliberate influence strategies or tactics?

Scoring Notes: Levels 2 and 3 refer to uncustomized or relatively unsophisticated means of persuasion. That is, the same argument or point could be made to any other person in the same general situation. Levels 4 through 6 are customized or personalized to the individuals or situations at hand, and imply some Organizational Awareness (OA) and/or Interpersonal Understanding (IU). Either or both of these are often scored as well, with sufficient evidence. If a person uses a number of customized efforts for the same purpose (e.g., relating to the same subplot of a story), score all those actions as 5 or 6. Do not score those actions separately.

Level	This Person:
1.	**States Intention but Takes No Specific Action:** Intends to have a specific effect or impact; expresses concern with reputation, status, appearance, etc., but does not take any specific actions.
2.	**Takes a Single Action to Persuade:** Uses direct persuasion in a discussion or presentation (e.g., appeals to reason, data, others' self-interest; uses concrete examples, visual aids, demonstrations, etc.). Makes no apparent attempt to adapt presentation to the interest and level of the audience.
3.	**Takes Multiple Actions to Persuade:** Takes two or more steps to persuade without trying to adapt specifically to level or interest of an audience. Includes careful preparation of data for presentation OR making two or more different arguments or points in a presentation or a discussion.
4.	**Calculates the Impact of One's Actions or Words:** Adapts a presentation or discussion to appeal to the interest and level of others. Anticipates the effect of an action or other detail on people's image of the speaker. OR takes a well-thought-out dramatic or unusual action in order to have a specific impact. Anticipates and prepares for others' reactions.
5.	**Uses Indirect Influence:** Uses chains of indirect influence: "Get A to show B so B will tell C such-and-such." OR takes two steps to influence, with each step adapted to the specific audience. Uses experts or other third parties to influence.
6.	**Uses Complex Influence Strategies:** Assembles political coalitions, builds "behind-the-scenes" support for ideas, gives or withholds information to have specific effects, uses "group process skills" to lead or direct a group.

Further examples from the framework will be introduced in the section of this book that deals with conceptualising competence. Here it is sufficient to note that it is impossible to use this framework without thorough familiarity with (a) the procedures required to elicit the basic data, and (b) the extensive examples of thoughts, feelings, and behaviours that do, and do not, fit into the various competence by level categories assembled in *Competence at Work*. It is, in particular, important to note that the descriptions given of the *levels* at which these two competencies may be displayed are summaries. Higher levels of the competencies actually involve (1) a greater breadth or completeness of action, (2) more complex thinking—taking more things, people, data, or causes into account, (3) longer time horizons, and (4) a greater breadth of impact.

By training people—much as one trains a chemist—in the procedures required to elicit the data and what to make of it—it has been possible, as will be shown in a later chapter by McClelland, to achieve inter-worker reliabilities of .9. "Profiles" of the competencies by levels that make for success in different kinds of job are available in *Competence at Work* and other publications listed in McClelland's later chapter.

References

Hay/McBer. (1996). *Scaled Competency Dictionary*. Boston: Hay/McBer.

Spencer, L. M., & Spencer, S. M. (1993). *Competence at Work*. New York: Wiley.

Chapter 10

Competence in Context:
Identifying Core Skills for the Future[1]

George O. Klemp, Jr.

This paper was written with two different audiences in mind: One audience is research practitioners who identify competencies required in the world of work, and the other is the one charged with helping students develop these competencies in higher education. One thing that both audiences have in common is the need to divine the nature of the workplace of the future so they can identify and develop the core skills that will take today's graduates into employment roles where they will flourish rather than leave them with an inventory of capabilities that are necessary but unfortunately not sufficient for success in the years to come.

What is meant by "core skills"? In the world of work, one might define them as "survival" skills, or capabilities needed to achieve minimally acceptable levels of performance in a job. They might also be defined as capabilities that distinguish outstanding from average performers in a variety of occupations. Or they might be defined as capabilities that enable a person to interact effectively in a wide variety of work environments and other aspects of life. Whatever the definition, it is important to define these skills in terms of the role they play in achieving outcomes important to individuals and/or the institutions that employ them. Core skills then become grounded in two factors: the requirements of tasks to be performed and the organizational, social, and other environmental contexts within which they are performed. Understanding these requirements, one can define the knowledge needed to carry out the tasks and the skills and abilities needed to translate knowledge into effective action.

For the purposes of this paper, I choose to define core competencies as those based on the differences between effective and less effective performance of job tasks in the context of large organizations. Since the beginnings of my work in this area over 20 years ago, as I have attempted to understand what makes the difference between exemplary and average performers in a wide variety of occupations, I have been struck by the realization that so many of our early discoveries have stood the test of time. In 1977, I wrote "Three Factors of Success," an essay on what I believed to be the areas of competence that were essential for effectiveness in the world of work. In a nutshell, these factors were:

1. Cognitive skill, including the ability to see patterns in information, to understand different sides of controversial issues, and to learn from experience;
2. Interpersonal skill, including demonstrating empathy for others, the ability to empower others through positive regard, and refraining from inappropriate impulsive behavior; and
3. Motivation, including the drive for achievement, the need for influence, and the disposition to take independent action, or initiative.

It is striking how stable these observations remain as indicators of success today. And with all that is known about the role of interpersonal skills and motivation as important determinants of success, it is even more remarkable that few institutions of higher learning have actively considered these factors in the design of curriculum. Writing this paper has provided an opportunity to examine these concepts anew, to build on the 20 years of research that has gone into articulating these concepts further, to peer a bit into the future of competencies and their relation to the changing requirements of the workplace, and to further articulate the role of educators in preparing their students for the future.

Job Competence Assessment vs. "Intelligence" Testing

Perhaps the place to begin is to briefly review the job competence assessment method as practiced by David McClelland and his colleagues. Although the notion of competence began with Robert White (1959), who labeled it a basic human drive to acquire personal skills and effectively manipulate the environment, McClelland (1973) can probably be credited with energizing the competence discussion in his article "Testing for Competence Rather Than for 'Intelligence.'" McClelland noted that the traditional route used by psychologists to determine predictors of success in work and other aspects of life is to conceive of a construct ("intelligence," for example), develop statistically reliable paper-and-pencil tests of the construct, and then administer these tests to groups of people who differ in performance of some outcome of interest. By contrast, McClelland argued that one should start with highly effective performers, learn what makes them different from others, and then develop measures of the capabilities demonstrated by the high-performing group. Competence, he argued, is something that can be empirically defined, and standardized tests constructed to capture performance should be more valid as predictors than theoretically derived proxy measures of the skills needed for success.

Barrett and Depinet (1991), in an article challenging McClelland's assertions about the invalidity of such tests, have assembled a variety of evidence from other researchers showing the predictive power of standardized testing. But what do such test scores predict? Although Hunter and Hunter's (1984) reviews using statistical meta-analysis techniques showed substantial correlation between intellectual aptitude and job performance in entry-level jobs, much of this may be due entirely to Ghiselli's (1966) finding that trainability in a new occupation, rather than actual job performance, is more readily predicted from IQ. Barrett and Depinet do not challenge McClelland's point that characteristics other than intelligence do predict occupational success (e.g., Campbell, Dunnette, Lawler, & Weick, 1970; Thornton & Byham, 1982). Finally, few of the studies that link aptitude and IQ to job performance are of complex professional or managerial jobs; those that investigated this relationship usually found that IQ correlates much higher with level of occupational attainment than with actual success in one's job (Matarazzo, 1972; Hope, 1984; Raven, Raven, & Court, 1998).

Though competency testing has not shown the promise that McClelland had hoped, the idea that performance is more than a matter of IQ and standardized testing has been made by many equally respected but less controversial researchers (e.g., Gardner, 1983; Sternberg, 1986). They and others make the point that "intelligence" is a complex, multidimensional attribute not measured well by traditional intelligence tests. Most agree that a general intelligence factor (g) is one of the bases of human capability but that its importance to job performance and success in other aspects of life is overstated. All the research of which I am aware assumes that a certain minimum (usually unstated) amount of general intelligence is needed to carry out the basic task requirements of any job. However, beyond this point, other attributes such as interpersonal skills and individual motivation take over in the performance equation.

As illustrated in other chapters of this book, what these other attributes are has been the subject of job competence assessment research. When compared to the records of average performers in the same job or role, the differences were often startling. The exemplary performers consistently demonstrated different ways of viewing similar situations; reported different mental, verbal, and behavioral responses; and reported higher-level outcomes than those reported by their less-accomplished peers. Accumulating these data over 20 years has enabled us to discover what makes top performers "tick" in professions ranging from insurance sales-persons, commodities traders, chief financial officers, inventors, geologists, health care professionals, adult educators, senior executives, and management consultants. We have aggregated these data into competency databases that can be sorted by occupational title, organizational level, industry, and numerous other demographic factors. Currently, however, these databases lack an underlying framework with which to organize competencies in ways that are more useful than a dictionary of personal attributes. The next sections of this paper suggest two directions for rectifying this situation: One considers competencies from a person-centered perspective, consistent with other theories of intellectual functioning; the other considers competencies in terms of the nature of work and the work environment—the context of performance.

The Person-Centered Approach: A "Supply-Side" Model

Most of the work on job competencies has taken what is essentially a person-centered approach: It identifies exemplars in an occupation or role, describes the competencies that are correlated with their effectiveness, and uses these so-called competency models as the basis for hiring, training, and promotion. When these competencies are described in behavioral terms (sometimes referred to as behavioral indicators), they become observable. When these behaviors are defined as they would be observed on the job, they become useful as agents for behavioral change through training and performance feedback; when these behaviors are described in terms of root processes, i.e., as generic indicators of competency demonstration, they are more useful as criteria for selection.

This way of viewing competencies describes the person who performs exceptionally well rather than the work the person performs. It is essentially a trait-based approach that defines characteristics of the high performer rather than characteristics of work that require certain competencies to be demonstrated. However, this approach lends itself to a taxonomy of abilities that can be related readily to the literature on cognitive development in complex occupations (e.g., Jaques, 1989) and theories of intellectual functioning from the world of cognitive psychology (e.g., Sternberg, 1986).

Given the interest in the relationship between intellectual and interpersonal competencies as topics for a higher education curriculum, Table 10.1 presents a taxonomy that relates sets of these skills in terms of common underlying processes. These processes are presented as a developmental sequence, beginning with basic pattern recognition. Pattern recognition involves the use of knowledge and experience to determine the meaning of new situations: When there is a match with previously understood patterns or concepts, the nature of the current situation is defined. Pattern recognition also involves simple matching of information to an ideal case—proofreading for errors or visual inspection of materials for flaws, for example. When viewed in the context of problem solving, we labeled the competency *skillful diagnosis,* such as would be demonstrated by a physician who observes symptoms and identifies the likely disease. In the context of interpersonal relationships, the competency that mirrors this process becomes *interpersonal sensitivity,* or the ability to "read" the feelings of others through verbal and non-verbal cues. The underlying process in both cases is the same; only the nature of the data is different.

Table 10.1 Taxonomy of Intellectual and Interpersonal Competencies

Underlying Principle	Process	Intellectual Manifestation	Interpersonal Manifestation
Recognition ↓	Recognizing patterns in data and verbal and nonverbal behavior, similarities between present and past situations, and discrepancies between observations and the ideal case	Skillful Diagnosis	Interpersonal Sensitivity
Use of Logic ↓	Applying cause-and-effect logic (inductive and deductive reasoning) to the process of solving problems and communicating with others	Analytic Thinking	Persuasion
Synthesis ↓	Constructing solutions that explain complex relationships among dissociated information (e.g., data, past experiences, and observed behavior)	Conceptual Thinking	Strategic Influence
Divergence/ Convergence	Thinking tangentially; dissociating normally associated elements and recombining them into meaningful new concepts	Creativity	Symbolic Influence

Moving down the table, the process of linking concepts and observation using the rules of logic constitutes the next level of functioning, which is labeled *analytic thinking* in the intellectual domain and *persuasion* in the interpersonal arena. These competencies differ in their targets (problems to be solved vs. people to be "sold") and the motives that underlie them; the drive behind analytic thinking is the *need for achievement,* or the concern for efficiency and personal excellence, while the drive behind persuasion is the need for power, or the concern for influence and impact on others. The next level of complexity, where available data are not sufficient to prove the case and critical information is missing, people construct their own reality by developing and acting on hypotheses about the way their world works. *Conceptual thinking* is the intellectual competency equivalent of synthesis, where disparate pieces of information are brought together and summarized and masses of data are aggregated and construed into patterns and themes with great explanatory power. The interpersonal competency, *strategic influence,* sometimes known as "political astuteness," is how people conceptualize the power relationships among people in organizations and use this understanding to get things done.

Finally, the process of divergent thinking goes beyond established concepts or frameworks and establishes entirely new ways of viewing the world. *Creativity* as an intellectual competency is demonstrated by research scientists and inventors through the process of breaking the bonds that connect ideas and observations in memory and imagining how these disassociated ideas might go together in new and interesting ways. Most creative breakthroughs in science and art occur when people put preexisting elements together in combinations that have never before existed. In the interpersonal world, divergent thinking manifests itself in *symbolic* influence, the creation of organizational visions and missions, and the use of symbolic acts to communicate and promote them. These visions are often very powerful precisely because they are new ways of viewing the familiar. A good example is that of AT&T, which changed its view of itself as "the phone company" to the company that "brings people around the world together." The power of this vision has energized employees in a way that the old one never did and is contributing to AT&T's competitiveness.

Table 10.2 represents 170 recent job competency studies from our database to illustrate the frequency with which exemplary professionals and managers in different industries and functions demonstrated aspects of each of the above competencies. *Skillful diagnosis* revealed itself to be a basic competency in these studies, meaning that it was sufficiently present in both exemplary and average performers so as not to be a distinguishing characteristic in the majority of cases; however, its social equivalent, *interpersonal sensitivity,* was a distinguishing competency in more than half of these studies. From this table I conclude that these competencies can be considered core skills, with the exception of *creativity* and *symbolic influence,* both of which occurred much less frequently among managers and professionals.[2]

Another underlying theme that may not be obvious in this person-centered approach but can be readily stated: The hierarchy of intellectual and interpersonal skills presented in Tables 10.1 and 10.2 also corresponds to how people carry out tasks of varying difficulty and complexity and under different levels of ambiguity. This brings us naturally to a bridge between taking an essentially psychological understanding of competency and an understanding based on the nature of the requirements imposed on us by our environment. If we are to take the latter perspective, we

Table 10.2 Frequency of Intellectual and Interpersonal Competencies among Exemplars in Professional and Managerial Positions

Competencies	Behavioral Indicator	Professionals (113 studies)	Managers (57 studies)
Intellectual			
Skillful Diagnosis	Applying knowledge and experience to new situations	30%	26%*
Analytic Thinking	Critically evaluating alternatives and priorities	63%	75%
Conceptual Thinking	Making connections to larger frames of reference	38%	6%
Creativity	Using available resources in novel ways	19%	23%
Interpersonal			
Interpersonal Sensitivity	Identifying unstated issues and feelings	62%	53%
Persuasion	Getting agreement through data-based argument	62%	67%
Strategic Influence	Using complex influence strategies	43%	44%
Symbolic Influence	Creating and reinforcing a vision or broad purpose	10%	35%

* This competency was a minimum requirement for most jobs in the Cambria database; as such, it seldom passed the threshold for distinguishing exemplary performers from their average counterparts.

need first to understand the challenges that confront people in the work-place, then to understand which competencies are needed to deal with these challenges successfully.

Despite the importance of the person-centered approach to identify-ing competency requirements, it has a number of problems. First, al-though competency models are developed from the study of people in real work settings, there is no way to reconstruct the work just by looking at the competencies themselves. For example, knowing that *persuasion* is a competency that distinguishes exemplary technical professionals from average ones doesn't reveal much about the nature of the work they do. This often makes it difficult to explain how core skills are related to the work of technical professionals, not to mention students who aspire to technical professional roles.

A second problem with person-centered competency models is that they are not necessarily good guides to future competency requirements because they are based on the past performance of exemplars. Most of our own clients need to go beyond what people do today and ask about competencies needed for future success in key jobs. In the absence of incumbents in the jobs of tomorrow, one can only speculate on future competency requirements based on a person-centered approach.

Third, a persuasive theoretical framework has yet to emerge to explain why certain competencies turn out to be associated with superior perfor-mance while other competencies do not. Although knowledge competen-cies tend to be face-valid to people who understand the content of a job (for example, technical knowledge), it is less obvious why other compe-tencies distinguish exemplary performers. We may agree that *analytic thinking* is a core skill for any professional or managerial job, but why is it a critical distinguishing competency in some jobs but not in others? What characterized those managerial jobs on Table 10.2 where job com-petency assessment did not find *analytic thinking* to be a distinguishing competency? It is important to understand why certain competencies are required as core skills to justify the attention placed on them in both education and employment.

The Context-Centered Approach:
A "Demand-Side" Model

To resolve these problems, we went back to the literature on job task analysis to see if any recent work had been done to examine the demand side of the performance equation—the characteristics of work and the environment in which it is performed. Initially, we found different ways to categorize jobs according to task requirements, but most of these were based either on their association with certain kinds of work (e.g., tasks associated with clerical vs. professional vs. supervisory jobs) or on the different types of broadly defined skills required (e.g., psychomotor vs. problem-solving vs. interpersonal skills). These taxonomies, in short, were not much better than our competency dictionary in explaining underlying relationships between tasks and skills. However, once one goes beneath the surface descriptions of task and context requirements, just as we have done for competencies identified through the person-centered approach, one finds underlying dimensions that describe the processes by which tasks are performed. These dimensions have become the foundation for a "demand-side" or "context-centered" approach to defining competency requirements for different jobs: They provide us with the basis for describing core skills in context for both the present and the future.

Obviously, knowledge requirements differ greatly from job to job. But competencies such as *analytic thinking* are often shared requirements of jobs whose tasks differ greatly. The dimensions of work requirements that I am about to describe have helped to sort out real differences between jobs that appear to be similar in many respects but that have very different demands placed on them. I will illustrate five such dimensions and show how they can be applied to the specific job to demonstrate how core skills can be defined in this manner. I will then illustrate three general trends in the workplace to draw some conclusions about core skills for the future.

The five job context dimensions are as follows:

1. *Judgement/decision-making.* This dimension reflects the amount of flexibility one has in performing one's work and the consequences of making good and bad decisions. Hackman and Oldham (1976), among others, have studied aspects of this dimension in their work on the relationship between job characteristics and motivation.
2. *Task complexity.* This dimension, common in the job analysis literature (e.g., Fine, 1974; Fleishman & Harris, 1962) relates to the multidimensionality and tangibility of work.
3. *Time span of discretion.* This dimension is defined by the time horizon required for thinking and planning. According to Jaques, who first coined the term (1964), this dimension is both a measure of the level of work to be done and the cognitive capacity required to do the work.

Table 10.3 Demand-Side Competency Analysis for Engineering Professionals

Underlying Dimension	Related Task Requirement	Required Competency	Required Level
1. Judgment/ Decision-making	Field is well-established; work is guided by precedent	Skillful Diagnosis	High
	Cost of mistakes is high	Attention to Detail	High
	Limited discretion in how tasks are performed	Initiative	Basic
2. Task Complexity	Diverse problems capable of more than one solution	Analytic Thinking (evaluation)	High
3. Time Span of Discretion	Problems must be solved quickly	Efficiency	High
	Projects normally completed in less than 6 months	Analytic Thinking (planning)	Basic
4. Interaction with Others	Interactions mostly with team members in sharing information	Clear Communication	Basic
	Some interaction with non-engineers	Persuasion (data-based)	Moderate
	Some interaction with senior managers requiring influence	Strategic Influence (Political Astuteness)	Moderate
5. Level of Uncertainty	Some events are unpredictable but must be dealt with quickly	Flexibility	Moderate

4. *Interaction with others.* This dimension reflects the contextual requirement of the level and type of dealings with other people inside and outside one's organization. McCormick, Jeanneret, and Mecham (1972) have incorporated a similar dimension in their *Position Analysis Questionnaire.*

5. *Level of uncertainty.* This dimension captures the relative predictability of job events and task requirements. It is grounded in information processing theory (Garner, 1962; Miller, 1974) and reflects the amount of mental work needed to make choices and define priorities for others under conditions of uncertainty.

Table 10.3 applies these dimensions to the work requirements of a mid-level engineering professional in a multinational oil company. These data are based on competency studies carried out on similar employee populations in the United States, Norway, Indonesia, Nigeria, Saudi Arabia, and Canada. The table extracts some of the common job requirements and then links them to competency requirements. Among the various competencies referenced, there are four from Tables 10.1 and 10.2 that appear as core competencies for these positions, albeit at different levels of skill: the intellectual competencies *skillful diagnosis* and *analytic thinking* and the interpersonal competencies *persuasion* and *strategic influence*. Aggregating across other technical professional jobs sharing similar demand characteristics, these competencies (except for *strategic influence*) emerge as core skills.

The importance of the above illustration is not that we have found another way to derive many of the same core skills identified by the person-centered approach, but that we can take a more objective look at future requirements in the workplace and draw conclusions about core skill requirements that go beyond speculation.

Implications for Core Skills for the Future

Clearly the demands of the workplace and the nature of work itself have changed dramatically during the last 10 years. Global competition among businesses is increasing, jobs are being redefined through re-engineering, and telecommunications and data processing are revolutionizing the workplace. Even the employment role of organizations has shifted in unanticipated directions. According to Drucker (1995), more work that used to be performed by full-time employees of large companies is being and will continue to be reassigned to smaller companies, part-time employees, and subcontractors.

When we take these changes into account, three key trends emerge that have direct implications for core skills in the workplace of the future:

1. ***Employees will be required to do more***. As organizations have flattened and work processes have been re-engineered, jobs have gotten bigger and skill requirements have increased. Organizational stovepipes, filled with people who have grown up in one kind of job, are giving way to more flexible career paths for those with talent. Consequently, employees will have to become more versatile and be more effective at leveraging people and resources. There will be a premium for people with in-depth technical and

specialized knowledge, but these individuals will also have to be more knowledgeable about the larger business context and about the disciplines of others with whom they interact.

2. **Relationships among employees will be more complex.** A major trend of the 1980s, customer focus, has resulted in new systems and structures whose success depends on maintaining closer external and internal business relationships. The latest wave of this trend is the "customer-intimate organization," in which employees at the front lines will be required to improvise solutions and to attend more closely to the needs of smaller customer segments. Even more work will be done in teams, including teams that transcend functional and geographic boundaries. New types of business-to-business relationships will require everyone to develop skill sets that stress interdependence, communication, and the ability to build and maintain productive work relationships.

3. **Employees will have to think more flexibly.** The journey of the past 10 years—from Theory X, Theory Y, and Theory Z to virtual management in managerless factories to employees as independent contractors to virtual corporations—makes the point that all theories of managerial style can become obsolete. Leaders, managers, and all other employees will need to be more flexible and open-minded about experimenting with new ways to get work done through others and even about fundamental notions about the nature of leadership.

These trends will continue. And the implications of these trends are that employees at all levels will need to operate with less structure and direction, to develop clearer lines of sight to their outside and inside customers, and to think "outside the box" of their job descriptions to add value. Overall, work requirements on all the job dimensions listed in Table 10.3 will change. Below are some of the changes I foresee and the impact of these changes on the definition of core skills in higher education.

1. **Judgement/decision-making:** People will be required to take more independent action and make more decisions of consequence. One implication for core skills is that there will be more emphasis on analytic thinking—people will need to identify alternatives and make recommendations without necessarily having all the data— and there will need to be more initiative/risk-taking on the part of employees at the front lines.

2. **Task complexity**: There are two major challenges here: Employees will need a broader perspective on their contribution and will also need to understand how their work adds value to the overall enterprise. The implication for core skills is that a greater level of conceptual thinking will be required to understand how work connects to the larger picture and the priorities of the organization. People will also be required to do more with fewer resources. The implication for core skills is the requirement for creativity of the type demonstrated by resourcefulness—using existing resources in new ways and finding custom-fitted solutions in place of tried-and-true ones.

3. **Time span of discretion**: The key to future business competitiveness can be summed up in one word: speed. Paradoxically, this will require people to think through potential obstacles over a longer time horizon and anticipate ways to overcome them. The implication for core skills is the need for greater efficiency and analytic thinking (particularly planning skill) for professionals and greater conceptual thinking (from the long-term perspective) for supervisors and managers.

4. **Interaction with others**: Professionals will have less solo and more group activity, more relationships with external stakeholders (e.g., customers), and a requirement for more frequent communication. The implication for core skills is a greater need for interpersonal sensitivity, even among highly skilled technical professionals. Managers will continue to emphasize team-building and strategic influence (getting organizational support for recommendations) and will place less emphasis on the power of position and more on symbolic influence to get others to take action.

5. **Level of uncertainty**: As the pace of change increases, people in all roles will have to create their own sense of purpose in work and will not be able to rely on their employer to provide that purpose for them. The implication for core skills, in addition to the obvious need for greater flexibility, is the need for self-directed continuous learning as an internalized capability rather than an institutional purpose.

Future core skill requirements, as seen through the lens of a demand-side analysis, include skills other than those shown in Tables 10.1 and 10.2. Nevertheless, if we restrict ourselves to the skills noted in those tables, we notice that conceptual thinking and creativity appear less often as competencies that differentiate exemplary from average managers and professionals today. Creativity, especially, is likely to be more important in the future than it has been in the past.

Conclusion

Retrospective analyses of competency requirements identified using traditional job competence assessment methods have provided valuable insights into core skills for occupational success. These analyses validated skillful diagnosis and analytic thinking as important skills and brought to light interpersonal sensitivity and persuasion as skills that help translate critical thinking into effective action in the workplace. There is also ample evidence that conceptual thinking is important and can be used to get things done in complex organizational environments through strategic influence. While higher education appears to be fulfilling its role in developing *skillful diagnosis* and *analytic thinking,* our data indicate that conceptual thinking and creativity are less prevalent among exemplary performers. Although the aforementioned interpersonal skills play a major role in performance, it appears that they were already attributes of the exemplary performers before their college experience or that they were developed outside the classroom.

What is the role of the academy in developing these skills? A key difference between learning in college and learning in the workplace is that the latter is largely experiential and on-the-job, and often takes place in interaction with colleagues, whereas the former is less connected with application to practical tasks (i.e., is "academic") and is normally accomplished through independent study. Perhaps one reason for this is higher education's emphasis on developing critical thinking skills and subject-matter expertise, whereas the emphasis in the workplace is on overall effectiveness. This difference drives much of the focus on individual attainment in the classroom, while developing skills requiring group interaction is left to extracurricular activities such as team sports, dramatics, political clubs, and other "non-academic" interests. Institutions of higher learning need not try to build all "core skill" development into the formal curriculum, which already seems well suited to provide critical thinking skills, but should instead ensure that their students have availed themselves of all the developmental opportunities that college has to offer.

A greater cause for concern, however, is what our analysis indicates will become core skills for the future: conceptual thinking and creativity being especially important. Though the trend in the professions is for people to become more specialized, there is also a trend—and a future requirement—for specialists to bridge multiple disciplines and to understand how their work relates to the "big picture" of the overall enterprise. When fully understood, the connections and interdependencies among one's own job, employees in different roles, customers, and other stakeholders give organizations and individuals a significant competitive advantage that is summarized in the term "organizational alignment." The ability to make cognitive connections to the work of different functions and areas of specialization will become a "survival skill" in the workforce of tomorrow.

Although I predict that the role that creativity will play in the future will increase, our research shows little evidence to suggest that this skill is adequately available among today's exemplary job incumbents. Organizations are attempting to hire people able to think "outside the box," to view old problems from different perspectives, and to invent tailored solutions. The type of creativity they seek is not the stuff of Nobel laureates but rather the ability to question assumptions about the way things have been done in the past and to be resourceful. Experiences can surely he designed into the college curriculum that encourage students to risk having the "wrong" answer in order to explore radical possibilities and to learn how to salvage benefit from the ashes of a failed experiment. Students still need a solid grounding in the paradigms underlying their disciplines before challenging them; however, the emphasis should shift from students' ability to recall and integrate facts about the disciplines to their ability to be inventive and engage in well-considered speculation. Indeed, encouraging students to explore novel possibilities is consistent with preparing them to live with greater amounts of uncertainty and risk in life after college.

Finally—and this cannot be emphasized enough—social skills will become increasingly important as work becomes more interconnected, the demographic diversity of the workforce increases, and organizational entities become more interdependent. Should higher education concern itself with this? I believe that institutions of higher learning do students a disservice when they ignore the need to prepare them for effective functioning in the world of work in all "core skills," including those in the interpersonal domain. Surely this means that classroom experiences must become more interactive: how might interpersonal skills be developed otherwise? Independent study, which develops the ability to work effectively on one's own, should be balanced with group problem-solving and team projects where students can benefit from each other's insights.

Examination and certification should address a student's understanding of the dynamics of the influence process and test the successful application of ideas in social settings.

In the introduction to this paper, I described the definition of core skills as being dependent on both task requirements and the environment in which they are performed. I then described the findings of competency research suggesting certain intellectual and interpersonal skills are at the core of effective functioning in the workplace today and a methodology that suggests additional core skill requirements for the future. Mastery of the content of one's discipline and a key set of intellectual skills forms the necessary foundation of effective performance. Successful functioning in the workplace, however, involves not only solving problems, reacting to events, and independent thinking but also implementing solutions, adapting to events, and thinking *inter*dependently. These realities require a larger set of skills than are usually thought of as core skills: they are nevertheless important considerations not only as core skills for today but as survival skills for tomorrow.

Notes

1. This paper was originally presented at the General National Vocational Qualifications conference "Core Skills in Higher Education," held in York, United Kingdom, April 1997.

2. The exceptions to this are senior managers and executives, for whom *symbolic influence* was a distinguishing competency in over 80% of the studies.

References

Barrett, G. V., & Depinet, R. L. (1991). A reconsideration of "testing for competence rather than for intelligence." *American Psychologist, 46*, 1012–1024.

Campbell, J. P., Dunnette, M. D., Lawler, E. E., & Weick, K. E. (1970). *Managerial Behavior, Performance, and Effectiveness.* New York: McGraw-Hill.

Drucker, P. F. (1995). The network society. *The Wall Street Journal,* March 25, A12.

Fine, S. A. (1974). Functional job analysis: An approach to a technology for manpower planning. *Personnel Journal, 53*, 813–818.

Flanagan, J. C. (1954). The critical incident technique. *Psychological Bulletin, 51*, 327–358.

Fleishman, E. A., & Harris, E. F. (1962). Patterns of leadership behavior related to employee grievances and turnover. *Personnel Psychology, 15*, 43–56.

Gardner, H. (1983). *Frames of Mind: A Theory of Multiple Intelligences.* New York: Basic Books.

Garner, W. R. (1962). *Uncertainty and Structure as Psychological Concepts.* New York: Wiley.

Ghiselli, E. E. (1966). *The Validity of Occupational Aptitude Tests.* New York: Wiley.

Hackman, J. R., & Oldham, G. R. (1976). Motivation through the design of work: Test of a theory. *Organizational Behavior and Human Performance, 16*, 250–279.

Hope, K. (1984). *As Others See Us: Schooling and Social Mobility in Scotland and the United States.* New York: Cambridge University Press.

Hunter, J. E., & Hunter, R. F. (1984). Validity and utility of alternative predictors of job performance. *Psychological Bulletin, 96*, 72–98.

Jaques, E. (1964). *Time-Span Handbook.* Arlington, VA: Cason Hall.

Jaques, E. (1989). *Requisite Organization.* Arlington, VA: Cason Hall.

Klemp, G. O. (1977). Three factors of success. In D. W. Vermilye (Ed.), *Relating Work and Education: Current Issues in Higher Education.* San Francisco: Jossey-Bass.

Klemp, G. O. (1982). Job competence assessment: Defining the attributes of the top performer. *ASTD, Research Series,* Vol. 8. (American Society for Training and Development, Washington, DC).

Klemp, G. O., & McClelland, D. C. (1986). What characterizes intelligent functioning among senior managers? In R. Sternberg and R. Wagner (Eds.), *Practical Intelligence.* Cambridge: Cambridge University Press.

Matarazzo, J. D. (1972). *Wechsler's Measurement and Appraisal of Adult Intelligence.* (5th ed.). Baltimore: Williams and Wilkinson.

McClelland, D. C. (1973). Testing for competence rather than for "intelligence". *American Psychologist, 28,* 1–14.

McCormick, E. J., Jeanneret, P. R., & Mecham, R. C. (1972). A study of job characteristics and job dimensions as based on the Position Analysis Questionnaire (PAQ). *Journal of Applied Psychology, 56,* 347–368.

Raven, J., Raven, J. C., & Court, J. H. (1998). *Manual for Raven's Progressive Matrices and Vocabulary Scales. Section 4: The Advanced Progressive Matrices.* Oxford, England: Oxford Psychologists Press; San Antonio, TX: The Psychological Corporation.

Spencer, L. M., & Spencer, S M. (1993). *Competence at Work.* New York: Wiley.

Sternberg, R. J. (1986). *Beyond IQ: A Triarchic Theory of Human Intelligence.* New York: Cambridge University Press.

Thornton, G. C., & Byham, W. C. (1982). *Assessment Centers and Managerial Performance.* San Diego, CA: Academic Press.

White, R. W. (1959). Motivation reconsidered: The concept of competence. *Psychological Review, 66,* 297–333.

Chapter 11

Professional Capability—Requirements and Accreditation in the Legal Profession

Diana Tribe

Editorial Introduction

We have reprinted this chapter, with one or two minor editorial changes, because it illustrates many of the problems that are likely to be encountered by those who—in many senses rightly—embark on competency-oriented education without considering the issues addressed in other chapters of this book. These include:

- The almost infinite regress into which one gets if one begins to atomise competence, teaching, and assessment.
- The way in which that atomisation then results in educational programmes which somehow fail to engage with the kinds of competence which led their organisers to move away from content-oriented education in the first place. (To avoid this problem it would be necessary to engage students' motives in such a way that they learn to "observe," "communicate," etc. while undertaking activities they care about.)
- The power that the most prestigious members of a professional group have to determine the content of armchair-based lists of the competencies "necessary" in a profession in such a way that those

This chapter was previously published as Chapter 11 in D. O'Reilly, L. Cunningham & S. Lester (Eds.) *Developing the Capable Practitioner*, Kogan Page, London (1999). It is © Kogan Page and is reprinted here by kind permission of the publisher.

lists end up missing the competencies actually required by most of those who have actually been through the educational programmes concerned—and especially the considerable number who will enter walks of life not directly associated with the profession.

- The way in which centralised specifications of the competencies required in a profession tend to fail to come to terms with the diversity of the competencies actually required.

- (Although Professor Tribe mentions the point only in passing), the fact that even cursory study of what the members of a professional group actually do rapidly reveals that even most of the "core" group do *not* engage in the behaviours that are most widely associated with the group—yet these images powerfully determine what it is thought the group concerned needs to learn to do (Professor Tribe's example is that few members of the legal profession undertake courtroom cross-examinations, while many spend a lot of time counselling clients.)

- The hegemony of courses designed to communicate temporary knowledge of bodies of specialist content despite (a) the tendency of such knowledge to go rapidly out of date and (b) the irrelevance of such knowledge to the future careers of most students.

- The unwillingness of professionals to spend time developing competencies that actually make a difference to their clients (because these competencies are invisible to their peers) and their preference for gaining credentials that *will* be visible to gatekeepers and thus advance them in their careers.

- The tendency to focus on doing whatever is necessary to improve the public image of the professional group concerned, especially by creating lofty statements which erect barriers that protect its members from competition.

- The tendency to think in terms of competencies that can be "taught" rather than in terms of motivational dispositions, the development of which can only be "facilitated."

Introduction

"If a broad approach to the definition of competence based education is taken, then it can be said that contemporary legal education at all stages is marked by a proliferation of statements of competency, learning outcome statements and skills guides which provide a specification of performance against which skills might be judged" (Jones, 1994).

The "Ultimate Aim" of a legal education, as described by the Lord Chancellor's Advisory Committee on Legal Education and Conduct, a body which gives statutory approval to training regulations for both branches of the legal profession, is "to produce humane, reflective, all-round lawyers" (1995a&b). How this is to be achieved, through the four stages of a lawyer's training—the undergraduate or "academic" stage; the postgraduate or "professional" stage; the professional skills or training contract stage; and the continuing professional development stage—is made less than clear, however, in the Advisory Committee's consultation papers.

The following analysis of the various stages of legal education illustrates that, although the training of lawyers is firmly controlled by the relevant professional bodies at each stage, there is no common approach between the different stages.

Definition of Skills and Competencies Which Form Part of Each Stage of Legal Education and Training

The Undergraduate Stage

In their Joint Announcement on Qualifying Law Degrees (which was approved by the Lord Chancellor's Department in 1994), the Law Society and the Bar not only outlined the academic content which is required to be taught at the academic stage of training (the seven foundation areas of legal study), but also identified the competencies with which students should be equipped at the academic stage: these are defined as "the intellectual and practical skills needed to research the law . . . to apply it to the solution of legal problems and to communicate—both in writing and orally—the results of such work". It is interesting to compare this analysis of the skills to be taught at the undergraduate stage with that of the Lord Chancellor's Advisory Committee on Legal Education, which reported in the same year and defined the aim of the initial stage of legal education as being "to get students to think like lawyers, constructively but critically."

The emergence of law degrees early in this century was marked by a struggle to achieve academic acceptance of the subject as one fit for study at university level. It is only over the past fifteen years that elements of what has been described as "clinical" skills or competence teaching have been widely incorporated into law teaching at the undergraduate level.

The content of such courses varies widely between institutions but seems generally to be influenced by notions of reflective practice and "capability". It may include the following:

(i) Vocational skills for the legal profession
(sometimes referred to as clinical legal education)

Here students are involved in training in a law centre (or simulated law centre) context, in order to develop the specific practitioner skills employed by solicitors and barristers. Skills commonly included are:

legal analysis
professional/ethical responsibility
advocacy
litigation management
legal advice
legal document drafting

(ii) General professional skills

The rationale behind the integration of general professional skills into law degrees is that not all students will necessarily enter the legal profession at the end of their undergraduate training: indeed, the evidence suggests that a decreasing number will actually do so. The following are typical of the skills involved:

time management
case management
chairmanship
negotiation
client interviewing
document drafting
advanced information technology skills
foreign language skills

(iii) Life skills connected with personal development

This training aims to help students maximise their future potential, not simply in relation to employment, but also in personal life. It is claimed that all undergraduate students need to develop these skills. They include:

oral and written communication
self-management
information retrieval
word processing
research/study skills

The introduction of skills teaching to undergraduate programmes has presented serious teaching problems. In some cases no attempt is made to teach the skills: rather, reliance is placed on student-centred learning where students are given tasks to complete, tasks which, it is assumed, will inculcate those skills thought desirable and necessary. Legal skills are also notoriously hard to assess and although the subjective element of assessment can be reduced through the development of standards, check lists, criteria and the like, these are perceived by critics as reductionist and simplistic. In practice they are often ignored, assessment being carried out, initially at least, on the basis of personal preference.

Universities vary in the extent and manner in which skills and competencies are integrated into the undergraduate curriculum. In some cases free standing compulsory modules (often in the foundation year of study) are offered, and the assessments based upon them contribute to the overall assessment of the student. In other cases, a more adventurous approach has been developed in which skills/competencies are integrated across the curriculum as a whole. Here they form a sub-set of the objectives for each subject studied, and subject tutors take responsibility for ensuring that these areas are covered in each subject. Thus, for instance, a Land Law tutor would ensure that the teaching of that subject included the development of communication skills (both oral and written), the making of presentations, working in groups and the development of research skills.

The Professional/Postgraduate Stage
The most significant changes over the past decade have occurred however at the postgraduate level. In 1989 the Council of Legal Education, which provides training for the Bar, developed a new "skills-based" course to prepare prospective barristers for pupillage in response to the criticism that the old Bar Finals course produced students with technical knowledge but without the practical skills required to be competent barristers.

In 1993 the Law Society followed this lead by introducing the Diploma in Legal Practice to replace the old Law Society Finals course for those who intend to qualify as solicitors: This Diploma is based around a set of "competence"-based standards which provide an integrated model for a competence-based approach to learning. The dominant mode for the course is one year of full time training, although there are alternatives (e.g., it may be integrated within a four year degree, as at the University of

Northumbria, or run part time over a two year period, or studied by distance learning, or even on a sandwich basis).

Jones (1994) indicates that the standards are based on:

(i)   Knowledge and tasks that are assessed through coursework and end of session examinations.

(ii)   Lawyering skills in five key areas (drafting, research, advocacy, interviewing, negotiation) which are not defined by the Law Society but rather stated in the form of outcome statements. There are no detailed guides to the assessment of these skills; course providers are expected to formulate their own detailed assessment criteria that specify the behaviours that need to be demonstrated in each area.

(iii)   Professional practice skills. These are made up of a core set of generic skills which are common within the range of professional activities referred to above and include, for instance, communication skills, client relationship skills, office practice skills, personal work management skills, Information Technology (IT) skills and personal development skills. No criteria for the assessment of the performance of these skills are provided by the Law Society, and it would appear that most course providers do not assess them as such.

Students on the Diploma in Legal Practice are assessed on their ability to complete the steps and procedures involved in certain key transactions and on their ability to perform a range of lawyers' skills. Only if successful are they able to move onto the next stage of legal education—supervised practice within a training contract.

As Maughn, Maughn and Webb (1995) suggest:

"there seems to be quite a contrast between what is happening at the academic stage and the vocational stage. Some of the progressive initiatives shown by the Law Schools at the academic stage are influenced by notions of reflective practice and capability and seek to go beyond the old paradigm of knowledge and skill. At the vocational stage the programme rests firmly on the knowledge and skills divide . . . the substantive law components are tested through coursework and examination . . . the skills are assessed separately. Such a separation serves only to solidify attitudes about the academic/vocational hierarchy."

Neither The Bar Vocational Course nor the Legal Practice Course has been without its critics. The Bar has had well-publicised difficulties with claims that a skills-based course discriminates against candidates from ethnic minorities, and it has been alleged that the skills basis for the Legal Practice Course has had the effect of diluting the provision of necessary legal technical knowledge for legal practice.

The Lord Chancellor's Advisory Committee in its June 1995 paper sought responses from interested parties to the question "Is the current balance at the vocational level between skills and knowledge appropriate?", whilst at the same time indicating the view that students "should be equipped with up-to-date skills for professional practice in the context of rapid and radical changes to the provision of legal services" and that they should be inculcated with a "professional attitude" and the notion of "lifelong learning".

The Professional Skills Course and Continuing Professional Development

For new recruits to the profession, the Professional Skills Course takes place during the training contract and the training contract itself incorporates a set of standards for the skills that trainees are to have developed during the training contract. "This provides a carefully structured set of standards that provide an integrated approach to post degree professional education" (Jones, 1994).

The Lord Chancellor's Advisory Committee reporting in 1995 defined the objectives of training for those solicitors for whom continuing professional development courses are now mandatory (almost the entire profession) as follows:

> The broad aim of continuing professional development should be to develop practice management skills as well as to enable qualified practitioners to update their expertise and widen their horizons. At a deeper level this kind of education should inculcate the notion of "lifelong learning" as being at the heart of lawyering. All lawyers must recognise the need to expand or update their proficiency, knowledge, skills and attitudes.

In practice however, the continuing professional development programme is only nominally controlled by the Law Society and individual practitioners have considerable latitude as to the type and quality of further training undertaken provided that they acquire the requisite number of training "points". Some attend courses offered by educational or commercial providers; others acquire the necessary "points" by certifying that they have used one of the training videos currently produced for that purpose. What this means is that the practitioner tends to concentrate on acquiring further information which s/he believes will be useful in expanding her/his expertise into new areas and away from those areas where there is perceived to be a declining market.

It would be surprising if practitioners showed more than a superficial interest in courses aimed at developing skills and competencies, and this tends to be borne out in practice (except perhaps for those larger firms who employ in-house educational trainers). This despite the acknowledged fact that many solicitors sadly lack the normal interpersonal and communication skills required to operate effectively in almost any walk of life.

How Can These Qualities Be Assured?

Quality assurance goes beyond the mere written definition of aims and outcomes and tends to be centred around the assessment process. For that reason it is of some interest to consider the methods of assessment used in the development of skills and competencies for lawyers.

A survey of law degrees carried out in 1989 (Tribe & Tribe) showed that the methods used for the assessment of skills varied very much from skill to skill within institutions, as well as between institutions. In some cases there was no formal assessment; all that was required for students to pass was their attendance. In others, assessment was based upon a mixture of attendance and written work, whilst in yet others this was combined with, or an alternative to, more innovative techniques such as filmed presentations, tribunal representation, or a comparison of the outcomes of negotiation exercises. In most institutions several methods were combined in use, and in at least three there was a schedule of component sub-skills which was used as a basis for the allocation of marks.

What was clear from the survey however was that there was a fundamental conceptual problem associated both with the delivery of skills teaching and with its assessment, in that there was a shortage of objective criteria by which to judge students' performance.

Put simply, the problem was perceived thus: if we assume that it is, for example, appropriate to teach the skills of interviewing to law students, we must identify the skills which make a good interviewer and then identify the behaviours (or sub-skills) which combine to make up those skills. These behaviours (or sub-skills) will then form the basis for a teaching programme and for subsequent student assessment.

We may argue, for instance, that in order to perform an interviewing task effectively, a student must be a competent listener, but this means that we must then identify the behaviours or sub-skills which will indicate this.

A breakdown of desirable *listening* behaviours might be as follows:

shows interest in the person who is speaking
shows interest in the subject under discussion
continues to listen when the subject becomes boring
does not allow prejudice to reduce attention
does not permit enthusiasm to carry them away
is not critical of the other person's speech or method of delivery
regularly summarises what is heard
checks for understanding
does not allow emotional reactions to affect understanding
concentrates when difficult ideas are being expressed
creates the right environment for listening
allows sufficient time for full understanding before reacting
makes a final review of understanding of facts

Even if such sub-skills can be conceptualised in this way, the problem is still short of solution, since each sub-skill remains capable of further breakdown into component low inference behaviours. For instance, the sub-skill "shows interest in the person who is speaking", may be identified by such behaviours as:

intermittent eye-contact
head nodding
smiling
avoiding looking at watch
avoiding interruptions from phone/colleagues

In any case it may be the balance between the sub-skills when they are combined together which is most important in the carrying out of the overall interviewing task.

If one cannot identify with sufficient clarity exactly what students should achieve, it is difficult to assess whether, and to what extent, they have achieved it. The unarticulated, idiosyncratic model "I cannot define it but I know it when I see it" works in only a very limited way.

Not surprisingly, although there are many skills training programmes within law courses in the UK, it is rare to find that their objectives have been clearly defined in the way suggested above. The study of Cort and

Sammons (1980) attempted such an analysis based, not upon empirical study of what it is that professional lawyers do, but rather on an observation of student attempts to carry out lawyer operations. This resulted in the identification of six major competencies. The Antioch Competency Based Model took this approach considerably further: here fifty three lawyering tasks are defined, each of which is then split down into approximately ten observable behaviours per task. Each of these is then in turn divided into several sub-sets with marks specifically allocated to each sub-set on a ten point scale. Individual ratings are eventually combined to give a score for each student. A variation on this method has been used at Mercer University where some of the original fifty three competencies are identified as being essential for students to acquire, whilst others are only desirable, thus providing additional complexities in an already complex system.

Whilst such systems appear to be systematically based, the identification of a set of sub-skills representing low inference behaviours is a difficult and time consuming task; moreover, there is no provision for assessing the manner in which the sub-skills are combined to produce the total competency in question. The production of written standards is frequently assumed to lead to a systematic basis for assessment, but there are in fact no objective criteria for the allocation of marks, which still proceeds on a subjective basis. Finally, written accounts of competences tend to be linear in form and provide only two dimensional models for what are essentially "three dimensional" activities.

Another fundamental problem related to the actual grading of skills activities by staff. Even supposing that skills can be identified and defined, what criteria should be used in allocating marks to their performance? What is the basis for distinguishing between 60% and 70% in a negotiation exercise when so much depends on context (i.e. the strength of the other negotiating party) that it is only possible to make rough numerical judgements about individual performances? Additionally, academic staff need extensive training to be able to use a skills schedule such as the Antioch model, and the whole system is time consuming and expensive; it seems extremely unlikely that such a method would recommend itself to British academics.

The difficulties referred to above in defining and assessing skills have meant that for many colleagues in the UK a written form of assessment in which students are asked simply to reflect on their acquisition of skills, was the natural and preferred method. Thus students might be asked to present a case book outlining negotiation planning, tactics used and outcomes achieved as a basis for assessment; it is argued that although this may indicate something about an individual student's self appraisal, it is not an objective test of his/her actual negotiation skills. It is understandable that staff prefer assessment based on written work however, since it can be assessed by more than one member of staff, it can be repeated if unsatisfactory, and sent to the external examiner in cases of doubt. Furthermore, there is a feeling among lecturing staff that such written assessment is in some way more "objective" and "reliable" than the assessment of practical work.

However, with the advent of the Legal Practice Course, which was introduced in some institutions in September 1993, law teachers at last began to move towards more universal and formalised practices. The Legal Practice Course requires students to demonstrate "competence" in the skills of drafting, research, advocacy, interviewing and negotiation before they can be awarded the Diploma necessary for entry into a training contract with a firm of solicitors. In some Universities the teaching and assessment of these skills is integrated into the subject content which runs alongside: thus the skill of interviewing may be assessed as an integral part of the Conveyancing course, and the skill of advocacy as an integral part of the Litigation course. This "transactional" approach is one originally favoured by the Law society on the grounds that it is the nearest approximation to the reality of a solicitor's practice. In other cases exemplars of skilled behaviour are videotaped to assist assessors in determining whether an individual students has displayed "competence" in a particular skill or not. Exemplars are certainly helpful when used to illustrate written standards, but exemplars themselves cannot be used as an alternative. Different assessors will view the same exemplar differently and perceive different aspects of the same exemplar as being critical (Wolf, 1993).

The Needs of Employers

It would seem reasonable to assume that the needs of employers of law graduates would vary depending on whether they enter the legal profession or some other employment context. However a small study carried out by staff at the University of Hertfordshire showed that the type of questions asked of referees by potential employers were relatively consistent regardless of the eventual employment context.

The questions listed below occur very regularly:

what degree classification do you expect/did this candidate achieve?
is this candidate trustworthy?
does this candidate have good interpersonal skills?
does this candidate have good research skills?
is this candidate a "clock watcher"?
is this candidate hard working/conscientious?
has this candidate a good level of literacy?
is this candidate "flexible" in approach?

The questions listed below appear regularly:

has this candidate usually been able to hand work in on time?
has this candidate usually been a regular attender at classes?
would this candidate be a suitable person to work in a large city firm?
would this candidate be a suitable person to work with legal aid clients?
can this candidate write a concise and accurate account of a set of
    facts?
did this candidate suffer from regular periods of absence due to ill
    health when a student?
does this candidate possess basic IT skills?

Some potential employers tend to phrase their questions more ob-
liquely, but on the whole seem to be searching for the same kind of competencies. They appear to take for granted the academic ability of graduates and to be unconcerned about the details of the curriculum studied.
What even a superficial analysis of these questions suggests is that the
type of graduates sought by potential employers (whether within the legal
profession or otherwise) are those who possess the skills/competencies
described variously as generic, transferable, personal, or professional practice, i.e.,

• general communications skills, which permeate communications
  outside and inside the office environment;
• client relationship skills;
• internal office practice skills including those involved in working
  with others: for example, delegation, team building, group leadership;

- the personal work management skills of time management, task priority setting, meeting deadlines, diary keeping, punctuality;
- IT skills both generic (the ability to use general computerised tools) and specific (the ability to use legally specific tools and applications);
- personal and professional development skills—the ability to determine personal priorities, seek out new forms of learning that maintain and advance personal expertise, learn through self-reflection and respond flexibly to change.

These "core" or generic skills are the ones that Universities have been urged to develop by a series of governmental initiatives over the past two decades (the Enterprise in Higher Education initiative, the Royal Society of Arts capability movement and the NAB/UGC statement) (Barnett, 1990). The intention is to produce a range of skills that will be of value in a variety of employment contexts.

As indicated above these skills are frequently, though not universally, incorporated to a greater or lesser extent within the undergraduate stage of a lawyer's training. Their existence is inferred from the standards defined by the professional bodies for students at the postgraduate stage, although they are not directly addressed at this stage. Nonetheless potential employers still seek assurance that individual applicants possess these skills.

References

Barnett, R. (1990). *The Idea of Higher Education.* Buckingham: SRHE/ Open University Press.

Cort, H. R., & Sammons, J. L. (1980). The search for "good lawyering": A concept and model for lawyering competences. *Clev St L Review, 29,* 397.

Jones, P. (1994). *Competences, Learning Outcomes and Legal Education.* Legal Skills Working Paper, Institute of Advanced Legal Studies, University of London.

Law Society and the Council of Legal Education. (1995). *Joint Announcement on Qualifying Law Degrees.* London: Law Society and the Council of Legal Education.

Lord Chancellor's Advisory Committee on Legal Education and Conduct. (1995a). *Review of Legal Education: The Vocational Stage* (Consultation Paper), June.

Lord Chancellor's Advisory Committee on Legal Education and Conduct. (1995b). *Review of Legal Education: The Foundation Stage* (Consultation Paper), June.

Maughn C., Maughn, M., & Webb, J. (1995). Sharpening the mind or narrowing it? The limitations of outcome and performance measures in legal education. *ALT International Journal of Legal Education, 29* (3), 255.

Tribe, D., & Tribe, A. J. (1989). Assessing law students. *Assessment & Evaluation in Higher Education, 13* (3), 195.

Wolf, A. (1993). *Assessment Issues and Problems in a Criterion-Based System.* London: Further Education Unit.

Chapter 12

Issues Raised by the Studies of Competence

John Raven

The aim of this commentary is not to summarise what has been said in the previous chapters but to draw out some further implications. Because the topics are interrelated, it may be useful to list the issues to be discussed. They are:

1. The conclusions that emerge from any competency study are, as in all science, heavily dependent on the frame of reference and assumptions of the scientist. The adoption of any particular methodology is no guarantee of "truth."
2. *Critical incident* and *Behavioural Event Interviewing* methodologies offer no panacea.
3. There is no justification for the preoccupation with low-level skills and abilities evident in some quarters of the competency movement. Indeed, setting the results summarised in the preceding chapters in the context of other work, and reflecting more deeply on their implications, suggests that even higher-level competencies than those highlighted are required to perform effectively in the roles and activities that emerge as most important in the workplace and society. A more adequate framework for thinking about competence will therefore be one that helps us to think more effectively about the qualities required to cope with societal and ethical issues. In other words, those involved in advancing the competency movement must embrace all the issues to which those who drafted the *Capability Manifesto* drew attention.
4. Even if it is accepted that high-level competencies are of fundamental importance in every area of society, a huge amount of research

and development remains to be done to develop the concepts, understandings, and tools that are needed to identify, nurture, place, develop, and utilise high-level competencies.

5. The question of how to guard against *in*competence—the fear of which has provided such an impetus to both the professionalisation and competence-specification and credentialling movements (and even the national curriculum in schools)—demands urgent and careful thought. Our present perspective is that its solution will depend on very different developments to those currently most widely envisaged and that it requires the development of high-level competencies in members of the population far removed from those most commonly targeted for training and re-education programmes.

We will now discuss each of these topics in turn.

1. The conclusions that emerge from any competency study are, as in all science, heavily dependent on assumptions accepted and rejected by the scientist.

Although Russ-Eft, Huff, and our summary of McBer's work may have given the impression that Behavioural Event Interviewing and Critical Incident methodology have been refined to the extent that they can be routinely applied to identify the competencies that are important in any occupational position, this impression is misleading.

One example of this comes from a study that we were unfortunately unable to include in this book. Leonard and Fambrough[1] studied the competencies required by research managers. However, in their work, they basically accepted the customer-contractor principle as a framework within which research should be conducted. Yet there is ample evidence that this framework is itself a grossly *inefficient* method of conducting either fundamental research[2] or what is generally termed research and development.[3] "Customers"—administrators—are rarely in a position to specify what needs to be done. The whole process of "calling for proposals," unless it is subverted by capable administrators who invert their job descriptions, *constrains* the scientific process. The effective management of research therefore involves subversion of the very system in which those concerned nominally believe. What competencies would a capable competence modeller require if he or she were to note and report this observation? What image of science would the research community require when evaluating his or her work? What competencies would the competency-modeller require to change both the image of the research community, the terms under which his or her own research was conducted, and the way research is generally conducted? Fambrough has in fact reported (in a personal communication) that incidents that provoked such reflections were omitted from their report because there were not enough of them to amount to a "significant" finding and they would thus have been viewed as "unscientific." They would have been unacceptable to those who sponsored the research, and the claim that the observations were not sufficiently substantiated to be "scientific" would have been used to discredit the researchers. Yet the fact is that it is the insights *forged in the course of research*—and not the findings "documented" in it—that advance understanding—that is, advance science.[4]

To reinforce these insights into the competencies *we* may need to possess and the limitations of our methodology, some of the results of our own studies of outstanding primary school teachers may be briefly introduced.[5] It emerged that those teachers who did the best—indeed the only educationally competent and ethically justifiable[6]—work *in* their classrooms were the ones who spent most time *outside* those classrooms seeking to gain control over the wider social and bureaucratic processes (such as the expectations of parents and the limited range of important competencies that show up on the tests currently used in the "quality control" operations of the "educational" system) that would otherwise have prevented them from nurturing high-level competencies—that is, that would have prevented them from behaving competently—in their classrooms. Yet such activities are not normally regarded as part of a teacher's job. Had we, as researchers, accepted the usual job descriptions we would not have come up with what can now be seen to be one of our most important findings—a finding that has major implications for the training of teachers, the job descriptions generated for teachers, the criteria of appraisal deemed appropriate, and the overall organisation and management of the educational system.

In a chapter that is reprinted later in this book, Schön likewise demonstrates that it is crucially important that investigators reflect on the significance of their observations. That is to say, the most important implications of research may well have to do with advancing our understanding of the competencies required by *researchers*, the arrangements required to advance scientific understanding, and the competencies required to diffuse a better understanding of the nature of science and the arrangements needed to advance it.

Another way of putting this conclusion is to say that the competencies identified as important depend on the implicit job description accepted by

(a) the organisation employing those concerned and (b) those building the competency model.

2. *Critical Incident* and *Behavioural Event Interviewing* methodologies offer no panacea: Indeed, they produce results that in some ways mislead us.

What was said in the last few paragraphs indicates that it is necessary to go well beyond Critical Incident and Behavioural Event Interviewing studies if we are to identify the competencies important in a job.

But more serious limitations emerge from considering the work of Adams and Burgess,[7] and, as Lynne Cunningham has shown, Kanter. One way of putting it is that focusing on "superstars" exacerbates the problems arising from acceptance of conventional thoughtways. Those who are interviewed are not encouraged to think about the crucial contributions to group performance made by those who are not regarded as superstars and those who are doing vitally important things that do not happen to be mentioned in their job descriptions—such as salesmen noting (and pushing through) important changes in organisational arrangements or soothing tensions between other members of staff. Such activities normally pass unnoticed, unmentioned, and invisible.

Yet, as we have seen, such contributions are vital to the success of the "parallel organisation activity" required for organisational survival, they are crucial to the success of research and development,[8] they are essential to Druskat's "emergent" group competencies, they are essential to scientific productivity,[9] and, indeed, they are essential to intelligent behaviour itself.[10]

Adams and Burgess's system was specifically set up to make such contributions visible or, put differently, to enable all the personnel in an organisation to identify the way in which each and every member of the organisation *is* a superstar and could become more superstar-like in a superstar organisation or a society displaying high-level emergent competencies of different kinds.

But there is a sense in which even the system trialled by Adams and Burgess does not go far enough. Groups have properties that cannot be discovered by investigating and summing the competencies of the individuals that make them up, just as copper sulphate has properties that cannot be discovered by summing the properties of copper, sulphur, and oxygen. Further, the parts *change*—or transform—each other. What a person *is* depends on the environment in which he or she lives and works. It depends on the concerns and competencies of other people in the environment. It depends on what others do and permit. It depends on what the organisational arrangements make it easy to do and difficult to do. The competencies identified as important depend on the organisational purposes deemed important.

3. There is no justification for the preoccupation with low-level skills and abilities evident in some quarters of the competency movement. Indeed, setting the results summarised here in the context of other work, and reflecting more deeply on their implications, suggests that even higher-level competencies than those highlighted are required to perform effectively in the roles and activities that emerge as most important in the workplace and society. A more adequate framework for thinking about "competence" will therefore be one that helps us to think more effectively about the qualities required to cope with societal and ethical issues. In other words, those involved in advancing the competency movement must embrace all the issues to which those who drafted the *Capability Manifesto* drew attention.

The work summarised in the papers in this section strongly reinforce Schön's claim that competence and incompetence do not usually stem from excellence or deficiencies in technical knowledge. Rather, they stem from excellence or inadequacy in dealing with what Schön calls "the swamp." Nevertheless limitations in the range of studies summarised here may give the impression that these conclusions apply only to *professional* competence. Nothing could be further from the truth. Flanagan and Burns have demonstrated the same thing among machine operatives,[11] Van Beinum among bus drivers,[12] and Sykes among construction site workers.[13] Flanagan and Russ-Eft have shown that the same is true of contributions to community activities[14] and Ian Cunningham, in his chapter in this volume, strongly suggests that similar high-level competencies are required to achieve a satisfying lifestyle.

The problems involved in a reductionist approach are well illustrated in Tribe's chapter. She nicely illustrates the dilemmas that arise when it comes to be recognised that a long-established, traditional, knowledge-based training programme is wildly off beam but when there is no simultaneous investment in empirical studies of what really makes for effectiveness and ineffectiveness among those actually employed in the profession. The quest for a competency-oriented curriculum then results in a listing of low-level skills that somehow misses the point. While the shortcomings of this then become visible, no guidance is available on what should be done instead. In retrospect, however, perhaps the most important observation to be made about what happened was that the *educators* concerned did not call for research as an aid to tackling their problem. It is, perhaps, this pervasive failure to see research as a route to finding ways of assessing the effectiveness of, and improving, provision in this vast domain of public expenditure that is the most alarming. In other words, perhaps the lack of the *competence to problematise* is among our most important deficiencies.

As noted, the most serious oversights in the competency studies we reviewed here have involved the competencies that are required to perform effectively and ethically when judged against wider criteria of performance.

It is not, of course, true that the importance of some of the required competencies has entirely evaded our researchers. Desjardins and Huff, for example, noted that some of their college principals actually set out not just to ensure the survival of their colleges through image-building and financial manipulation but to find better ways of benefiting the students by helping them to develop the competencies they would need to contribute most effectively to society. Some realised that this meant finding ways of nurturing in students the competencies required to consider the long-term social consequences of their actions and act on those insights—in other words, nurturing the competencies required to both act morally in the narrow sense and ethically in the sense of trying to influence the workings of their society. This meant helping them to develop both the ability to build up their own understanding of how society worked and the commitment to influence it.

We have already mentioned that our own work with teachers showed that for them to behave competently, it was necessary for them to intervene outside their classrooms to gain control over social and economic forces that otherwise prevented them from competently nurturing high-level competencies in their pupils.[15] But, although in some ways a dramatic enough claim in itself, this formulation understates the position. The reality is that it is *unethical* for teachers *not* to engage in these activities because failure to nurture at least *some* high-level talents in *all* of their pupils both damages the life chances of those pupils—often assigning them to degrading lives in which they suffer demeaning treatment at the hands of the "welfare" services—and deprives society of their talents. Worse, by not challenging myths about "ability" and the social order, their failure contributes to the perpetuation of an unethically divided and dysfunctional society that is plunging toward the destruction of the lives and livelihoods of all.

It emerges from these observations that educators have, in the past, typically behaved in ways that are both incompetent and unethical. If they are to cease to be open to this accusation, they will have to show that they have contributed in one way or another, directly or indirectly, to the development of multiple-talent frameworks for thinking about ability, tools to administer multiple-talent educational programmes, a better understanding of how high-level competencies are to be nurtured, a better understanding of the constraints on their behaviour, or ways of influencing those constraints.

Russ-Eft's study of managers, and others brought together by the Spencers,[16] clearly indicate the need to have some managers who take the initiative to intervene in extra-organisational social, political, and economic processes for the benefit of their organisations.

But such a statement only raises the question of where the boundaries of "their organisations" are to be drawn. Barnard has argued that reconciling the conflicting demands that arise when one draws such boundaries in different places creates value and ethical dilemmas, the resolution of which, in the end, becomes the most important and critical task of senior management.[17] Do "their organisations" consist of their employees, the community members they support, or their shareholders? Although many may think that individual firms have no legal responsibility to the community, such is not the case. A crucial explicit (if perhaps fraudulent) justification for enacting the legislation that made it possible to form liability companies and corporations in the first place was that it would facilitate action that would benefit the community as a whole and enable them to be held accountable for so doing. At the time, some even had their charters revoked by their communities for not doing so.[18] So, how are we to find out whether companies are in fact acting in the best interests of the community and how would managers have to behave to get them to do so?

But this is not the only reason for insisting that managers need to focus on such issues. Many of the managers studied by those who have worked with Critical Incident and Behavioural Event Interviewing methodology have been, either directly or indirectly, employed in or by the public sector. Under these circumstances, one might have anticipated that one of the criteria of effectiveness applied to their work would have been the ability to act effectively in the public interest. Unfortunately, both the rarity of references to such activity in the summaries of results, the thinness of the Spencers' discussion of applications of their work in the public sector, and our own work with public sector managers[19] suggest that it is rare for public sector managers themselves, or those who identified incidents of effective or ineffective behaviour among them, to, in any sense, identify the "organisation" on whose behalf those managers were charged with the task of finding ways of intervening in sociological, political, and economic processes as being society itself.

Similar observations can be made about the competencies required by psychologists, doctors, and others. Reform of our living and working arrangements is crucial to mental and physical health in the short term—the largest-selling drugs currently being tranquillisers and drugs to control ulcers to alleviate the stresses and other symptoms stemming from these arrangements—and still more radical reform of such arrangements is clearly crucial if there are going to be *any* human beings around in the not-too-distant future.

It follows that we are not ourselves immune from the accusations of incompetence and unethical behaviour we have been levelling at others.

If we are to behave more competently—which means ethically—we will need to better understand the context in which we are working. Why is it that the atomistic version of Competency Based Education is so pervasive and dislodgable? We will explore the answer to this question more fully in a later chapter. What we have seen here is that part of the problem is that there is little understanding of how to conceptualise high-level competencies, how to nurture them, and how to assess them for formative, summative, or placement purposes. But there may be more important forces at work. One sees the way in which not only all public discussion but virtually all professional discussion of educational goals (including discussion among researchers) has been dramatically narrowed—on a worldwide basis—over the past 20 years. One notes how this has become linked to the need to legitimise and perpetuate a deeply—and unethically—divided society both within and between countries. One sees how researchers have, on the one hand, come to recognise that it is futile to seek to promote discussion of a wider agenda—because no one will listen and there is little possibility of getting funds for (or opportunities to carry out) research in the area—and, on the other, come to accept money for studies that preclude investigation and discussion of (and therefore render invisible) many of the wider aspects of competence discussed here. It is hard to avoid noting the parallel between what is happening in this area and the way in which authoritarian and totalitarian regimes have more generally—by controlling the terms and framework of public discussion and linking personal advancement to that agenda—been able to promote and advance extremely unethical social systems. Conspicuous examples include Hitler and Mao. In the context of such reflections, it does not seem so far fetched to suggest that behind the "reforms" of the educational system may lie a desire to cement acceptance of the right of others to prescribe what one will know, do, and think, the right of others to determine what will count as "ability" so that other talents will remain invisible and unutilised, and the right of others to deprive one of opportunities to enquire and investigate.

If there is any truth in such suggestions it follows that we will *really* need to develop the competencies required to engage in collective social action if we are to behave competently.

4. Even if it is accepted that high-level competencies are of fundamental importance in every nook and cranny of society, a huge amount of research and development is required to develop the concepts, understandings, and tools that are needed to identify, nurture, place, develop, and utilise high-level competencies. And the adoption of Critical Incident and Behavioural Event Interviewing methodology will *not* lead us to some of the key insights we require.

Spencer, Huff, Russ-Eft, and others have used Behavioural Event Interviewing and related methods to generate vitally important insights into the competencies that differentiate between more and less effective performance in a wide range of occupational and social roles. Yet their work provides us with little insight into the patterns of motivation and talent that lead people to carry out effectively one or other of the wide range of activities that are required in every occupational or social position, how people who are likely to carry out one or another of these sets of activities are to be identified, how the development of these competencies is to be nurtured whether through on- or off-the-job developmental programmes, or even to distinguish between the main different types of contribution that may be required in any role position or in "parallel organisation activity." Still less does it help us to think about emergent properties of groups or the different roles that need to be performed for different "emergent competencies" to arise.

Nor does it provide us with a basis from which to develop the tools managers need to:

- think about the motives and talents of subordinates and how best to place and develop them;
- structure the network-based working relationships required for "parallel organisation activity,"
- create groups having different emergent properties
- recognise the currently invisible but essential contributions which people make to such emergent group properties.

Likewise it gives us little help when setting out to develop the tools that teachers and lecturers need to orchestrate and monitor the development of students engaged in multiple-talent, group-based, individualised, competency-oriented, developmental programmes and recognise the particular talents that those students have developed.

Despite these limitations, if one compares and contrasts the kinds of activity that Schön, Huff, and Spencer have shown to be so important with skills of the kind listed by Tribe, a number of features that seem to distinguish high-level, generic, competencies from skills do suggest themselves.

It is immediately obvious that one of the key features of high-level competencies is their *self-motivated* nature. It would make hardly any sense for someone to tell Huff's college principals to go and do the things that emerged as important. It was the individual him or herself who defined the situations in which the behaviour was appropriate and (often "intuitively") worked out what needed to be done. It follows that certain types of motivational predisposition are an integral part of these high-level competencies. Certain components of competence—such as the tendency to monitor and learn from the effects of one's actions—are required to carry out these self-initiated activities effectively, but the one cannot be separated from the other. It is quite inappropriate, therefore, to attempt to view or designate high-level competencies as skills or abilities. Nor are they "aspects of personality." The kinds of thing people are predisposed to do and the abilities required to do them effectively are certainly important. But one cannot be separated from the other. The required skills or abilities cannot be somehow detached from the motivational context in such a way that they can be separately practised and assessed.

Competence in the kind of communication that is required when trying to put someone at ease cannot be developed in the course of making presentations of company development plans. Sensitivity to the cues that lead to the recognition of new activities a college might undertake cannot be developed in the course of developing sensitivity to, and awareness of the implications of, the colours of hues under a microscope. Nevertheless, these competencies are not situation specific in the sense in which typing is situation specific. The tendency to engage in them is, in some sense, omnipresent but evoked by cues that the person concerned defines as relevant. Clearly, possession or lack of possession of such competencies cannot be "tested" by creating situations that *someone else* deems relevant to their evocation and display. Such a test would indicate that the person being assessed does not do what someone else thinks he or she should do. But it would not reveal what the person concerned is motivated to do and good at doing. Note the implication that it does not make sense even to try to assess such things as "the ability to communicate" by presenting set tasks. What people will communicate about, how they will communicate, and how effectively they will communicate depends on whether their motivational predispositions are engaged. In a given situation one person will contribute in one way while another will see it as an opportunity to contribute to (or undermine) the process in a very different way.

Clearly, a whole new way of thinking about competence, its development, and its assessment is needed. We need a methodology that elicits an individual's definitions of situations and ways of contributing to them. And then a system for classifying such information.

**5. The question of how to guard against *in*competence—
the fear of which has provided so much impetus to both
the professionalisation and the competence-specification
and credentialling movements—demands urgent and careful
thought. Our present perspective is that finding a way forward
will depend on developments that are very different indeed
from those currently most widely envisaged and that it will
depend on the development of high-level competencies in
members of the population far removed from those most
commonly targeted for training and re-education.**

The observation and fear of incompetence has fuelled numerous efforts to specify everything that surgeons, psychologists, bus drivers, and others may one day need to know. Unfortunately, surgeons not only specialise in the conduct of very different types of operation, some surgeons organise research teams, others edit journals, and others service committees of the Medical Associations. The specialist knowledge they require changes rapidly. Likewise, some psychologists test children, others provide psychotherapy, others run countries, and so on. Worse still, most incompetence arises not from deficiencies in technical knowledge but from an inability to deal effectively with the social context—Schön's "swamp."

But the problem of incompetence runs even deeper than this. Here, we have already noted the problems posed by the destruction by teachers of the minds and competence of children and their failure to initiate through their professional organisations the developments needed to introduce an effective educational system, by the inability of public servants' to initiate and learn from the effects of their actions in such a way as to prevent the collapse of the biosphere and their inability to introduce the organisational capabilities required to deal with personal and organisational incapability.

What is needed is new thinking about the nature of competence followed by network working among the members of occupational groups (with recognition of the different types of contribution required for effective network working) and network-based supervision designed to limit displays of incompetence and ensure—by exposing behaviour to the public gaze—that people act in ways that are likely to be in the long-term public interest (which implies studies of the kinds of activity that are likely to lead to radical change in the way we do things). Thus, new organisational arrangements, new job descriptions, and new staff appraisal procedures are all required.

Clearly a great deal of "parallel organisation activity" is required to evolve these. Two questions emerge as paramount: "How can people develop the competencies required to contribute to this process?", and "What are the wide variety of ways in which people can contribute to that process?"

Yet the development of new thinking about organisational arrangements, the evolution of new job descriptions, the development of new staff appraisal procedures, and the study of the consequences of alternative ways of doing things are all quintessentially jobs for psychologists. Once again, therefore, the outcome of our reflections is to underline the need to reconsider both the image that psychologists have of themselves and that others have of themselves in the light of the observations we have made about the *nature* of a "learning society"—an "information society"—and the developments that are most central to its effective operation.

Notes

1. Leonard & Fambrough (1996).

2. See Raven (1995) for summaries of the evidence, but see Roberts (1967) for an example.

3. Again, see Raven (1995), but see especially Kanter (1985).

4. The point has been more fully argued by Donnison (1972).

5. Raven, Johnstone, & Varley (1985); Raven (1994).

6. See Raven (1997, 2000).

7. Adams & Burgess (1989). We greatly regret being unable to include a chapter summarising this important, but out of print, work.

8. See Raven (1984/1997).

9. Taylor, Smith, & Gheselin (1963).

10. J. Raven, J. C. Raven, & Court (1998).

11. Flanagan & Burns (1955).

12. Van Beinum (1965).

13. Sykes (1969).

14. Flanagan & Russ-Eft (1975).

15. Similar conclusions emerge from the work of Klemp, Huff, & Gentile (1980) and Schneider, Klemp, & Kastendiek (1981).

16. Spencer & Spencer (1993).

17. Barnard (1938).

18. Grossman & Adams (1993).

19. Raven & Dolphin (1978).

References

Adams, E., & Burgess, T. (1989). *Teachers' Own Records*. Windsor, England: NFER-Nelson.

Barnard, C. (1938). *The Functions of the Executive*. Cambridge, MA: Harvard University Press.

Donnison, D. (1972). Research for policy. *Minerva, X*, 519–537.

Flanagan, J. C., & Burns, R. K. (1955). The employee performance record. *Harvard Business Review, 33*, 95–102.

Flanagan, J. C., & Russ-Eft, D. (1975). *An Empirical Study to Aid in Formulating Educational Goals*. Palo Alto, CA: American Institute for Research.

Grossman, R. L., & Adams, F. T. (1993). *Taking Care of Business: Citizenship and the Charter of Incorporation*. Cambridge, MA: Charter Inc.

Kanter, R. M. (1985). *The Change Masters: Corporate Entrepreneurs at Work*. Hemel Hempstead: Unwin Paperbacks.

Klemp, G. O., Huff, S. M., & Gentile, J. D. G. (1980). *The Guardians of Campus Change: A Study of Leadership in Nontraditional College Programs*. Boston: McBer and Co.

Leonard, D., & Fambrough, M. (1996). *Project Management at ****'s Research Center: Identifying a Model of Superior Performance*. Unpublished Report. Cleveland, OH: Case Western Reserve University.

Raven, J. (1984/1997). *Competence in Modern Society: Its Identification, Development and Release*. Unionville, NY: Royal Fireworks Press (1997); Oxford, England: Oxford Psychologists Press (1984).

Raven, J. (1994). *Managing Education for Effective Schooling: The Most Important Problem is to Come to Terms with Values*. Unionville, New York: Trillium Press; Oxford, England: Oxford Psychologists Press.

Raven, J. (1995). *The New Wealth of Nations: A New Enquiry into the Nature and Origins of the Wealth of Nations and the Societal*

Learning Arrangements Needed for a Sustainable Society. Unionville, NY: Royal Fireworks Press; Sudbury, Suffolk: Bloomfield Books.

Raven, J. (1997). Educational research, ethics and the BPS. Starter paper and peer reviews by P. Mortimore, J. Demetre, R. Stainthope, Y. Reynolds, & G. Lindsay. *Education Section Review, 21* (2), 3–26.

Raven, J. (2000). Ethical dilemmas. *The Psychologist, 13,* 404-406

Raven, J., & Dolphin, T. (1978). *The Consequences of Behaving: The Ability of Irish Organisations to Tap Know-How, Initiative, Leadership and Goodwill.* Edinburgh: Competency Motivation Project.

Raven, J., Johnstone, J., & Varley, T. (1985). *Opening the Primary Classroom.* Edinburgh: Scottish Council for Research in Education.

Raven, J., Raven, J. C., & Court, J. H. (1998). *Manual for Raven's Progressive Matrices and Vocabulary Scales. Section 4: The Advanced Progressive Matrices.* Oxford, England: Oxford Psychologists Press; San Antonio, TX: The Psychological Corporation.

Roberts, E. B. (1967). Facts and folklore in research and development management. *Industrial Management Review, 8,* 5–18.

Schneider, C., Klemp, G. O., & Kastendiek, S. (1981). *The Balancing Act: Competencies of Effective Teachers and Mentors in Degree Programs for Adults.* Boston: McBer and Co.

Spencer, L. M., & Spencer, S. M. (1993). *Competence at Work.* New York: Wiley.

Sykes, A. J. M. (1969). Navvies: Their work attitudes. *Sociology, 3,* 21ff. and 157ff.

Taylor, C. W., Smith, W. R., & Ghiselin, B. (1963). The creative and other contributions of one sample of research scientists. In C. W. Taylor & F. Barron (Eds.), *Scientific Creativity: Its Recognition and Development.* New York: Wiley.

Van Beinum, H. (1965). *The Morale of the Dublin Busman.* London: Tavistock Institute of Human Relations.

PART IV

CONCEPTUALISING COMPETENCE

We have now reviewed evidence underlining the importance of generic high-level competencies in both workplaces and society. It would seem to follow that such qualities should lie at the heart of the competency-based education movement. Yet this has not been, and is not, the case.

Historically, as far as schools are concerned, Fraley (1981) has shown in her *Education and Innovation: The Rhetoric and the Reality* that, despite their advocacy for more than a century and the investment of millions of pounds and dollars, most "progressive" and "open" education programmes have failed to operate effectively. Furthermore, most of those which did work either died or were closed down. More recent attempts to implement educational programmes aiming to nurture qualities such as initiative, self-confidence, problem-solving ability, and the ability to understand and influence society—programmes such as the Technical and Vocational Education Initiative in the UK and the competency-oriented education movement in the United States—have not been notably more successful.

Currrently, we are confronted by a huge, multibillion-dollar worldwide programme of central-government-mandated activities that aims to specify the competencies "required" by those who are to be employed in almost all occupations, train those competencies, and assess them as prerequisites for entry (see Burke, 1989 and Wolf, 1995 for an indication of the scale of this enterprise). Yet as Wolf and others have shown, the activity has largely been corrupted back into "educational" activities very like those which had been so justifiably—and severely—criticised.

Equally, while there has, in the international staff-selection industry, been much talk of moving away from selection on the basis of "ability" and "personality" to selection on the basis of "competence", most of what has happened has consisted of a vast renaming exercise.

As we shall see later, there are many deep-seated reasons for these failures. But one reason is undoubtedly the absence of and agreed-upon conceptual framework for thinking about competence or capability and how its components are to be nurtured. Despite the need, however, our trawl of the literature for contributions to re-thinking has not unearthed as much as we would have liked. We will therefore mainly have to content ourselves with the thought that this book may help to problematise the issue.

References

Burke, J. (Ed.). (1989). *Competency-Based Education and Training.* London, England: The Falmer Press.

Fraley, A. (1981). *Schooling and Innovation: The Rhetoric and the Reality.* New York: Tyler.

Wolf, A. (1995). *Competence-Based Assessment.* Buckingham: Open University Press.

Chapter 13

The Crisis of Professional Knowledge and the Pursuit of an Epistemology of Practice

Donald Schön

Introduction: The Crisis of Confidence in Professional Knowledge

Although our society has become thoroughly dependent on professionals, so much so that the conduct of business, industry, government, education, and everyday life would be unthinkable without them, there are signs of a growing crisis of confidence in the professions. In many well-publicized scandals, professionals have been found willing to use their special positions for private gain. Professionally designed solutions to public problems have had unanticipated consequences, sometimes worse than the problem they were intended to solve. The public has shown an increasing readiness to call for external regulation of professional practice. Laymen have been increasingly disposed to turn to the courts for defense against professional incompetence or venality. The professional's traditional claims to privileged social position and autonomy of practice have come into question as the public has begun to have doubts about professional ethics and expertise (Hughes, 1959). And in recent years, professionals themselves have shown signs of a loss of confidence in professional knowledge.

Yet, in 1963, the editors of *Daedalus* could introduce a special volume on the professions with the sentence, "Everywhere in American life the professions are triumphant" (Lynn, 1963). They noted the apparently limitless demand for professional services, the "shortages" of teachers and physicians, the difficulty of coordinating the proliferating technical specializations, the problem of managing the burgeoning mass of technical data. In the further essays which made up the volume, doctors, lawyers, scientists, educators, military men, and politicians articulated variations on the themes of professional triumph, overload, and growth. There were only two discordant voices. The representative of the clergy complained of declining influence and the "problem of relevance", (Gustafson, 1963) and the city planner commented ruefully on his profession's lagging understandings of the changing ills of urban areas (Alonso, 1963). Yet in less than a decade the discordant notes had become the dominant ones and the themes of professional triumph had virtually disappeared.

In 1972, a colloquium on professional education was held at the Massachusetts Institute of Technology (MIT). Participants included distinguished representatives of the fields of medicine, engineering, architecture, planning, psychiatry, law, divinity, education, and management. These individuals disagreed about many things, but they held one sentiment in common—a profound uneasiness about their own professions. They questioned whether professionals would effectively police themselves. They wondered whether professionals were instruments of individual well-being and social reform or were mainly interested in the preservation of their own status and privilege, caught up in the very problems they might have been expected to solve. They allowed themselves to express doubts about the relevance and remedial power of professional expertise.

It is perhaps not very difficult to account for this dramatic shift, over a single decade, in the tone of professional self-reflection. Between 1963 and 1972 there had been a disturbing sequence of events, painful for professionals and lay public alike. A professionally instrumented war had been disastrous. Social movements for peace and civil rights had begun to see the professions as elitist servants of established interests. The much-proclaimed shortages of scientists, teachers, and physicians seemed to have evaporated. Professionals seemed powerless to relieve the rapidly shifting "crises" of the cities, poverty, environmental pollution, and energy. There were scandals of Medicare and, at the end of the decade, Watergate. Cumulatively, these events created doubts about professionally conceived strategies of diagnosis and cure. They pointed to the overwhelming complexity of the phenomena with which professionals were trying to cope. They led to skepticism about the adequacy of professional knowledge, with its theories and techniques, to cure the deeper causes of societal distress.

Sharing, in greater or lesser degree, these sentiments of doubt and unease, the participants in the MIT colloquium tried to analyze their predicament.

Some of them believed that social change had created problems ill-suited to the traditional division of labor. A noted engineer observed that "education no longer fits the niche, or the niche no longer fits education". The dean of a medical school spoke of the complexity of a huge healthcare system only marginally susceptible to the interventions of the medical profession. The dean of a school of management referred to the puzzle of educating managers for judgment and action under conditions of uncertainty.

Some were troubled by the existence of an irreducible residue of art in professional practice. The art deemed indispensable even to scientific research and engineering design seemed resistant to codification. As one participant observed, "If it's invariant and known, it can be taught; but it isn't invariant".

Professional education emphasized problem-solving, but the most urgent and intractable issues of professional practice were those of problem-finding. "Our interest", as one participant put it, "is not only how to pour concrete for the highway, but what highway to build? When it comes to designing a ship, the question we have to ask is, which ship makes sense in terms of the problems of transportation?"

And representatives of architecture, planning, social work, and psychiatry spoke of the pluralism of their schools. Different schools held different and conflicting views of the competences to be acquired, the problem to be solved, even of the nature of the professions themselves. A leading professor of psychiatry described his field as a "babble of voices".

Finally, there was a call for the liberation of the professions from the tyranny of the university-based professional schools. Everett Hughes, one of the founders of the sociology of the professions, declared that "American universities are the products of the late 19th and early 20th centuries. The question is, how do you break them up in some way, at least get some group of young people who are free of them? How do you make them free to do something new and different?"

The years that have passed since the 1972 colloquium have tended to reinforce its conclusions. In the early 1980s, no profession can celebrate itself in triumphant tones. In spite of the continuing eagerness of the young to embark on apparently secure and remunerative professional careers, professionals are still criticized, and criticize themselves, for failing to adapt to a changing social reality and to live up to their own standards of practice. There is widespread recognition of the absence or loss of a stable institutional framework of purpose and knowledge within which professionals can live out their roles and confidently exercise their skills.

In retrospect, then, it is not difficult to see why participants in the 1972 colloquium should have puzzled over the troubles of their professions. They were beginning to become aware of the indeterminate zones of practice—the situations of complexity and uncertainty, the unique cases that require artistry, the elusive task of problem-setting, the multiplicity of professional identities—that have since become increasingly visible and problematic. Nevertheless, there is something strange about their disquiet. For professionals in many different fields do sometimes find ways of coping effectively, even wisely, with situations of complexity and uncertainty. If the element of art in professional practice is not invariant, known, and teachable, it does appear occasionally to be learnable. Problem-setting is an activity in which some professionals engage with recognizable skill. And students and practitioners do occasionally make thoughtful choices from among the multiple views of professional identity.

Why, then, should a group of eminent professionals have been so troubled by the evidence of indeterminacy in professional practice?

It is not, I think, that they were unaware of the ways in which some practitioners cope reasonably well with situations of indeterminacy. Indeed, they might easily have counted themselves among those who do so. Rather, I suspect, they were troubled because they could not readily account for the coping process. Complexity and uncertainty are sometimes dissolved, but not by applying specialized knowledge to well-defined tasks. Artistry is not reducible to the exercise of describable routines. Problem-finding has no place in a body of knowledge concerned exclusively with problem-solving. In order to choose among competing paradigms of professional practice, one cannot rely on professional expertise. The eminent professionals were disturbed, I think, to discover that the competences they were beginning to see as central to professional practice had no place in their underlying model of professional knowledge.

In the following pages, I shall describe this underlying model, this implicit epistemology of practice, and I shall outline a fundamental dilemma of practice and teaching to which it leads. I shall propose that we seek an alternative epistemology of practice grounded in observation and analysis of the artistry competent practitioners sometimes bring to the indeterminate zones of their practice. I shall attempt a preliminary description and illustration of the "reflection-in-action" essential to professional artistry, and I shall suggest some of its implications for professional education.

The Dominant Model of Professional Knowledge

The epistemology of professional practice which dominates most thinking and writing about the professions, and is built into the very structure of professional schools and research institutions, has been clearly set forth in two essays on professional education. Both of these treat rigorous professional practice as an exercise of technical rationality, that is, as an application of research-based knowledge to the solution of problems of instrumental choice.

Edgar Schein (1974) proposes a threefold division of professional knowledge:

1. An *underlying discipline* or *basic science* component upon which the practice rests or from which it is developed.
2. An *applied science* or *"engineering"* component from which many of the day-to-day diagnostic procedures and problem-solutions are derived.
3. A *skills and attitudinal* component that concerns the actual performance of services to the client, using the underlying basic and applied knowledge.

In Schein's view, these components constitute a hierarchy which may be read in terms of application, justification, and status. The application of basic science yields engineering, which in turn provides models, rules and techniques applicable to the instrumental choices of everyday practice. The actual performance of services "rests on" applied science, which rests, in turn, on the foundation of basic science. In the epistemological pecking order, basic science is highest in methodological rigor and purity, its practitioners superior in status to those who practice applied science, problem-solving, or service delivery.

Nathan Glazer, in a much-quoted article, argues that the schools of such professions as social work, education, divinity, and town planning are caught in a hopeless predicament (Glazer, 1974). These "minor" professions, beguiled by the success of the "major" professions of law, medicine, and business, have tried to substitute a basis in scientific knowledge for their traditional reliance on experienced practice. In this spirit, they have placed their schools within universities. Glazer believes, however, that their aspirations are doomed to failure. The "minor" professions lack the essential conditions of the "major" ones. They lack stable institutional contexts of practice, fixed, and unambiguous ends which "settle men's minds" (Glazer, 1974), and a basis in systematic scientific knowledge. They cannot apply scientific knowledge to the solving of instrumental problems, and they are, therefore, unable to produce a rigorous curriculum of professional education.

Can these fields (education, city planning, social work, and divinity) settle on a fixed form of training, a fixed content of professional knowledge, and follow the models of medicine, law, and business? I suspect not because the discipline of a fixed and unambiguous end in a fixed institutional setting is not given to them. And *thus* (my emphasis) the base of knowledge which is unambiguously indicated as relevant for professional education is also not given (Glazer, 1974).

Glazer and Schein share an epistemology of professional practice rooted historically in the positivist philosophy which so powerfully shaped both the modern university and the modern conception of the proper relationship of theory and practice.[1] Rigorous professional practice is conceived as essentially technical. Its rigor depends on the use of describable, testable, replicable techniques derived from scientific research, based on knowledge that is objective, consensual, cumulative, and convergent. On this view, for example, engineering is an application of engineering science; rigorous management depends on the use of management science; and policy-making can become rigorous when it is based on policy-science.

Practice can be construed as technical, in this sense, only when certain things are kept clearly separate from one another. Deciding must be kept separate from doing. The rigorous practitioner uses his professional knowledge to *decide* on the means best suited to his ends, his *action* serving to "implement" technically sound decisions. Means must be clearly separated from ends. Technical means are variable, appropriate or inappropriate according to the situation. But the ends of practice must be "fixed and unambiguous", like Glazer's examples of profit, health, and success in litigation; how is it possible otherwise to evolve a base of applicable professional knowledge? And finally, research must be kept separate from practice. For research can yield new knowledge only in the protected setting of the scholar's study or in the carefully controlled environment of a scientific laboratory, whereas the world of practice is notoriously unprotected and uncontrollable.

These tenets of the positivist epistemology of practice are still built into our institutions, even when their inhabitants no longer espouse them. Just as Thorstein Veblen propounded some 70 years ago, the university and the research institute are sheltered from the troublesome world of practice (Veblen, 1968). Research and practice are presumed to be linked by an exchange in which researchers offer theories and techniques applicable to practice problems, and practitioners, in return, give researchers new problems to work on and practical tests of the utility of research results. The normative curriculum of professional education, as Schein describes it, still follows the hierarchy of professional knowledge. First, students are exposed to the relevant basic science, then to the relevant applied science, and finally to a practicum in which they are presumed to learn to apply classroom knowledge to the problems of practice. Medical education offers the prototype for such a curriculum, and its language of "diagnosis", "cure", "laboratory", and "clinic" have long since diffused to other professions.

From the perspective of this model of professional knowledge, it is not difficult to understand why practitioners should be puzzled by their own performance in the indeterminate zones of practice. Their performance does not fit the criteria of technical rationality; it cuts across the dichotomies built into the positivist epistemology of practice. Artistry, for example, is not only in the deciding but also in the doing. When planners or managers convert an uncertain situation into a solvable problem, they construct—as John Dewey pointed out long ago—not only the means to be deployed but the ends-in-view to be achieved. In such problem-setting, ends and means are reciprocally determined. And often, in the unstable world of practice, where methods and theories developed in one context are unsuited to another, practitioners function as researchers, inventing the techniques and models appropriate to the situation at hand.

The Dilemma of Rigor or Relevance

For practitioners, educators, and students of the professions, the positivist epistemology of practice contributes to an urgent dilemma of rigor or relevance.

Given the dominant view of professional rigor, the view which prevails in the intellectual climate of the universities and is embedded in the institutional arrangements of professional education and research, rigorous practice depends on well-formed problems of instrumental choice to whose solution research-based theory and technique are applicable.[2] But real-world problems do not come well formed. They tend to present themselves, on the contrary, as messy, indeterminate, problematic situations. When a civil engineer worries about what road to build, for example, he does not have a problem he can solve by an application of locational techniques or decision theory. He confronts a complex and ill-defined situation in which geographic, financial, economic, and political factors are usually mixed up together. If he is to arrive at a well-formed problem, he must construct it from the materials of the problematic situation. And the problem of problem-setting is not a well-formed problem (Rein & Schön, 1977).

When a practitioner sets a problem, he chooses what he will treat as the "things" of the situation. He decides what he will attend to and what he will ignore. He names the objects of this attention and frames them in an appreciative context which sets a direction for action. A vague worry about hunger or malnourishment may be framed, for example, as a problem of selecting an optimal diet. But situations of malnourishment may also be framed in many different ways.[3] Economists, environmental scientists, nutrition scientists, agronomists, planners, engineers, and political scientists debate over the nature of the malnourishment problem, and their discussions have given rise to a multiplicity of problem-settings worthy of *Rashomon*. Indeed, the practice of malnourishment planning is largely taken up with the task of constructing the problem to be solved.

When practitioners succeed in converting a problematic situation to a well-formed problem, or in resolving a conflict over the proper framing of a practitioner's role in a situation, they engage in a kind of inquiry which cannot be subsumed under a model of technical problem-solving. Rather, it is through the work of naming and framing that the exercise of technical rationality becomes possible.

Similarly, the artistic processes by which practitioners sometimes make sense of unique cases, and the art they sometimes bring to everyday practice, do not meet the prevailing criteria of rigorous practice. Often, when a competent practitioner recognizes in a maze of symptoms the pattern of a disease, constructs a basis for coherent design in the peculiarities of a building site, or discerns an understandable structure in a jumble of materials, he does something for which he cannot give a complete or even a reasonably accurate description. Practitioners make judgments of quality for which they cannot state adequate criteria, display skills for which they cannot describe procedures or rules.

By defining rigor only in terms of technical rationality, we exclude as non-rigorous much of what competent practitioners actually do, including the skillful performance of problem-setting and judgment on which technical problem-solving depends. Indeed, we exclude the most important components of competent practice.

In the varied topography of professional practice, there is a high, hard ground which overlooks a swamp. On the high ground, manageable problems lend themselves to solution through the use of research-based theory and technique. In the swampy lowlands, problems are messy and confusing and incapable of technical solution. The irony of this situation is that the problems of the high ground tend to be relatively unimportant to individuals or to society at large, however great their technical interest may be, while in the swamp lie the problems of greatest human concern. The practitioner is confronted with a choice. Shall he/she etc remain on the high ground where he can solve relatively unimportant problems according to his standards of rigor, or shall he descend to the swamp of important problems and non-rigorous inquiry?

Consider medicine, engineering, and agronomy, three of Glazer's major or near-major professions. In these fields, there are areas in which problems are clearly defined, goals are relatively fixed, and phenomena lend themselves to the categories of available theory and technique. Here, practitioners can function effectively as technical experts. But when one or more of these conditions is lacking, competent performance is no longer a matter of exclusively technical expertise. Medical technologies like kidney dialysis or tomography have created demands which stretch the nation's willingness to invest in medical care. How should physicians behave? How should they try to influence or accommodate to health policy? Engineering solutions which seem powerful and elegant when judged from a relatively narrow perspective may have a wider range of consequences which degrade the environment, generate unacceptable risk, or put excessive demands on scarce resources. How should engineers take these factors into account in their actual designing? When agronomists recommend efficient methods of soil cultivation that favor the use of large land-holdings, they may determine the viability of the small family farms on which peasant economies depend. How should the practice of agronomy take such considerations into account? These are not problems, properly speaking, but problematic situations from which problems must be constructed. If practitioners choose not to ignore them, they must approach them through kinds of inquiry which are, according to the dominant model of technical rationality, unrigorous.

The doctrine of technical rationality, promulgated and maintained in the universities and especially in the professional schools, infects the young professional-in-training with a hunger for technique. Many students of urban planning, for example, are impatient with anything other than "hard skills". In schools of management, students often chafe under the discipline of endless case analysis; they want to learn the techniques and algorithms which are, as they see it, the key to high starting salaries. Yet a professional who really tried to confine his practice to the rigorous applications of research-based technique would find not only that he could not work on the most important problems but that he could not practice in the real world at all.

Nearly all professional practitioners experience a version of the dilemma of rigor or relevance, and they respond to it in one of several ways. Some of them choose the swampy lowland, deliberately immersing themselves in confusing but crucially important situations. When they are asked to describe their methods of inquiry, they speak of experience, trial and error, intuition or muddling through. When teachers, social workers, or planners operate in this vein, they tend to be afflicted with a nagging sense of inferiority in relation to those who present themselves as models of technical rigor. When physicians or engineers do so, they tend to be troubled by the discrepancy between the technical rigor of the "hard" zones of their practice and the apparent sloppiness of the "soft" ones.

Practitioners who opt for the high ground confine themselves to a narrowly technical practice and pay a price for doing so. Operations research, systems analysis, policy analysis, and some management sciences are examples of practices built around the use of formal, analytic models. In the early years of the development of these professions, following World War II, there was a climate of optimism about the power of formal models to solve real-world problems. In subsequent decades, however, there was increasing recognition of the limited applicability of formal models, especially in situations of high complexity and uncertainty (Ackoff, 1979). Some practitioners have responded by confining themselves to a narrow class of well-formed problems—in inventory control for example. Some researchers have continued to develop formal models for use in problems of high complexity and uncertainty, quite undeterred by the troubles incurred whenever a serious attempt is made to put such models into practice. They pursue an agenda driven by evolving questions of modeling theory and techniques, increasingly divergent from the contexts of actual practice.

Practitioners may try, on the other hand, to cut the situations of practice to fit their models, employing for this purpose one of several procrustean strategies. They may become selectively inattentive to data incongruent with their theories,[4] as some educators preserve their confidence in "competency-testing" by ignoring the kinds of competence that competency-testing fails to detect. Physicians or therapists may use junk categories like "patient resistance" to explain away the cases in which an indicated treatment fails to lead to cure (Geertz, 1973). And social workers may try to make their technical expertise effective by exerting unilateral control over the practice situation, for example, by removing "unworthy" clients from the case rolls.

Those who confine themselves to a limited range of technical problems on the high ground, or cut the situations of practice to fit available techniques, seek a world in which technical rationality works. Even those who choose the swamp tend to pay homage to prevailing models of rigor. What they know how to do, they have no way of describing as rigorous.

Writers about the professions tend to follow similar paths. Both Glazer and Schein, for example, recognize the indeterminate zones of professional practice. But Glazer relegates them to the "minor" professions, of which he despairs. And Schein locates what he calls "divergent" phenomena of uncertainty, complexity, and uniqueness in concrete practice situations, while at the same time regarding professional knowledge as increasingly "convergent". He thinks convergent knowledge may be applied to divergent practice through the exercise of "divergent skills"—about which, however, he is able to say very little (Schein, 1974). For if divergent skills were treated in terms of theory or technique, they would belong to convergent professional knowledge; and if they are neither theory nor technique, they cannot be described as "knowledge" at all. Rather, they function as a kind of junk category which serves to protect an underlying model of technical rationality.

Yet the epistemology of practice embedded in our universities and research institutions, ingrained in our habits of thought about professional knowledge, and at the root of the dilemma of rigor or relevance, has lost its hold on the field that nurtured it. Among philosophers of science, no one wants any longer to be called a positivist.[5] There is a rebirth of interest in the ancient topics of craft, artistry, and myth, topics whose fate positivism seemed once to have finally sealed. Positivism and the positivist epistemology of practice now seem to rest on a particular view of science, one now largely discredited.

It is timely, then, to reconsider the question of professional knowledge. Perhaps there is an epistemology of practice which takes full account of the competence practitioners sometimes display in situations of uncertainty, complexity, and uniqueness. Perhaps there is a way of looking at problem-setting and intuitive artistry which presents these activities as describable and susceptible to a kind of rigor that falls outside the boundaries of technical rationality.

Reflection-in-Action

When we go about the spontaneous, intuitive performance of the actions of everyday life, we show ourselves to be knowledgeable in a special way. Often, we cannot say what we know. When we try to describe it, we find ourselves at a loss, or we produce descriptions that are obviously inappropriate. Our knowing is ordinarily tacit, implicit in our patterns of action and in our feel for the stuff with which we are dealing. It seems right to say that our knowing is in our action. And similarly, the workaday life of the professional practitioner reveals, in its recognitions, judgments and skills, a pattern of tacit knowing-in-action.

Once we put technical rationality aside, thereby giving up our view of competent practice as an application of knowledge to instrumental decisions, there is nothing strange about the idea that a kind of knowing is inherent in intelligent action. Common sense admits the category of know-how, and it does not stretch common sense very much to say that the know-how is in the action—that a tightrope walker's know-how, for example, lies in, and is revealed by, the way he takes his trip across the wire, or that a big league pitcher's know-how is in his way of pitching to a batter's weakness, changing his pace, or distributing his energies over the course of a game. There is nothing in common sense to make us say that know-how consists in rules or plans which we entertain in the mind prior to action. Although we sometimes think before acting, it is also true that in much of the spontaneous behavior of skillful practice we reveal a kind of knowing which does not stem from a prior intellectual operation.

As Gilbert Ryle (1949) put it:

> "What distinguishes sensible from silly operations is not their parentage but their procedure, and this holds no less for intellectual than for practical performances. "Intelligent" cannot be defined in terms of "intellectual" or "knowing how" in terms of "knowing that"; "thinking what I am doing" does not connote "both thinking what to do and doing it". When I do something intelligently . . . I am doing one thing and not two. My performance has a special procedure or manner, not special antecedents."

Andrew Harrison (1978) has expressed a similar thought by saying that when someone acts intellectually, he "acts his mind".

Examples of intelligence in action include acts of recognition and judgment, as well as the exercise of ordinary physical skills.

Michael Polany (1967) has written about our ability to recognize a face in a crowd. The experience of recognition can be immediate and holistic. We simply see, all of a sudden, the face of someone we know. We are aware of no antecedent reasoning and we are often unable to list the features that distinguish this face from the hundreds of others present in the crowd.

When the thing we recognize is "something wrong" or "something right", then recognition takes the form of judgment. Chris Alexander has called attention to the innumerable judgments of "mismatch"—deviations from a tacit norm—that are involved in the making of a design (Alexander, 1964). And Geoffrey Vickers has gone on to note that not only in artistic judgment but in all our ordinary judgments of quality, we "can recognize and describe deviations from a norm very much more clearly than we describe the norm itself" (Vickers, 1978). A young friend of mine who teaches tennis observes that his students have to be able to feel when they're hitting the ball right, and they have to like that feeling, as compared to the feeling of hitting it wrong, but they need not, and usually cannot, describe either the feeling of hitting it right or what they do to get that feeling. A skilled physician can sometimes recognize "a case of . . ." the moment a person walks into his office. The act of recognition comes immediately and as a whole; the physician may not be able to say, subsequently, just what led to his initial judgment.

Polany has described our ordinary tactile appreciation of the surface of materials. If you ask a person what he feels when he explores the surface of a table with his hand, he is apt to say that the table feels rough or smooth, sticky or slippery, but he is unlikely to say that he feels a certain compression and abrasion of his fingertips—though it must be from this kind of feeling that he gets to his appreciation of the table's surface. Polany speaks of perceiving from these fingertip sensations *to* the qualities of the surface. Similarly, when we use a stick to probe a hidden place, we focus not on the impressions of the stick on our hand but on the qualities of the place which we apprehend through these tacit impressions. To become skilful in the use of a tool is to learn to appreciate, as it were, directly, the qualities of materials that we apprehend *through* the tacit sensations of the tool in our hand.

Chester Barnard (1968) has written of "non-logical processes" that we cannot express in words as a process of reasoning, but evince only by a judgment, decision, or action. A child who has learned to throw a ball makes immediate judgments of distance which he coordinates, tacitly, with the feeling of bodily movement involved in the act of throwing. A high-school boy, solving quadratic equations has learned spontaneously to carry out a program of operations that he cannot describe. A practiced accountant of Barnard's acquaintance could take a balance sheet of considerable complexity and within minutes or even seconds get a significant set of facts from it, though he could not describe in words the recognitions and calculations that entered into his performance. Similarly, we are able to execute spontaneously such complex activities as crawling, walking, riding a bicycle, or juggling, without having to think, in any conscious way, what we are doing, and often without being able to give a verbal description even approximately faithful to our performance.

In spite of their tacit complexity and virtuosity, however, our spontaneous responses to the phenomena of everyday life do not always work. Sometimes our knowing-in-action yields surprises. And we often react to the unexpected by a kind of on-the-spot inquiry which I shall call *reflection-in-action*.

Sometimes this process takes the form of ordinary, on-line problem-solving. It need not even be associated with a high degree of skill but may consist in an amateur's effort to acquire skill. Recently, for example, I built a wooden gate. The gate was made of wooden pickets and strapping. I had made a drawing of it, and figured out the dimensions I wanted, but I had not reckoned with the problem of keeping the structure square. I noticed, as I began to nail the strapping to the pickets that the whole thing wobbled. I knew that when I nailed in a diagonal piece, the structure would become rigid. But how would I be sure that, at that moment, the structure would be square? I stopped to think. There came to mind a vague memory about diagonals—that in a square, the diagonals are equal. I took a yard stick, intending to measure the diagonals, but I found it difficult to make these measurements without disturbing the structure. It occurred to me to use a piece of string. Then it became apparent that I needed precise locations from which to measure the diagonal from corner to corner. After several frustrating trials, I decided to locate the center point at each of the corners (by crossing diagonals at each corner), hammered in a nail at each of the four center points, and used the nails as anchors for the measurement string. It took several moments to figure out how to adjust the structure so as to correct the errors I found by measuring, and when I had the diagonal equal, I nailed in the piece of strapping that made the structure rigid.

Here—in an example that must have its analogues in the experience of amateur carpenters the world over—my intuitive way of going about the task led me to a surprise (the discovery of the wobble) which I interpreted as a problem. Stopping to think, I invented procedures to solve the problem, discovered further unpleasant surprises, and made further corrective inventions, including the several minor inventions necessary to make the idea of string-measurement of diagonals work.

Ordinarily, we might call such a process "trial and error". But it is not a series of random trials continued until a desired result has been produced. The process has a form, an inner logic according to which reflection on the unexpected consequences of one action influences the design of the next one. The "moments" of such a process may be described as follows:

- In the context of the performance of some task, the performer spontaneously initiates a routine of action that produces an unexpected outcome.
- The performer notices the unexpected result which he construes as a surprise—an error to be corrected, an anomaly to be made sense of, an opportunity to be exploited.
- Surprise triggers reflection, directed both to the surprising outcome and to the knowing-in-action that led to it. It is as though the performer asked himself, what is this?, and at the same time, what understandings and strategies of mine have led me to produce this?
- The performer restructures his understanding of the situation—his framing of the problem he has been trying to solve, his picture of what is going on, or the strategy of action he has been employing.
- On the basis of this restructuring, he invents a new strategy of action.
- He tries out the new action he has invented, running an on-the-spot experiment whose results he interprets, in turn, as a "solution", an outcome on the whole satisfactory, or else as a new surprise that calls for a new round of reflection and experiment.

In the course of such a process, the performer "reflects", not only in the sense of thinking about the action he has undertaken and the result he has achieved, but in the more precise sense of turning his thought back on the knowing-in-action implicit in his action. He reflects "in action" in the sense that his thinking occurs within the boundaries of what

I call an action-present—a stretch of time within which it is still possible to make a difference to the outcomes of action.

These are examples of reflection-in-action drawn from some of the familiar contexts of professional practice:

- A designer, hard at work on the design of a school, has been exploring the possible configurations of small, classroom units. Having tried a number of these, dissatisfied with the formal results, she decides that these units are "too small to do much with". She tries combining the classrooms in L-shaped pairs and discovers that these are "formally much more significant" and that they have the additional, unexpected educational advantage of putting grade one next to grade two and grade three next to grade four.
- A teacher has a young student, Joey, who disturbs her by insisting that an eclipse of the sun did not take place because "it was snowing and we didn't see it". It occurs to the teacher that Joey does not know that the sun is there, even if he can't see it, and she asks him, "Where was the sun yesterday"? Joey answers, "I don't know; I didn't see it". Later, it occurs to her that his answer may have reflected, not his ignorance of the sun remaining in the sky, but his interpretation of her question. She thinks that he may have read her as asking, *Where* in the sky was the sun? With this in mind, she tries a new question: "What happened to the sun yesterday"?, to which Joey answers, "It was in the sky".

In such examples as these, reflection-in-action involves a "stop-and-think". It is close to conscious awareness and is easily put into words. Often, however, reflection-in-action is smoothly embedded in performance; there is no stop-and-think, no conscious attention to the process, and no verbalization. In this way, for example, a baseball pitcher adapts his pitching style to the pecularities of a batter, a tennis player executes split-second variations in play in order to counter the strategies of his opponent. In such cases, we are close to processes we might recognize as examples of artistry.

When good jazz musicians improvise together, they display a feel for the performance. Listening to one another and to themselves, they feel where the music is going and adjust their playing accordingly. They are inventing on-line, and they are also responding to surprises provided by the inventions of the others. A figure announced by one performer will be taken up by another, elaborated, and perhaps integrated with a new melody.

The collective process of musical invention is not usually undertaken at random, however. It is organized around an underlying structure—a shared schema of meter, melody, and harmony that gives the piece a predictable order. In addition, each of the musicians has ready a repertoire of musical figures that he can play, weaving variations of them as the opportunity arises. Improvisation consists in varying, combining, and recombining a set of figures within the schema that gives coherence to the whole performance. As the musician feels the directions in which the music is developing, out of their interwoven contributions, they make new sense of it and adjust their performances to the sense they make. They are reflecting-in-action on the music they are collectively making, though not, of course, in the medium of words.

Their process is not unlike the familiar improvisation of everyday conversation, which does occur in the medium of words. A good conversation is both predictable and, in some respects, unpredictable. The participants may pick up themes suggested by others, developing them through the associations they provoke. Each participant seems to have a readily available repertoire of kinds of things to say, around which we can develop variations suited to the present occasion. Conversation is collective verbal improvisation which tends to fall into conventional routines—for example, the anecdote (with appropriate side comments and reactions) or the debate—and it develops according to a pace and rhythm of interaction that the participants seem, without conscious attention, to work out in common. At the same time, there are surprises, in the form of unexpected turns of phrase or directions of development. Participants make on-the-spot responses to surprise, often in conformity to the kind of conversational role they have adopted. Central to the other forms of improvisation, there is a conversational division of labor that gradually establishes itself, often without conscious awareness on the part of those who work it out.

In the on-the-spot improvisation of a musical piece or a conversation, spontaneous reflection-in-action takes the form of a kind of production. The participants are involved in a collective *making* process. Out of the "stuff" of this musical performance, or this talk, they make a piece of music, or a conversation—in either case, an artifact that has, in some degree, order, meaning, development, coherence. Their reflection-in-action becomes a reflective conversation—this time, in a metaphorical sense—with the materials of the situation in which they are engaged. Each person, carrying out his own evolving role in the collective performance, "listens" to the things that happen, including the surprises that result from earlier moves, and responds, on-line, through new moves that give new directions to the development of the artifact. The process is reminiscent of Carpenter's description of the Eskimo sculptor, patiently carving a reindeer bone, examining the gradually changing shape, finally exclaiming, "Ah seal"!

That one can engage in spontaneous reflection-in-action without being able to give a good description of it is evident from experience. Typically, when a performer is asked to talk about the reflection and on-the-spot experimenting he has just carried out, he gives at first a description which is obviously incomplete or inaccurate. And by comparing what he says to what he has just done, he can often discover this for himself.

Clearly, it is one thing to engage spontaneously in a performance that involves reflection-in-action, and quite another thing to reflect on that reflection-in-action through an act of description. It is still another thing to reflect on the resulting description. Indeed, these several, distinct kinds of reflection can play important roles in the process by which an individual learns a new kind of performance. A tennis coach (Galloway) reports his use of an exercise in which he repeatedly asks his students to "say where their racket was when they hit the ball"; he intends to help them get more precisely in touch with what they are doing when they hit the ball, so that they will *know* what they are doing when they try to correct their errors. Seymour Papert used to teach juggling by informing would-be jugglers that they are susceptible to a variety of kinds of "bugs"— that is, to typical mistakes ("bugs" by analogy with computer programming)—such as "throwing too far forward" or "overcorrecting" an error. He would ask them from time to time to describe the "bug" they had just enacted.

Professional practitioners, such as physicians, managers, and teachers, also reflect-in-action, but their reflection is of a kind particular to the special features of professional practice. "Practice" has a double meaning. A lawyer's practice includes the kinds of activities he carries out, the clients he serves, the cases he is called upon to handle. When we speak of practicing the performance, on the other hand, we refer to the repetitive yet experimental process by which one learns, for example, to play a musical instrument. The two senses of "practice", although quite distinct, relate to one another in an interesting way. Professional practice also includes repetition. A professional is, at least in some measure, a specialist. He deals with certain types of situations, examples, images, and techniques. Working his way through many variations of a limited number of cases, he "practices" his practice. His know how tends to become increasingly rich, efficient, tacit, and automatic, thereby conferring on him and his clients the benefits of specialization. On the other hand, specialization can make him narrow and parochial, inducing a kind of overlearning which takes the form of a tacit pattern of error to which he becomes selectively inattentive.

Reflection on spontaneous reflection-in-action can serve as a corrective to overlearning. As a practitioner surfaces the tacit understandings that have grown up around the repetitive experiences of a specialized practice, he may allow himself to notice and make new sense of confusing and unique phenomena.

A skillful physician, lawyer, manager, or architect continually engages in a process of appreciating, probing, modeling, experimenting, diagnosing, psyching out, and evaluating, which he can describe imperfectly if at all. His knowing-in-action is revealed and presented by his feel for the stuff with which he deals. When he tries, on rare occasions, to say what he knows—when he tries to put his knowing into the form of knowledge—his formulations of principles, theories, maxims and rules of thumb are often incongruent with the understanding and know-how implicit in his patterns of practice.

On the other hand, contrary to Hannah Arendt's observation that reflection is out of place in action, skillful practitioners sometimes respond to a situation that is puzzling, unique, or conflicted, by reflecting at one and the same time on the situation before them and on the reflection-in-action they spontaneously bring to it. In the midst of action, they are able to turn thought back on itself, surfacing, criticizing and restructuring the thinking by which they have spontaneously tried to make the situation intelligible to themselves. There are, for example:

- Managers who respond to turbulent situations by constructing and testing a model of the situation and experimenting with alternative strategies for dealing with it.
- Physicians who, finding that "80% of the cases seen in the office are not found in the book", treat each patient as a unique case, constructing and testing diagnoses, inventing and evaluating lines of treatment through processes of on-the-spot experiment.
- Engineers who discover that they cannot apply their rules of thumb to a situation because it is anomalous or peculiarly constrained (like the shattering of windows on the John Hancock building in Boston), and proceed to devise and test theories and procedures unique to the situation at hand.

- Lawyers who construct new ways to assimilate a puzzling case to a body of judicial precedent.
- Bankers who feel uneasy about a prospective credit risk, even though his "operating numbers" are all in order, and try to discover and test the implicit judgments underlying their uneasiness.
- Planners who treat their plans as tentative programs for inquiry, alert to discovering the unanticipated meanings their interventions turn out to have for those affected by them.

Many such examples of reflection on reflection-in-action occur in the indeterminate zones of practice—uncertain, unique, or value-conflicted. Depending on the context and the practitioner, such inquiry may take the form of on-the-spot problem-solving, or it may take the form of theory-building, or reappreciation of the problem of the situation. When the problem at hand proves resistant to readily accessible solutions, the practitioner may rethink the approach he has been taking and invent new strategies of action. When he encounters a situation that falls outside his usual range of descriptive categories, he may surface and criticize his initial understandings and proceed to construct a new, situation-specific theory of the phenomena before him. (The best theories, Kevin Lynch observed, are those we make up in the situation.) When he finds himself stuck, he may decide that he has been working on the wrong problem, and evolve a new way of setting the problem.

The objects of reflection may be anywhere in the system of understanding and know-how that a practitioner brings to his practice. Depending on the centrality of the elements he chooses to surface and re-think, more or less of that system may become vulnerable to change. But, systems of intuitive knowing are dynamically conservative, actively defended, and highly resistant to change. They tend not to go quietly to their demise, and reflection-in-action often takes on a quality of struggle. In the early minutes and hours of the "accident" at the Three Mile Island nuclear power plant, for example, operators and managers found themselves confronted with combinations of signals they could only regard as "weird", unprecedented, unlike anything they had ever seen before.[6] Yet they persisted in attempting to assimilate these strange and perplexing signals to a situation of normalcy—"not wanting to believe", as one manager put it, that the nuclear core had been uncovered and damaged. Only after 12 hours of fruitless attempts to construe the situation as a minor problem—a breach in a steam line, a build-up of steam in the primary circulatory system—did one anonymous key manager insist, against the wishes of others in the plant, that "future actions be based on the assumption that the core has been uncovered, the fuel severely damaged".

Many practitioners, locked into a view of themselves as technical experts, find little in the world of practice to occasion reflection. For them, uncertainty is a threat; its admission, a sign of weakness. They have become proficient at techniques of selective inattention, the use of junk categories to dismiss anomalous data, procrustean treatment of troublesome situations, all aimed at preserving the constancy of their knowing-in-action. Yet reflection-in-action is not a rare event. There are teachers, managers, engineers, and artists for whom reflection-in-action is the "prose" they speak as they display and develop the ordinary artistry of their everyday lives. Such individuals are willing to embrace error, accept confusion, and reflect critically on their previously unexamined assumptions. Nevertheless, in a world where professionalism is still mainly identified with technical expertise, even such practitioners as these may feel profoundly uneasy because they cannot describe what they know how to do, cannot justify it as a legitimate form of professional knowledge, cannot increase its scope or depth or quality, and cannot with confidence help others to learn it.

For all of these reasons, the study of professional artistry is of critical importance. We should be turning the puzzle of professional knowledge on its head, not seeking only to build up a science applicable to practice but also to reflect on the reflection-in-action already embedded in competent practice.

We should be exploring, for example, how the on-the-spot experimentation carried out by practicing architects, physicians, engineers and managers is like, and unlike, the controlled experimentation of laboratory scientists. We should be analyzing the ways in which skilled practitioners build up repertoires of exemplars, images and strategies of description in terms of which they learn to see novel, one-of-a-kind phenomena. We should be attentive to differences in the framing of problematic situations and to the rare episodes of frame-reflective discourse in which practitioners sometimes coordinate and transform their conflicting ways of making sense of confusing predicaments. We should investigate the conventions and notations through which practitioners create virtual worlds—as diverse as sketch-pads, simulations, role-plays and rehearsals—in which they are able to slow down the pace of action, go back and try again, and reduce the cost and risk of experimentation. In such explorations as these, grounded in collaborative reflection on everyday artistry, we will be pursuing the description of a new epistemology of practice.

We should also investigate how it is that some people learn the kinds and levels of reflection-in-action essential to professional artistry. In apprenticeships and clinical experiences, how are textbook descriptions of symptoms and procedures translated into the acts of recognition and judgment, and the readiness for action characteristic of professional competence? Under what conditions do aspiring practitioners learn to see, in the unfamiliar phenomena of practice, similarities to the canonical problems they may have learned in the classroom? What are the processes by which some people learn to internalize, criticize and reproduce the demonstrated competence of acknowledged masters? What, in short, is the nature of the complex process we are accustomed to dismiss with the term, "imitation"? And what must practitioners know already, what kinds of competences, what features of stance toward practice, must they already have acquired in order to learn to construe their practice as a continuing process of reflection-in-action?

Clearly, just as some people learn to reflect-in-action, so do others learn to help them do so. These rare individuals are not so much "teachers" as "coaches" of reflection-in-action. Their artistry consists in an ability to have on the tip of their tongue, or to invent on-the-spot, the method peculiarly suited to the difficulties experienced by the student before them. And, just as professional artistry demands a capacity for reflection-in-action, so does the coach's artistry demand a capacity for reflection-in-action on the student's intuitive understanding of the problem at hand, the intervention that might enable them to become fruitfully confused, the proposal that might enable them to take the next useful step.

The development of forms of professional education conducive to reflection-in-action requires reflection on the artistry of coaching—a kind of reflection very nicely illustrated by the studies of case teaching conducted over the past ten years at the Harvard Business School. If educators hope to contribute to the development of reflective practitioners, they must become adept at such reflection on their own teaching practice.

In this way, perhaps, we will be heeding Everett Hughes' call for a way of undoing the bonds that have tied the professional schools to the traditions of the late 19th century university. At least, and at last, we will be getting some groups of young people who are free of those bonds, making them free to do something new and different.

Notes

1. For a discussion of Positivism and its influence on prevailing epistemological views, see Habermas (1968). And for a discussion of the influence of Positivist doctrines on the shaping of the modern university, see Shils (1978).

2. I have taken this term from Simon (1972) who gives a particularly useful sample of a well-formed problem.

3. For an example of multiple views of the malnourishment problem, see Berg, Scrimshaw and Call (1973).

4. I have taken this phrase from the work of psychiatrist, Harry Stack Sullivan.

5. As Bernstein (1976) has written: "There is not a single major thesis advanced by either nineteenth century Positivists or the Vienna Circle that has not been devastatingly criticized when measured by the Positivists' own standards for philosophical argument. The original formulations of the analytic-synthetic dichotomy and the verifiability criterion on meaning have been abandoned. It has been effectively shown that the Positivists' understanding of the natural sciences and the formal disciplines is grossly oversimplified. Whatever one's final judgment about the current disputes in the post-empiricist philosophy and history of science . . . there is rational agreement about the inadequacy of the original Positivist understanding of science, knowledge, and meaning."

6. Transcript of *Nova*, 29 March, 1983, "60 Minutes to Meltdown".

References

Ackoff, R. (1979). The future of operational research is past. *Journal of Operational Research Society,* 30(2), 93–104.

Alexander, C. (1964). *Notes Toward the Synthesis of Forum.* Cambridge, MA: Harvard University Press.

Alonso, W. (1963). Cities and city planners, *Daedalus,* 838.

Barnard, C. (1968). *The Functions of the Executive* (2nd Ed., p. 306). Cambridge, MA; Harvard University Press.

Berg, A., Scrimshaw, H. S., & Call, D. L. (Eds.). (1973). *Nutrition, National Development and Planning.* Cambridge, MA: MIT Press.

Bernstein, R. (1976). *The Restructuring of Social and Political Theory.* New York: Harcourt, Brace, Jovanovich.

Geertz, C. (1973). *The Interpretation of Cultures, Selected Essays by Clifford Geertz.* New York: Basic Books.

Glazer, N. (1974). The schools of the minor professions. *Minerva, XII(3),* 363.

Gustafson, J. (1963). The clergy in the United States. *Daedalus,* 743.

Habermas, J. (1968). *Knowledge and Human Interests.* Boston, MA: Beacon Press.

Harrison, A. (1978). *Making and Thinking.* Indianapolis: Hacket.

Hughes, E. (1959). The study of occupations. In R. Merton, & V. Broom (Eds.), *Sociology Today.* New York: Basic Books.

Lynn, K. (1963). Introduction to "The Professions". *Daedalus,* 649.

Polany, M. (1967). *The Tacit Dimension* (p.12). New York: Doubleday.

Rein, M., & Schön, D. (1977). Problem-setting in policy research, In: C. Weiss, (Ed.), *Using Social Research in Public Policy Making.* Lexington, MA: D. C. Heath.

Ryle, G. (1949). On knowing how and knowing that. In *The Concept of Mind* (p.32). London: Hutcheson.

Schein, E. (1974). *Professional Education* (pp. 43–44). New York: McGraw Hill.

Shils, E. (1978). The order of learning in the United States from 1865 to 1920: The ascendancy of the universities. *Minerva,* XVI (2).

Simon, H. (1972). *The Science of the Artificial.* Cambridge, MA: MIT Press.

Veblen, T. (1968). *The Higher Learning in America* (Reprint of the 1918 edition). New York: Kelley.

Vickers, G. (1978). Unpublished memorandum, MIT.

Chapter 14

Beyond Competences: Lessons from Management Learning

Ian Cunningham

Summary

This chapter goes beyond discussion of competence and competencies. Cunningham believes it is axiomatic that we want people who are competent at what they do. He argues that focusing on just the competence to do things is too limited as an aim of learning. As an alternative, the concept of capability succeeds in promoting a necessarily wider perspective.

Reference is made to a wide range of philosophical concepts and theories, and critical observation of current practice, to illustrate that more priority should be given to deciding *what* needs to be learned before addressing the processes and structures for learning.

Examples are drawn from the managerial world. However, it is suggested that there may be general lessons for education and training in the evidence and arguments quoted, within this broad case for a holistic approach to learning.

Introduction

In discussing capability there is a tendency for many people to see this concept as implying a largely mental/cognitive activity. I see it as involving also:

This chapter was previously published as Chapter 17 in D. O'Reilly, L. Cunningham, & S. Lester (Eds.), *Developing the Capable Practitioner*, Kogan Page, London (1999). It is © Kogan Page and is reprinted here by kind permission of the publisher.

- feelings and emotions
- physical aspects
- issues of values, morals and spirituality
- social factors, for example, to do with relationships with others.

This perspective has been labeled "holistic," and I will try to give my view of how this concept can be applied to good learning. As well as basing comments on practical experience and on authors quoted, I have also drawn on research conducted on chief executives and other top managers. This research was carried out in the United States and the United Kingdom with a view to developing fundamental concepts and models that are usable cross culturally (Cunningham, 1988, 1999). (My colleague Graham Dawes also contributed to the research in the United States.)

The Social Domain

A major problem with the educational world in the United Kingdom is the individualistic orientation to learning. The focus on individuals must, of course, have a central place in planning learning, and I shall address this level. But before doing that I want to argue that in organizational life there is also an important focus on learning at the group or team level and on whole-organization learning (as exemplified by the current concerns to develop learning organizations). Beyond the organization, there is a need to consider learning at the community level and in whole societies (as indicated in the learning society concept). And, lastly, there is the growing awareness of global learning needs, environmentalists being one group that has highlighted this issue.

I do not have space to do justice to these wider issues, but perhaps one example will help at least to record the dangers of self-centered individualism. In education, when learners help each other and share their learning it is called cheating and people get punished for it. In the world outside educational establishments it is absolutely essential that people "cheat." Organizations, communities, and whole societies cannot function effectively in the modern world unless people share their learning. Unless educational institutions address this issue they will continue to undermine attempts to create learning organizations, learning communities, and learning societies.

Feelings and Emotions

Let me next comment on "emotional learning." Mike Dixon, a columnist for the *Financial Times*, once commented to me that in management,

"Thinking is embedded in feeling." This phrase struck a chord. Managers think out of an internal context of feelings and emotions: thoughts are not produced out of other thoughts. We think what it is possible for us to think as a result of the other dimensions of ourselves (as mentioned above—the emotional, the physical, the spiritual, and the social).

> Keutzer (1982), drawing on the work of Paul McLean and others, suggests that neurophysiological evidence supports the view that evolution of the neocortex has produced a split between the archaic (emotional) structures of the brain and the "thinking cap" that governs rational thought. Emotion is the older partner—and, it is suggested, the more powerful. Given the inevitable conflicts between reason and emotion, the reasoning part is "compelled to provide spurious rationalizations for the senior partner's urges and whims" (Keutzer, 1982). Goleman (1995) makes a similar point when he says that "the emotional faculty guides our moment to moment decisions". Indeed, the popularity of Goleman's book provides evidence that many people want to take seriously the research evidence he cites to support his argument for the centrality of "emotional" intelligence.

Bramley (1977), from her experience as a student counselor, argues that many students cover up emotional problems in unbalanced intellectual development. But, if we take Keutzer's hypothesis seriously, we can see that this strategy is misguided. And, as Bramley comments, "When and if a student realizes, on attainment of a good degree, that his intellectual ability cannot give him love and security for which he yearns, he may become very ill indeed, and certainly several suicidal young people whom I have known come into this category."

All this was well known in ancient times and in diverse cultures. To take one example, from the Middle East: "Your reason and your passion are the rudder and the sails of your seafaring soul. If either your sails or your rudder be broken, you can but toss and drift, or else be held at a standstill in mid-seas" (Gibran, 1972).

Unfortunately, the lessons have not been learned in the managerial world—or they have been forgotten or driven out in the learning environments of business schools. I will quote just one example. *The Boston Globe* of 13 October 1986 wrote up the 25-year class reunion of the Harvard Business School MBAs who graduated in 1961. Whilst it noted that there were positive comments about Harvard's role in making participants successful, significant concerns were also raised. Edwin Stanley (Chairman of Stanley Investment and Management Inc.) said "Business School did us a disservice with a compass locked on true north." His criticism was of a narrowly focused ambition to succeed. Amos Hostetter (Chairman of Continental Cablevision) went further when he claimed that his personal life had been "sublimated" to business success. "I was being a coward and afraid of intimacy," he commented. One of the wives present criticized those who were raising these concerns. She said "I feel sorry for you guys. You shouldn't expect Harvard to teach you how to be human in your professional lives."

I think that response was unfair. Business schools claim to equip people for managerial roles. If they pretend that personal feelings and values have no place, or they force the sublimation of these in a pseudo-rational analytical atmosphere, then they do deserve to be criticized. La Bier's clinical research on young managers produced clear evidence of this problem. He found that there were managers who superficially were climbing the corporate ladder with apparent consummate skill and who behaved in ways that were totally "normal." However, from in-depth clinical study, he found that they were, to use his words, "quite sick." He described them as "dominated by irrational passions of power lust, conquest, grandiosity, and destructiveness or, conversely, by cravings for subjugation and humiliation" (La Bier, 1986).

On the other hand, he found another group who seemed to display some neurotic symptoms but were psychologically normal. These he saw as growing up through learning about and struggling with the difficulties of corporate life. This could be painful, and they sometimes showed it (for example through anxiety feelings or sleepless nights). The problem is that, as William Temple alluded to earlier this century, we are taught to think together and feel separately, whereas we need to think separately and feel together. That is the mark of good collaborative practice such as teamwork.

Evans and Bartolomé (1980) discuss these issues, drawing on writers such as Vaillant and Schein. They agree with the latter that "the distinguishing characteristic of a top level executive is not his skill or ability but his emotional competence." They show how, for instance, a successful manager may have to do an unpleasant task such as firing someone. He or she will feel bad about it, but will face up to it and do it. In other words the manager will experience negative feelings, but deal with them appropriately. [Also see Schein (1978) and Vaillant (1977)].

Metafeeling

The term I use to elucidate this emotional sophistication is metafeeling. This is, the emotionally mature person may feel bad, but they feel OK about feeling bad. They know that life has its ups and downs and they accept it. They experience crises but work them through.

Metafeeling, then, is about how we feel about how we feel. People go to sad films, cry a lot, and say how much they enjoyed it. They feel good about feeling sad. However, a person could experience some difficulty in life (for example loss of job), feel sad about it (reasonably), then feel bad about feeling sad. This can lead to a downward spiral of depression.

Some Buddhist monks have a routine of getting up in the morning, thinking of all the problems they and others have or could have, then laughing out loud about them. They recognize problems and the negative feelings around them. They are not covered up or pretended away. But they are put in perspective.

Biorhythm evidence suggests that we go through cycles of ups and downs. It is suggested that we inevitably have emotional highs and lows, irrespective of what is going on in the world around us. Whilst I am not sure that the wilder claims about biorhythms are not too fanciful, it seems undeniable that people do experience patterns of internal changes, for example, hormonal changes, that have an effect on our emotional states. If we accept this, then we can metafeel OK—we can know that we will not be on top form every day of our lives and that these variations are not to be blamed on anyone—least of all ourselves.

Connectedness

One of the important aspects of good learning seems to be about connecting. This includes internal connecting, which integrates:

- thinking
- feeling
- the physical (the body)
- believing/valuing (including spiritual beliefs)

These internal processes need to come together. Holistic learning is not about developing each aspect sequentially. When we learn in the best sense, we have feelings about what we think and we integrate these in our value/belief systems. A useful concept in explaining this connection is *Centeredness*.

We also engage in External Connecting—that is, we interact with the world around us. *Grounding* is the concept I will use to explore this. I will take the two concepts of Centering and Grounding in turn. They both came from Eastern thinking and are most visibly used in martial arts training, but they are best seen as "learning for life" in its broadest sense.

Centering

In some approaches to learning developed in China and Japan (such as Tai Ji and Aikido), the concept of the Center is important. It can be viewed as the center of a single person, as their center of gravity around which the body revolves (not literally!). It can also be seen that a person's Center is the center of the universe from their point of view. It's the place from which to connect to others (people, things, animals, etc.). So it has an ecological sense; the Center is the harmonizing focus of energy fields and patterns of relationships.

This can all sound like pretty flaky, esoteric stuff if the language and way of thinking is new. But it is highly practical. There is a demonstrable difference between Centered and Uncentered people. Let me elaborate some features of Centeredness.

Harmony

"Harmony is an attunement of opposites, a unification of many, a reconciliation of dissentients" said Theon of Smyrna. Harmony is not, in music, unison. It is the aesthetic "centering" of difference (different voices, different instruments). We each have these differences within us. Some psychologists and psychotherapists refer to our different parts as "subpersonalities." Berne (1964, 1974), in developing Transactional Analysis, used the idea of "ego states," which he labeled "Parent," "Adult," and "Child." Irrespective of their theoretical base, there is much agreement among psychotherapists that a key part of their work can be in helping a person integrate or harmonize or come to terms with these differences.

In terms of developing a holistic sense, the harmonizing required here is of head, heart, and guts. Particularly as applied to centered managers, we are thinking of the person who:

- Demonstrates harmonized energy.
- Shows congruence and coherence in integrating theory and practice. (In doing so one would bring together "theory-in-use" and "espoused theory," as suggested by Argyris & Schön, 1974.)
- Is able to work with difference and ambiguity, and has the self-awareness to do this.
- "Listens to the inner voice"—this is a term Bennis (1989) uses about highly effective leaders. (Bennis was influenced by Ralph Waldo Emerson's essay "Self-Reliance.") The inner voice, if it is to be heard and believed, comes from the center.

- Is able to be inside and outside at the same time—Postman and Weingartner (1969) call this "the anthropological perspective," meaning that one can understand the rituals, norms, and culture of the group or organization (the insider perspective) and is able to stand outside, examine them, and operate out of the inner voice.
- Has personal theories and meanings that may not conform to the textbook (see McLean et al., 1982).

Balance

It is not that centered managers always feel "in balance," but that they are aware of the value of balance. They recognize polarities and dualities and address them as such. However, we can get inappropriate balance as in the suggestion that the balanced middle manager has a chip on both shoulders! Without a centered way of operating, and attention to some of the factors above, balance on its own is insufficient.

I will mention some polarities that are relevant here, but they are not exhaustive of all the possibilities (see Cunningham, 1984).

Doing/Being

Centered managers are aware of what they do and who they are. The verb "to be" crops up in their language (e.g., "I am . . . ") (see Cunningham, 1992).

A related polarity is:

Proactivity/Reactivity

Proactivity is usually lauded as more desirable than reactivity. But it is clear from my research that this criticism is of the wrong kind of reactivity. Wise reactivity is at the heart of the best customer care practices— flexible, thoughtful, caring responses to customer requests and demands. Proactive organizations that push their technology onto the market with little reactive wisdom in their responses to the market tend to come unstuck eventually.

Taoists use the polarity yin/yang. This is often translated as yin (feminine) and yang (masculine), but the concepts are looser and more sophisticated (Cunningham, 1984). They can, for instance, be seen as subsuming proactivity (in yang) and reactivity (in yin). Taoists emphasize the complementarity and inter-penetration of these seeming opposites. The Taoist principle of mutuality suggests that it is not possible to have one pole without the other. The analogies are that there is no night without day, no light without dark, and no valley without hills.

Theory/Practice

This is a classic polarity that comes up a great deal in discussions about management. Business schools justify an overweening interest in theory by quoting aphorisms such as; "There is nothing so practical as a good theory." In their turn managers attack academics. Two jokes indicate this:

1. *Question*: If you push the professor of marketing and the professor of finance off the roof of the university, which one hits the ground first?
   Answer: Who cares?
2. *Question*: Why are academics buried 30 feet under the ground?
   Answer: Because deep down they're OK.

A root cause of these divides is a dichotomy between what could be labeled two "worlds." Firstly there is a world of Theory which tends to be concerned with teaching generalizations about management in a classroom. As a shorthand I have called this the "S" world, because such teaching gives managers *solutions* to apply to their problems. They tend to be taught *specializations* (Human Resource Management, marketing), *subjects* (economics, sociology) and systems (Information Technology, Operations Research). This "S" world can also include precise *skills* and often includes particular *structures*.

The other world is a world of Practice (the "P" world). It is where managers learn most of what they need to learn. (Research suggests 80-90% of the abilities successful managers use come from this world.) Managers learn by experience and from received wisdom (e.g., more experienced managers, mentors, etc.). The learning is job based and is often a response to live *problems*. For example, when a new IT system is put in, managers have a problem if they do not know how to use it. So they learn. Such learning is very *people* oriented; it is often about changing patterns of work and learning new *processes*. The "P" world is readily recognizable by managers.

There are two difficulties with these two worlds. Firstly there is the "S to P" issue. This is where managers are taught *solutions* and then have to find *problems* or *people* to use them on. Or, even worse, they distort problems to fit the solutions they have available.

To take my own career as an example, I was trained initially as a chemist. At one time I was offered a job as a research chemist in a pharmaceutical company. If I had taken it I might have been presented with the problem of alleviating or even curing a particular mental illness (say depression). The solution I was trained to provide was a chemical one. Presented with such a problem the only solution I would conceive of would be a new drug. My training had convinced me to look for chemical solutions to such problems.

Some years after leaving the world of research chemistry I became involved in the field of psychotherapy. Here, presented with problems of mental illness, the therapist will commonly talk to the patient/client. He or she will look for solutions to the problem within the confines of the particular theoretical framework within which he or she has been trained. What the therapist will not usually do is search for a chemical solution to the problem, just as the average chemist would not think of refusing to search for a new drug and suggesting psychotherapy instead.

Mental illness presents major problems in Western countries. It is arguable that developing apt solutions to these problems is hampered by the inability of the various professions involved to talk to each other (and this problem seems to get worse as the subject boundaries are strengthened through increasing specialization).

This issue affects the managerial world quite broadly, and in training it leads to difficulties such as "the transfer of training" problem (a trainer euphemism for "we taught them things that are no use in their work and therefore they don't apply them").

A different issue from the "S to P" syndrome is "P" only. This is where managers say "I've learned all I need from experience. I don't need to explore new ideas being promoted by a bunch of ivory-tower academics." The difficulty with this approach is that experience is all about the past. If, as we assume, the future is not going to be like the past, experience-only learning will become very limited.

As Fiedler (1992) has shown in his research, highly experienced managers/leaders function well in situations that require little or no learning. These especially include situations with high job stress, such as fire-fighting. Someone leading a group of fire-fighters will draw on experience very heavily. They will not, in the middle of a fire, stop to think about learning issues. They work to well-rehearsed grooves, and stopping to think could be a dangerous activity. On the other hand, the evidence of Fiedler (and others) suggests that in the low job-stress world of the average organization, intellectual and creative ability is more likely to predict good leadership performance than experience. Note that I say that the average organization has low "job stress," not necessarily low "interpersonal stress"; that is, managers may not get on with each other (hence producing interpersonal stress) but their jobs are not inherently stressful (e.g., dangerous, as in fire-fighting).

The two dangers I have identified, namely "S to P" and "P only" need addressing. The answer seems to be "P to S," that is going from problems to solutions, or from people to systems, etc. The point is that experience cannot be the only teacher. New ways of doing things are needed. There is a value in the expert, the professional, the academic. But they should be more in a role of responsiveness to the needs of people, problems, patterns, and processes than they often are. This example shows the need for balance to be driven more from one direction. That is not to deny, though, the need for balance. And sometimes the backroom boffin will come up with a solution to a problem no one knew we had (or that we ignored).

Grounding

I have emphasized so far the idea of Centering, and I have suggested the importance of internal balance and harmony. However, this is not enough. For instance, I quoted Bennis on "listening to the inner voice." But suppose the inner voice is coming from some disconnected, crazy place? At worst it could be a schizophrenic delusion.

Also, Centered managers can be lively, creative entrepreneurs, but without connection to the wider society they may go off at tangents. The manager who is Centered and Grounded has a sense of these wider connections. They are the ones who take environmental and ecological issues really seriously. They do not just see their role as complying with the law or avoiding bad publicity if they pollute rivers. They see themselves as integrally involved in the planet and all life upon it.

Grounding can be grounding in:

- Spiritual and religious beliefs that provide a well-worked-out faith.
- Professional values—a sense of belonging to something bigger than the organization. (As one civil engineer in a public organization said to me "If my employers were to ask me to build something I thought might be unsafe or unwise, I'd refuse because my professional values override my loyalty to my employer.")
- Family and community—a feeling of belonging and of intimate connection to others.

Grounding connects the inner to the outer worlds (and vice versa). It provides a solid base from which the manager can operate. Grounded managers are not pushovers. This is literally true. I often demonstrate this in groups by using Ki Aikido techniques to show how if a person physically grounds themselves they literally cannot be pushed over. If, on the other hand, they are not physically grounded, they can be knocked sideways with a gentle push on the shoulders. People in organizations often intuitively recognize these differences. They recognize who is a lightweight and therefore easy to defeat in a conflict. And they recognize who not to take on in a fight.

Centering and Grounding need to be brought together. Grounding without Centering can lead to inertia and lack of change: Centering without Grounding can lead to burnout.

Morality and Ethics

Rushworth Kidder (1992) has claimed to be the first Western journalist to visit the Chernobyl nuclear power plant after the accident there. He discovered that the accident had occurred because two engineers conducted an unauthorized experiment on reactor number four. In order to do this they had to override six separate computer-driven alarm systems. Now these engineers were highly competent, highly able men. The accident did not occur because of human error, in the sense of someone making an unknown mistake. As Kidder commented, the accident was "not a question of technology. It's a matter of ethics." By this he meant that he saw the engineers' actions as requiring "an ethical override." The question I have from this is "What was missing in their development and learning that left out ethics (or at least this kind of ethical issue)?"

Another incident points to this same problem. Richard Grabowski was, by all accounts, a brilliant aerospace engineering student. He was offered jobs with two prestigious companies, both of which would have involved designing weapons systems. On October 16 1985, while considering these job offers, he committed suicide. His suicide note read:

> If I were to live out my potential, I would only destroy life . . . I have such un-
> bounded respect for the practical application of physical ideas that I would go so
> far as to murder humans . . . I am incapable of love. I am incapable of compas-
> sion. I can only respect rational, physical ideas. It is for this reason that I must die.
> If I were to continue living, I would only prolong my death. I cannot "live" by any
> sense of my imagination producing weapons. (Quoted in Skolimowski, 1986).

That is pretty terrifying stuff. What, again, was there in this person's learning and development that created this awful end for him? We can guess that examination of morality and ethics—and the struggles we need to make with moral and ethical choices—was missing. But in an era where old certainties no longer exist, where postmodern views of knowledge encourage a nihilistic relativism, new bases for action are necessary. This points to a moral basis for managerial activity—and therefore the need to learn to make moral choices.

I am not seeking to preach a particular moral position. That discussion, to do it full justice, belongs elsewhere. My point is about learning. It is possible to argue that rather than seeing ethics as an interesting option in the business school curriculum, we need to begin managerial learning with an examination of issues of morality, ethics, values, and social responsibility. Deciding what it is right and good for a manager to learn must begin by treating decisions about rightness and goodness as moral questions.

There is much debate at present about what a good company is, or should be. Many, myself included, would say that the "bottom line" is insufficient justification for the existence of a company or for measuring its success (goodness). Struggles with moral dilemmas, such as the interplay between the need for profit, the needs of employees, and the needs of the planet, are at the heart of the strategic learning that is needed in business. And moral development is both a learning issue and learnable.

Indeed in Murdoch's (1992) statement that "learning is moral progress" we have a clue as to how to proceed. She points out that good learning develops wisdom and subtler visions, and it diminishes crass egoism. This kind of learning does not come from didactic preaching. It comes from individuals working openly with colleagues to explore moral dilemmas. Haste (1993) suggests that moral development comes from two factors. "First, a caring community of which the individual feels a valued member, where mutual respect and justice are enacted, not just preached. Second, an environment which continually encourages reflection on the wider implications—including personal responsibility—of everyone's actions."

The evidence of people coming out of higher education is that universities provide precisely the opposite environment. Indeed, in terms of all the criteria for holistic learning that I have identified, universities score badly. It is not that academic, cognitive development is unimportant—on the contrary, it is of crucial importance. But my thesis is that an unbalanced education that assumes that human beings are merely walking brains does not even work in its own terms. The denial of the emotions, of moral issues, and of the social context of learning also produces poor cognitive activity.

Conclusion

This paper has explored facets of "good learning." Whilst it has over-lapped into the wider field of what makes a good manager, I have tried to keep the analysis within bounds. Hence there is much more that could be said about issues only alluded to here. The paper is based on work more fully explored elsewhere (see Cunningham, 1999; Cunningham, Bennett, & Dawes, 2000). The latter text also goes into detail on practical ways of solving some of the problems discussed here. However, as I indicated at the start of this paper, we need to get clear on what is worth learning before we can address ways of meeting these needs—hence the focus of this piece.

References

Argyris, C., & Schön, D. (1974). *Theory in Practice.* San Francisco: Jossey-Bass.

Bennis, W. G. (1989). *On Becoming a Leader.* Reading, MA: Addison Wesley.

Berne, E. (1964). *Games People Play.* London: Penguin.

Berne, E. (1974). *What Do You Say After You Say Hello?* London: Andre Deutsch.

Bramley, W. (1977). *Personal Tutoring in Higher Education.* Guildford, Surrey: Society for Research into Higher Education.

Cunningham, I. (1984). *Teaching Styles in Learner-Centered Management Development.* Unpublished doctoral dissertation, Lancaster University.

Cunningham, I. (1988). Patterns of managing for the future. *Industrial Management and Data Systems* (Jan./Feb.), 18–22.

Cunningham, I. (1992). The impact of who leaders are and what they do. In K. E. Clark, M. B. Clark, & D. P. Campbell (Eds.), *Impact of Leadership.* Greensboro, NC: Center for Creative Leadership.

Cunningham, I. (1999). *The Wisdom of Strategic Learning* (2nd ed.). Aldershot, Hants: Gower.

Cunningham, I., Bennett, B., & Dawes, G. (Eds.). (2000). *Self-Managed Learning in Action.* Aldershot, Hants: Gower.

Evans, P., & Bartolomé, F. (1980). *Must Success Cost So Much?* London: Grant McIntyre.

Fiedler, F. E. (1992). The role and meaning of leadership experience. In K. E. Clark, M. B. Clark, & D. P. Campbell (Eds.), *Impact of Leadership.* Greensboro, NC: Center for Creative Leadership.

Gibran, K. (1972). *The Prophet.* London: Heinemann.

Goleman, D. (1995). *Emotional Intelligence.* New York: Bantam.

Haste, H. (1993). Guilt and the struggle to teach right from wrong. *Guardian Education,* (March), 2–3.

Keutzer, C. S. (1982). Physics and consciousness. *Journal of Humanistic Psychology, 22*(3), 74–90.

Kidder, R. (1992). Ethics: A matter of survival. *The Futurist* (March/April), 10–12.

La Bier, D. (1986). Madness stalks the ladder climbers. *Fortune* (1 September), 61–64.

McLean, A. J., Sims, D. B. P., Maugham, I. L., & Tuffield, D. (1982). *Organization Development in Transition.* Chichester: Wiley.

Murdoch, I. (1992). *Metaphysics as a Guide to Morals.* London: Chatto and Windus.

Postman, N., & Weingartner, C. (1969). *Teaching as a Subversive Activity.* London: Penguin.

Schein, E. M. (1978). *Career Dynamics.* Reading, MA: Addison-Wesley.

Skolimowski, H. (1986). Destruction through education. *The Scientific and Medical Network Newsletter, 31,* 1.

Vaillant, G. E. (1977). *Adaptation to Life.* Boston: Little, Brown.

Chapter 15

The McClelland/McBer Competency Models

John Raven

We have seen how the staff of David McClelland's consulting firm—McBer—conducted their competency studies in the 1970s and 1980s and evolved a framework for describing the nature and levels of those competencies. This was first published in full by Lyle and Signe Spencer in 1993 and updated and condensed into the *Scaled Competency Dictionary*, in 1996.

Here our first step will be to back up somewhat so as to be able to set that framework in another context. Although our discussion will largely focus on the *measurement* procedures that have been used instead of being organised around an abstract discussion of what is meant by the terms that have been used to summarise research results, our concern will, in reality, be with the way of thinking that lies behind the measures. Despite the fact that there is a sense in which this chapter belongs with those on the *assessment* of competence, it is necessary for it to appear here because it provides an *operational definition* of the terms used in the McBer conceptual framework.

As we saw in Table 9.1 in our chapter summarising McBer's framework for organising the results of their Behavioural Event Interview-based studies of competence, the first generic competence they speak about is Achievement orientation. The table summarising their definition of this and how its levels are to be determined and described is reproduced in Table 15.2 below.

Before examining it we will, however, go back 40 years. During the early 1950s, McClelland and his co-workers sought to study a number of the "motives" identified by Murray (1938) experimentally. They started with a number of biological motives—the need for food, sex, and so on—

and moved on to other motives such as the need for achievement, friends, and power.

What they did was starve people, make them sexually aroused, arouse their achievement motivation, and so on and then look to see what effects this had on the stories those concerned made up about what the characters in ambiguous pictures (a form of the Thematic Apperception Test known as the Test of Imagination) were thinking about, feeling, and doing.

This led to a coding system for analysing the content of these stories in ways which would summarise the effects of the experimental manipulations in terms of the concerns expressed by the stories' authors and the thoughts, feelings, and behaviours those authors attributed to the characters in their stories.

This coding framework was then applied to the stories people told when specific motives had *not* been aroused and to such things as stories in children's readers at different periods in history. This yielded insights into different people's motives (and their competence to pursue them) and how population concerns changed over time (and with what social consequences).

One of the most significant findings from this work was that the things people saw the characters in their stories thinking about, feeling, and doing when specific motives were aroused were the *same* regardless of the motive that was aroused. People whose need was for food, sex, achievement, friends, or power all saw the characters in their stories doing the same kinds of things to satisfy those needs. Thus, they made plans, anticipated obstacles, turned their feelings and emotions into the task, sought the help of others, and persisted over a long period of time. Although neither McClelland nor any of his colleagues commented on it at the time, *the authors of the stories, in effect, saw the characters doing things which would enable them competently to satisfy their needs.*

The detailed coding systems that were developed by McClelland and his co-workers to assess the "strength" of people's Achievement, Affiliation, and Power "motives" were published in long appendices to a book edited by Atkinson published in 1958 under the title *Motives in Fantasy, Action and Society.*

After having demonstrated the importance of the Achievement, Affiliation, and Power motives in determining individual and community life, McClelland and his colleagues began to wonder if these motives could be aroused and developed. The framework they developed for this purpose is outlined in a later chapter in this book.

Here what is important is that it occurred to them that one way in which it might be possible to encourage Achievement-oriented individuals to behave more *competently*—although they did not use that term then—would be to teach them the scoring system for the *need* Achievement motive.

The appendices to the Atkinson book by McClelland et al. were much too long and technical to be used for this purpose, so McClelland and Litwin condensed them into "*Brief Scoring Manuals*" for Achievement, Affiliation, and Power motivation.

Extensive extracts from the *Brief Scoring Manual* for *need* Achievement are reproduced as Table 15.1.

Table 15.1 Extracts from: *A Brief Scoring Manual for Achievement Motivation* by D. C. McClelland and G. H. Litwin (1967)

I. Deciding Whether or Not a Story Shows Achievement Motivation

In deciding whether or not an imaginative story shows evidence of the achievement motive, we first look to see if one of the characters is concerned about attaining an achievement goal. That is, does one of the characters have as his goal some sort of success in a situation which requires excellent performance? We have found there are four types of stories containing reference to an achievement goal, which we call Achievement Imagery. They are:

1. *Desire for Success in Competition with Others.* One of the characters is engaged in a competitive activity where winning or doing as well as or better than others is a primary concern. Typical examples are wanting to win a race, or contest, wanting to show the boss he can do the job well, feeling proud about being a winner, feeling sad about being a loser.

2. *Competition with a Self-Imposed Standard of Excellence.* Often the standard of excellence does not involve competition with others, but with a self-imposed standard of high-quality performance. Typical examples include wanting to do a good, thorough, workmanlike job, wanting to find a better method, working carefully on the plan, etc. A distinction should be made between intensity and quality. Working hard, or working fast, is evidence of concern over a standard of excellence only when the task demands intense effort. The worker may only want to get done by five o'clock. But a concern for accuracy, or quality, does imply a self-imposed standard of excellence.

3. *Unique Accomplishment.* One of the characters is involved in accomplishing other than an ordinary task which will mark him as a personal success. Inventions, artistic creations, and other extraordinary accomplishments fit in this category.

4. *Long-Term Involvement.* One of the characters is involved in attainment of a long-term achievement goal. Being a success in life, becoming a good machinist, doctor, lawyer, successful businessman, and so forth are all examples of career involvement which permit scoring for achievement motivation. However, mere mention of a job, or career, or even career goals, is not a sufficient basis for scoring. There must be evidence of involvement in a *long-term* career goal and this means some statement of wanting, or feelings about, goals that lie 5 to 10 years away.

Table 15.1 (Continued)

If a story shows evidence of Achievement Imagery, through one or more of the categories described above, we give that story one (1) point to begin with.

Other stories, not showing such evidence, are scored Doubtful (TI), and are given a score of zero (0); or they are scored Unrelated Imagery (UI) . . . The difference between Doubtful and Unrelated stories is usually that Doubtful stories contain some reference to a commonplace task, or solving a routine problem, but do not meet the criteria described above, while the unrelated stories contain no reference whatsoever to achievement. Stories scored TI or UI are not scored further.

Below are examples of three stories which show achievement motivation. The fourth story is scored UI because it contains no evidence of Achievement Imagery.

1. The boy is watching the older man do something that *the boy is trying to learn to do*. The boy was trying to do this but he was doing it wrong and the old man is showing him how. The boy is a little downhearted. He *knows he can do it if he tries a little harder*. The man is calm and patient with the boy and is trying to teach him. The boy will watch and the man will allow the boy to try again and the *boy will do well because I think he is determined to do it*. (Competition with a standard of excellence.)

2. The boss is talking to an employee. The boss wants the employee, an engineer, to start working on a *specially designed carburetor for a revolutionary engine*. The job will come off OK, and the engine will *revolutionize* the automobile industry. (Unique accomplishment)

3. *The boy is thinking about a career as a doctor. He sees himself as a great surgeon performing an operation.* He has been doing minor first aid work on his injured dog, and has discovered that he enjoys working with medicine. He thinks he is suited for this profession and sets it as an ultimate goal in life at this moment. (Long-term involvement)

4. The boy is daydreaming of some picture he may have seen or is projecting himself into the future, putting himself into the situation as it would be if he were a man. The boy has seen a movie. The boy is thinking of how he would like to be in the situation as seen.

II. Determining the Strength of Achievement Motivation

Once we have decided that a story contains evidence of the achievement motive and given it one point, we may go on to determine the strength of the motive. We do this by seeing if the phrases and expressions of the story can be fitted into the pre-established *scoring categories* which follow. When one (or more) of these categories appears in a story, we give an additional point (or points). If one story contains evidence of, say, five of these categories, and another evidence of only three, we can say that the writer of the first has greater achievement motivation than the writer of the second. The categories are as follows: a story gets one additional point for each category of response included. A given category is scored only once per story.

A. Stated Need for Achievement (N)
Someone in the story states the desire to reach an achievement goal. Expressions such as "He *wants* to be a doctor," "He *wants* to finish the painting," "He *hopes* to succeed"

Table 15.1 (Continued)

are the clearest examples. Need should not be inferred from the activity described in a story. It may seem obvious to the scorer that characters who are working furiously toward an achievement goal must want to succeed. But Need is scored only when there is a definite statement of desire to attain an achievement goal.

B. Activity (A)

Activity is scored when something is actively being done by one of the characters within the story in order to attain an achievement goal. The activity may be overt or mental and its outcome may be successful, doubtful, or unsuccessful. For example, the statement "The man worked hard to make money and failed," would be scored Activity since it contains the necessary three elements of Activity: an activity (work), a goal (making money), and an outcome (failure).

C. Goal Anticipation (Ga+, Ga-)

Someone in the story anticipates, or expects, goal attainment or frustration and failure. The Anticipation is Positive when someone is thinking about the success he will achieve, expects that the invention will work, dreams of himself as a great surgeon. The Anticipation is Negative when someone is worried about failure, is concerned over the possibility that the invention won't work, expects the worst, or is wondering whether or not he will succeed. Both Positive and Negative Anticipations may be scored in the same story, but each may be scored only once

D. Personal and Environmental Blocks (Bp, Bw)

Stories are scored for Blocks when the progress of goal-directed activity is blocked or hindered in some way. Things do not run smoothly. There are obstacles to be overcome before the goal may be attained. The Block may be a previous failure or personal lack which must be overcome before further progress toward the goal is possible, or the Block may be a present environmental or personal factor. If the Block is located within the individual (lack of confidence, a conflict to be overcome, inability to make decisions, or some past failure), it is called a Personal Block (Bp). When the block to be overcome is part of the environment, that is, when it is located in the world at large such as "The invention was almost finished when the gasket broke," "His family couldn't afford to send him to medical school," it is called an Environmental Block (Bw). Both personal and environmental blocks may occur and be scored in the same story, but each is scored only once per story.

E. Help (H)

Help is scored when somebody in the story aids a character in the story who is engaged in an achievement-related activity. Someone aids, sympathizes with, or encourages the person striving for achievement. The assistance is in the direction of the achievement goal. For example, "The experienced machinist is trying to straighten things out for the apprentice and is encouraging him." Help must always be considered from the point of view of the character or characters in the story who are striving for achievement.

F. Feelings (F+, F-)

Feelings associated with goal attainment, active mastery, or frustration of the achievement-directed activity are scored. When someone in the story feels good at active mas-

Table 15.1   (Continued)

tery or definite accomplishment. "He *enjoys* painting," "He is proud of his accomplishment," "They are very *satisfied* with their invention," F+ is scored. When someone in the story feels bad at failure to attain an achievement goal "He is *disturbed* over his inability," "He is *discouraged* about past failures," "He is *disgusted* with himself," F- is scored. Both Positive and Negative Feelings may occur and be scored in the same story, but each may be scored only once per story. Feelings are only scored when associated with the achievement-related activities of the story, as is the case for all our other categories.

G. Achievement Theme (Th)
Achievement Theme is scored when it is evident that the major plot or theme of the story is concerned with achievement. Striving for an achievement goal and eventual attainment of the goal may be the central plot of the story. The decision to be made by the scorer is whether or not the whole story is an elaboration of the achievement-related activity sequence. If there is a major counterplot, or if there is any doubt about achievement being central to the plot, Achievement Theme is not scored. Note that we may score for achievement motivation without the story being scored for Achievement Theme. The latter is scored only when achievement becomes the principal concern of the story.

The scoring system works like this:

1) Examine the story for the presence of any one of the four clear signs of Achievement motivation—that is, for evidence of a desire for success in competition with others, competition with a self-imposed standard of excellence, concern with unique accomplishment, or long-term involvement. If none of these are present, make no further attempt to score the story for Achievement motivation.

2) If there is clear evidence of a concern with Achievement motivation, *count up* how many of the following are present in relation to that kind of activity: Actual behaviour, positive feelings about goal achievement and/or negative feelings about failure, anticipation of obstacles from the environment and/or personal limitations and taking steps to surmount them; seeking help (or being helped), and using one's feelings or emotions to carry out the task effectively.

Note that, although McClelland and his colleagues did not draw attention to it, undertaking many of the activities listed under 2) is likely to make for competence in carrying out the activity.

The scoring systems for Affiliation and Power worked in exactly the same way except that, for Affiliation, for example, the clear sign is a concern for "establishing, maintaining, or restoring a positive affective relationship with another person", a desire to be liked or accepted or forgiven. Motive "strength" is scored by counting up *exactly the same things*. Thus it is not true that "love is blind." Those who are concerned about, and good at establishing, warm relationships with others make plans, anticipate obstacles, monitor the effects of their actions and modify their behaviour accordingly, turn their emotions into the task, seek the help of others, persist over a long period of time, and so on. The same applies to Power, although it turned out that it is necessary to score the strength of socialised and personal power separately.

There are many important things to note about this scoring system. For example, it makes nonsense of the attempt to separate the cognitive, affective, and conative components of effective behaviour. What one thinks about is based on one's feelings, and it is feelings that beckon and encourage one to pursue—check out—possible ways forward. Likewise, it is negative feelings that tell one that one has "lost the scent." One initiates "experimental interactions with the environment" on the basis of hunches or feelings and then monitors the effects of one's actions and changes one's behaviour. These are not internally consistent "dimensions" of behaviour: The *more* of these activities one undertakes in the course of conducting a self-motivated activity, the more successful one is likely to be.

Not only does thinking involve feeling and persistence; *it does not make sense to attempt to assess the **ability** to think except in relation to an activity the individual concerned is strongly motivated to achieve.* No one is going to do all these difficult, demanding, time-consuming, and frustrating things that are required to "think" effectively when they care about the activity. So it does not make sense to make general statements to the effect that a particular individual is good or bad at thinking.

Now, to jump forward 40 years, these insights seem somehow to have got lost in the *Scaled Competency Dictionary*.

As will be seen from Table 15.2, although, as we noted in a previous chapter, the "level" at which all competencies are said to be displayed depends on more than can be listed in a summary table, the level of competence at which self-motivated Achievement activities is being displayed (shown by the numbers down the left hand side) is now being assessed primarily from the breadth and depth of the *conceptual* analysis being undertaken (albeit that that involves wider organisational consider-

Table 15.2 Summary of Scoring System for *Achievement Orientation (ACH)* from McBer's *Scaled Competency Dictionary* (1996)

Achievement Orientation: A concern for working well or for surpassing a standard of excellence. The standard may be one's own past performance (striving for improvement); an objective measure (results orientation); outperforming others (competitiveness); challenging goals one has set; or even what anyone has ever done (innovation). Thus a unique accomplishment also indicates ACH.

Core: Does the person think about meeting and surpassing goals and taking calculated risks for measured gains?

Level	This Person:
1.	**Wants to Do Job Well**: Tries to do the job well or right. May express frustration at waste or inefficiency (e.g., gripes about wasted time and wants to do better) but does not cause specific improvements.
2.	**Creates Own Measures of Excellence**: Uses own specific methods of measuring outcomes against a standard of excellence not imposed by others. May focus on new or more precise ways of meeting goals set by management. (Code specifically for spontaneous interest in measuring outcomes or performance excellence.)
3.	**Improves Performance**: Makes specific changes in the system or in own work methods to improve performance (e.g. does something better, faster, at lower cost, more efficiently; improves quality, customer satisfaction, morale, revenues), without setting any specific goal. (The improvement *must* be noticeable and could be measurable. Code even if outcome is still unknown, or if it is less successful than hoped.)
4.	**Sets and Works to Meet Challenging Goals**: "Challenging" means there is about a 50-50 chance of actually achieving the goal—it is a definite stretch, but not unrealistic or impossible. *OR* refers to specific measures of baseline performance compared with better performance at a later point in time: e.g., "When I took over, efficiency was 20% flow it is up to 85%." (Goals which are not clearly both challenging and achievable should, however, be coded at level 2—as evidence of competing against a standard of excellence. If scoring for level 4, don't score for 3 for the same actions or activity in story.)
5.	**Makes Cost-Benefit Analyses**: Makes decisions, sets priorities or chooses goals on the basis of *calculated* inputs and outputs: makes *explicit* considerations of potential profit, Return-on-Investment or cost-benefit analysis. Analyzes for business outcomes. (To code, the person must show: 1) specific mention of costs *and* 2) specific benefits, *and* 3) a decision based on the balance between them.)
6.	**Takes Calculated Entrepreneurial Risks**: Commits *significant* resources and/or time (in the face of uncertainty) to increase benefits, (i.e., improve performance, reach a challenging goal, etc.). In scoring for level 6, you should also code for evidence of lower levels as they occur to capture the richness and depth of ACH thinking.

Table 15.3 Summary of Scoring System for *Analytical Thinking* (*AT*) from McBer's *Scaled Competency Dictionary* (1996)

Analytical Thinking: Understanding a situation by breaking it apart into smaller pieces, of tracing the implications of a situation in a step-by-step way. Analytical Thinking includes organizing the parts of a problem, situation, etc., in a systematic way; making systematic comparisons of different features or aspects; setting priorities on a rational basis; identifying time sequences, causal relationships or If-Then relationships.
Core: Does the person understand cause-and-effect chains and relationships?

Level	This Person:
1.	**Breaks Down Problems**: Breaks problems into simple lists of tasks or activities, without assigning values. Makes a list of items with no particular order or set of priorities.
2.	**Sees Basic Relationships**: Takes apart problems into pieces. Links together pieces with a single link: A leads to B; can separate into two parts: pro and con. Sorts out a list of tasks in order of importance.
3.	**Sees Multiple Relationships**: Breaks down a problem into smaller parts. Makes multiple causal links: several potential causes of events, several consequences of actions, or multiple-part chains of events (A leads to B leads to C leads to D). Analyzes relationships among several parts of a problem or situation. Anticipates obstacles and thinks ahead about next steps. (Code level 2 as a default if you are unsure about the complexity of the problem or situation broken down by interviewee.)
4.	**Makes Complex Plans or Analyses**: Uses several analytical techniques to break apart complex problems into component parts. Uses several analytical techniques to identify several solutions and weighs the value of each. (This is more than the linear breaking down of problems in level 3. Code level 4 for *multiple* causal-leading to more than one possible solution.)

ations and longer time horizons). Furthermore, as can be seen from Tables 15.3 and 15.4, both Analytic Thinking and Conceptual Thinking are being coded *independently of the activity in relation to which they are being displayed.*

According to the earlier model, the strength of Achievement motivation depends as much, if not more, on the extent to which the affective and conative components of effective behaviour are engaged as it does on the extent of cognitive activity. Further, as we have seen, it follows from the earlier model that analytic and conceptual thinking are *subsidiary* activities that cannot be measured or take effect on their own. They don't have *direct* consequences. People will only reveal the level at which

Table 15.4 Summary of Scoring System for *Conceptual Thinking* (*CT*) from McBer's *Scaled Competency Dictionary* (1996)

Conceptual Thinking: The ability to identify patterns or connections between situations that are not obviously related, and to identify key or underlying issues in complex situations. It includes using creative, conceptual or inductive reasoning.

Core: Does the person match patterns? Assemble many pieces into a coherent whole? Create new ways to look at things?

Level	This Person:

1. **Uses Basic Rules**: Uses simple rules ("rules of thumb"), common sense, and past experiences to identify problems. Recognizes when a current situation is exactly the same as a past situation.

2. **Sees Patterns**: When looking at information, sees patterns, trends, or missing pieces. Notices when a current situation is similar to a past situation, and identifies the similarities.

3. **Applies Complex Concepts**: Uses knowledge of theory or of different past trends or situations to look at current situations. Applies and modifies complex learned concepts or methods appropriately; e.g., statistical process control, TQM demographic analysis, managerial styles, organizational climate, etc. This is evidence of more sophisticated pattern recognition.

4. **Clarifies Complex Data or Situations**: Makes complex ideas or situations clear, simple, and/or understandable. Assembles ideas, issues, and observations into a clear and useful explanation. Restates existing observations or knowledge in a simpler fashion. (The coder should look for evidence of the ability to see a simpler *pattern* within complex information.)

5. **Creates New Concepts**: Creates new concepts that are not obvious to others and not learned from previous education or experience to explain situations or resolve problems. (To score level 5, the coder should be convinced that the concept is new and should be able to cite specific evidence. Do not also score for Innovation.)

---

they are capable of displaying these abilities while they are carrying out tasks they care about. According to the earlier model, it is therefore a mistake to present and discuss them in the way they are presented in the *Scaled Competency Dictionary 1996* and discussed in *Competence at Work*. The same goes for such traits as "self-confidence," "information-seeking," and "initiative." People who are good at carrying out affiliative tasks show a great deal of self-confidence and initiative *in that area*. They display a lack of self-confidence and initiative if they are confronted with an intellectual or power task.

What is more, the role of feelings, persistence, getting help, and so forth in carrying out "analytic thinking" etc. effectively is entirely missing from the later model.

This is not to say that the earlier model was necessarily the correct one. What we have here are two hard-to-reconcile frameworks for summarising extremely important programs of research. Because the tension between the two has the potential to provoke both conceptual re-thinking and a swathe of research we will return to it in a later chapter. Here it is perhaps sufficient to conclude by asking for the correlation between *n*. Ach assessed using the much-trumpeted 1958 method and assessed using the—equally much-trumpeted—behavioural-event-interviewing method. It is hard to avoid the suspicion that it may not be much higher than that between Thematic Aptitude Test-based *n*. Ach and "personality test"-based *n*. Ach.

References

Atkinson, J. W. (Ed.) (1958). *Motives in Fantasy, Action and Society*. New York: Van Nostrand.

Hay/McBer. (1996). *Scaled Competency Dictionary*. Boston: Hay/McBer.

McClelland, D. C., and Litwin, G. (1967). *A Brief Scoring Manual for Achievement Motivation*. Boston, MA: McBer & Co.

Murray, H. A. (1938). *Explorations in Personality*. New York: Oxford University Press.

Spencer, L. M. & Spencer, S. M. (1993). *Competence at Work*. New York: Wiley.

Chapter 16

Leadership Competencies: Putting It All Together

George O. Klemp, Jr.

Introduction

Practically every major company has ideas about what it takes to be an outstanding leader. Many of these organizations have developed formal "competency models"—descriptions of knowledge, skills, personal characteristics, and behaviors of effective leaders. The models are typically used for a number of purposes, including assessment of current senior managers, identification of high-potential executive talent, performance appraisal, and leadership development.

For the past 10 years, Cambria Consulting has developed a significant number of leadership competency models for Fortune 500 businesses and financial services organizations. It was in this connection that we came into contact with the Corporate Leadership Council (CLC).[1] In 1997, the CLC gave Cambria access to its database of leadership competency models from selected member organizations. Our tasks were to put these different competency models into a coherent framework, to identify common leadership competency trends, to examine relationships among competencies and organizational strategies, and to clarify how competencies can be used in the early identification and development of leadership talent. This paper presents a summary of this research.

Much has been written about leadership in the popular and academic press, from first-person "how-I-did-it" accounts to predictions about the nature of leadership in the 21st century. The importance of this study is that it is based not on theory but on the criteria that organizations are actually using to make judgments about current and potential leaders. It speaks to what is seen as important in today's world and hopefully can serve as a reference for other organizations in re-examining their own leadership competencies.

Conceptualizing Competencies

Exhibit 16.1 lists some of the companies that shared their leadership competency models for this study. The Corporate Leadership Council's files provided 42 of these models, and Cambria Consulting's clients supplied an additional 20. These organizations are quite varied in size and type of business, and although most are based in North America, many are truly global in scope. In addition, almost all of the competency models were developed within the past five years and are in current use.

It was immediately apparent that these models were very different from each other on the surface. Although one could certainly discern common themes, the competency terminology varied substantially. Different models used different words to describe essentially the same concepts (for example, compare "taking charge" with "decisiveness" or "managerial courage"). The level of detail with which competencies were presented differed as well, ranging from short lists with no definitions to lengthy lists arranged hierarchically and defined by precise behavioral indicators. Pulling the different leadership models together required us to create what was essentially a Rosetta stone—a common language to translate competencies from different models into a framework that could be analyzed.

The first step in establishing this common language was to distinguish between two different types of competencies:

Exhibit 16.1 Sample Companies Represented

Allied-Signal	General Electric
Alcoa	Hewlett Packard
American Express	International Paper
AT&T	Johnson & Johnson
Bank One	Knight-Ridder
BP-Amoco	Merck
Canadian National	Mobil
Chase	PepsiCo
DuPont	Siemens-Rolm
EDS	Sun Microsystems
Ford	Unilever

Practices—what people do on the job to get results. For example, a leader might "set vision and direction," "focus on the customer," and "make decisions."

Attributes—knowledge, skills, and other characteristics that people bring to the job that enable them to carry out leadership tasks. For example, a leader might possess "strategic thinking," "initiative," and "high energy" as personal attributes.

Attributes are the raw ingredients of performance: They are the capabilities needed by people to do their jobs. Practices are what people do with the attributes they possess and are described by observable on-the-job behavior. Practices also depend on the presence of attributes: For example, one cannot "make tough decisions" (a practice) without a high degree of "self-confidence" (an attribute). Having the required attributes, however, does not necessarily guarantee that the required behaviors (practices) will be demonstrated (for example, not all highly self-confident people make tough decisions when the situation calls for them), but it certainly increases the likelihood that the behaviors will be demonstrated consistently over time.

A content analysis of the 62 leadership models revealed 30 attributes and 30 practices, presented in Exhibits 16.2 and 16.3, that were used to

Exhibit 16.2 Leadership Attributes Menu

Accountability	Decisiveness	Judgment
Achievement Drive	Dependability	Learning Orientation
Analytic Thinking	Directive/Controlling	Political Astuteness
Attention to Detail	Energy/Enthusiasm	Presence/Charisma
Business Acumen	Flexibility/Adaptability	Responsiveness
Communication Skill	Global Perspective	Risk-taking
Composure/Self-control	Influence Skill	Self-confidence/Courage
Conceptual Grasp	Initiative/action-orientated	Strategic Thinking
Cooperativeness	Integrity/Honesty/Ethics	Technical/Functional Knowledge
Creativity	Interpersonal Astuteness	Tenacity/Persistence

Exhibit 16.3 Leadership Practices Menu

Act as a Role Model	Develop Strategy	Manage Complexity
Align the Organization	Drive Change	Manage Conflict
Build Business Relationships	Drive for Improvement	Manage Diversity/ Value Others
Build Teams	Empower Others Performance	Manage
Communicate	Focus on the Customer	Motivate Others
Cooperate/Team Player	Get Results	Plan and Organize
Create a High-performance Climate	Hire & Staff	Promote Learning
Delegate	Influence the Organization	Set Vision & Direction
Develop Creative Solutions	Make Decisions	Take Charge
Develop People	Manage Across Boundaries	Total Quality Management

code the leadership competencies from all the models into a common database. Over 99% of the competencies from our sample of leadership models could be coded into these categories. The coding process revealed three types of leadership models: those comprised mostly of attributes, those comprised mostly of practices, and those that were a mixture of the two. Of the competency models in our database, 8% were essentially pure attribute models, 27% were essentially pure practice models, and 65% were a mixture of attributes and practices. I believe that there are two reasons for most of these models being "mixed." One is that this is the way senior managers talk about other senior managers, for example, as people who both "have the right stuff" and "do the right things." The other is that until now there has not been a clear distinction between practices and attributes to provide rigor and conceptual clarity to the development of competency models.

Key Findings

Our original charge was to discern whether there was a set of leadership competencies that could be termed "universal" that was applicable to all leaders in all situations. The answer to this question came by examining the scope of the different leadership models (number and type of competencies) and the nuances of the language used to label and define the competencies themselves.

The Scope of the Models

How many competencies does the typical leadership model contain? The answer depends largely on whether competencies are defined as practices or as attributes. Leadership models based mostly on attributes tend to have more competencies on average than models based mostly on practices. However, the sheer number of competencies in a model is less significant than the philosophy that determines the choice of how many leadership competencies to include in the model. From this perspective, the models in the current database are of two types:

Comprehensive models based on dictionaries that include anything deemed worth assessing or observing in a current or potential leader. Rather than assigning priorities to competencies in terms of what is most important, these models contain long menus of competencies that can be used for different applications.

Selective models that focus on a few high-impact competencies. These models implicitly assume that other "baseline," "enabling" or "minimum" competencies exist but focus instead on the competencies that differentiate "outstanding" from "average" leaders.

The companies in our database have apparently made a choice either to focus on a few high-leverage competencies for special emphasis or to adopt a more comprehensive list of competencies to describe requirements for any conceivable leadership role. The selective models, which typically contain 10 or fewer competencies, tend to highlight what is most valued for future success. By contrast, the comprehensive models, which typically contain 20 competencies or more, present assessment and development possibilities that can be used to define a wide variety of job requirements, hiring criteria, and/or development plans.

Meanwhile, a few organizations in our database have adopted a hybrid approach, whereby a small set of key leadership competencies (usually five or less) is grafted onto a larger competency dictionary that can be used for many purposes. The "key" competencies are viewed as essential to anyone in a leadership role, while the others depend on the requirements of the leadership situation. This potentially has the virtues of both selective and comprehensive models and could well be an emerging best practice.

The Role of Language

The terms used to label and define competencies in different leadership models showed different sensitivities to the nuances of language and the messages that the competency models communicate to the broader organization. The leadership models fell into two categories, depending on the language used to describe the competencies:

> **Generic** models that have adopted a standard language from preexisting competency lists. Examples of generic competencies include "dealing with ambiguity," "strategic agility," "managerial courage," "developing others," and "valuing diversity."
> **Customized** models that have adopted a special language to give each competency special emphasis and character unique to the organization. Examples of customized competencies include "build key relationships," "claim the future," "provide structure and direction," "data-driven," and "foster entrepreneurial thinking."

Generic leadership models are typically developed from standard competency lists. Because they are generic, they say little about a particular organization's business or strategy. Models developed from the same competency dictionary tend to look alike, despite being from companies of different scope and in different industries. In fact, in a number of cases where the same company provided competency models for different roles, there was almost no difference between the competencies of first-level managers and executives. However, generic competency lists can often be useful as starting points for organizations new to competency-based approaches.

Customized models, on the other hand, are usually characterized by language that has a flavor all its own and reflects the culture and the aspirations of the organization. These models also tend to be more selective, reflecting what is most important to the enterprise. Whether they have been created out of standard competency lists or from scratch, a certain care and attention has clearly been given to how the competencies were labeled and organized. In these models, the competency language communicates things that go beyond basic definitions of attributes or practices, such as the organization's position in the marketplace; its relationships to customers, suppliers, and the communities where it operates; and how employees are valued.

Competency models that are both selective and customized have a number of advantages, not the least of which is their ability to communicate expectations for leaders throughout the organization in a distinctive way. Tailoring the competency language to reflect the organization's strategy and culture with language that resonates within the organization makes the competencies more accessible and business-focused.

So which competencies best characterize leaders in the organizations surveyed? Again, the answer depends on whether competencies are defined as practices or as attributes.

The Top Leadership Practices

When competencies are defined as practices, eighteen of the thirty competencies emerge as the most common (see Exhibit 16.4). The percentages in the exhibit reflect the number of leadership competency models in which the practice was represented. Recalling that only 27% of the models in our database were defined entirely as practices and that 65% of the models were a mix of attributes and practices, the frequencies reported in Exhibit 16.4 would certainly have been higher if all of the leadership models had been developed using the language of leadership practices.

Exhibit 16.4 Top Leadership Practices

Key Practices		Other Practices	
Develop People (64%)	Get Results (55%)	Build Teams (36%)	Cooperate/ Team Player (36%)
Focus on the Customer (52%)	Communicate (52%)	Develop Creative Solutions (34%)	Create a High-performance Climate (32%)
Set Vision & Direction (46%)	Build Business Relationships (43%)	Drive Change (32%)	Act as Role Model (29%)
Make Decisions (41%)	Manage Performance (39%)	Manage Diversity (29%)	Develop Strategy (25%)
Influence the Organization (38%)		Take Charge (23%)	

In interpreting these results, the fact that many leadership practices are not universally represented suggests that leadership is situational: Different leaders face different challenges, and different challenges require different behaviors. Also, some of these practices may have been regarded as "baseline" by some of the organizations choosing a "selective" approach and therefore would have been absent from their competency models.

Perhaps the most surprising finding is the presence of "develop people" at the top of the list, ahead of "get results." My own experience working with some of the companies in our database leads me to believe that developing people is more of an aspiration than a reality, given the varying attention paid to it by senior managers. I surmise that the reason it is included in so many of the leadership competency models is that there is a significant gap between what leaders typically do and what the organization would like them to do, particularly given the great need for executive talent and the fact that leaders play a pivotal role in developing their own replacements.

The Top Leadership Attributes

To determine which competencies defined as attributes were represented most often, the leadership models were coded into our database in two ways. First, the competencies already defined as attributes were coded into the 30 attribute categories shown in Exhibit 16.2. Next, the competencies defined as practices were decomposed into attributes from the definitions and behavioral indicators provided by the source organizations and encoded into the 30 attribute categories. The resulting database contained the frequencies with which each attribute was referenced in each model and the number of models in which each attribute was represented at least once. The results that follow are based on the percentage of leadership models in which an attribute was noted at least once, without any additional weighting of importance based on the frequency of their occurrence in any given model.

From this perspective, 10 attributes achieve "universal" status by being found in 60% or more of the models, with an additional 10 attributes being found in 40% to 60% of the models (see Exhibit 16.5). Again, since different leadership situations require different behaviors, we conclude that not all of the possible leadership attributes are needed to perform effectively in a given leadership role. Many of the attributes cited most frequently are rooted in either the character of the individual

Exhibit 16.5 Top Leadership Attributes

Key Attributes		Other Attributes	
Integrity/Honesty/ Ethics (77%)	Achievement Drive (76%)	Initiative/Action- orientated (58%)	Communication Skill (52%)
Interpersonal Astuteness (73%)	Learning Orientation (73%)	Energy/ Enthusiasm (50%)	Political Astuteness (50%)
Directive/ Controlling (66%)	Influence Skill (64%)	Analytic Thinking (48%)	Accountability/ Commitment (48%)
Strategic Thinking (64%)	Conceptual Grasp (63%)	Cooperativeness (48%)	Decisiveness (44%)
Flexibility/ Adaptability (61%)	Self-confidence/ Courage (60%)	Judgment (44%)	Business Acumen (40%)

(e.g., "integrity"), personality characteristics (e.g., "flexibility") or capacities (e.g., "conceptual grasp"), none of which are particularly easy to develop. Logically, such attributes should be the focus of selection or early identification of talent.

Distinguishing leadership practices from leadership attributes can help answer the question of whether leaders are "born" or "made." Leaders are "born" to the extent that they develop certain qualities or characteristics early in life and have the opportunity to nurture their native capacities, motivations, and preferences. However, not everyone who has the necessary attributes will emerge as a leader. Leadership comes from a combination of having the raw ingredients of capability and being thrust into situations that require one to rise to the challenges of leadership. While the presence of role models and mentors can speed the process, and recognizing that education also plays an important part in preparing leaders with know-how essentials, there is no substitute for experience and accountability in molding people with the right attributes into capable leaders.

What's Missing?

In our view, the results presented above do not fully reflect the importance of certain competencies to effective leadership. The gaps are principally at the attribute level, where the following are either underrepresented in our data or are missing altogether.

Business Acumen. Real business know-how and a broad perspective on how business deals are done are critical to effectiveness as a senior manager. Financial, technical, or functional knowledge is a foundation competency, whether it is already present in the leader or is acquired on the job. It was therefore surprising that only 40% of the competency models in our sample included this competency. We suspect that this is so for two reasons: 1) business acumen is a tacit requirement or is assumed to be a baseline competency, and 2) competencies defined as attributes are heavily biased toward the language of personal characteristics.

Ambition. Shakespeare noted the inconsistency between being "ambitious" and being an "honorable man" in Mark Antony's famous funeral oration in *Julius Caesar*. Yet the evidence is that many (if not most) leaders are indeed highly ambitious people. Aspiring leaders have high career aspirations, are attracted to challenge, have the desire to run a business someday, and are driven by the need for power. People with these characteristics, of course, do not necessarily make good leaders, but it is almost certain that ambition is one of the key ingredients of effectiveness: effective leaders have to *want* to lead.

Putting It All Together

With competencies defined as practices and attributes, and different leadership models emphasizing different mixes of each, are there any truly universal themes? If you have ever seen an impressionist painting up close, you know that the specks and globs of paint are distinctive from each other but appear as an incoherent blur—all texture, but with no discernible forms or shapes. Only when you step back do you see that the distinct forms, shapes, and images literally become the "big picture." Like the up-close viewer, we have been immersed in so many of the details that it was difficult to see the broader patterns of leadership competency: the ingredients (attributes) and the behaviors (practices) seem only to add up to another laundry list.

Nevertheless, a view from a distance reveals a set of nine "meta-competencies" that combine different attributes and practices. This set of meta-competencies, which I call the "nine-bucket model," captures what I believe is the core of effective leadership, regardless of differences among leadership competency models.

First, the five core leadership attribute buckets:

- **"IQ"** (Intellectual horsepower). Effective leaders need high general intelligence to handle the complexities inherent in an executive role, exemplified by strong conceptual grasp, analytical capability, strategic thinking, and the ability to make swift judgments in ambiguous or novel situations. In effective senior leadership, there seems to be no substitute for high intelligence: 97% of the leadership competency models reflect this attribute.
- **"EQ"** (Emotional intelligence). Effective leaders are also astute about reading people and their unspoken feelings, are able to anticipate the reactions of others to what they may say or do, are in touch with the morale and climate in the work environment, and are aware of the interpersonal and political dynamics operating between individuals and throughout the organization. This theme was present in 84% of the leadership models.
- **"Know"** (Business and technical acumen). Knowledge is the foundation of effective performance. I include wisdom in this category even though I understand the limits of factual knowledge in making sound decisions and using understanding gained from experience. This theme was present in 55% of the leadership models (a low estimate of its importance, as noted earlier).
- **"Grow"** (Personal development). Effective leaders are inquisitive and thirsty for knowledge, are eager to take on new situations and learn by doing, and are mentally flexible and willing to consider other views. They also see mistakes as valuable learning opportunities and encourage others to do the same. This theme was present in 81% of the leadership models.
- **"Ego"** (Strong sense of self). Effective leaders are self-confident and decisive, but they must have a healthy ego that allows them to admit when they are wrong and to surround themselves with highly capable people without being threatened. A healthy ego is also the foundation for acting with honesty, integrity, and strong ethics. This theme was present in 92% of the leadership competency models.

Next, the four core leadership practice buckets:

- **"Tell"** (Giving direction). Taking charge is the sine qua non of leadership. Effective leaders set direction, focus on results, make decisions, delegate authority, control discussions, manage performance, and hold others accountable. The authority to do these things is theirs, and they use it to get things done. This theme was present in 82% of the leadership models.

- **"Sell"** (Influencing others). As a counterpoint to "telling," effective leaders are masters of influence. They are highly persuasive in one-on-one discussions, work formal and informal influence channels effectively, build effective coalitions and teams, create a high-performance climate, and support all of these activities through skillful and frequent communication. This theme was present in 76% of the leadership models.

- **"Initiate"** (Making things happen). Effective leaders are highly proactive: They drive change, take risks, shake things up, push for improvements (even in the best-run operations), and take decisive action rather than let circumstances or events drive their behavior. Characteristically, many are also impatient and restless, always looking for new opportunities to act. This theme was present in 79% of the leadership models.

- **"Relate"** (Building relationships). Effective leaders understand the importance of strong relationships built on trust and respect. They build these relationships at many levels, both outside (with customers, business partners, community, and government) and inside (with peers, superiors, and employees at lower levels) the organization, and they leverage these relationships to get things done. This theme was present in 79% of the leadership models.

These nine meta-competencies hold up well across almost all of the leadership competency models in our database, despite differences among organizations and the challenges of particular leadership roles.

Recommendations

Our findings suggest that there are, indeed, some universal competencies, despite differences in how competencies are conceptualized, labeled, and defined. We have sought to understand the connections between competencies and strategy and how competencies are used in selection, high-potential identification, performance management, succession planning, and leadership development. The following are some concluding thoughts about best practices that were gleaned from the leadership models available to us and our experience consulting for organizations about using competency models to drive human resource strategy:

- **Be selective.** Whether leadership competencies are defined as attributes or practices, keep their number to 10 or fewer. If a broad dictionary approach is being considered, it should try to emphasize the few competencies with the biggest impact on organizational performance. Chances are that the other competencies will fall into place if your leaders attend to developing and demonstrating the most important ones first.
- **Select for attributes, manage to practices.** Although specific leadership practices may vary substantially with business and role requirements, the attributes of effective leaders are more fixed and consistent across situations. In general, attributes are more appropriate for early identification of talent and practices are more appropriate for assessing the performance of incumbent leaders. More specifically:
  1) Consult the four attribute meta-competencies that are most difficult to develop ("IQ," "EQ," "Grow" and "Ego") to identify people with leadership potential.
  2) Assess results achieved using the four practice meta-competencies ("Tell," "Sell," "Initiate" and "Relate") to evaluate how well people currently in leadership roles are performing.
  3) Use all nine meta-competencies to identify people who are ready to take the next step into the executive ranks.
- **Use the nine-bucket model as a template.** This model can be used as a framework to determine how well rounded a particular leadership competency model is, assuming every competency model should include something in each of the nine meta-competency buckets. Gaps in a particular leadership model might be there for a good reason or might reveal important areas that need attention.
- **Refresh your competencies over time.** Leadership competencies should be reviewed and revised periodically. This is especially true when competencies are defined as practices and behaviors that are fine-tuned to business strategy and situation requirements. A number of companies, including General Electric, AT&T, and PepsiCo, have updated their leadership models periodically to reflect the changing business priorities and capabilities needed for the future. As business conditions and strategic imperatives change, it only makes sense that the competencies be reexamined and repositioned.
- **Keep your concepts clear.** There is nothing particularly wrong with "mixed" models that include both practices and attributes, but

be clear about the purposes and applications of each. Attributes are the ingredients needed for leadership effectiveness, but possessing them does not mean that one will be a good leader. The proof points are the leadership practices that transform capability into action. The power of attributes is in their ability to predict leadership potential, while the power of the practices is in their definition of what effective leaders actually do.

Note

1. The Corporate Leadership Council is a division of the Advisory Board, a for-profit association based in Washington, D.C., that publishes studies and research briefs on best management practices for the benefit of its membership, with a special focus on how its members can identify and develop future leadership talent.

Chapter 17

The Conceptualisation
of Competence

John Raven

Background

What may be termed the competency movement—which Spady (1977) long ago described as a "bandwagon in search of a definition"—has its origins in the conspicuous irrelevance of much knowledge-based "education"—including most in-service training courses—to occupational performance (see, e.g., Berg, 1973) and the failure of educational qualifications to predict occupational success (see, e.g., McClelland, 1973; Raven, 1977; and Hunter & Hunter, 1984 for reviews). The movement seeks to break the hegemony of what Schön (1983) termed the technico-rational model of competence. It argues that people need to learn how to do what they will later have to do. Given this orientation, some 80% of those involved in the competency movement then set about trying to specify the specific knowledge and skills required to be a competent travel clerk, train driver, teacher, or psychologist. The other 20% argued that such specific knowledge and skills are easily acquired, rapidly obsolescent, and contribute little to the conspicuous differences between competent and incompetent performance of occupational roles. They argue that the competencies on which attention needs to focus consist of qualities such as initiative, problem-solving ability, and the ability to build up one's own understanding of how the organisation and society in which one works and lives operate and thereafter intervene effectively in it. Such competencies may be termed generic high-level competencies. But they are hard to identify, difficult to nurture, and still harder to assess using conventional psychometric methods.

The problems that these observations pose have been sidestepped in the international network of competency specification and training programmes by legislating that occupational groups, aided by consultants, must generate their own specifications of the competencies that prospective members of those groups will have to acquire and demonstrate as a condition of entry. Given the absence of both a research base and a tradition of consultancy in this area, a huge variety of poorly researched conceptual frameworks has mushroomed to meet this bureaucratically generated "need." This way of proceeding allows the consulting firms to attach the words "competency-oriented" to the tools and procedures they already have at hand to identify, nurture, and test qualities previously described as knowledge, skills, aptitudes, abilities, attitudes, or personality. The net result has been, as Wolf (1995) has shown, a vast renaming and proliferation of the very kinds of activity that were so much open to criticism in the first place. This will inevitably lead to a discrediting of the competence-based education movement and its replacement by another, almost certainly equally poorly founded, bureaucratic "initiative" proffered as a solution to the problem.

Given the threats to their existence posed by the comments of researchers such as Barrett and Depinet (1991) on the one hand and the imminent discrediting of the all-hype-and-no-substance movement with which the term competence-based education has become associated on the other, those with a serious scientific interest in competence (or even a humane interest in the reform of education) urgently need to put their house in order, state their position more coherently, and, as McClelland so forcefully states in his chapter in this volume, initiate the research and development required to establish a more defensible position.

It has proved necessary to emphasise that this critique has been written with the intention of advancing scientific understanding and stimulating further work. This is because the authoritarian image of science that is carefully nurtured in many schools and universities causes authors whose work has been criticised to be regarded as unsound and thus unworthy of further support. It is therefore necessary to state in no uncertain terms that nothing that is said here is intended to give this impression. In my opinion, the work of the McBer team, culminating in the Spencers' book, came so close to developing a framework that would *revolutionise* thinking about competence and human resource management that it would be a mistake not to do what I can to help to ensure that that revolution is carried through.

The need to develop different, but interrelated, frameworks for think-ing about human competencies and occupational role requirements.

The effectiveness of *Competence at Work* is seriously undermined by its conflation of thinking about human competencies—defined as genetically and environmentally determined patterns of competence to carry out cer-tain self-motivated activities—with an attempt to describe the competen-cies required to perform different types of occupational roles effectively.

To illustrate the point, "managerial competence" is not a competence *as it occurs in human beings*. Managerial competence is determined by an interaction between role requirements and personal qualities. What is more, people in the same occupational position actually perform different kinds of jobs. What we need is a framework that will enable us to think more clearly about the different types of managerial roles that need to be performed; a better framework for thinking about the competencies of people who are (or who might become) managers; a better framework for thinking about the personal, organisational, and societal consequences of filling different types of managerial position with different types of people; and better ways of placing, developing, and utilising the competencies of managers and recognising particular contributions they have made.

The need to situate all discussion of "abilities" in the context of the motives in relation to which they are, or are expected to be, displayed.

Following a tradition that has acquired hegemony over the past century, psychologists persistently think and write as if qualities such as "concep-tual ability," "self-confidence," and "internal locus of control" are disposi-tions that are generalisable across all domains of life. It is thus not alto-gether surprising that, despite their 30 years' immersion in research into the motive-based conceptualisation and assessment of competence, the Spencers regularly fall into the same trap. Yet such qualities cannot be assessed without reference to the specific motivational dispositions of the person being assessed.

Let us consider the trait of "self-confidence" to illustrate the point.

People display enormous amounts of self-confidence when doing things they care about and of which they have experience—such as putting other people at ease, creating mayhem in a classroom, or ingratiating them-selves with their superiors. They lack self-confidence or internal locus of control in other areas. As a result, if one sets them a task that they are not strongly predisposed to undertake (or asks them questions about their confidence to undertake such a task) one, not surprisingly, concludes that they "lack self-confidence."

As we saw in the chapter in which we introduced the McBer framework, the same is also true of such things as "analytic ability." Conceptualising, analysing, and problem-solving are all difficult and demanding activities that no one will undertake or display except in relation to activities they have a strong internal predisposition or motivation to undertake. This means that the assessment procedures most commonly employed by psychologists—which present everyone with the *same* problem (such as a Piagetian task) with a view to seeing how well they do—are off beam. The results tell us more about the respondents' motivation to undertake tasks of that kind than they do about their actual ability to make their own observations, reason, and learn from experience.

"Analysing" is not only difficult and demanding. It is also primarily affective and conative. It involves sensitivity to fleeting feelings on the fringe of consciousness that tell one that one has a problem, "playing" with tentative insights until one stumbles upon one that "fits," experimenting with relevant aspects of the environment in order to learn more about it, "monitoring"—usually in a feeling-based rather than a "cognitive" way—the effects of one's actions in order to "learn" more about the nature of the problem and the effectiveness of one's strategies, changing one's behaviour accordingly, and so on. *All* of these activities need to be carried out effectively if one is to undertake "non-cognitive," "non-achievement" activities such as putting people at ease. Yet, when carried out in such contexts they, given our current psychometric procedures, usually escape notice—and if an astute psychologist happens to notice them, he or she is inclined to be puzzled about how to categorise them, being reluctant to designate them as "thinking."

The above formulation points to another psychometric problem. If it is true that people will not display their talents, abilities, and skills unless their motives are aroused, it follows that if we wish to assess their self-confidence, analytic ability, or knowledge in anything approaching a conventional way, we will need either to study them while they are doing things they care about or set them tasks that engage with their motives. Thus, if we are to draw justifiable inferences from people's behaviour, the *first* thing we need to know is whether the task they have been set engages with their motives and thus whether it creates an opportunity for them to display their talents.

Beyond that, there is the question of whether the tasks people have been set in the past have engaged with their motives and in this way created opportunities for them to develop the competencies of which they are capable.

Our first question must always be: "*In relation to what* will this person display his or her intelligence?" rather than "How intelligent is this person?" What the Spencers—and especially Elliot Jaques—describe as thinking at different *levels*—such as thinking about how to put people at ease compared with thinking about how society works—is (at least in the absence of further evidence along the lines supplied by Maistriaux, 1959), in reality, thinking about different *topics*.

So what are people going to "think" *about*? Are they going to think about putting people at ease or making scientific discoveries or creating a climate of innovation or advancing themselves in an occupational setting by doing whatever will create a good impression on their superiors or by knifing the competition or about how to intervene in worldwide economic and social processes in order to reap maximum financial rewards and publicity for their organisation?

The need to capitalise on the full revolutionary potential of McClelland's motive-scoring framework.

The scoring system that McClelland and his co-workers developed (in the early 1950s) to index the strength of *need* Achievement, *need* Affiliation, and *need* Power that was described in our chapter summarising that framework actually handles all of the problems so far mentioned in an elegant (if psychometrically revolutionary) way. Yet Spencer and Spencer (and even McClelland himself) do not seem to realise—and certainly have not capitalised upon—this.

As we saw in the earlier chapter, one uses a framework such as that summarised in Grid 1 to score *Test of Imagination* protocols and (potentially) *Behavioural Event Interviews*. To do this, one first reads over a transcript of a story written about a picture or a record of an *event*, asking, essentially, What kind(s) of activity is the person who told this story or described this incident strongly motivated to carry out? When one has answered that question, one starts asking questions such as "In relation to those activities (and *only* in relation to those activities) does the respondent make plans, anticipate obstacles, and try to think of ways round those obstacles?", that is, does he or she engage in *cognitive*

Grid 1 A Model of Competence

Examples of Potentially Valued Styles of Behaviour

| Achievement | | | | Affiliation | | | | | Power | |

Column headings (left to right):
1. Doing things which have not been done before.
2. Inventing things.
3. Doing things more efficiently than they have been done before.
4. Developing new formal scientific theories.
5. Providing support and facilitation for someone concerned with achievement.
6. Establishing warm, convivial relationships with others.
7. Ensuring that a group works together without conflict.
8. Establishing effective group discussion procedures.
9. Ensuring that group members share their knowledge so that good decisions can be taken.
10. Articulating group goals and releasing the energies of others in pursuit of them.
11. Setting up domino-like chains of influence to get people to do as one wishes without having to contact them directly.

Examples of components of effective behaviour

Cognitive

Thinking (by opening one's mind to experience, dreaming, and using other sub-conscious process) about what is to be achieved and how it is to be achieved.

Anticipating obstacles to achievement and taking steps to avoid them.

Analysing the effects of one's actions to discover what they have to tell one about the nature of the situation one is dealing with.

Making one's value conflicts explicit and trying to resolve them.

Consequence anticipated:
Personal: e.g. "I know there will be difficulties, but I know from my previous experience that I can find ways round them."
Personal normative beliefs: e.g. "I would have to be more devious and manipulative than I would like to be to do that."
Social normative beliefs: e.g. "My friends would approve if I did that": "It would not be appropriate for someone in my position to do that."

Affective

Turning one's emotions into the task:
Admitting and harnessing feelings of delight and frustration: using the unpleasantness of tasks one needs to complete as an incentive to get on with them rather than as an excuse to avoid them.

Anticipating the delights of success and the misery of failure.

Using one's feelings to initiate action, monitor its effects, and change one's behaviour.

Conative

Putting in extra effort to reduce the likelihood of failure.

Persisting over a long period, alternatively striving and relaxing.

Habits and experience

Confidence, based on experience, that one can adventure into the unknown and overcome difficulties, (This involves knowledge that one will be able to do it plus a stockpile of relevant habits).

A range of appropriate routineised, but flexibly contingent behaviours, each triggered by cues which one may not be able to articulate and which may be imperceptible to others.

Experience of the satisfactions which have come from having accomplished similar tasks in the past.

activities? "Does he or she turn his or her feelings into the task and use these feelings to initiate action and monitor the results?", and so forth, that is, does he or she engage in *affective* activities? And "Does he or she exercise willpower and persist for a long period of time?", that is, is there evidence of *conation*? One puts a tick (or check mark) in each cell of the Grid under the appropriate heading for each of the components of competence that the author of the stories sees his or her characters displaying while carrying out activities he or she was strongly motivated to carry out. As noted in the earlier chapter, the components of competence listed down the side of the Grid are not purely theoretical but emerged from a series of studies of what people actually do when they are starved, sexually aroused, or otherwise motivated—and it has since been extensively validated. One then adds up the number of ticks in each column. The resulting scores obviously have nothing in common with internally consistent factor scores. They are much more like multiple regression correlations calculated by weighting a number of independent predictors of performance and adding them up. (In this case all predictors have been given unit weight.) These scores indicate the likelihood that the person concerned will effectively carry out activities of the kind he or she cares about. That is, they are indices of *competence*. Conceptually, what we have down the side of the grid is a set of components of competence that, if brought to bear to carry out any activity, will help to ensure that that activity will be carried out effectively.

An additional benefit of the completed grid is that it prompts us to replace such questions as "How capable is this person of thinking analytically?" by questions like: *"In the course of carrying out what kinds of activity does this individual display his or her analytic ability?"*

As one reviews the grid it is obvious that we need something akin to Dalton's atomic theory to tell us how the potentially motivating activities listed across the top group together and which components of competence down the side belong together or perhaps subsume others. We need a framework of descriptors that, in some sense, tells us which observable behaviours are elemental motives or components of competence and which are compounds. In a sense, this is what the Spencers set out to develop, but, at least from the perspective developed here, one reason why they did not quite succeed was that they got off on the wrong foot, seemingly failing to recognise and capitalise upon one of the greatest strengths of the very framework on which their work builds most heavily.

Level of task or level of competency?

In their book, the Spencers at several points become involved in discussions of "levels of competence." They suggest, for example, that thinking about how society works reveals a higher level of competence in thinking than thinking about how to persuade a customer to buy a product. But is that really the case? It seems to me that the answer is, probably, "No." What we have here is thinking about different kinds of things. We need to clarify the different kinds of activity people may think about. A high competency score should tell us how effectively people are likely to carry out particular kinds of tasks. A competency score computed as described above tells us *how many* of the previously mentioned list of multiple and substitutable competencies someone deploys to carry out activities they are strongly motivated to carry out. Thus a high competency score obtained in relation to a "low-level" achievement task tells us that the person is likely to carry out such tasks extremely well. But, in and of itself, it tells us nothing about how well they are likely to carry out other types of achievement tasks. If we want to find out whether they will carry out a "high-level" achievement task effectively, we need to ask about such tasks. We must beware of conflating the "level of competence" index with some possible "order" in the "levels" of task that are to be undertaken. We need to unscramble our indices of competence from our indices of what kinds of activity people find engaging. It may or may not be the case that we can order achievement (and affiliation and power) tasks on the basis of their impact on organisations or society, just as it is possible to arrange chemical elements in cycles in the periodic table. But, at least in the absence of further evidence, we cannot assume that competence to carry out tasks having greater impact is built on, and implies competence to carry out, tasks having lesser impact. The "size" or nature of the task to be undertaken or motivated activity to be executed should not be mixed up with the problem of identifying the main components of competence that can be brought to bear to carry out the activity effectively.

Although, therefore, there is no doubt that we could do with a better framework for thinking about, classifying, and ordering motives and competencies, it therefore seems unlikely that the Spencers' current attempt to define competency clusters meets the need.

Respondent versus operant measures.

I have argued that the way of thinking that lies behind Grid 1 provides us with a basis on which to build a more appropriate framework for thinking about competence and its assessment than any other used in the past. It also enables us to escape from some important mental straitjackets that have, in the past, ensnared many psychologists.

The most pervasive of these have involved the concepts of unidimensionality and internal consistency in measurement. As we have seen, competence is a value-based and internally heterogeneous quality—a fact which was implicitly, but not explicitly, acknowledged in McClelland's 1958 scoring system.

Not having explicitly recognised these things, McClelland generated alternative explanations of why his measures of n. Ach., n. Aff., and n. Pow. did not correlate well with measures purporting to assess the same constructs that were developed using more conventional (internal-consistency–based) psychometric procedures and yielded different patterns of correlation with other variables.

While these "explanations" embodied observations that were important in themselves, they also carried prescriptions that, although they are actually irrelevant, have ensnared the Spencers and are likely to limit the options we believe to be open to us unless they are recognised for what they are.

Two of the most important have to do with the distinctions between operant and respondent measures and between "motives" and "values."

McClelland argued that the stories people wrote in response to his *Test of Imagination* pictures yielded samples of behaviour that were much less constrained by the nature of the stimulus than the answers they selected in response to multiple-choice "personality" tests. He called the former "operant" measures and argued that one learned more about people from examining such samples of behaviour than one could from pre-formatted multiple-choice tests.

Having now understood how radically McClelland's n. Ach., n. Aff. and n. Pow. scores differ from those derivable from conventional psychometric tests, it is obvious that it is not necessary to employ the distinction between operant and respondent measures (however important that is in itself) to explain the failure of most "personality" questionnaire scores purporting to index these or related constructs to correlate in similar ways with other indices of behaviour. Questionnaires purporting to measure n. Ach. and similar variables simply do not index the same constructs as do McClelland's measures. More specifically, they do not index the *competence* with which people are likely to be able to undertake tasks they care about. It is therefore not necessary to latch onto the distinction between operant and respondent to explain the discrepancies.

McClelland also argued—and the Spencers reiterate the party line—that measures of motives must be sharply distinguished from measures of values. What we have placed beyond all dispute is that McClelland's motive measures are imbued with values! The distinction McClelland draws is therefore a red herring that prevents us exploring avenues that are potentially very important from the point of view of view of finding a way forward.

To explain the generally poor correlation between "attitudes" and behaviour, all one has to do is to recognise that:

- There are all sorts of good reasons why people are unable to translate their values into effect—such as the virtual impossibility of pursuing certain lifestyles given the way society is organised, the behaviour of other people in the workplace, and pressures from other people;
- People are unlikely to be fully aware of the things they are strongly motivated to do; and
- Most of those who have constructed "personality" questionnaires have not adequately explored the way people think and feel about the domain of issues they are dealing with, have not attempted to sample that domain with appropriate questions, or have not investigated the ways in which the questions are actually interpreted by those who answer them.

The need to question the conventional job description/job designation framework and the assumption of "hierarchy" and acknowledge the importance of "distributed competence."

A pervasive problem in the competence movement has been acceptance of the conventions employed to think about and delineate occupational groups. Most workers in the area have accepted the myth that people having the same professional designation or job title are actually performing similar jobs. In fact, people having the same job title perform a huge range of very different functions. Thus, some psychologists carry out one type of basic research, others another; some publicise other people's work and claim it as their own; some raise funds for their organisations; some make good "hatchet men," doing whatever is necessary to advance themselves in their careers; some offer direct support to clients, and so on. One manager sets about creating a vibrant and innovative organisation. Another plays the international stock market and sets about creating a facade that leads to confidence in—and therefore investment in—the company. Another intervenes in the political system to get laws mandating the use of the company's products or services onto the statute books. Another sets about creating a good impression on his or her superiors so as to obtain advancement in his or her career, and so on.

The attempt to identify the competencies required by a psychologist, doctor, teacher, or manager in any generic way is therefore fundamentally misguided. Much more fine-grained analyses are required to find out what different people are actually doing . . . and often to find ways of enabling them to get credit for what they have, in reality, contributed to their organisations. What competencies are required to contribute in one or other of a number of very different ways to one's organisation? And which sets of concerns and patterns of competence have what short- and long-term consequences for the individuals concerned, for their organisations, and for society as a whole when set in the context of different organisational and societal arrangements?

Nor is this the end of the problems: The range of activities that need to be undertaken by those occupying any one occupational designation is far too wide for any one person to carry out. A *range* of people with different motives and patterns of competence is required at any job level if the job as a whole is to be carried out effectively. No one—not even a superstar—can do all that needs to be done.

One implication of the complexity is that—as I have shown elsewhere (Raven et al., 1998)—it is simply not possible to validate measures in the simplistic correlational way that is most widely advocated in textbooks on educational and psychological measurement. Instead, it will be necessary to generate a framework that will enable us to work with descriptive statements about the kinds of activity that people in some sense value or are strongly motivated to carry out, the patterns of competence they are capable of displaying while carrying out those activities, the features of the environment that are relevant to the development and display of their idiosyncratic motives, the emergent properties of the groups or organisations that emerge as they interact with others, and the consequences of interactions between people and their environments.

Making descriptive statements about people, their environments, and the way one engages with the other to produce transformations in both seems to me to have much more in common with the way in which chemists go about their work than it has with the "variable"-based work of physicists (which is what most educational and psychological measurement theoreticians and practitioners have in the past tried to emulate).

If we adopt the chemical analogy, the key questions become: What are the descriptors (analogous to the "elements" of chemistry) that are to be used to characterise the kinds of activity people are strongly motivated to carry out and the components of competence they display while doing so? What are the key descriptors required to characterise the features of the environment that engage with, or repel, these motivational predispositions? How are we to think about and describe the emergent properties of groups and identify the basic properties of individuals within them? In this context we may note that, to pursue the analogy, the properties of copper sulphate are very different from, and in a sense unpredictable from, the properties of the copper, sulphur, and oxygen that make it up (and the properties of copper sulphate certainly cannot be predicted from any additive combination of these components and they are not observable *in* any of the components) and the identification of any of the elements within the compound is a difficult and demanding process. It follows that not only may the key properties on which we need to focus be "group" competencies, the competencies an individual will display will depend heavily on those with whom they are working. The addition or subtraction of an almost invisible member of a group—especially one equivalent to a catalyst in the "environment" of others—may radically change not only the apparent characteristics of the group but also the apparent qualities of all of the others within it. Clearly, no one of the chemicals is more "important"—any more of a "superstar"—than the others. These observations suggest that our very concern with "superstars" reflects and reinforces an unjustified preoccupation with hierarchy and authority—a suggestion that is strongly confirmed in the work of Kanter (1985) and Adams and Burgess (1989)—and suggests that what we are witnessing is a legitimisation of a dysfunctional *sociological* process. And what environmental conditions or organisational arrangements (analogous to temperature and pressure) result in the interactions between people having different kinds of consequence?

Lest we be overawed by the apparent enormity of the task of unscrambling such an apparently complex network of relationships, we should note that this is *exactly* what chemists have succeeded in doing.

One immediately practical implication of these observations is that the effective performance of any organisational role requires the appointment of a number of people who do very different (and complementary) things. Another is that the effectiveness of any person's actions very much depends on what other people do. And a third is that the effectiveness of an organisation depends on the *balance* of people—even within a single job designation—who do very different things. Our focus cannot therefore be on *selection;* it must be on the identification of the motives and talents of individual members of staff and their release, development, and deployment.

A Dictionary—or an Atomic Theory?[1]

The Spencers set out to develop a framework for thinking about competence that would have more in common with atomic theory than a dictionary, but, in the light of the enormity of the task, they found it necessary to content themselves with an intermediary objective. While I have myself been unable to get even as far as they did, I feel that they would have got further if they had built on our own attempt (already summarised in Grid 1) to reconceptualise the motive-scoring framework developed by McClelland and his colleagues in the 1950s (McClelland et al., 1958). As we have already seen, the scores generated by that framework are best understood as indices of competence to undertake intrinsically motivating activities effectively, not as indices of "motive strength." To move toward an "atomic" theory, it will be necessary to fill out, and more effectively systematise, the list of descriptors across the top and down the side of the grid and, at the same time, resolve some of the problems inherent in McClelland's framework.

Perhaps the most important of these problems is the way in which the preoccupation with doing something *better* appears both as a sign of achievement motivation (across the top of the grid) and as a component of competence that contributes to the effective execution of *any* kind of task (down the side of the grid).

This problem stems at least in part from the instructions used to arouse achievement motivation in the original (1953) experiments. These had the effect of arousing *different kinds* of achievement motivation in different people. This was a necessary experimental ploy because this was the only way in which the motivation of enough people could be influenced to get *any* detectable effect.

The Spencers encountered a problem when attempting to delimit *need* Achievement—but tried to resolve it by excluding hobbies and sport from the framework—and failed to connect the problems they had with the conceptualisation of *need* Achievement with those they encountered in dealing with *need* Affiliation and *need* Power.

The basic problem is that setting standards of excellence, monitoring one's performance, and trying to do something *better* is, in the McClelland scoring system, treated as one of the three clear signs of *achievement* motivation. Yet such activities are crucial to the effective performance of *any* kind of task—whether it is connected with the values of achievement, affiliation, or power. It follows that neither having high standards and a concern with excellence nor persisting over a long period of time to achieve them lie at the heart of n. Ach.

The cluster of activities that are most often referred to as "achievement-oriented activities" seem to revolve around financial success (as in entrepreneurial behaviour), technological innovation (including the technology of organisational design), and activities, such as sport, in which competition seems appropriate. The clarity of the *criterion* of excellence also seems to have something to do with our willingness to say that such activities belong to the "achievement" cluster: Standards of excellence in connection with putting people at ease or even when competing for power seem somehow less clear cut.

But the cluster of activities about which one easily agrees to describe using the words "achievement-oriented" also seems to include thinking of better ways of identifying, developing, and utilising the talents of superiors and subordinates; releasing the know-how, creativity, and initiative of others and thus creating a hive of innovation; developing better ways of thinking about society; and acting in the public interest.

Instead of grouping together what seem to be very different kinds of activity—and rather arbitrarily excluding others—we have, in our own work, found it helpful to be much more specific about the kinds of activity that people seem to be somehow strongly motivated to undertake. And we have further found (1) that these specific motives seem to be very persistent over the life cycle and (2) that it seems to be as difficult for people to transfer their competencies from a specific area of activities that lie within the achievement domain to other activities within the same domain as it does to transfer them to activities listed under the affiliation or power headings.

The Spencers' attempt to resolve the confusion inherent in the original scoring system for n. Ach by limiting n. Ach to activities relevant to work gets them into further difficulties when they try to handle the problems posed by activities from other domains that apparently need to be carried out to achieve goals in the achievement domain. Examples would be thinking out how to influence the political process in order to raise the funds needed to carry out an experiment to test a new theoretical hypothesis or how to maintain a "warm" network of contacts to keep tabs on new options. Thinking out how to put people at ease, conducting "experiments with the problem" of putting people at ease, and soothing flared tempers can all be very important tasks to carry out at work. And they are all activities that would seem possible to undertake either in the service of achievement ends or as ends in themselves. But our experience is that people who are not inherently strongly motivated to carry out such activities cannot (and do not) carry them out effectively, however painfully obvious it is to them that they *need* to do so in order to undertake some other activity that strongly attracts. It seems to me, therefore, that the way to handle the problem is to say that a particular cluster of specific motives (identified from those listed across the top of the grid) and competencies (from down the side of the grid) is required if any one individual is to carry out some activity that calls for those motives and competencies effectively or to accept the need for a small "team" of people each member of which possesses key ingredients of the overall cluster. (Of course, as I have shown in Raven [1984/1997], there are many more potentially engaging or valued activities than are shown across the top of the grid and many more potentially important components of competence than are actually shown down the side of the grid: the grid was produced for heuristic purposes only.)

The Spencers' treatment of "calculated" entrepreneurial risks is another area in which they have incorporated problematic thinking from the McClelland tradition into their framework without sufficient examination. Entrepreneurs are well known for their tendency to engage in activities that appear to others to be risky. But it turns out that it is not the calculation of risk that is important—for their behaviour is much less risky than others take it to be. In the first place, they tend to be much more knowledgeable than others about personal and environmental resources that can be brought to bear to achieve their goals and that markedly reduce the risk element. In the second place, they tend to be much better than others at monitoring the effects of their actions and capitalising on what is learned—often changing the goal to make the best of "chance" observations. They are also much more likely to make use of a series of pilot experiments to try things out and learn from the results before launching into a full-scale change. So the key issue is not that they are more willing to take "calculated" risks but that they are more competent at dealing with an evolving situation.

Moreover, it is not only in relation to entrepreneurial activities that the behaviours that are described as "risky" when they occur in connection with entrepreneurial tasks have to be taken. The same subset of activities is required to conduct affiliation and power tasks successfully. And, indeed, the same terminology emerges. The Spencers actually quote a power-oriented person who, having identified a chain of domino-like activities that would probably produce the effect he desired said "I took a risk." He did indeed. And in a sense it was more "calculated" than many entrepreneurial risks. But what was really important was the other things he did to minimise risk and turn chance observations to advantage. It is not on the risk-taking that we need to focus. What is important is (1) the particular idiosyncratic—and often tacit—knowledge that is brought to bear and (2) the strategies that are deployed to learn from, and handle, the developing situation.

These are not the only behaviours that fall out more cleanly if reconceptualised in terms of the grid framework. Qualities such as "initiative," which the Spencers treat as a "molecular" component of n. Ach., do so too.

If we are to move forward it will also be necessary to use words such as "intention" and "understanding"—which everyone working in the area regularly finds themselves obliged to use—with greater care because they create an endless network of trip wires arising from their too-cognitive connotations. What is important in the former is the predisposition, not the intention, to undertake certain activities. "Interpersonal understanding"—like the "understanding" of effective entrepreneurs, managers, scientists, and authors—is, despite what the words seem to imply, not usually conscious or articulate. It usually involves unconscious or tacit knowledge of both a knowing-how and a knowing-that variety. Use of the word "understanding" is liable to orient people toward textbook-based courses as a means of "learning" how to do it.

Impact and Influence

Just as the conceptualisation of the achievement cluster needs to be reworked, so, too, does the power or influence cluster. However, unlike the achievement cluster, this has already been subject to revision since 1958 (Winter, 1973). My own work suggests that *different people* are concerned to influence those above them and those below them. But perhaps that is not right: Perhaps there are those who seek to ingratiate themselves with those above them and wish to wield authority over those below them—that is, people who are more concerned with their own position in a hierarchy of authority than with the influence they have on others or, at least, the way they wish to influence those above them is very different from the way they want to influence those below them. Either way, it seems to be necessary to distinguish a concern to influence superiors from a concern to influence those below one.

Then there is the problem that the kind of person who seeks to *understand* wider social, economic, political, and systems processes is not usually the kind of person who has good "intuitive" strategies for influencing those processes. I am not sure that a concern with interpersonal power is at all the same thing as a concern to understand and influence systems processes. The end to which the ability to influence social processes and mass perceptions is exerted seems very important. One meets so many senior public servants and politicians who engage in Machiavellian strategies to advance themselves without the least concern with the public interest. So, again, the need seems to be to distinguish between the different *types* of activity that have been grouped together in this cluster and to spell out the strategies—or components of competence—that could be deployed to undertake any one of them effectively.

There is one final problem to be mentioned under this heading. I have been very surprised in my own work to have uncovered the extent to which behaviour is governed by perceptions and, in particular, perceptions of how society works, how one's own organisation works, and one's own role and that of others within those organisations and society.

That is why these cognitions are now listed among other components of competence down the side of Grid 1. What I have found is that the greatest source of incompetence in modern society is the inability and unwillingness to engage with the wider social, economic, and political processes that primarily determine what one *can* do in one's job. Of course, as the Spencers show, some people are much more interested in understanding and influencing these processes than are others. But perceptions and understandings—like understandings of other concepts such as "management" and "democracy"—seem to influence the competence to carry out all valued activities effectively. So here again we encounter the problem of conceptually unscrambling the requirements for the effective performance of different kinds of activity from motivational predispositions.

Concluding Comment

The Spencers have provided us with the most important text that has ever been published on competence at work. Yet it hardly provides a basis on which to build the radical reform of our educational system and employment practices that is needed. It does not provide us with the information needed to rationalise the misguided, international, mandatory competence specification, training, and testing movement that has been wished upon us with the aid of terms that we ourselves helped to coin. It does not even lead directly to an adequate rejoinder to Barrett and Depinet's criticisms. It needs to be reworked. We need an atomic theory of competence. By this I mean an agreed-upon framework of descriptors to use to make *statements* about individual patterns of motivation and competence, about groups and their emergent competencies, about environments, about how individuals and their environments interact and transform each other, and about the short- and long-term, personal and social, consequences of alternatives. Contrasting theses need to be developed. An army of creative, inventive, thoughtful researchers who are able to get beyond the constraints of both traditional psychometric and educational thoughtways on the one hand and of academic life in general on the other are required. Yet even to rework the database in which the book is rooted is problematic, because few of the studies have been published. In the end, then, it emerges that one of the central issues to be clarified and addressed is how to conduct urgently needed policy research that will help us to reform our society in more appropriate ways than those being wished upon us by the Department of Education and Employment. This issue, hardly glimpsed by the Spencers, turns out to be the central issue to which university staff and students dedicated to the true aims of such institutions would turn their attention. Here, without doubt, lies a role for Higher Education for Capability

Note

1. I have also published a critique of the British government's competency programme in Raven (1995).

References

Adams, E., & Burgess, T. (1989). *Teachers' Own Records*. Windsor, England: NFER-Nelson.

Barrett, G. V., & Depinet, R. L. (1991). A reconsideration of testing for competence rather than intelligence. *American Psychologist, 46* (10), 1012–1024.

Berg, I. (1973). *Education and Jobs: The Great Training Robbery*. London: Penguin Books.

Hunter, J. E., & Hunter, R. F. (1984). Validity and utility of alternative predictors of job performance. *Psychological Bulletin, 96*, 72–98.

Jackson, P. W. (1986). *The Practice of Teaching*. New York: Teachers College Press.

Kanter, R. M. (1985). *The Change Masters: Corporate Entrepreneurs at Work*. Hemel Hempstead: Unwin Paperbacks.

Maistriaux, R. (1959). *L'Intelligence et le Caractere*. Paris, France: Presses Universitaires de France.

McClelland, D. C. (1951). *Personality*. New York: Sloane, Dryden, Holt. Reprinted in 1953 by Irvington Publishers, New Jersey.

McClelland, D. C. (1973). Testing for competence rather than for "intelligence." *American Psychologist, 28*, 1–14.

McClelland, D. C. (1975). *Power: The Inner Experience*. New York: Irvington.

McClelland, D. C, Atkinson, J. W., Clark, R. A., & Lowell, E. L. (1958). A scoring manual for the achievement motive. In J. W. Atkinson (Ed.), *Motives in Fantasy, Action and Society*. New York: Van Nostrand.

Miron, D., & McClelland, D. C. (1979). The impact of achievement motivation training on small businesses. *California Management Review, XXI*, 13–28.

Raven, J. (1977). *Education, Values and Society: The Objectives of Education and the Nature and Development of Competence*. Oxford, England: Oxford Psychologists Press.

Raven, J. (1984/1997). *Competence in Modern Society: Its Identification, Development and Release.* Unionville, NY: Royal Fireworks Press (1997); Oxford, England: Oxford Psychologists Press (1984).

Raven, J. (1987a). Learning to Teach in Primary Schools: Some Reflections. *Collected Original Resources in Education, 11,* F3, D07.

Raven, J. (1987b). Tell Them About Teacher Training. *Collected Original Resources in Education, 11,* F3, F13.

Raven, J. (1988a). The assessment of competencies. In H. D. Black and W. B. Dockrell (Eds.), *New Developments in Educational Assessment: British Journal of Educational Psychology, Monograph Series No.3,* 98–126.

Raven, J. (1988b). Developing the talents and competencies of all our children. *Gifted International, 5,* 8–40.

Raven, J. (1989). Parents, education and schooling. In C. Desforges (Ed.), *British Journal of Educational Psychology, Monograph Series No.4, Special Issue on Early Childhood Education,* 47–67.

Raven, J. (1994). *Managing Education for Effective Schooling: The Most Important Problem is to Come to Terms with Values.* Unionville, NY: Trillium Press; Oxford, England: Oxford Psychologists Press.

Raven, J. (1995). *The New Wealth of Nations: A New Enquiry into the Nature and Origins of the Wealth of Nations and the Societal Learning Arrangements Needed for a Sustainable Society.* Unionville, NY: Royal Fireworks Press; Sudbury, Suffolk: Bloomfield Books.

Raven, J., & Dolphin, T. (1978). *The Consequences of Behaving: The Ability of Irish Organisations to Tap Know-How, Initiative, Leadership and Goodwill.* Edinburgh: The Competency Motivation Project.

Raven, J., Johnstone, J., & Varley, T. (1985). *Opening the Primary Classroom.* Edinburgh: Scottish Council for Research in Education.

Raven, J. C., Raven, J., & Court, J. H. (1998). *Manual for Raven's Progressive Matrices and Vocabulary Scales. Section 4, The Advanced Progressive Matrices.* Oxford, England: Oxford Psychologists Press; San Antonio, TX: The Psychological Corporation.

Schön, D. (1983). *The Reflective Practitioner*. New York: Basic Books.

Spady, W. G. (1977). Competency-based education: A bandwagon in search of a definition. *Educational Researcher, 6* (1), 9–14.

Spencer, L. M., & Spencer, S. M. (1993). *Competence at Work*. New York: Wiley.

Winter, D. G. (1973). *The Power Motive*. New York: Free Press.

Winter, D. G., McClelland, D. C., & Stewart, A. J. (1981). *A New Case for the Liberal Arts*. San Francisco: Jossey Bass.

Wolf, A. (1995). *Competence-Based Assessment*. Buckingham: Open University Press.

PART V

FACILITATING THE DEVELOPMENT OF CAPABILITY

The quest for material for this Part of our book has been a frustrating experience. We are aware of educational programmes that *work*—work, that is, in the sense that they offer genuinely *educational*—developmental—experiences for those involved. Put another way, they work in the sense that they *draw out the talents* of those involved. Put like that, and given that the word "educate" comes from the Latin root *educere*, meaning "to draw out", it follows that these are the *only* programmes that can legitimately claim to be *educational*.

Unfortunately, *few of even these programmes clearly set out what they are trying to do and how they are trying to do it*. Here, as we see it, lies the central problem of the educational system—and the high-level (or "generic") competency-oriented education movement in particular.

How can any educational programme validate a claim to be effective if the goals that are to be achieved and the criteria to be used to judge its effectiveness remain obscure?[1]

But the situation is, in fact, even more remarkable than these observations suggest. This is because, despite the absence of discussion of *goals*, there are thousands of descriptive—that is, non-theoretically grounded—accounts of practice! There are, for example, enough books on "progressive" or "open" education to fill a library. Yet not more than a handful of these make explicit the qualities that are to be nurtured, let alone the ways in which the processes that are described at such length are expected to promote their development.[2] Similarly, when teachers have been asked to say what they understand by the term "progressive education,"[3] very few say anything that would lead one to believe that they think that it involves some kind of reprioritisation of goals.

Yet the educational—developmental—processes to be employed to help people to learn to lead, to invent, to put people at ease, to create political disruption, to persuade, to argue, to fight, to be socially at ease, to communicate, to be at harmony with nature—or any other of the myriad of things that people might usefully learn to do—*must* be different from those required to get them to "learn" in the constricted sense in which that term is most commonly used.

The main consequence of this is that most accounts of how competence-oriented education is to be implemented are capable of being read— and are in fact usually read—as accounts of alternative ways of promoting only that form of "learning" that is commonly understood when the word is used.

This is even true of most of the material included here. The version of "action learning" developed and promoted by Reg Revans has—despite its corruption into the phrase "people learn better if they are actively involved"—very little to do with achieving conventional learning outcomes more effectively. The same is true of at least one of the variants of independent study offered at what was the North East London Polytechnic (NELP) and described by its former and current heads (John Stephenson and Dave O'Reilly). Yet it is quite clear that many of the difficulties encountered by "action learning" stem from Revans' failure to spell out its distinctive goals. Likewise, it is evident from both O'Reilly's chapter in a later Part of this book and Robbins'[4] book on the subject that the collapse of Independent Study at NELP was, at least in part, a product of failure to secure agreement on what was to be achieved and how it was to be achieved. Although Stephenson documents some of the outstanding, diverse, benefits that students derived from the experience, O'Reilly, in a later chapter, refers to some of the tensions that arose from failure to distinguish the programme's core objectives from the acquisition of credentials on the one hand and "humanistic" activities on the other.

But these have not been the only sources of frustration in putting together this material. There have been at least three major exceptions to the generalisations made above. The first is the work of Donald Schön at the Massachusetts Institute of Technology. In *The Reflective Practitioner* Schön summarises his studies of the high-level competencies required for effective performance in a wide range of occupational settings. In *Educating the Reflective Practitioner* he reports the results of his efforts to design and implement an appropriate educational programmme. We would have loved to have included a summary of the processes employed and the barriers encountered. Unfortunately, none of the numerous

publications Schön sent us to consider reprinting in this book summarised
this work

Then again, we desperately wanted to include material relating to the
goals and processes employed at Alverno College.[5] Unfortunately (at least
from our point of view!) Alverno's staff declined to let us publish a series
of excerpts from their booklets and, for space reasons, we were unable to
include the whole. The result has been that "the best has (again) driven
out the good" and we have no material at all to speak for this outstanding
work.

The third exception has been the work associated with the name of
David McClelland. In this case, we have been able to include it—but only
by ourselves summarising it and integrating it with the results of our own
work.

Notes

1. Of course, it is necessary to specify *both* goals *and* process. In later Parts of our book we will see that many committees *have* specified goals such as the development of problem solving ability, self-confidence, the ability to work with others, and the ability to understand and influence organisations and society. But they have failed to specify either the processes to be employed to nurture such qualities or the means to be used to find out whether they have been achieved. As we shall also see later, where performance goals have been specified as outcomes, they have tended to consist of low level skills or information.

2. See Raven (1991 or 1994) for the literature review on which this statement is based.

3. For example, Bennett (1976).

4. Robbins (1988).

5. Alverno (1992, 1992, 1994).

References

Alverno College Faculty. (1992). *Liberal Learning at Alverno College.* Milwaukee, WI: Alverno.

Alverno College Faculty. (1992). *Valuing in Decision-making,* Milwaukee, WI: Alverno.

Alverno College Faculty. (1994). *Student Assessment-as-Learning at Alverno College.* Milwaukee, WI: Alverno.

Bennett, N. (1976). *Teaching Styles and Pupil Progress.* London: Open Books.

Raven, J. (1991). The wider goals of education: Beyond the 3Rs. *Educational Forum, 55* (4), 343–363.

Raven, J. (1994). *Managing Education for Effective Schooling: The Most Important Problem Is to Come to Terms with Values.* Unionville, New York: Trillium Press; Oxford, England: Oxford Psychologists Press.

Robbins, D. (1988). *The Rise of Independent Study.* Milton Keynes: Open University Press.

Chapter 18

Facilitating the Development
of Competence

John Raven

An idea that has proved useful when thinking about, and organising material relating to, facilitating the development of competence is the concept of a "developmental environment."

In developmental environments people:

- have opportunities to consider their values and resolve value conflicts in an open and supportive atmosphere in which their views, concerns, and decisions are respected.
- have opportunities to experience the consequences of behaving in different ways with the assurance that mistakes will neither bring ridicule at the time nor have serious negative long-term consequences.
- are encouraged to evolve, and practise, new styles of behaviour while undertaking activities they are strongly motivated to carry out.
- can think about their organisations and their society and come to understand and perceive these institutions (and their operation) in new ways that have marked implications for their own behaviour.
- are given (or can evolve) new concepts to help them to think about their behaviour, the world in general, and the consequences of alternatives.
- are exposed to role models—either in real people or in literature—that enable them to see, and share in, other ways of thinking, feeling, and behaving; to observe the consequences; and to try the behaviours for "fit." (Exposure to others whose behaviour brings

satisfactions that one wants oneself is a strong incentive to engage in the behaviour!)

- are encouraged to set themselves high (but realistic and measurable) goals, are encouraged to monitor progress toward them, and are helped and supported by others when they are unable to live up to their own expectations.
- are provided with support, encouragement, and help *when they make mistakes*. Under these circumstances, it is particularly important for colleagues to identify and encourage what was worthwhile in the activity and to refrain from threatening inquisitions into the causes of failure. Colleagues should, in particular, refrain from implying that they know better than the person concerned what he or she should have done. After all, the person who undertook the activity knew more about both the situation in which he or she was working and his or her own abilities and limitations than did the others.
- are encouraged by having their accomplishments recognised and commented upon.

We will put flesh on this skeleton in a moment. But first we should reiterate two observations made in earlier chapters. First, competent behaviour is very much dependent on an absence of inhibitions arising from motive or value conflicts. Second, the development of competence depends on opportunities to practise important components of competence while carrying out activities one cares about. Value clarification and value engagement are therefore crucial to the development of competence.

The most systematic discussion of the features required in effective attitudinal and motivational change programmes is to be found in an article published by David McClelland in 1965. In it, he draws together, summarises, and builds on a great deal of previous research. He deals first with the legitimacy of trying to influence values. He meets the objection that explicit value-clarification activities consist of brainwashing by pointing out that such activities enable people to choose between outcomes that previously remained implicit or were made explicit only in the minds of orators, politicians, or religious leaders. In making such considerations explicit, one is, therefore, freeing people from the possibility of brainwashing. Knowledge of both the personal and social consequences of pursuing alternative values is, therefore, not only central to value clarification, it is also critical to the legitimisation of activities that clarify values and develop competence.

He then notes that people often have latent or relatively inarticulate values which they can be helped to articulate. Once brought into full consciousness they can be pursued more effectively. McClelland notes that the problem is not so much to *change* people's values as to discover, reinforce, strengthen, and expand relevant pre-existing thoughtways and associations. Providing people with the vocabulary they need to think about their values—and doing so in such a way that they can see that others who share their values also obtain other satisfactions they would like—can do much to facilitate the process. McClelland argues—again citing research evidence—that this can best be done in a warm, open, trusting, honest atmosphere that recognises the stresses involved in personal self-examination and that accepts, without pressure, personal decisions that go counter to those of the overall group. In the absence of such warmth and acceptance, people feel threatened and retreat into entrenched positions. In the absence of the leisure needed to formulate, and try out, new strategies, they fall back on thoughtways and behaviours which have met with at least some success in the past. What has to be done is to feed them information that enables conflicting beliefs (such as "I am not an achieving type" or "Achievers are nasty, personally motivated, and underhanded") to be resolved. This can be facilitated by providing those concerned with the concepts they need to think about their values, the components of competence, the institutional structures in which they live and work, and the consequences of their beliefs and actions. Although consequences are often anticipated but not valued, there is much to be gained from discussing the long-term social consequences of alternative courses of action—the moral consequences of the actions. This has the effect of reinforcing and strengthening people's awareness of the ways they feel they *should* behave. As Fishbein has shown, such considerations exert a powerful influence on behaviour.

Value change can also be facilitated by emphasising that people *can* and *do* change. Witness the efficacy of McClelland's own programmes (about two-thirds of the participants ended up thinking, feeling and behaving in ways which characterised only one-third at the beginning—see McClelland & Winter, 1969; Gorman & Molloy, 1972; Miron & McClelland, 1979) and the fact that people change their behaviour quite dramatically when they change the role they are enacting. The same person will behave quite differently when he says to himself "I am now being a parent," "I am now being a teacher," or "I am now being a manager." The label "I am behaving now as a parent, teacher, or manager"—or "high achiever"—has a marked effect on a whole range of behaviours.

Words and ways of thinking about people, things, and situations exert a marked influence on behaviour. This is why the pen is mightier than the sword. Hence, it is important to introduce new definitions of the role of the worker and the manager and new understandings of participation, delegation, and democracy into our everyday thinking. However, for such role definitions to exert effective control over behaviour it is necessary for those concerned to know a great deal about how people who occupy the relevant roles think, feel, and behave. Most people have just no idea how people with other motivations and dominant values think, feel, and behave. Those who run programmes to help people clarify their values must, therefore, supply the necessary information. This can be done with the aid of research findings and case histories, and it can be reinforced through role-playing. Such activities are particularly likely to be effective if they require the participants to invent the desired thoughtways for themselves rather than merely repeat what they have been told.

The salience of particular concerns can also be enhanced by determined, preferably collective, decisions to talk about such things as achievement issues, innovation, and so forth throughout the day and to minimise discussions of housekeeping issues, cost-checking, and risk-avoidance. This again results in raised consciousness about certain activities and further prevents the tendency to think about distracting issues in future.

In order to ensure that people have the detailed store of knowledge, feelings, and behaviour which is needed if they are to change their behaviour, it is frequently desirable to teach them *in detail* how to *assess* the nature and strength of value-laden competencies in others. This gives them the vocabulary they need to think about their overriding values and the components of competence they use to pursue them. The beauty of such frameworks is that they often enable people to put into words things they know but have not previously been able to articulate for themselves. In this way, it is possible to reinforce and strengthen existing thoughtways rather than seek to impose new ones. The whole process can then be strengthened by encouraging those concerned to role-play a variety of styles of behaviour (including their cognitive and affective components) so that they can try them for fit and establish what sort of person they would like to be.

Following exercises in which those concerned learn competency scoring systems, apply them to case histories, and role-play the behaviours, they can practise them "for real" in educational simulations and "games." This provides them with a *real* opportunity to do such things as scan the environment for opportunities, plan challenging but realistic achievement programmes, monitor the effects of their actions to learn more about that with which they are dealing, and so forth. They are, once again, able to make these processes explicit and *label* them and their components so that they can think more effectively about—and monitor—their own behaviour in the future.

Such role-playing exercises are also important because they allow people to practise and perfect new ways of behaving in a situation in which the consequences of a mistake are not as serious as they would be in real life. To a degree, new habits—new ways of thinking, feeling, and behaving— can be practised and perfected in this way so that they can be produced smoothly in appropriate real-life situations.

The fact that we have once more emphasised the centrality of the *person*—his or her values, patterns of competence, thoughtways, and general patterns of behaviour—should again be underlined. This contrasts sharply with the widely held view that the function of vocational training is to foster specific skills. What we have argued is that *general* thoughtways and patterns of feeling and behaving come into play in *every* situation. Specific skills—such as keyboarding—are situation specific. Put another way, the exercise of specific skills is dependent on particular things (such as keyboards) being present in the environment. They are therefore unable to have a very pervasive influence on behaviour. More generic competencies influence the tendency to obtain access to appropriate information technology and work out how to apply it effectively.

Having thoroughly reviewed a series of potentially enticing new ways of thinking, feeling, and behaving, the next step taken by those involved in McClelland's programmes is to make decisions about how they wish to change, to make explicit and rehearse the reasons for change, and, above all, to commit themselves to change, preferably with a specific action plan describing goals they are to achieve by particular dates. Beyond that, the establishment of a review mechanism whereby those concerned get together to monitor progress toward their goals, to see what can be done to overcome obstacles, and to provide support for persisting with the desired behaviour—almost certainly in the face of opposition from less enlightened colleagues—is essential.

Much of what has been said relates to off-the-job developmental programmes. But a great deal can also be accomplished on the job. Opportunities can be created to discuss values—on a group or individual basis—in many situations. People can be encouraged to make explicit and discuss their value dilemmas and, when they do, they can be supplied with relevant information on the consequences of alternatives.

Opportunities can be taken to not only correct inappropriate expectations but also to do something about widely shared expectations that discourage desired behaviour. Managers can make their own values explicit and make it clear that pursuit of these values leads to satisfactions which others want. They can involve their colleagues in their own struggles to resolve value dilemmas. They can support and encourage colleagues and subordinates who are pursuing valued goals that they, themselves, believe are important. They can help their subordinates to make contact with a network of other people with similar values. They can move people with crucially important values into environments in which they will be supported, rather than derided, by others. They can influence the *overall* organisational climate of the workplace and the support provided by others for particular types of activity.

All these processes can be greatly facilitated if the group concerned collects data (perhaps using *The Edinburgh Questionnaires*) on shared values, perceptions, expectations, and definitions. They can then collectively examine these data—and their own personal contribution to it—with a view toward clarifying what the personal, organisational, and social consequences are likely to be. The implications of the data so collected can be highlighted by comparing and contrasting it with that obtained by others. In this way, those concerned can be encouraged to evolve *new* perceptions and understandings as well as clarify their own values. The effectiveness of these strategies can be enhanced if a deliberate effort is made to encourage the participants to use these data to develop a picture of how *an outsider* would see the organisation and its staff, how he or she would compare it with others, and what he or she would, on the basis of those results, expect the future to hold for the organisation and its staff.

This abstract description of key features of developmental environments will now be fleshed out from programmes of research and action research which I have carried out with businessmen, teachers, and parents.

Developmental Environments in Business Settings

In the course of McClelland's programmes for the owners and managers of small businesses, which are held with small groups in residential settings, participants are first taught the scoring system for McClelland's *Test of Imagination*. This deals with three major motive clusters (affiliation, power, and achievement) and with 10 major components of competence (including anticipating obstacles, enthusiasm for the task, getting help from others, and monitoring the effects of one's actions). In this way, participants are provided with words they can use to think about and discuss motives, valued styles of behaviour, and components of competence that might be utilised to carry out valued activities effectively. They analyse their own personal patterns of values and motivation using this conceptual framework and, as a result, become thoroughly familiar with it. They also analyse case history material. They engage in educational games that are designed to emphasise what it feels like to behave in different ways and to experience the emotional and objective consequences of alternatives. Participants study research and case history material that illustrate the consequences of alternatives. They are encouraged to think about how they would like to change, the effects of others' behaviour on them, and the effects of their behaviour on others. At the end of the programme the groups arrange to continue meeting so that they can support each other when they encounter difficulties.

Raven and Dolphin (1978) examined naturally occurring work environments for evidence of the presence or absence of many of these characteristics. Environments which appeared to promote growth seemed to be characterised by such things as an effort being made to identify the motives and talents of each individual and take steps to recognise, develop, and capitalise upon those talents and abilities—an atmosphere in which there was an expectation of high standards and support for innovation but an absence of pressure for results (which has the effect of stifling the willingness to experiment with new ideas and new ways of thinking). Opportunities to participate in managerial activities, study the goals of the organisation, and influence decisions also seemed to be important. For that to happen it seemed to be necessary for the managers concerned to feel confident that they were in a growth situation in which their subordinates were not vying to do them out of a job. Managers also seemed to need time to develop confidence in their subordinates' goodwill and ability—and especially to decide which types of developmental experience would prove most productive.

Data collected by myself, Graham, Berrill, and others using *The Edinburgh Questionnaires* point to the widespread existence of environments which are barely developmental. In these environments, people are *not* able to go on learning new things; their talents are not recognised, developed, and rewarded; they do not have responsibility for their work and an opportunity to influence decisions or innovate; they are not credited with the specialist information which they and only they have; they are not viewed as people who have useful information to contribute; there is little variety in what they do and little opportunity to identify the types of task which lead them to be optimally motivated or to tap multiple motivations to perform any one task; they are not encouraged to try out new activities and new ways of thinking and experience the consequences; and their colleagues and managers do not portray, and encourage them to share in, effective innovatory behaviour.

Klemp, Munger, and Spencer (1977) and Jaques (1976) have shown that one of the most important sets of activities distinguishing more from less effective managers is the time they spend thinking about the talents of their subordinates, how to redeploy both those staff members and others to capitalise upon those motives and talents, and how to develop them. Graham and Raven (1987) showed that Japanese managers are much more likely than British or American managers to think that it is important to do these things, and Dore and Sako (1989) showed that Japanese managers do indeed spend much more time on it.

Klemp, Munger, and Spencer also showed that effective managers tended to encourage subordinates to participate in doing their own jobs. This enabled the subordinates to become clearer about what was to be achieved and how it was to be achieved. The managers shared their concern with innovation—the thoughts, feelings, and anxieties involved in initiating behaviour on the basis of hunches—and then monitoring (in a feeling-based way) the effects of that action in order to learn more about the problem and the effectiveness of their strategies and then take further action to regain control of the situation. They shared their efforts to understand the wider socio-political situation which so much determined their behaviour and their attempts to think out how to get together with others to influence it. They shared their thinking and strategies dealing with the assessment, development and deployment of subordinates. In all these ways they enabled their subordinates to see and share in normally private psychological components of competence and see their effectiveness—and in this way develop those components of competence. Their subordinates learned *how* to adventure into the unknown, how to study social and political processes in such a way as to be able to influence them, and how to release the energies of, deploy, and develop subordinates.

Schön (1983) has provided somewhat similar accounts of how master architects and town planners developed the talents of juniors, of how research and development managers developed their subordinates, and of how psychotherapists developed their skills.

Developmental Environments in the Home

Further insights into the environmental factors which promote development emerged from our studies of child-rearing in the home. In our research at the preschool level (Raven, 1980), we found that mothers who
valued the development of initiative, independence, self-confidence, the
ability to make one's own observations, the ability to think for oneself,
and the ability to achieve personal goals effectively explicitly and systematically set out to foster these qualities in their children. The developmental environments they created permitted their children to practise the
qualities which have just been mentioned, together with other components of competence that were listed in my chapter on the nature of
competence in relation to goals that the children personally cared about.
They created opportunities for their children to find out what interested
them and what they were good at, and discussed their children's feelings
and behaviour—and the effectiveness of their behaviour—with them. They
did not interfere in what their children were doing, but reacted sensitively,
with a specific view to promoting their growth, only when they were
having difficulties which they could not overcome on their own. They
rewarded their children's success by sharing in their feelings of delight at
accomplishments and by helping to create more opportunities for them to
do the types of thing they enjoyed. They encouraged their children to set
goals, plan the sequences of activities which would be required to achieve
them, and to monitor their own performance. They gave their children a
vocabulary for thinking about these processes: They talked to them about
planning, experimenting, thinking about what had happened, trying to
find out what went wrong, and how to do better next time. They encouraged their children to evolve goals as they went along and saw what "gave"
in their environments and what interested them.

In addition, they set out to demonstrate competent behaviour to their
children in such a way that their children could learn from them. They
tried to create opportunities for their children in which the children could
behave competently and they discussed their own behaviour with them.
They tried to create opportunities for their children to take responsibility,
manage others, make discretionary judgements, and follow up those judgements by activities which would keep the programme of activities on
target and lead it to reach its goals. They created opportunities for their
children to share in their own, normally private, thoughts and feelings.
Thus, they would talk about what they were doing, why it was important,
and their feelings about it. They would create opportunities for their children

to participate in their own attempts to clarify their goals and the route to be taken to reach them. Their children, therefore, shared in the process of clarifying values, prioritising goals, considering the long-term consequences of their actions, and reconciling value conflicts. They shared in the process of anticipating obstacles to goal achievement and planning strategies to reach them which involved getting help and cooperation from other people. They learned how to adventure into the unknown on the basis of initial insights and partial understandings, monitor the effects of their initial actions to learn more about the situation and the effectiveness of their strategies, and take corrective action where necessary. They shared their parents' feelings of frustration and misery at failure and delight in success.

The parents also set out to earn their children's respect instead of, as some other parents did, simply demanding it. In order to achieve this goal, the parents found themselves discussing the long-term social consequences of their actions with their children. To do this they shared with their children their understanding of the world, how it operated, and what they believed to be right and wrong. In order to justify their children's respect, they found it necessary to try to behave in ways that were above reproach. They, therefore, found themselves discussing not only the constraints on their behaviour but also the whole complex of factors which influenced decisions and the relative weights that have to be placed on alternatives (instead of merely laying down prescriptive moral codes which cannot be simply related to most of the day-to-day decisions which have to be taken).

The effects of attempting to treat children with respect—as people who were entitled to their own views and opinions—were also significant. They discovered how serious-minded and competent their children really were. This reinforced their tendency to rely on their competence rather than believe that children needed to be taught, restricted, confined, and disciplined. This created an ascending spiral in which they were able to create demanding opportunities for their children to adventure on their own, exercise discretion and initiative, and take responsibility for their own behaviour. This led to a further advance in their competence. There came to be less and less need for demeaning restrictive rules.

Insights from Studies of the Backgrounds of Creative and Innovative Individuals
The work we have just summarised dealt with the ways in which the child-rearing strategies of parents who wished to foster independence, initiative,

and adventurousness in their children differed from the child-rearing strategies of others. Many of the same results have been obtained when studies have been made of the backgrounds of highly creative and innovative individuals in our society.

A study by Rosen and d'Andrade (1959) is of particular importance, but many others have been summarised by McClelland (1961, 1982) and McClelland and Winter (1969). There have also been a large number of studies of the background and upbringing of highly innovative and creative people. These include the studies made by MacKinnon (1962), Taylor and Barron (1963), Barron and Egan (1968), Bloom (1985), and Walberg and Stariha (1992). Since the composite picture emerging from these two sets of studies is very similar, they may be discussed together here.

Highly creative people, and people high in *need* achievement, tend, firstly, to have been encouraged to be independent at an early age, to go about town on their own, and to choose their own films and friends. Their decisions are not made for them; their parents have a great respect for their ability to think and decide for themselves.

Second, they are more likely than others to have been encouraged to try hard for things for themselves—as children they are given little assistance in doing things but are given strong approval when they complete them. In contrast, fathers of people low in concern with achievement tend to give explicit directions to their children, to interfere in what they are doing, and to express irritation when their children do not do what they want them to do.

Third, children who are highly motivated to achieve had been expected to develop their own moral code—none was forced upon them, although their parents did make it clear what their own code was. This code particularly stressed forthrightness; honesty; respect for others; pride, diligence, and joy in work; and making the most of one's abilities. In general, the parents seemed to have a remarkable respect for their children and their ability to reason, act, and cope on their own.

Fourth, they had been exposed to models of intelligent, thoughtful, hard-working, and resourceful behaviour—mostly by their parents but occasionally by others in their environment. Effective achievement-oriented behaviour, including its thinking, feeling, and behavioural components, was also often portrayed for them in great detail, and in a context of evident warmth and approval, in the stories that were read to, and told to, them as children. A well-known series of books that exemplify these characteristics are those describing the achievements of Babar the King (de Brunhoff, 1953).

It is important to distinguish between *achievement* training and *independence* training—both of which occur in the backgrounds of highly achievement-oriented individuals. Independence training consists of training people to cope on their own—to be independent of others. Independence training is often present in situations where it is important that the children learn to look after themselves—such as on public housing estates. Achievement training, on the other hand, involves a great deal of contact between children and parents, expectations of high levels of performance, and the willingness of parents to work with their children to help them to set challenging but realistic goals and help them to anticipate obstacles.

Facilitating the Growth of Competence
Among Primary School Pupils

In our work in schools my colleagues and I have collected extensive evidence showing that the great majority of classrooms fail to promote the growth of the components of competence we have been concerned with in this book. Indeed, the majority of classrooms currently stunt the growth of these qualities. They therefore fail our children and our society (Raven, 1977; Raven & Varley, 1984; Raven, Johnstone, & Varley, 1985; Raven 1994).

We have also described a large number of educational procedures that are intended to, and do, enable a number of teachers to nurture the wider aspects of competence. Relevant processes include project-based education, discussion lessons, and enquiry-oriented studies. We have described in some detail the work of a number of teachers who achieve these goals effectively (Raven, 1977, 1994; Raven, Johnstone, & Varley, 1985). Accounts of the ways in which activities such as project work can be used to achieve educational goals will be found in *Education, Values and Society* (Raven, 1977). Here it is more appropriate to summarise some of the results of our attempt to portray the processes used by one teacher to promote the general development of her pupils.

In order to achieve the broader goals of which we have spoken, this teacher organised her entire programme of work around project-based enquiry-oriented activities carried out in the environment around the school. These enquiries were organised around a topic, or theme. One such theme covered "the local area and its surroundings." Under this umbrella pupils carried out a number of projects, some individual and some group. One group project involved a re-examination of a local archaeological excavation. Another involved a study of population movements over time, a study of the history of each house and the occupations of its changing occupants, a study of changes in patterns of agriculture, and a study of the current social structure of the area—who was related to whom and what they talked about. All projects involved original research. However, some also involved the initiation of social action—such as getting something done about pollution in the local river. Such a project might be used both as a tool of social research and as a means of promoting the development of the understandings and competencies required to initiate effective social action. Within each project, pupils had personal projects, distinctive areas of specialisation, and distinctive roles. Thus, one pupil undertook a study of butterflies and their habitats whilst another studied the history of a hay rake. The project work that was carried out did not consist—as it so often does—of merely looking material up in reference books, although carrying out an original enquiry or initiating and monitoring some social action might involve tracing and using *specialist* books, research reports, or original accounts of scientific investigations or archaeological excavations. More commonly, if information was wanted, it was obtained by interviewing "ordinary" people or from church records, tombstones, old newspapers, or catalogues unearthed in attics.

But all of this, although extremely unusual, was not what was most distinctive about the work of this particular teacher. Most striking were her unusual concerns. Like Barnes and Young (1932) and Curtis (see Cremin, 1961), she was not preoccupied, as were most teachers, with coursework—with covering a syllabus. But neither was she preoccupied with a particular process—such as creating a "democratic" classroom or encouraging an interest in architecture. Instead she focused on the high-level competencies which the pupils were to develop *in the course of their work*. These competencies included reading, writing, spelling, and counting. But they also included communicating, observing, finding the information that was needed to achieve goals (which often had to be collected by observation or by talking to people rather than reading books), inventing, persuading, and leading. In this context even the three R's took on a different complexion. Learning to read, for example, came to include such things as learning to use structure to locate material that might just possibly contain interesting information, learning to use what was read to stimulate lateral thinking, and learning to quickly discard what was not relevant to one's purposes. Writing came to involve such things as the use of allusion and innuendo to influence the reader. Communicating came to include gesture, artwork, diagrams, and body language.

Project work of this kind—though not other kinds of project work—was fairly typical of the relatively small proportion of teachers who successfully nurtured the kinds of competence we have been concerned with in this book. One key feature of the approach was that it enabled them to discover each pupil's distinctive interests and talents. These interests might lie in the types of behaviour that made them enthusiastic (such as finding better ways of doing things, getting people to work together, or getting something done about a particular problem—such as pollution) or they might lie in particular content (such as Celtic civilisation or aerodynamics). The approach also enabled different pupils to learn to undertake different activities. It confronted the pupils with the fact that there are endless *new* problems out there waiting to be understood and solved: There is no need for them to be put in the position of having to master tired, out-of-date knowledge and the strategies to be used to reproduce solutions to problems that have already been solved. (Incidentally, one great advantage of tackling new problems is that the teacher cannot tell pupils how to act but has to show them how to be adventurers, learners, detectives, and discoverers. Another is that unique combinations of up-to-date, high-level, specialist [rather than out-of-date and low-level] knowledge are required if progress is to be made.) As a result of adopting this approach it was possible for the teachers to create developmental environments in which pupils practised and developed a selection of high-level competencies (such as leadership, initiative, the ability to observe and to think, or the ability to understand and influence society) in the course of undertaking activities they cared about. Since competence involves such things as the willingness to persist for a long period of time in the face of frustration—and often in the face of the scorn of others—it was important for the teachers to ensure that the pupils experienced the satisfactions which come from undertaking different sorts of task successfully. (Examples include conducting an experiment, putting a group at ease, persuading a local council to change its decisions, or communicating some important ideas to parents.) In this context the teacher's task was to notice what motivated each pupil, invent an opportunity for the pupil to pursue his or her interests (so that the pupil would, in the process, develop some high-level competencies), monitor the pupil's response to that experience and take corrective action when necessary, and to support the pupils by helping them to tackle problems which would otherwise have discouraged them and led them to give up. But they did not only create opportunities for their pupils to practice—and thereby develop—

high-level competencies. They also, like good parents and good managers, coached their pupils by creating opportunities for their pupils to see the normally private psychological components of competence ... and the consequences. Thus, they created opportunities for their pupils to share in their own thinking and prioritising. They shared their hopes and fears. They talked about their hunches, the auras that excited and beckoned them, the cues that told them when things were going to pay off and when they were going wrong—and thus when corrective action had to be taken. They shared their constant re-formulations of their goals and the problems that needed to be surmounted to reach them—re-formulations which occur as a result of (often playlike) rumination and reflection on the effects of hunch-based actions or "experimental interactions with the environment" (Jackson, 1986). In all these ways they modelled components of competence in such a way that pupils could copy them, and they let the pupils see that these processes were effective in helping them to reach their goals (and Bandura, 1977, has shown that people are particularly likely to copy effective behaviours). Some teachers shared their planning and anticipations; their concern with excellence, innovation, and efficiency; their disdain for petty regulations; their anticipation of obstacles and their search for ways round them; their concern with aesthetics; and their feeling of being in control of their destinies. They demonstrated how to capitalise upon whatever resources were available—indeed how to select their purposes in the light of the resources that were available and achieve those purposes instead of, as was characteristic of many other teachers, complaining about the lack of resources to do what they wanted to do. In these ways these teachers communicated their values to their pupils and portrayed effective, competent behaviour in such a way that pupils could emulate it. It was not only the overt behaviour which was portrayed in this way for the pupils, but the entire pattern of thinking, feeling, and striving that normally lies behind it. By deliberately avoiding the role of expert and provider of wisdom—by regularly (and successfully) trying to do things that they themselves did not initially know how to do—they showed their pupils how to be learners and innovators. By demonstrating in their own behaviour how thoughts, feelings, and persistence lead to satisfactions that the pupils also wanted, they strengthened the pupils' tendency to engage in the relevant behaviours. They portrayed the strategies of enquiry, anticipation of reactions, and experimentation that are required to build up an understanding of a complex biophysical or social process and the strategies required to intervene in it, anticipate the way aspects of the system would react, and take corrective action when necessary. By accepting pupils' suggestions, they showed them that authorities and leaders are not best regarded as sources of information and organisation, but as people who, at best, help other people to articulate and share what they know, to acknowledge what others have contributed (and lead others to feel capable of achieving), and to be motivated to achieve their own goals. Some of these teachers, like some parents, realised that, if pupils are to learn from mentors who portray the cognitive, affective, and conative components of high-level competence, mentor and disciple must share at least some enthusiasms, talents, and concerns (Gardner, 1990). Since there is no possibility that a single teacher's values could mesh with those of all his or her pupils, they realised that it was essential to place children with other adults outside the school who shared their values and to engage a range of other adults with them in the class's activities so that pupils could see people successfully exercising important components of competence whilst undertaking activities that they (the pupils) cared about. They also used stories, literature, and historical material to illuminate the intra-psychic, cognitive, affective, and conative components of competence and illustrate the personal and social consequences of pursuing different kinds of valued activity and deploying different patterns of competence in different types of society having different institutional arrangements and dominant cultural concerns. (One might add that they could, with advantage, also have prepared case history materials and materials derived from psychological research for this purpose.) In a similar way, their pupils learned a great deal from, and came to rely more extensively on, their fellow pupils. They developed a partnership in learning. Aided by a vocabulary supplied by their teachers, they became able to think about, and value, the contributions of others. The teachers would encourage them to identify the particular talents and contributions of their fellows and enlist their help in trying to find ways of tapping the energies of other—perhaps in some ways disruptive—pupils. In this way the teachers helped their pupils to develop and use multiple-talent concepts of competence and ability instead of classifying their fellows only as "smart" or "dumb." They made explicit both the fact that not everyone contributes in the same way to a group process and also to the thought processes that contribute to effective leadership and management (that is, to the processes that are involved in identifying, developing, and using the talents of each member of the work group). By engaging their pupils in this process the teachers therefore helped them to develop the competencies required for effective leadership and management.

Fostering Competence in the University

In the most important study yet published of the ability of the university to promote value change and the development of competence, Winter, McClelland, and Stewart (1981) compared the effects of several different types of college in the United States. Unlike the researchers who conducted many earlier studies (summarised in Jacob, 1956) and the vast majority conducted since (Pascarella and Terenzini, 1991), they used measures that were both tailored to, and sensitive to, the effects that the educators concerned desired and to those that could be anticipated after examining the programmes. The study showed that the colleges had very different effects on their students. Ivy-league colleges (the equivalent of Oxbridge) bred a sense of importance, destiny, and leadership that was, in fact, followed through into activities that conferred major benefits on society in later life. They fostered the willingness and the ability to think critically and to handle cognitive complexity—especially the cognitive complexity involved in understanding social problems.

These colleges achieved such goals neither through academic course work nor through dormitory residence ("the enemy . . . of critical thinking is student social life centred in dormitories or other living units") but by:

- exposing students to diverse experiences. These experiences came, in particular, from contact with, and working with, others who had very different backgrounds, values, and preoccupations. These experiences were, however, only effective if the college insisted that the students analyse and integrate their experiences in an effective way instead of merely "accepting" them, chatting about them, and compartmentalising them.
- demanding that their students cope with new, unfamiliar, and, particularly, challenging experiences involving diversity, variety, and challenge to their assumptions and thoughtways. These demands could not, however, be general—they had to be in relation to areas of activity that the students cared about.
- creating a wide variety of opportunities for students to engage in types of activity (leadership, innovation, research, etc.) that were new to them and providing support while they haltingly tried out the activities they selected in relation to goals they cared about.
- establishing with the students new, personally challenging, tasks to be executed to high standards—but simultaneously providing support and encouragement to ensure goal achievement.

- insisting on high standards in *independent* academic work. This involved preparing theses or conducting seminars and participating in original research with faculty members.
- avoiding prescriptive rules that choked students off from particular types of experience or demanding that they cover prescribed content for vocational reasons: time to explore, daydream, reflect, and integrate is a crucial component of any effective educational programme that is too often missing because it is precluded by pressure for results.

It will be readily apparent that many current trends in university education are away from, rather than toward, the development of these features.

It would appear that we can again abstract from this study the importance of providing opportunities to explore and clarify values, to practise new styles of behaviour, to engage in independent study, and to develop relevant competencies in the course of independent study. We can also underline the importance of specialist information and the importance of contact with appropriate role models. Once again, however, opportunities to make a personal analysis of the workings of the socio-economic system and explore their implications seem to have been emphasised too lightly.

Conclusion

The creation of developmental environments in higher education will require staff to:

- change from a concept of teaching as "telling" to a concept of teaching as "facilitating growth."
- focus on the competencies that are to be fostered instead of on the information (content) that is to be conveyed.
- think about students' "abilities" instead of their "level of ability."
- help students to study their incipient interests and competencies; help them to generate individualised, competency-oriented, developmental experiences to harness those interests and promote the development of those competencies; and monitor each student's reactions to those experiences and take corrective action when necessary.
- become specialists in human development and education instead of, or as well as, subject specialists.

Clearly, if competency-based education is to be introduced into higher education, radical change will be required in the roles of higher education staff, whether as perceived by staff members themselves, students, or higher education administrators. Nevertheless, it is important to reiterate that Winter, McClelland, and Stewart's work shows that it is the adoption of precisely such a role—the *traditional* role of the university mentor—that distinguishes the staff of ivy league (Oxbridge) colleges from those who work in other institutions and that it is the adoption of this role that results in their differential effectiveness. By portraying such behaviour, higher education staff would incidentally help their students to develop a more appropriate image of effective management.

References

Bandura, A. (1977). *Social Learning Theory*. Englewood Cliffs, NJ: Prentice Hall.

Barnes, E. A., & Young, B. M. (1932). *Unit of Work: Children and Architecture*. New York: Bureau of Publications, Teachers College, Columbia University for Lincoln School of Teachers College.

Barron, F., & Egan, D. (1968). *Leaders and Innovators in Irish Management*. Dublin, Ireland: Human Sciences Committee.

Bloom, B. S. (Ed.). (1985). *Developing Talent in Young People*. New York: Ballantine Books.

Cremin, L. A. (1961). *The Transformation of the School*. New York: Knopf.

De Brunhoff, J. (1953). *Babar the King*. London: Methuen.

Dore, R. P., & Sako, M. (1989). *How the Japanese Learn to Work*. London: Routledge.

Gardner, H. (1990). The difficulties of school: Probable causes, possible cures. In Literacy in America, *Daedalus, Proceedings of the American Academy of Arts and Sciences, 119*, 85–113.

Gorman, L., & Molloy, E. (1972). *People, Jobs and Organisations*. Dublin: Irish Productivity Centre.

Graham, M. A., & Raven, J. (1987). *International Shifts in the Workplace: Are We Becoming an "Old West" in the Next Century?* Provo: Brigham Young University Dept. of Organizational Behavior.

Jackson, P. W. (1986). *The Practice of Teaching*. New York: Teachers College Press.

Jacob, P. E. (1956). *Changing Values in College*. New York: Harper Bros.

Jaques, E. (1976). *A General Theory of Bureaucracy*. London: Heinemann.

Klemp, G. O., Munger, M. T., & Spencer, L. M. (1977). *An Analysis of Leadership and Management Competencies of Commissioned and Non-Commissioned Naval Officers in the Pacific and Atlantic Fleets.* Boston: McBer.

McClelland, D. C. (1961). *The Achieving Society.* New York: Van Nostrand.

McClelland, D. C. (1965). Toward a theory of motive acquisition. *American Psychologist, 20,* 321–333.

McClelland, D. C. (1982). What behavioral scientists have learned about how children acquire values. In D. C. McClelland (Ed.), *The Development of Social Maturity.* New York: Irvington Press.

McClelland, D. C., & Winter, D. G. (1969). *Motivating Economic Achievement.* New York: Free Press.

MacKinnon, D. W. (1962). The nature and nurture of creative talent. *American Psychologist, 17,* 484–494.

Miron, D., & McClelland, D. C. (1979). The impact of achievement motivation training on small businesses. *California Management Review, XXI,* 13–28.

Pascarella, E. T., & Terenzini, P. T. (1991). *How College Effects Students.* San Francisco: Jossey-Bass.

Raven, J. (1977). *Education, Values and Society: The Objectives of Education and the Nature and Development of Competence.* Oxford, England: Oxford Psychologists Press.

Raven, J. (1980). *Parents, Teachers and Children: An Evaluation of an Educational Home Visiting Programme.* Edinburgh: Scottish Council for Research in Education. Distributed in North America by the Ontario Institute for Studies in Education, Toronto.

Raven, J. (1994). *Managing Education for Effective Schooling: The Most Important Problem is to Come to Terms with Values.* Unionville, NY: Trillium Press; Oxford, England: Oxford Psychologists Press.

Raven, J., & Dolphin, T. (1978). *The Consequences of Behaving: The Ability of Irish Organisations to Tap Know-How, Initiative, Leadership and Goodwill.* Edinburgh: Competency Motivation Project.

Raven, J., Johnstone, J., & Varley, T. (1985). *Opening the Primary Classroom*. Edinburgh: Scottish Council for Research in Education.

Raven, J., & Varley, T. (1984). Some classrooms and their effects: A study of the feasibility of measuring some of the broader outcomes of education. *Collected Original Resources in Education, 8* (1), F4 G6.

Rosen, B. C., & D'Andrade, R. G. (1959). The psychological origins of achievement motivation. *Sociometry, 22*, 185–218.

Schön, D. (1983). *The Reflective Practitioner*. New York: Basic Books.

Taylor, C. W., & Barron, F. (Eds.). (1963). *Scientific Creativity: Its Recognition and Development*. New York: Wiley.

Walberg, H. J., & Stariha, W. E. (1992). Productive human capital: Learning, creativity, and eminence. *Creativity Research Journal, 5* (4), 323–340.

Winter, D. G., McClelland, D. C., & Stewart, A. J. (1981). *A New Case for the Liberal Arts*. San Francisco: Jossey Bass.

Chapter 19

Stimulating Self-Directed Learning through a Managerial Assessment and Development Course[1]

Richard E. Boyatzis

There appear to be no images, metaphors, or models for management from natural life. Although the role of manager has been identified as similar to that of warrior, taskmaster, coach, technician, juggler, parent, or facilitator, none of these is adequate to capture the complexity of the management job, or what it means to be a manager. Therefore, we may conclude that management is an unnatural act, or at least there is no "natural" guidance for being a manager. If management is an unnatural act, then development and preparation to be a manager must be intentional. Unfortunately, most people and most organizations have used the "life experience" or "sink or swim" approach to management development—a congratulatory letter from your 'boss, a handshake, and a new title. Early preparation and lifelong development is being increasingly cited as the key to the development of managers (Kotter, 1988; McCall, Lombardo, & Morrison, 1988; Dreyfus, 1990).

The role of graduate management education (i.e., an MBA program) can be to help people explicitly begin this process, regardless of their earlier experiences in high school, college, or work. But do MBA programs help prepare people for management jobs? Given that the primary mode of teaching in graduate management schools has been the traditional academic transmission of knowledge, we must question whether knowledge is enough. Studies of effective managers (Campbell, Dunnette, Lawler, & Weick, 1970; Boyatzis, 1982; Kotter, 1982; Luthans, Hodgetts, & Rosenkrantz, 1988) suggest that knowledge is necessary but not sufficient for superior performance as a manager. Graduate management programs based on the approach of building knowledge in the student are not adequate to prepare people for management.

The Managerial Assessment and Development course at Case Western University School of Management sets the individual on his/her path to development throughout the MBA program. Unlike a typical academic course, it stimulates students to consider drawing from all of their courses, from non-course developmental experiences, and from work and leisure experiences in order to make the maximum progress toward their personal development goals. Therefore, it seems particularly important to examine this course in detail.

The Managerial Assessment and Development Course

The Goal
The goal of the Managerial Assessment and Development course is to learn a method for assessing one's knowledge and abilities that are relevant to management and for developing, to implement plans for acquiring new management-related knowledge and abilities throughout one's career and to be aware of one's own values and the values of others.

The Philosophy and Theory of Self-Directed Learning
The course is based on the belief that a person learns most effectively when in control of the learning process and can choose developmental activities best suited to his or her personal situation. It is believed that a person learns most effectively when building on their current capability and experiences and not repeating material already known. Another belief is that feedback is necessary as a basis for planning growth and development. The course is designed with an assumption that a person should, during their graduate management program, add value to themselves as an asset and grow in their abilities and knowledge related to the management role.

The theory of self-directed change, which leads to self-directed learning, proposes a self-perpetuating change process initiated by a person (Kolb & Boyatzis, 1970a&b; Kolb, 1971; Boyatzis, 1982; Boyatzis, 1999, in press; Boyatzis, Murphy, & Wheeler, 2000). Change and learning occur when a person:

a) articulates an image of where he or she is with regard to a particular characteristic (i.e., The Real), and
b) articulates an image of where he or she would like to be with regard to that same characteristic (i.e., The Ideal), then

c) perceives and experiences a discrepancy between The Real and The Ideal, which is

d) converted into a goal. This is

e) translated into a plan to achieve the change, or learning goal, and then

f) action and feedback as to progress occurs and

g) feeds back information to the ongoing assessment of The Real and The Ideal states, which begins the cycle again.

Using the theory of self-directed change as the guiding principle, control of the change process is placed firmly in the student's hands. In fact, of course, students are in control of the change process anyway. What this approach does is avoid the delusion of faculty control.

Through the use of self-directed change and learning, the student can use all of his or her experiences during the months or years of the MBA program as opportunities for learning. It is potentially far more efficient to access *all* of their experiences and to have students feel responsible for linking them into their agendas for learning rather than to have the faculty responsible for creating the complete experience.

Faculty typically conceptualize and then deliver only one type of experience—a course. A student typically spends about 2,500 hours in classes and doing homework for classes in a two-year full-time MBA program. Allowing for an average of seven hours of sleep each night, the student is awake for approximately 10,500 hours during this same time period. *What are they learning during the other 8,000 hours?* Arousing and beginning the self-directed change process and guiding it through the use of the individualized learning plan makes all 10,500 hours opportunities for self-directed learning.

To engage self-directed change, the process should provide three components: (1) an assessment process, not merely a self-assessment process; otherwise the determination of the current state is more a function of social desirability and reference group expectations than performance capability; (2) the generation of development, or learning, plans to help the student focus his or her efforts and energy; and (3) vehicles for the reflection and integration of experiences to create learning.

A part of the philosophy on which the course is based requires respecting the individual, especially in terms of his or her experiences, theories, views, affect, values, and so forth. Since MBA students have worked and developed theories, or at least images, of themselves and how others should function, their personal theories or implicit images should be elicited prior to working on examining them (Hunt, 1987).

Early in the course, students are asked to write several essays. One essay concerns their expectations about learning, including the role of student and faculty. Another concerns their philosophy of management. Yet another concerns their ideas about an ideal model of management (i.e., the way a manager should act).

Building the Model of Management

Each student determines his or her learning agenda (i.e., goals) using a management model developed at the Case Western School of Management. However, students are also encouraged to set out to master other things that are not included in the model but that are likely to be of interest to them or likely to be useful in their intended career. The model itself has 22 abilities, 11 knowledge areas, and scope for the acknowledgment of value orientations and values. The abilities, knowledge areas, and value themes are shown in Figure 19.1.

The domains of substantive and procedural knowledge included in the model were built up from the American Association of Collegiate Schools of Business framework published in 1987. All of these disciplines are represented among the specialties of Weatherhead School of Management (WSOM) staff.

The abilities included in the model emerged from the empirical studies of the competencies that contributed to superior performance in management and related individual contributor jobs conducted by McBer and summarized in other chapters in this book.

The WSOM model seeks to identify and work on specific abilities, not clusters of abilities. A cluster of abilities might be called interpersonal communications. In the WSOM model, this cluster is broken into oral communications, written communications, empathy, and networking.

While "cluster" models may be useful in some settings, the increased specificity of the WSOM model is important because it is the framework around which the student builds his or her individual learning plan. To guide development efforts regarding abilities, the student needs behavioral specificity and situational guidance as to when and where to best use the ability (i.e., guidance through "intent").

The model of value themes was generated through faculty discussions. They represent shared concerns and perspectives most highly valued by the faculty and staff. The entire model, including knowledge, abilities, and value themes were discussed and altered through numerous discussions with all concerned. The final set represents a shared view of what we (i.e., stakeholders of the WSOM MBA program) hope our graduates will have and be like when they graduate. It does not limit the student, and

Figure 19.1 The Model of Management Abilities, Knowledge, and Values Used at the WSOM (adapted from Boyatzis, 1982)

Goal and Action Management Abilities
1. Efficiency orientation
2. Planning
3. Initiative
4. Attention to detail
5. Self-control
6. Flexibility

People Management Abilities
7. Empathy
8. Persuasiveness
9. Networking
10. Negotiating
11. Self-confidence
12. Group management
13. Developing others
14. Oral communication

Analytic Reasoning Abilities
15. Use of concepts
16. Systems thinking
17. Pattern recognition
18. Theory-building
19. Using technology
20. Quantitative analysis
21. Social objectivity
22. Written communication

Knowledge Areas
1. Accounting
2. Banking and finance
3. Economics
4. Labor and human resource policy
5. Marketing
6. Management information and decision systems
7. Operations research
8. Operations management
9. Organizational behavior
10. Policy
11. Managerial statistics

Value Themes
Creating economic, intellectual, and human value.
(a) Managing in a complex, diverse, and interdependent world;
(b) Innovating in the use of information and technology;
(c) Developing the manager as team leader and team member;
(d) Stimulating professionalism, integrity, and social responsibility.

in that sense it is not a "cookie-cutter" describing specifications for standardized parts. Students are encouraged to place different weighting on the various characteristics in the model according to their personal dreams, aspirations, and careers. They are encouraged to add other characteristics that may be appropriate as well.

Determining Strengths and Weaknesses

An essential basis on which to build students' programs is an assessment of strengths and weaknesses. The designation levels are: consistently and frequently shown (i.e., a strength), occasionally shown, and rarely shown or not known. The latter may occur because of lack of prior opportunity to determine possession and use of the ability of knowledge area or lack of adequate information on which to make a judgment. The emphasis is placed on the degree to which the person "demonstrates" the ability or knowledge. This avoids the question of whether the person has, or possesses, the ability or knowledge but does not use it.

Another outcome of the initial assessment process is determination of the level of priority of each ability and knowledge area for the student's future job(s) and career(s). From the first class, through the various papers and assignments, and into the construction of their learning goals and learning plan, the student is asked to anchor his or her thoughts and plans on the job or types of jobs, career, type of organization, and life that he or she sees as a desirable future. Therefore, when determining the third output, the level of priority for future development, the student is viewing himself or herself in the context of his or her desired future.

Students use three sources of information about their abilities, knowledge, and values during the course to determine their strengths and weaknesses:

1) their own view of where they stand on each ability, where they stand with regard to each body of knowledge, and where their preferences are regarding value orientations and values;
2) the views and reactions of others (e.g., the members of their executive action team, colleagues and/or a manager at work, family and friends); and
3) coded assessment instruments and exercises.

The students are told that no one of these sources of information is inherently more or less accurate than any other. Each source adds different information and each has different vulnerabilities to distortion and error. It is the student's responsibility to figure out what it means, with the guidance provided by the course structure, faculty, and facilitator. Some students have found it useful to think about each of these sources of information as a different voice. In this sense, a major activity of the course is for students to have a dialogue among the three voices and seek a consensus among them. It is believed that a person develops a more accurate view of current strengths and weaknesses from consideration of all three sources of information (i.e., listening to all three voices) than from merely considering one source of information. The course methods and activities are designed to communicate and reinforce the message that the student is in charge of interpreting and integrating all of the information provided.

Commitment to Growth: The Ladder of Commitment

To gain maximum benefit from this course and the entire MBA program, students must confront a series of questions about their development and future. Students are informed that their growth during the program depends on their commitment to learning and change. They are told that people do not change unless they want to change and perceive the benefit of a change.

The following questions are presented to the students as representing the logical development of commitment to learning and growth. It is difficult to seriously consider the answer to the second question and continue learning in the MBA program until the first has been answered, and so forth. In other words, progress in the course depends on students confronting each question and achieving an answer before proceeding. The questions are:

1) Are abilities and knowledge relevant to success in management or my intended future career?
2) Do I believe abilities can be developed? Do I believe knowledge can be acquired?
3) Do I think the specific abilities addressed in personal development program and the particular knowledge areas addressed at the WSOM are important?
4) Do I think I have little of this ability or knowledge area, or seldom use it? (At this point, each ability and each knowledge area requires separate commitment.)

5) Do I want to change my use of this particular ability or knowledge area in the next few years?

6) How can I pursue my goals to change and grow?

Components of the Course

The course is designed to incorporate five basic elements:

1) assessment of abilities, knowledge, and values;
2) feedback and interpretation as to levels of these abilities and knowledge areas;
3) documentation of current capability and past performance in these areas;
4) development of a learning plan for the period of the person's program; and
5) formation of executive action teams

Approximately one week is devoted to introductory activities, including exercises to help the students get to know the other members of their executive action team. Two weeks are devoted to assessment exercises. One week is spent on a lecture and case studies explaining the model of management used in the course (i.e., the 22 abilities, 11 knowledge areas, and value themes), and preparation for the feedback. Six weeks are spent on feedback and interpretation. Two weeks are devoted to the development of a personal learning agenda (i.e., learning goals) reflecting life and career goals. Two to three weeks are devoted to development of the student's learning plan. This includes viewing (at home) videos of faculty from each department describing potential career paths, their electives, and personal interests. Other developmental resources within the university and community are identified and discussed, and students are also encouraged to seek resources in their current workplaces, which is particularly appropriate for evening MBA students. In addition, students review a set of tests oriented to helping them identify their learning style (i.e., preference), learning skills, and learning flexibilities; this information is considered particularly important in developing a realistic and personalized learning plan.

The assessment of abilities involves collating information from three sources: assessment instruments and exercises, self-assessment, and views of others. The assessment instruments and exercises require students to directly demonstrate the ability being examined.

The assessment exercises and instruments include:

1) a group discussion exercise (which is videotaped)
2) a critical incident interview (which is audiotaped)
3) a presentation exercise (which is videotaped)
4) Learning Style Inventory, Learning Skills Profile, and Adaptive Style Inventory
5) Technology Applications Questionnaire
6) Personal Orientation Questionnaire on value orientations
7) a value survey
8) a written comparative analysis of business case studies

The Learning Style Inventory (LSI) is a measure of a person's dispositions, or preferences, with regard to how he or she learns (Kolb, 1984). The LSI asks respondents to rank nine sets of four descriptors as being more or less appropriate designations of the way they learn. Four learning modes are assessed with this measure: (1) concrete experience; (2) reflective observation; (3) abstract conceptualization; and (4) active experimentation.

The Learning Skills Profile is a card-sort in which the student is asked to describe himself or herself by sorting 72 statements of skills into various categories reflecting different levels of skill acquisition and mastery (Boyatzis & Kolb, 1991, 1995). Based on the underlying theory of experiential learning (Kolb, 1984), the items are organized into 12 skill scales. A respondent is asked to sort 72 cards into as many stacks as appropriate corresponding to seven categories: (1) I have no skill or ability in this area; (2) I am now learning this skill or activity; (3) I can do this with some help or supervision; (4) I am a competent performer in this area; (5) I am an outstanding performer in this area; (6) I am an exceptional performer in this area; or (7) I am a creator or leader in this area.

Each of the 72 cards has a statement describing a specific skill or activity. The respondent can form one stack, two stacks, or so on up to a maximum of seven. The statements are scored according to the stack into which the respondent places each card. Twelve scales result from the scoring. They are: leadership skills; relationship skills; help skills; sense-making skills; information-gathering skills; information-analysis skills; theory skills; quantitative skills; technology skills; goal-setting skills; action skills; and initiative skills. The reliability and validity data available suggest that each scale is an appropriate measure of the skills it represents (Boyatzis & Kolb, 1991, 1999).

The Adaptive Style Inventory (ASI) is the third part of a system of tests assessing learning dispositions and skills (Boyatzis & Kolb, 1999;

Mainemelis, Boyatzis, & Kolb, 1999). While the Learning Style Inventory assesses a person's preference for ways of learning, the ASI assesses the degree to which a person can respond to the opportunities for learning in various types of settings. That is, the ASI addresses the issue of whether the person can adapt and be flexible in their way of learning to respond to specific situations (Kolb, 1984). It is scored in terms of a total score indicating integrative flexibility (i.e., integrating learning from all possible "ways" of learning). It also provides scores as to the person's flexibility in responding to situations offering learning through concrete experience, reflective observation, abstract conceptualization, and active experimentation (i.e., the four modes of the experiential learning cycle that are assessed in the Learning Style Inventory; Kolb, 1984).

The presentation exercise is primarily an assessment of the student's oral communication ability. In the exercise, the student is asked to prepare and make a 10-minute presentation on an organization for whom they would like to work. The student is provided with a two-page list of issues to consider in identifying their "ideal work organization." If they are not sure of the type of organization or industry in which they want to work, they are asked to identify an organization that intrigues them. They are instructed to approach the presentation as if they were recruiting MBA students to work for it. The presentation is followed by a five-minute question and answer period. The entire presentation and question-and-answer period is videotaped for later coding and analysis.

The oral communication ability is composed of six indicators; each indicator can be coded as a zero, one, or two level. A total oral communication ability score is the sum of the person's scores on each of the six indicators. The presentation exercise is conducted with half of the person's executive action team present, or about six people. Each person takes a turn making their presentation and answering questions.

The group discussion exercise is a 45-minute exercise conducted with half of the executive action team. The group is given three business problems and asked to discuss each and make a recommendation to top management as to how to respond to the situations. The exercise is videotaped for later coding and analysis. The group discussion exercise is coded for: efficiency orientation, planning, initiative, attention to detail, flexibility, empathy, persuasiveness, networking, negotiating, group management, developing others, systems thinking, pattern recognition, and social objectivity. A person can be coded for having shown each ability once per business case. Self-confidence is coded for each person at the end of the one hour; each person is assessed as to how consistently and clearly he or she demonstrated self-confidence according to the codebook.

The individual interview is a one-hour critical incident interview (Flanagan, 1954; Boyatzis, 1982; Raven, 1992; Spencer & Spencer, 1993). It consists of approximately 45 minutes of an in-depth reconstruction of three to five recent events in which the student felt effective or ineffective at work or during school projects and internships; an attempt is made to have half of the incidents reported represent effective events and about half represent ineffective events. The interview is coded for all of the abilities except use of concepts, theory-building, and written communications.

The students are given the raw data, or information (e.g., the audiotape of the semi-structured interview), the scoring keys, and the coding of these exercises. The audiotapes and videotapes are coded by advanced doctoral students and faculty who have taken a graduate seminar on thematic analysis and have participated in approximately 12 days of training through a computer-based coder training program. At the end of the training, the prospective coders take a test, and only those who have passed the interrater reliability test beyond the .70 level of agreement on the 15 frequently coded abilities become coders for the course.

The self-assessment has three components: abilities, knowledge, and values. The self-assessment on knowledge occurs through a Core Requirements Self-Assessment Workbook. It provides the outlines of each of the 11 required courses, which correspond to the 11 disciplines covered in the WSOM program. Students are asked to determine the degree to which they recognize, understand, and have past formal education or work experiences using these concepts. For example, for any concept identified, the student is asked to list examples of events or times at work where they used the concept. If a student determines, or believes, that he or she has such familiarity with more than 50% of the concepts in a particular required course, he or she is encouraged to either take a test to determine a waiver of the course or meet with a faculty member from that department to determine the possibility of a waiver. If a student waives one of the required courses, he or she can take an extra elective at any point in their program.

The second self-assessment occurs through the Self-Assessment of Abilities Workbook. Students are asked to assess themselves on each ability prior to receiving the information from the assessment instruments and exercises.

The third self-assessment involves values. The student examines his or her value orientations through the Personal Orientation Questionnaire. He or she then develops a personal vision statement and assesses the relative importance of various specific values through a survey.

Others' views of their abilities and knowledge is encouraged and required for their written analysis (i.e., the various homework assignments requiring interpretation of the "three voices" of information). Students are asked to solicit information from members of their executive action team, colleagues at work, family, and friends as to their perceived strengths and weaknesses. A version of the Self-Assessment of Abilities Workbook is provided, without labels and the detail requested from the student, for collection of this information from others.

The feedback and interpretation component is designed to allow the student to set their own pace. Discussion in the executive action team is among a group of students who are all going through the same process at the same time. The faculty and facilitators take steps to ensure that individuals can determine when, if, and how they discuss or invite discussion of their information. The only exception to this involves the discussion of observations of information generated in "public settings" that is videotaped, such as the group discussion exercise or the presentation exercise. The scores and assessments are provided only to the student. The only other people aware of the information are the facilitators and faculty of the course. No one is allowed to see or examine the information without the student's invitation and permission. The process allows for individual students to seek out the facilitator and faculty for separate conversations, if desired.

The executive action teams are groups of 10 to 12 students. The students are randomly assigned to the teams to maximize diversity, avoid people forming groups with others they already know, and avoid groups being formed of people who are comfortable with their similarity to each other. Each team has a facilitator and corporate executive advisor. The facilitator is typically an advanced doctoral student, or sometimes a faculty member, with training and experience in small groups, career counseling, stimulating learning, and guiding structured experiences. The corporate executive advisor is either a CEO, president, or executive director of an organization or reports to someone with that title if the organization is sufficiently large. The executive advisor may be from the private, public, health care, or education sector, and is not to be confused with members of the mentor program, in which each student develops a relationship with a middle-level manager or advanced professional. The team assignments during the first semester include work during the Managerial Assessment and Development course and other selected activities. One of the objectives of the executive action team is to help in the building of a sense of peer group, which is considered to be the most potent source of influence on growth and development during college years (Astin, 1993).

During the second semester, team assignments may include special developmental activities to be decided by the team members, such as oral communications workshops, negotiating workshops, and so forth. It is also expected that team assignments during the second semester will include discussion and integration of material covered in the various courses taken and experiences in their own work organizations, such as study groups and tutorials.

Toward the end of the course, each student develops an individualized Learning Plan to maximize their use of the resources and course offerings at the WSOM and to stimulate a process of self-directed learning. The Learning Plan is reviewed and approved by the facilitator and faculty to ensure compliance with the MBA degree requirements. It builds upon the student's previous academic and work experiences and current capabilities and knowledge in order to ensure the most effective and efficient use of the MBA experience. The Learning Plan should become the student's document and guide. It is hoped that the student would modify their Learning Plan each semester. These modifications might include changing plans, adding learning objectives not previously identified, deleting those learning objectives already accomplished, and so forth.

At the last class, students are asked to complete a course evaluation and provide their permission to allow the use of their information in research and/or in the training of future faculty and facilitators of the course. If any student does not give permission, their individual information is destroyed after completion of the course. If a student gives permission, steps are taken to protect their confidentiality for the duration of the studies, which are currently conceived as 50 years.

Relationship to the WSOM Themes
Within the WSOM overall theme of "creating economic, intellectual, and human value," the primary purpose of this course is to create human and intellectual value. By helping students learn how to increase their own capability and how to help others add to their current capability, students are adding to their value and others' value as human resources. Since people create economic and intellectual value, we believe that helping

people increase their capability and the capability of others is a prerequisite to the creation of economic and intellectual value.

The course helps students learn about and actually create, or add, value through helping them learn a method for assessing and developing knowledge, abilities, and values. This method will be of use to them throughout their careers as a stimulus to lifelong learning. The course experiences help to create human value by directly addressing a number of key abilities. Working in the executive action teams provides many opportunities to give and receive feedback and to offer help and guidance to each other. The students work on communications skills while discussing the various topics and aspects of the course. Since the executive action team is composed of 12 diverse students, they learn about the differences in how people from different backgrounds, cultures, genders, and other social groups hear, interpret, and act upon information and actions of others. Interactions with their executive advisor, as well as interactions with their colleagues in the executive action team, provide practice in enhancing their ability to build and use social networks. Creating their own Learning Plan and helping others to do likewise enhances their planning ability.

Working with others in the executive action team also addresses the WSOM theme of "developing the manager as leader and team member." The WSOM theme of "stimulating professionalism, integrity, and social responsibility" is an integral part of the course at several levels. First, students learn and confront integrity in terms of learning about themselves. The courage to candidly engage in self-examination and question beliefs and assumptions previously held about oneself requires integrity. Second, the theme of social responsibility is discussed in terms of a person's responsibility to other students in terms of giving and receiving feedback (i.e., listening and sharing insights and views).

Reactions to the Course

Reactions to the Course from Students
Students evaluate the Managerial Assessment and Development course on a five-point scale from "dissatisfied to satisfied." Although many students valued the course, their frustration and difficulty in coming to terms with information about their abilities from all sources initially led too many to question the usefulness of the course. This led to course modification. Alumni, in giving recruiting presentations to current students about their organizations, have often remarked about the importance of the

issues raised and addressed in this course, and how their appreciation of it increased as they re-entered the workforce.

Regression analysis on the ratings of the course showed that, although ratings of faculty were important, the loadings of the ratings of the facilitator and executive action team activities confirmed student comments about their importance. The role of the facilitator is critical in creating and stimulating group development and a constructive focus on course activities. The quality and preparation of facilitators is essential in enabling the course to meet its objectives and the students' needs.

Student activism increased. The number of student clubs has increased. Student-initiated participation in faculty deliberations has increased. Students also initiated and developed a student's honor code (i.e., a code of ethics).

Following the development of their Learning Plans, students participate in ability-development workshops at a significantly greater rate than previously, and demand that many more such workshops be offered than they previously did.

From Faculty

Faculty have continued to show enthusiasm and support for the new program. Although not every faculty member is excited about this new course, and some still quietly question its appropriateness in higher education, the overall mood is supportive. Two faculty committees have been formed to address increased developmental opportunities for abilities and "the second transcript."

The "second transcript," or "portfolio," aims to provide recruiters with a portfolio alongside the normal academic transcript focusing on courses and grades. This will document the person's possession and use of the various abilities. While some of these abilities may be apparent during the first interview, many will not be. Typically, recruiters have 20 or so minutes to conduct an initial interview, assuming of course the student has passed the "paper screen." It is expected that recruiters will view this second transcript as a significant aid in accomplishing their task.

In the earlier stages of design of the course, faculty brought their differing models of abilities (or competencies) into the discussions of "which" abilities should be in our model. Discussions of empirical validity, appropriateness to a desired future world, and epistemological preferences took time. At the same time, there were still faculty who did not believe in the power of competencies (called "abilities" in the WOSM model) to affect managerial performance. Differences in work experience, academic discipline, and epistemological differences resulted in some intellectually exciting discussions about these issues and others that were frustrating.

Once the pilot of this course was complete, preparations for the "scale-up" for full implementation were a logistical nightmare. Recruiting and training 20 facilitators, 8 coders, 7 faculty, and 20 executive advisors in the spirit of the course as well as the mechanics took a great deal of effort. Acquiring the appropriate equipment for the new level of videotaping and audiotaping activity, as well as the dilemma of finding secure places to store equipment and student files, including large numbers of tapes, became organization-wide issues. Finding rooms to conduct the course, with each executive action team needing a room sufficient to allow 13 people plus equipment, involved numerous staff of the school and an expanding number of "discussions" with faculty whose classes had to be moved from their typical classrooms.

The initial implementation of the course, described in this chapter, was clearly not the end of the story but merely a stage in the process. Continuous improvement in the course structure; materials; the training of facilitators, coders, and faculties; and perceived integration into the MBA program are necessary. They demand an expanding group of people who are strongly committed to the course and eager to lead the effort.

From Executives

The executives involved in the executive action teams as executive advisors have been tremendously excited. They offer unsolicited testimonials of their excitement at meetings and approach faculty and the dean in restaurants and cultural or entertainment events outside the school. At the end of each year about 80% of the executive advisors volunteer for a further year.

Formal Evaluation

Background

The few formal attempts to systematically examine the effect of management development have generated confusing results. Most of the time, any positive effects of training and development programs atrophy or extinguish within six to twelve months of program completion. We appear able to help people develop skills, such as listening or planning through training. We appear able to help people become socialized into corporate cultures and experience pride of belonging to an organization through training, special events, rewards, and recognition programs. But the evidence and confidence that we can develop managerial talent (i.e., the competencies or abilities) is scarce, elusive, and disappointing.

Only a few management schools have compared their graduates to their students at the time of entry into the program (Albanese et al., 1990). Many more have, for example, studied their alumni or employers and prospective employers. Some schools have examined the student change from specific courses (Bigelow, 1991; Specht & Sandlin, 1991). More student change outcome studies have been conducted in under-graduate programs (Winter et al., 1982; Mentkowski & Strait, 1983; Mentkowski et al., 1991; Pascarella & Terenzini, 1991; Astin, 1993; Banta, 1993).

Some MBA programs result in improvement in some abilities (Boyatzis & Sokol, 1982; Development Dimensions International [DDI], 1985). Boyatzis and Sokol showed that students had significantly increased on 40% and 50% of the variables assessed in two MBA programs, while DDI reported that students in the two MBA programs in their sample signifi-cantly increased on 44% of the variables assessed. They also decreased significantly on 10% of the variables in the Boyatzis and Sokol study. Unfortunately, the samples were not random and may have been subject to volunteer effects. Given the common criticisms of MBA graduates, it is difficult to believe that many MBA programs were attaining even these modest gains.

Boyatzis and Renio (1989) and Boyatzis, Renio-McKee, and Thomp-son (1995) reported results from two outcome studies of student changes among full- and part-time MBA students at the Weatherhead School of Management in the late 1980s. These results showed that graduating full-time students had significantly more analytic skills and self-confidence than at entry. There was strong evidence of improvement on 32% (6 of 19) of the abilities (i.e., competencies) assessed and a significant decrease on one ability. The part-time students improved on analytic abilities and flexibility. They showed strong evidence of improvement on 21% (4 of 19) of the abilities assessed and a significant decrease on two abilities.

Boyatzis (1991) compared the student-change outcome data from the first of these studies in 1987–1988 with faculty intent. Data on objectives were collected from each faculty member. One of the instruments was the same as a measure used in the student-change studies. Comparison of faculty objectives with student-change data showed remarkable similarity. This was both good news and bad news. Students improved on those abilities that the faculty had targeted, or said they addressed in their courses, such as information analysis and quantitative analysis. Unfortunately, on skills the faculty did not feel they addressed, such as leadership and goal setting, the students did not show improvement.

Figure 19.2

Value-Added to *Full-Time* Students from the Old Vs. the New MBA Programs

Evidence of Value-Added	Old Program			New Program		
	Goal and Action Mgt.	People Mgt.	Analytic Reasoning	Goal and Action Mgt.	People Mgt.	Analytic Reasoning
STRONG EVIDENCE		Self-conf.	Use of concepts; Systems thinking Quantitative analysis; Use of tech.; Written com.	Efficiency orientation; Planning; Initiative Flexibility	Self-conf.; Networking; Developing others Oral com.	Use of concepts; Systems thinking Pattern recog.; Social obj.; Quantitative analysis; Use of tech.; Written com.
SOME EVIDENCE	Efficiency orientation; Initiative; Flexibility	Empathy; Networking	Social Obj.	Self-control; Attention to detail; Negotiating	Group mgt.; Empathy; Persuasive	
NO EVIDENCE	Planning (Attention to detail & Self-control were not coded)	Persuasive; Negotiating; Developing others; Oral com.				
NEGATIVE EVIDENCE			Pattern recog. (verbal)			

Value-Added to *Part-Time* Students from the Old Vs. the New MBA Programs

Evidence of Value-Added	Old Program			New Program		
	Goal and Action Mgt.	People Mgt.	Analytic Reasoning	Goal and Action Mgt.	People Mgt.	Analytic Reasoning
STRONG EVIDENCE	Flexibility		Systems thinking; Quantitative analysis Social objectivity	Efficiency orientation; Planning; Initiative Flexibility	Empathy; Self-conf.; Persuaive; Networking Oral Com.; Developing others	Use of concepts; Social obj.; Use of tech. Pattern recognition; Quantitative analysis; Written com.
SOME EVIDENCE	Efficiency orientation	Negotiating	Written Com.	Attention to detail; Self-control	Group mgt	Systems thinking
NO EVIDENCE	Planning; Initiative (Attention to detail & Self-control were not coded)	Persuasive; Self-conf.; Networking; Group mgt.; Developing others; Oral com.	Use of concepts; Pattern recognition			
NEGATIVE EVIDENCE		Empathy	Use of tech.			

Design of Formal Evaluation of the Current Program

As part of a projected 50-year longitudinal study, seven cohorts of students are being assessed as they graduate from the program (i.e., four samples of graduating full-time and three samples of graduating part-time students) and every five to seven years until they retire (Boyatzis, Wheeler, & Wright, in press).

In this part of our chapter, results from the 1992–1994 and 1993–1995 samples of full-time students, and the 1994 and 1995 studies of graduating part-time students are reviewed in the context of results from the 1987–1988 and 1988–1989 full-time and part-time students, 1990–1992 and 1991–1993 full-time samples, which were reported in detail in Boyatzis, Cowen, and Kolb (1995).

Results

As we have seen, all entering students complete a number of exercises and tests, including the Learning Skills Profile, the videotaped presentation exercise, the videotaped group discussion exercise, and the audiotaped critical incident interview. Similar information was collected later. Detailed comparison revealed that full-time students improved on 71%, and part-time students improving on 81%, of the abilities assessed, as summarized in Figure 19.2. There is some evidence that students improved on an

---

Note: In addition to the behavioral code used with audiotapes and videotapes, the following correspondence can be used to classify findings from the various measures used in all of the studies:

Efficiency Orientation = Learning Skills Profile (LSP) Action scale, and Thematic Apperception Test (TAT) N-Ach (McClelland, 1985);

Planning = LSP Goal Setting scale;

Initiative = LSP Initiative scale; Flexibility = LSP item 5 of the Sense-making scale;

Empathy = LSP Relationship scale and TAT N-Aff and Profile of Non-verbal Sensitivity (Rosenthal et. al., 1979);

Persuasiveness = LSP Leadership scale and TAT N-Pow; Self-confidence = LSP Total score;

Networking = LSP Relationship and Information Gathering scale;

Negotiating = LSP item 5 of the Leadership scale;

Group Management = LSP item 6 of the Leadership scale;

Developing Others = LSP Help and Goal Setting scales;

Oral Communications = LSP item 2 of the Leadership scale;

Use of Concepts = LSP Information Analysis scale;

Systems Thinking = LSP Theory scale;

Pattern Recognition = LSP Sense Making scale and for verbal pattern recognition the Test of Thematic Analysis (Winter & McClelland, 1978);

Quantitative Analysis = LSP Quantitative scale;

Use of Technology = LSP Technology scale;

Social Objectivity = LSP item 1 of the Information Gathering scale; and

Written Communications = LSP item 2 of the Information Analysis scale.

additional 29% of the abilities assessed in the full-time program and 14% in the part-time program.

Overall, this is not only a dramatic increase in impact on abilities from the old MBA program, but it is also substantially greater than the impact of other MBA programs assessed in various studies. The composite results suggest that competencies can be developed, in particular those abilities related to managerial effectiveness. Since positive impact on these abilities was a major objective in the redesign of the curriculum, the results also support the idea that faculty did effectively change the curriculum, which suggests that other human resource development professionals can similarly change their programs and have greater impact.

Design Issues for Management Schools

There were 10 major concerns in the development of the WOSM program, and it may be important to faculty in other schools setting out to develop or implement similar courses to have our reflections upon them.

1. Basing Personal Development Programs on Self-assessments Alone versus All the Information Available in the Three Voices of Data

The attempt to broaden the base of information used by students in designing their personal development programs is grounded in the observation and finding that self-assessment is filled with error (Goleman, 1985). Others have attempted to address this problem by introducing data from assessment centers. The addition of information from coders trained to high reliabilities on the coding system, the coding of video and audiotapes, and feedback from the members of the executive action teams goes, we believe, one step further, providing students with more opportunities to help them confirm, disconfirm, and clarify the information from various sources.

2. Feedback Alone versus Time Devoted to Interpretation

Use of assessment centers often results in more time being spent on assessment than on feedback. We hope we have shifted the balance in favor of feedback and interpretation. When little time is devoted to interpretation, students often do not change their prior understanding of concepts such as self-confidence, empathy, and persuasiveness. For example, in such interpretation discussions, students argue about whether networking is a useful ability or merely office politicking (and therefore "bad"). Comparison of their experiences at work (i.e., thinking about managers they have observed) and examination of each other's behavior enables students to further refine their understanding of such concepts and arrive at an appropriate assessment of their own levels of ability and their probable importance in their future careers.

3. Ad Hoc Opportunities for Growth versus a Detailed Learning Plan

It is apparent that merely offering students assessment, feedback, and interpretation would not result in the best use being made of the MBA program. People are more likely to make use of their experiences if they form part of an intentional plan for development (Kolb & Boyatzis, 1970b). The development of a Learning Plan provokes deep thought and specificity about future career interests and a structure for thinking about the best use of the time available. The Learning Plan should also provide a basis and a method for ongoing (i.e., lifelong) self-directed development. Finally, it functions as a type of learning contract for the student (Knowles, 1986).

A number of schools have explored the use of competence (ability) development courses, often called leadership development. Whether in modules, residencies (i.e., workshops), or special luncheon sessions, participants typically engage in training or skill-building activities directly, without prior assessment or the development of a learning plan. Although it may be easier for faculty to fit such courses into their framework of expectations about what courses should look like, students often find them frustrating, reporting that they do not understand their relevance or utility, or that they become bored. The latter is perhaps because they feel they have already developed and refined the skills being nurtured.

From our perspective, these courses are not engaging self-directed change and learning to the extent possible. Development is not an automatic process: People must change themselves. Others cannot do it for them. For this reason, they must *want* to change and must take the initiative in doing so. They must conceptualize how and why they want to change themselves. They must have clear targets or images of desired states (i.e., learning or development goals) to change toward.

Self-directed change and learning is also a much better use of time than alternatives. If one believes that development of managerial skills can occur only while engaged in coursework or workshops, one has committed oneself to an awesome learning or delivery schedule! If a student discovers a discrepancy between his or her ideal state and current state on a skill, formulates a goal for change, and constructs a plan for working toward that goal, he or she can be using any or all of his or her experiences: inside and outside of class, in part- or full-time jobs, in projects and internships, in clubs and associations, in leisure activities, in civic and volunteer social service or religious or community activities, or at play.

4. Workshop versus Course Format

Among faculty, discussion of whether activities such as assessment and developmental planning are "credible, proper, academic experiences" becomes most intense when a number of institutional and pedagogic issues are raised: a course versus a workshop; semester-long versus intensive work; required versus elective courses; and graded versus pass/fail work. For the same reasons, there is a heated debate about the question of whether the activity should be a fully-fledged academic course. Often, the search for academic credibility on the part of faculty is an integral part of these activities becoming an accepted part of the curriculum.

In parallel with this, it is often difficult to keep students' attention if their work does not form part of a course. Their prior socialization into "education" leads them to want to be "taught" through a course format. This often leads to low participation rates in activities that do not conform to traditional academic structures. Yet experiential learning, which is necessary for skill development, appears as confusing, or possibly even threatening, to students in such contexts. They may say they are "distracting" them from their "real" academic activities. Developing ways of engaging students' implicit theories of management, work, learning, and careers seems to be a useful starting point in challenging the effects of prior socialization. Making their implicit theory or expectations of learning a topic for class discussion seems important, but again difficult, especially in a workshop format.

5. Intensive Experience versus a Semester in Length

A full semester appears necessary for the preparation of learning plans for several reasons. First, students need time to absorb, reflect, and integrate the information. Changes in self-image do not come easily, and MBA students are no different from other students in this regard. In addition, since previous research has shown that a supportive interpersonal and social environment is important for experimentation and learning of this sort, students need time to build relationships within their executive action teams.

6. Elective versus Required Course

The desirability of having this type of course as a required course rather than an elective course comes from the observation that the students who volunteer for such developmental assessments are often those that already have many abilities and knowledge areas. The students who lack numerous abilities are typically least likely to be aware of their deficits, and therefore would not want to do something to improve. For example, the engineer who has been technically trained and has worked in a technical environment may not think that interpersonal and communication abilities are important to management. He or she may not have been exposed to "effective" management at work and have not seen any role models. Such a student would not utilize one of their elective slots for a developmental assessment elective, especially when they could take an extra computer applications or finance course!

Another reason to make the course required is to encourage all students to recognize their strengths and attend to development of their "flat sides." That is, seek to address abilities and knowledge areas that are important for effectiveness as a manager but for which they are currently deficient.

7. Pass/Fail versus Graded Work

The granting of grades provides a set of benchmarks for students during the course. Pass/fail coursework does not. Since the course is different from most academic courses (i.e., it emphasizes self-exploration; intra- and interpersonal processes; and addresses development of the whole person, not just acquisition of knowledge), students find it useful to have assignments graded during the early and middle parts of the course. Pass/fail work, unfortunately, is not often viewed as empowering, but as a message that the work is of less importance, particularly when students are wrestling with conflicting time demands from other assignments. Grades make expectations of performance clear. In our course, the grades are based on the specificity, clarity, and comprehensiveness of students' analysis and logic, not on whether they possess an ability or knowledge area.

8. Individual Development versus Social Context

Creating a social structure in which students can explore and learn appears vital to most graduate environments, but is particularly important in management schools. The models of management in technical and professional fields that supply people for management often focus on rugged individualism. Asking for help is seen as sinful; failure is equated with ignominy. In our course, students are told that they are in a relatively "safe" environment in which they can experiment and fail on the path toward learning.

Since all management jobs require working with others, the executive action teams provide opportunities for students to begin building perspectives and skills in understanding and working with others. Since they are randomly assigned to these groups, they also must deal with the diversity and heterogeneity of the groups. Hopefully, the diversity becomes a source of insight rather than a source of fear.

The executive action teams are an important learning vehicle in the course. Students use consensual validation as a method of learning about their abilities and knowledge. The utility of small groups to facilitate learning was first noted in Western civilization in ancient Greece, replicated in the tutorial concept at Oxford and Cambridge Universities, and most recently by faculty at the International Management School at Buckingham in the United Kingdom (Prideaux & Ford, 1988a&b), where they are called learning teams. For all of these reasons, the social context of learning appears to benefit from establishing executive action teams and using the course structure as a way to help them get started.

9. Connectedness

It was felt that students should feel connected to others and the school. Previously, there were too many convenient ways a person could become isolated. The development of relationships within the executive action team during the course begins a set of relationships, and at least a process, that is useful throughout the remainder of their program and later in life. In evaluation surveys, students often report that members of their executive action teams got together outside of class to study together for another course, meet with their executive advisor, have a social event, or engage in some other developmental activity during the semester. It is hoped that most of the members of the executive action team will continue to meet for such activities.

10. Lockstep versus Individualized Curriculum Plans

Lastly, a lockstep program (i.e., one in which all students take the same required courses in the same sequence) would be philosophically inconsistent with the WSOM new MBA program. Therefore, each student has the opportunity to individualize their course selection within guidelines established by the faculty of each department.

Closing Comment

While faculty exhort students to challenge "what is known and go beyond the limits of current understanding," it is difficult to do it ourselves. Years in graduate school are a long socialization period, reinforced through the years of assistant professorship and the journey to tenure. It is no wonder that our assumptions about what and how to provide graduate education are deeply rooted and relatively unyielding. The spirit of the WSOM MBA program and the Managerial Assessment and Development course is to explore, experiment, and learn better ways to prepare our students for management careers. We have rediscovered an atmosphere of excitement and learning among the faculty that facilitates creative encounters with other stakeholder groups in our community. This has been extended in executive education with inclusion of the course in the Professional Fellows Program, designed for 45- to 65-year-old advanced professionals seeking intellectual stimulation during life and career transitions; the longitudinal studies show that students in this program have similar results to other students in the WSOM MBA program (Ballou, Bowers, Boyatzis, & Kolb, 1999).

The number of schools exploring methods to develop "the whole student" is growing exponentially each year. A candid exchange of results and experiences "in process" is vital to our growth. We offer the story of our experience in this spirit, not as a set of answers we have found, but as a set of discoveries that are sometimes frustrating and often exciting.

Note

1. This is a much modified and updated version of Chapter 4 from Boyatzis et al., *Innovation in Professional Education: Steps in a Journey from Learning to Teaching* (San Francisco: Jossey-Bass, 1995). A short version of that chapter previously appeared in 1994 in the *Journal of Management Education, 18* (3), 304–323. A considerably longer account, summarizing other aspects of the work of Richard Boyatzis and his colleagues at Case Western's School of Management appeared in 1996 in *Capability, 2* (2), 25–41. Richard Boyatzis was previously managing director of McBer. It has therefore been possible here to omit summaries of the work of McBer that is presented more fully by other McBer authors elsewhere in this book.

The author would like to thank Dr. Harry Evarts, formerly vice president of the American Management Associations (AMA), for his support and colleagueship in developing the first version of this course in 1979 for the AMA Competency Development Program.

References

Albanese, R. (Chair), Bernardin, H. J., Connor, P. E., Dobbins, G. H., Ford, R. C., Harris, M. M., Licata, B. J., Miceli, M. P., Porter, L. W., & Ulrich, D. O. (1990). *Outcome Measurement and Management Education: An Academy of Management Task Force Report.* Presentation at the Annual Academy of Management Meeting, San Francisco, CA.

Astin, A. W. (1993). *What Matters in College? Four Critical Years.* San Francisco: Jossey-Bass.

Ballou, R., Bowers, D., Boyatzis, R. E., & Kolb, D. A. (1999). Fellowship in lifelong learning: An executive development program for advanced professionals. *Journal of Management Education, 23* (4), 338–354

Banta, T. W. (Ed.). (1993). *Making a Difference: Outcomes of a Decade of Assessment in Higher Education.* San Francisco, CA: Jossey-Bass.

Bigelow, J. D. (Ed.). (1991). *Managerial Skills: Explorations in Practical Knowledge.* Newbury Park, CA: Sage.

Boyatzis, R. E. (1982). *The Competent Manager: A Model for Effective Performance.* New York: John Wiley & Sons.

Boyatzis, R. E. (1991). Faculty intent and student outcome. In J. D. Bigelow, (Ed.), *Managerial Skills: Explorations in Practical Knowledge.* Newbury Park, CA: Sage.

Boyatzis, R. E. (1994). Developing the whole student: A required MBA course called Managerial Assessment and Development. *Journal of Management Education, 18* (3), 304–323.

Boyatzis, R. E. (1999). Self-directed change and learning as a necessary meta-competency for success and effectiveness in the twenty-first century. In R. R. Sims & J. G. Veres III (Eds.). *Keys to Employee Success in Coming Decades* (pp. 15–32). Westport, CT: Quorum Books.

Boyatzis, R. E. (in press). Developing emotional intelligence. In C. Cherniss, R. E. Boyatzis, & M. Elias (Eds.), *Research and Theoretical Advances in Emotional Intelligence: Volume 1.*

Boyatzis, R. E., Cowen, S. S., & Kolb, D. A. (1995). *Innovation in Professional Education: Steps on a Journey from Teaching to Learning.* San Francisco, CA: Jossey-Bass.

Boyatzis, R. E., & Kolb, D. A. (1991). Assessing individuality in learning: The learning skills profile. *Educational Psychology, 11* (3&4), 279–295.

Boyatzis, R. E., & Kolb, D. A. (1995). Beyond learning styles to learning skills: The executive skills profile. *Journal of Managerial Psychology, 10* (5), 3–17.

Boyatzis, R. E., & Kolb, D. A. (1999). Performance, learning, and development as modes of growth and adaptation throughout our lives and careers. In M. Peiperl, M. B. Arthur, R. Coffee, & T. Morris (Eds.), *Career Frontiers: New Conceptions of Working Lives* (pp. 76–98). London: Oxford University Press.

Boyatzis, R. E., Murphy, A., & Wheeler, J. (2000). Philosophy as the missing link between values and behavior. *Psychological Reports, 86*, 47–64.

Boyatzis, R. E., & Renio, A. (1989). The impact of an MBA program on managerial abilities. *Journal of Management Development, 8* (5), 66–77.

Boyatzis, R. E., Renio-McKee, A., & Thompson, L. (1995). Past accomplishments: Establishing the impact and baseline of earlier programs. In R. E. Boyatzis, S. S. Cowen, & D. A. Kolb, *Innovation in Professional Education: Steps on a Journey from Teaching to Learning.* San Francisco, CA: Jossey-Bass.

Boyatzis, R. E., & Sokol, M. (1982). *A Pilot Project to Assess the Feasibility of Assessing Skills and Personal Characteristics in Collegiate Business Programs.* St. Louis, MO: Report to the AACSB.

Boyatzis, R. E., Wheeler, J., & Wright, R. (in press). *Competency development in graduate education: A longitudinal perspective.* Conference Proceedings of the First World Conference on Self-Directed Learning, GIRAT, Montreal.

Campbell, J. P., Dunnette, M. D., Lawler, E. E., & Weick, K. E. (1970). *Managerial Behavior, Performance, and Effectiveness.* New York: McGraw-Hill.

Development Dimensions International (DDI). (1985). *Final Report: Phase III.* St. Louis, MO: Report to the AACSB.

Dreyfus, C. (1990). *Scientists and engineers as effective managers: A study of the development of interpersonal abilities.* Unpublished doctoral dissertation, Case Western Reserve University, Cleveland.

Flanagan, J. C. (1954). The critical incident technique. *Psychological Bulletin, 51,* 327–335.

Goleman, D. (1985). *Vital Lies, Simple Truths: The Psychology of Self-Deception.* New York: Simon and Schuster.

Hunt, D. E. (1987). *Beginning with Ourselves: In Practice, Theory, and Human Affairs.* Cambridge, MA: Brookline Books.

Knowles, M. S. (1986). *Using Learning Contracts: Practical Approaches to Individualizing and Structuring Learning.* San Francisco: Jossey-Bass.

Kolb, D. A. (1971). *A cybernetic model of human change and growth.* Unpublished Working Paper #526-71. Sloan School of Management, MIT.

Kolb, D. A. (1984). *Experiential Learning: Experience as the Source of Learning and Development.* Englewood Cliffs, NJ: Prentice Hall.

Kolb, D. A., & Boyatzis, R. E. (1970a). On the dynamics of the helping relationship. *Journal of Applied Behavioral Science, 6* (3), 267–289.

Kolb, D. A., & Boyatzis, R. E. (1970b). Goal-setting and self-directed behavior change. *Human Relations, 23* (5), 439–457.

Kotter, J. P. (1982). *The General Managers.* New York: Free Press.

Kotter, J. P. (1988). *The Leadership Factor.* New York: Free Press.

Luthans, F., Hodgetts, R. M., & Rosenkrantz, S. A. (1988). *Real Managers.* Cambridge, MA: Ballinger Press.

Mainemelis, C., Boyatzis, R. E., & Kolb, D. A. (1999). Learning styles and adaptive flexibility: Experiential learning theory. ORBH Working Paper, 99-7.

McCall, M. W., Lombardo, M. M., & Morrison A. M. (1988). *The Lessons of Experience: How Successful Executives Develop on the Job.* Lexington, MA: Lexington Books.

McClelland, D. C. (1985). *Human Motivation.* Glenview, IL: Scott, Foresman.

Mentkowski, M., & Strait, M. (1983). *A Longitudinal Study of Student Change in Cognitive Development, Learning Styles, and Generic Abilities in an Outcome-Centered Liberal Arts Curriculum.* Final Report to the National Institutes of Education from Alverno College, Milwaukee, WI.

Pascarella, E. T., & Terenzini, P. T. (1991). *How College Affects Students: Findings and Insights from Twenty Years of Research.* San Francisco, CA: Jossey-Bass.

Prideaux, G., & Ford, J. (1988a). Management development: Competencies, contracts, teams, and work-based learning. *Journal of Management Development, 7* (3), 13–21.

Prideaux, G., & Ford, J. (1988b). Management development: Competencies, contracts, teams, and work-based learning. *Journal of Management Development, 7* (1), 56–68.

Raven, J. (1992). A model of competence, motivation, and behavior, and a paradigm for assessment. In H. Berlak, F. M. Newmann, E. Adams, D. A. Archbald, T. Burgess, J. Raven, & T. A. Romberg, *Toward a New Science of Educational Testing and Assessment.* Albany, NY: SUNY Press.

Rosenthal, R., Hall, J. A., Archer, D., di Matteo, M.R. et al. (1979). *The PONS Test Manual: Profile of Nonverbal Sensitivity.* New York: Irvington Publishers.

Specht, L., & Sandlin, P. (1991). The differential effects of experiential learning activities and traditional lecture classes in accounting. *Simulations and Gaming, 22(2)*, 196–210.

Spencer, L. M., & Spencer, S. M. (1993). *Competence at Work: Models for Superior Performance.* New York: John Wiley & Sons.

Winter, D. G., & McClelland, D.C. (1978). Thematic analysis: An empirically derived measure of effects of liberal arts. *Journal of Educational Psychology, 70* (1), 8–18.

Winter, D. G., McClelland, D. C., & Stewart, A. J. (1982). *A New Case for the Liberal Arts.* San Francisco, CA: Jossey-Bass.

Chapter 20

Essentials of Action Learning

Reg W. Revans, 1978
Edited and revised by David Botham, 1998

Editorial Introduction

This paper remains remarkably fresh and clearly indicates many of the constraints that must be overcome if one is to have effective competency-oriented education—"education" being a term which, it may be important to remind ourselves, means "developing" or "drawing out", not "putting in." The needs (however problematic) to move from "teaching" to "facilitating growth," to individualise developmental programmes in relation to people's motives, and to resist the temptation to think that all should master fundamental bodies of knowledge could not be more clear. Reading between the lines, it could not be more apparent why "action learning" has so often been corrupted into its opposite and why authentic versions have invariably been rejected by institutions of higher education.

The Assumptions of Action Learning

Action learning makes the following assumptions:

1. The logical structure (paradigm) of the learning process is assimilated to that of the conscious (quasi-rational) decision and both are assimilated to the scientific method.

This paper was previously published in this form in *Link-Up with Action Learning*, Vol. 1, No.2, August-October, 1997, pp. 2–4. It is reprinted here by kind permission of the author and editor.

2. In consequence, there can be no learning unless the subject receives inputs about its own outputs, or feedback about its performance; to learn anything the subject must see the effects of using the new knowledge. Hence the principle of insufficient mandate "without authority to change one's ideas about the world one cannot change the world itself"; the distinctions made between research, action, and learning are false.

3. Subjects learn only of their own volition and never at the will of others (unless this is accommodated into the subject's volition for the time being as a bribe, prize, or incentive) they are not taught by others, but learn "within themselves," largely by the reorganisation or extension of what they already know.

4. The volition to learn is most readily engendered by the lure of success (in managerial terms, the desire to seize some opportunity) or by the dread of calamity (in the same terms, to solve some problem). Such opportunities and such problems must be "real," in the sense that they engage the personal value systems of the learners, offering real rewards for success and real penalties for failure. Learning exercises (so called) that do not engage personal value systems may actually prevent subjects from perceiving what their own value systems may be, and those who do not know what they finally believe in can never take real decisions about real problems in real time. Such learning exercises (so called) lack authenticity and encourage self-deception.

5. During the efforts to seize such opportunities or to solve such problems subjects may need to be conscious of what they are doing, in the sense of being able to describe their behaviour in words or symbols, what they believe themselves to be doing (such as in defining their objectives) may appear very differently to external observers, and a comparison between two or more different sets of impressions may (by invoking item 2 above) already start the learning process before any visible trial action is taken.

6. In action learning programmes these external observers are *without exception* other action learners, and the action learning set (that is, the cardinal element of action learning) provides that subjects learn with and from each other during the nascent interchanges that both precede and follow trial action in the field of the opportunity or of the problem.

7. The role of the professional teacher in action learning is thus confined to providing (or helping to provide) the conditions in which

subjects can learn with and from each other. The learning of the subject derives, on the one hand, from the criticism, advice, and support of the other and equal subjects in the set, and, on the other hand, from the outcome of the real-time action taken upon the real world of the problem or opportunity (except that, from time to time, the teacher may be able to supply the demand of the subjects as they arise from their operational endeavours).

8. Action learning has no syllabus, no texts, and no experts; it will make use of any existing idea (howsoever absurd) since it seeks one goal only: "Can we do what we set out to do, and by what evidence do we know whether we have done it?" In achieving this the utility (validity) of our ideas are automatically tested, precisely as they are in the application of the scientific method.

Implications for Applying Action Learning

Action learning must be specifically adapted for the chosen field of its application, and the following conditions must be observed:

1. Professional practitioners as a class are characterised by their obligation to take responsibility for anticipating and influencing the future; they are supposed to plan ahead and so work in conditions of ignorance, risk, and confusion.

2. Practitioners must, on this account, develop an ability to identify what are likely to be the most fertile questions to ask when nobody around them knows (or can be expected to know) what to do; there is a little evidence to suggest that too great a loyalty to some particular branch of knowledge (or expertise) may inhibit this freedom to choose fresh and unfamiliar lines of enquiry.

3. Since we do not know how to develop the general capacity to identify what may be useful questions in conditions of ignorance, risk, and confusion, we can only proceed empirically, namely, by putting professional practitioners into such conditions to attack real opportunities or problems and to observe the outcome.

4. Such a line of support demands that we accept working under the same conditions as those from whom we expect that support. This leads to our having to adopt certain organisational forms into which our learning processes are to fit; they are described as "the learning community, the project, the set, the induction programme" and so forth; it also means the allocation of specific roles to a variety of

participants, such as the steering committee, the sponsors, the clients, the fellows, (perhaps, the coordinators), the set advisers, and, above all, the initiators.

5. Within these conditions imposed by the treatment of real-world tasks, there is some freedom of design in the project or exercise to develop the general capacity to pose fertile questions in conditions of ignorance, risk, and confusion. Since this is an empirical essay set to particular practitioners to tackle some task about which nobody knows what to do (at least at the outset), there are four options open to the designer:

(a) a familiar task tackled in a familiar setting (of which the most evident example is the practitioner's own job);

(b) a familiar task tackled in an unfamiliar setting (the Hospitals Internal Communications Project exploited this option in exchanging teams to visit each others' places of work);

(c) an unfamiliar task in a familiar setting (action learning programmes internal to the same enterprise, such as within GEC, enable those normally employed in one function, say, production, to tackle the opportunities or problems in another, say, personnel or marketing);

(d) an unfamiliar task in an unfamiliar setting. The original Interuniversity Programme in Belgium was of this nature and continues with minor variations to be so. One variation is that each practitioner works on two tasks in two unfamiliar settings with two fellow colleagues; each fellow is *primo* on his/her "own" project task and *secondo* on the other.

6. Previous experience (which is always being added to) suggests that the fellows (participant-managers) in action learning programmes may be helped by brief preparatory (induction) seminars intended to convey:

(a) a brief vocabulary of debate thought useful in action learning sets; this emphasises six concepts—decision, information, risk, learning, system, and value;

(b) the distinction between diagnosis and therapy in the treatment of tasks; these become the distinction between the design and the negotiation of the decisions or strategy; elementary diagnostic (design) questions are:

What are we trying to do?

What is stopping us from doing it?

What might we be able to do about it?

Elementary therapeutic (negotiation) questions are:

Who knows about this task?

Who cares about this task?

Who can do anything about this task?

(c) the concept of the sequential development of the project, in order to permit the most economical use of the time available to the practitioners in tackling their tasks. There are, it seems, six identifiable stages—analysis, development, procurement (forming the diagnostic phase), assembly, application, and review (forming the therapeutic phase);

7. Action learning programmes are not, in general, intended to tackle puzzles, namely, questions to which an answer may be said to exist even if that answer is difficult to find. Action learning is intended to help to develop the ability to tackle problems or opportunities, for which different persons, all of whom are experienced, intelligent, and motivated, might well advocate different courses of action, all reasonable; it is in the set discussions of such differences that the participants are more clearly aware of their own value systems and of their own obliquities of perception (option 5b) may help with complex puzzles;

8. Action learning sets are not supposed to be psychotherapeutic sessions, dedicated to self-understanding by self-disclosure (although they are bound to contribute to this), nor are they clinics run partly by the participants, partly by a set adviser, to explain to the practitioners their responses to each other in terms of such-and-such models of individual and group psychology (although they are bound to make each more aware of the impact he/she has upon others . . . at least upon those particular others); there are, it seems, so many models of inter-personal behaviour that it would confuse most sets, if their members were to become aware of how many possible such models are mentioned in the literature. It is preferable for the exchanges between the participants to be confined strictly to the progress of the projects in hand, for which the six questions of 6(b) above provide all the operational discipline necessary for clear thought.

Chapter 21

Inputs and Outcomes:
The Experience of Independent Study
at the North East London Polytechnic

John Stephenson

*There is an awful truthfulness about independent study. It is about yourself
and there is no getting away from it. (Former student)*

Introduction

In 1974, the North East London Polytechnic (NELP) gained approval
from the UK body then responsible for quality control in higher education
for a course that had no specified content, no prescribed reading lists, no
timetables, and no formal examinations. The course proposal consisted
of a rationale, a set of procedures and criteria for validating programmes
of study prepared by students themselves, and arrangements for the provision of specialist supervision and basic skill support. Students had to
plan and negotiate approval for their own programmes leading to the
new award, thus turning traditional practice of course design and control
on its head.

Although capability objectives were explicit in but few of the papers
prepared while the programme was being developed, most were (perhaps

This chapter is a compilation of extracts from *Capability and Quality in Higher
Education,* edited by John Stephenson and Mantz Yorke (London: Kogan Page, 1998)
and John Stephenson's Professorial Lecture delivered in 1990. In the latter, he summarised
the results from a major research project on the student experience of independent
study. We have preserved the style of the latter, as an illustrated lecture, although it jars
slightly with the tone of the earlier part of the chapter. The material from the Kogan Page
book is © Kogan Page and is reproduced with their permission.

intentionally) sufficiently ambiguous to be capable of being read as if the programme had such an orientation. But the programme was not only unusual in its (potential) objectives and manner of working; it also sought to attract students who would have had difficulty gaining entrance to, and persisting in, traditional university courses.

For these reasons, among others, a great deal of time was set aside to provide students with opportunities to think about themselves, how to get what they wanted from the programme, and how to justify any claim that they had done it. We will return to these procedures in a moment, but first it is desirable to say a little more about the emerging concept of capability that informed the development of the programme.

The Underlying Concept of Capability

The concept of capability which underlay the NELP programme first came to more general notice with the publication of its *Capability Manifesto* by the Royal Society for Arts in 1980. This focused on the limited value of education when it is seen solely as the pursuit of knowledge and intellectual skills for their own sake. "Individuals, industry and society as a whole benefit," the *Manifesto* asserted, "when all of us have the capacity to be effective in our personal, social and working lives." Capability was viewed an all-round human quality, observable in what Weaver (1994) described as the ability to engage appropriately and sensitively in "purposive and sensible" action, not just only in familiar and highly focused specialist contexts but also in response to new and changing circumstances.

Capability is not just about skills and knowledge. Taking effective and appropriate action within unfamiliar and changing circumstances involves ethics, judgements, the self-confidence to take risks, and a commitment to learn from the experience. A capable person has culture, in the sense of being able to "decide between goodness and wickedness or between beauty and ugliness" (Weaver, 1994).

Delivering Student Capability in Higher Education

Delivering student capability in higher education has major implications for the culture, structures, procedures, practices, and management of universities and their programmes of study. The organisational arrangements required to deliver capability-oriented educational programmes have more recently (Stephenson & Yorke, 1998) been described as the "Capability Envelope" (Figure 21.1). This sets out to:

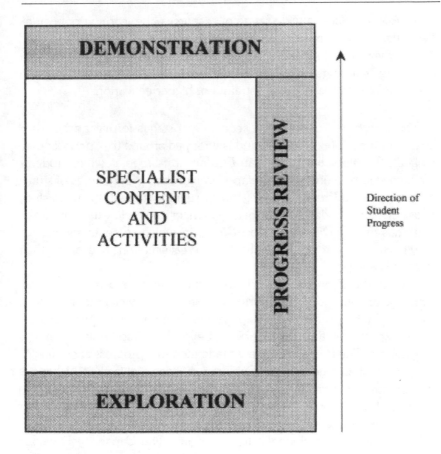

Figure 21.1 Capability Envelope

- Give students responsibility to formulate and manage their own *strategic educational development* according to their distinctive circumstances and longer-term aspirations.
- Ensure that students develop intellectual, specialist, and personal skills and qualities relevant to effective performance in life and at work.
- Meet the needs of key stakeholders such as professional bodies, custodians of academic standards, future clients (in the case of vocationally oriented programmes), and the community at large.
- Where necessary, accommodate current modes of delivery of specialist content.

- Accommodate a wide range of resources and learning opportunities and the greater availability of resources through electronic and other media in the community and at work.
- Create arrangements that can be implemented within the specialist and general resource constraints of higher education.

The Capability Envelope is a sequence of stages formally established as part of the total programme and is wrapped around the specialist content. The Envelope begins with an *Exploration Stage,* in which students are helped to plan and negotiate approval for their programmes of study; continues with a *Progress Review Stage* running through the main study phase, in which students are helped to monitor and review their progress; and ends with a *Demonstration Stage,* in which students show what they have learnt through its application to real situations relevant to their intended career.

Each of these three stages relates to the other two, giving an overall coherent structure to the learners' programme of development which is managed by the learner. The Exploration Stage builds on the students' prior experience and looks ahead beyond the completion of the programme. The Progress Review Stage monitors progress according to the plans that emerge from the Exploration Stage and facilitates changes in response to experience and evolving aspirations. What is demonstrated at the end of the programme is what was planned at the beginning or renegotiated on the way. A final critical review of the whole process provides a basis for the students' further plans. The Capability Envelope provides both a structure and a process for the autonomous management of lifelong learning, whether on campus, at work, or in life generally. People who adopt the central features of the Envelope as a habit are, we argue, independently capable.

Exploration Stage

Like explorers, autonomous learners need to construct a map of the terrain, acquire a set of tools by which to navigate, be aware of where they are starting from, and have some notion of a possible destination. The purpose of the Exploration Stage is to help students to prepare plans for the rest of their programme and to secure academic registration of those plans as leading to an approved qualification.

In order to prepare plans that meet the demanding requirements of registration, learners need with the support of institutional staff to:

- appraise their experience and become aware of their strengths and weaknesses,
- explore their career or other long-term aspirations,
- identify the specialist expertise and personal skills and qualities they will need in order to achieve those aspirations,
- plan an appropriate programme of learning activities,
- give thought to how they will demonstrate the relevance of what they have learned to their intended career or employment, and
- become aware of the general requirements of the award for which they are working.

The above activities can be conducted in peer groups with tutor supervision supported by a programme of exploratory activities, specialist inputs, and contacts with key stakeholders. In professional courses such as medicine and civil engineering, for instance, dialogue with professional practitioners at these early stages is essential. Career advisers also have a key role to play. Once likely areas of study have been identified, projects, placements, or assignments can be used to help students become familiar with key concepts and essential components and to provide some initial exposure to the good practice that they are aiming to attain.

The interests of key stakeholders, such as professional bodies and employer groups, and the general requirements of the university for the level of the intended award, can be accommodated formally through the general criteria for the approval of student plans and the composition of the groups charged with judging the appropriateness of those plans. Non-negotiable content, such as formal legal requirements for some professional courses, can be part of the criteria for approval, provided students have the right to show where, how, and at what stage such requirements will be demonstrated within the programme as a whole.

The amount of time needed for an Exploration Stage will depend upon the scale of the programme being prepared. For whole degree programmes, it can last 10 to 12 weeks. For shorter one-year programmes, anything from two to four weeks of intensive activity may suffice.

The Exploration Stage can be a valuable learning experience in its own right for which credit can and should be given. Much of this learning relates to personal qualities that come from the experience of taking responsibility within an uncertain environment. The process of planning and negotiation promotes the development of general and specialist skills and an understanding of the scope, key features, and relevance of the area of study.

Progress Review Stage
Once programmes are approved and running, students need time and opportunity to monitor their progress, review their aspirations in the light of experience, and judge the continuing relevance of their studies to those aspirations. "Learning sets" are particularly useful for these purposes; they provide students with opportunities for dialogue, intellectual challenge, personal support, and exchange of experience with peers.

The formal agenda for these sets can include:

- the preparation of learning logs or personal reviews of learning,
- the renegotiation or clarification of plans in response to experience,
- preparation of student feedback on the relevance of particular learning activities provided by the institution,
- formulation of demands that the institution provide different things,
- negotiation of access to remedial assistance,
- attention to conceptual and practical issues related to the final demonstration of learning, and
- efforts to raise students' awareness of the emotional, intellectual, and practical aspects of taking responsibility for managing their own development.

The Capability Envelope provides time, space, and tutorial support for learning sets to meet at regular intervals throughout the students' programme. The frequency of supervised meetings can vary, but on a long programme (e.g., an undergraduate degree programme) once a month can be sufficient.

The Progress Review Stage is the main means through which students retain ownership of their programmes of study. As with the Exploration Stage, the Progress Review Stage provides opportunities for significant learning derived from both reflection on, and consolidation of, specialist material and in relation to their planned future. In recognition of this learning, students should receive credit towards their final award, thereby justifying the allocation of scarce resources to this valuable activity.

Demonstration Stage
In this stage, students are helped and given time and space to prepare a demonstration of *what they can do* as a result of the studies they have completed, allowing assessment to be based on the students' *integration and application* of component specialist skills and knowledge in the context of their intended vocational, personal or professional aspirations.

The form of this demonstration of capability will be that which is most appropriate to the nature of the student's programme and can include a range of formats such as performances, exhibitions, project reports, and dissertations.

The NELP Experience of a Capability Approach

In 1984, 10 years after the NELP programme had been established and with over 1,000 students having passed through it, it seemed appropriate to ask questions about the effects the experience of independent study had had on the students themselves. A random selection of diplomats who were at least two years out of the Polytechnic were asked to evaluate, with the wisdom of hindsight, their experience of independent study in the context of their life histories to date. Two aspects emerged as key features of independent study: motivation and the growth of capability.

Student Motivation

People who meet with independent study students invariably remark on their high level of motivation and their strong personal identification with their studies. Examination of their explanations of the reasons why they applied, why they persevered, and how they have benefited reveals a range of motivating factors mainly characterised by the personal benefit they most desired from their higher education. Pursuit of these personal benefits is all embracing, impinging on all aspects of students' interactions with their programmes and the polytechnic. They have the status of being the students' primary needs.

Six primary needs were distinguished:

- Respect
- Identity
- Value
- Commitment
- Qualification
- Transformation

These different needs are first identifiable in students' reasons for applying. Need for *respect* is illustrated by those who feel that their educational qualifications, jobs, or personal circumstances do not accurately present their true potential and ability to the outside world. Phil told me that he was tired of people explaining long words to him just because he was a window-cleaner. He could feel people saying "Christ, let's throw clods of earth at him" whenever they saw him with his ladder. Meryl felt patronised by the professionally qualified people for whom she worked as a secretary. Both Phil and Meryl needed the respect they felt would come from participation in higher education and having recognised educational achievement. Any higher education course would do.

Typical of those with a need for identity was Tim, who had spent many years doing a range of jobs but could not see how he related to any one of them. Jean did not dare to reveal or trust her real interest in poetry, and Brian wanted a chance to look around for something to which he could commit himself. They wanted the chance to "sort themselves out."

The need for *value* is felt by students who have built up some expertise largely by their own efforts. They need time to take stock or make sense of their experience and to have it recognised. Bob felt that people saying "Oh, he's self taught" did not adequately recognise his artistic ability, and Delia was looking for "some theory, to have a central focus" for her experiences as a community worker.

The need for *commitment* is felt by those who know the future they want for themselves, and they want the opportunity to make it happen, to absorb themselves in their new direction. Gary turned down a scholarship to Oxford because he could not see its relevance. He felt that Independent Studies at NELP would help him become what he wanted to become.

Qualifications are to some extent relevant to all groups, but for some, the need for a qualification dominates all other considerations. Paul applied because it was the only way he could get a qualification in computing. The School of Independent Study provided him with a back-door entrance. He had been turned down for an Higher National Diploma because he had no qualifications; he is now head of the computer department in a City of London merchant bank.

The need for *transformation* involves all aspects of students' lives. These students feel they are severely constrained by circumstances and are looking to raise the level of their whole quality of life, including their careers. Julie, at the age of 18, felt totally dominated by her parents; Doreen was constantly put down by her boyfriend and employers. Each needed to break out.

Those with needs for respect or qualification would have preferred a conventional course. At that time, one was not available. This was also true to some extent for those looking for transformation.

It is likely that these highly personal needs can be found amongst any group of students. However, the research suggested that independent study makes two things possible. It makes it possible for students to acknowledge the importance of such personal needs, and, more importantly, it enables students themselves to take actions that ensure those needs can be met through their programmes of study.

With the absence of predetermined content, independent study students find themselves, in many cases reluctantly (as we shall see), in the position of having to argue for and justify what they want to do and to do so on the basis of their own distinctive experience and longer-term ambitions. This aspect of the planning of independent study programmes puts students in touch with a life-change perspective to their education and requires them to take an active rather than a passive role in the satisfaction of their needs as part of that life-change process. As a consequence, it is possible to characterise students' experiences by the actions they take in meeting their needs.

Students may be said to belong to the following categories:

Earners of Respect
Searchers For Identity
Provers of Value
Builders of Commitment
Takers of Qualifications
Transformers

Independent study students are not able to be passive receivers. For instance, commitment has to be built, not received. Identity has to be searched for, not received. Respect has to be earned, not received. Value has to be proved, not received. Qualifications are taken, not received. Transformation has to be initiated and carried out, not received. The boldfaced words (e.g. *earners*) characterise the nature of different student interactions with their programmes and the Polytechnic. Independent study students are not just students; they are builders, provers, earners, takers, searchers, or transformers.

The importance of these different motivations is seen when comparing the experiences of different students. Compare these reactions to the experience of planning their own programmes:

First, the *builders* of commitment: Gary found it "quite exciting" to be "responsible for getting it together," and validation of his proposed programme made him feel "educationally supported" in what he wanted to do and made him feel "enormously privileged". He was building his own future and the system was helping him do it.

In stark contrast, the *takers* found the business of planning to be "a chore," and an unnecessary "waste of time". This was Moira's view: "I just wanted to get on with it but we had to play the system. I was putting things down just to get the Statement (contract) through." When her programme was validated, Moira rejoiced because "it meant the headache had stopped" and she could at last get on with her work.

Having to plan their own courses put great pressure on the *searchers* of identity. They wanted to commit themselves to something but did not know to what. This was Brian's experience:

> It helped me clarify the path that my life had taken to that present point . . . it was a kind of catharsis, getting it out of my system . . . The process of validation was saying something about me, in that I'd clarified what it was that I wanted to do, and that felt pretty good. It was almost like a liberating experience.

Yet a further contrast can be seen with the *earners* of respect. They needed to be seen to be succeeding in higher education, so they planned courses according to the subjects most likely to lead to their success. "Find a reasonable tutor, one who was available and who told you what to do," seemed to be their major concern at that time. Validation of their proposals was important because it meant they had passed a Part One and were still on the course. Validation of their proposal also meant that they were being taken seriously.

Similar variations can be seen in the way students interact with their tutors, judge their own progress, and prepare for their assessments. I can give only the briefest flavour.

The takers, for instance, liked it best when their tutors gave them assignments and feedback directly relevant to getting their qualification. They leave as soon as they have the qualification that will take them forward.

Earners of respect liked getting good grades for their assignments, being involved in discussion and, above all, being taken seriously by tutors and other students. Because the Diploma in Higher Education is not recognised amongst their acquaintances, they proceed to the Degree. If that is not recognised, they proceed to a Masters Degree. When they feel generally respected for their ability and worth, they begin to look for something to which they can commit themselves.

Searchers of identity are very wary of getting too engrossed into a programme until they have tested it out as being what they really want. Formal assignments and grades do not help the searchers as much as successfully putting a possible identity to the test. Once an identity is found, progress is dramatic. Jean, the closet poet, described the most significant moment of her whole independent study experience thus:

> *I put forward the proposal that I wanted to do my own poetry and he (my tutor) was very nasty and he said "give me your poetry" and that was the first time ever that I had handed it over to someone who wasn't sympathetic. It was one of the biggest risks I had ever taken.*
>
> *I knew he had it in him to turn round and say "This is crap." He didn't. He said "Thank goodness, you CAN write poetry."*

With this confirmation, Jean progressed very rapidly and gained a degree in her own poetry. She is now publishing her work and is using poetry writing as an aid to the dying.

Builders judge their own progress in the field for which they are preparing themselves. Tutors are useful in helping them talk things through. Gary, for instance, became impatient with having to complete his programme once he realised that he had acquired the skills he needed in order to practice his new vocation.

The significance of all this is threefold:

First, students with very different needs are able to use independent study for their own purposes, and to get what they want out of it. Flexibility relates to student need as much as to content.

Second, student motivation is strong because students are able to relate their studies, and how they pursue them, to their own personal needs;

Third, awareness of the characteristics of different primary needs can help tutors and students get the most out of their interactions. The kind of feedback most useful for a taker, for instance, would not be too helpful to a searcher.

The Internal Dimension

What sense can be made of these different kinds of experience? What light do they shed on the underlying processes of independent study?

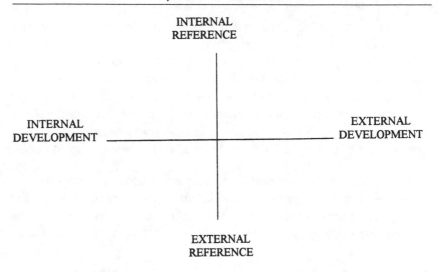

INTERNAL
REFERENCE

INTERNAL
DEVELOPMENT

EXTERNAL
DEVELOPMENT

EXTERNAL
REFERENCE

Figure 21.2 Students' Primary Focus Grid

At first sight, it might appear that the differences between students can be characterised as being "intrinsic" or "extrinsic." To some extent that is right, but only up to a point. There are two different aspects:

1. the focus of reference and
2. the focus of development,

each of which has an internal and an external dimension, as illustrated in the diagram above (Figure 21.2).

The *focus of development* refers to the general purpose of the student. An *internal focus of development,* for instance, refers to a concern about changing the self. An *external focus of development* refers to a concern to develop skills and knowledge for some outward context or application.

The *focus of reference* refers to a student's general inclination towards self-direction or towards the direction or opinions of others.

When they are presented in a grid form, there are four basic general student orientations. It is possible to place each of the student styles within the grid (Figure 21.3).

Figure 21.3 shows, for instance, that whilst both commitment and qualification are about the external application of skills and knowledge, the essential difference between them is that commitment involves much

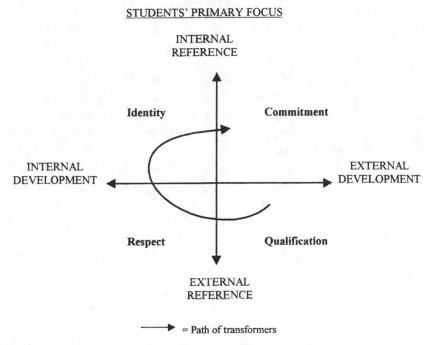

STUDENTS' PRIMARY FOCUS

INTERNAL
REFERENCE

Identity   Commitment

INTERNAL   EXTERNAL
DEVELOPMENT   DEVELOPMENT

Respect   Qualification

EXTERNAL
REFERENCE

⟶ = Path of transformers

Figure 21.3 Motivational Types According To Students' Primary Focus

more of an internal focus of reference than does a concern for qualifications alone.

Similarly, the concern for identity and the concern for respect are both about the internal development of the student. The qualitative differences between the experiences of the searcher and the earner are accounted for by their different focus of reference.

Concern for proving the value of your own experience involves both an external and an internal focus of development because the students concerned are so closely identified with their own expertise. The transformers move rapidly from section to section.

The qualification sector is the only sector without any internal dimension, either of reference or of development. The takers of qualifications were the students who most wanted to join a conventional course, if only they could find a conventional course to take them.

The intriguing question is whether conventional courses are able to meet needs other than the need for qualification. Do people who are strongly internally referenced keep away from education? Do they suppress their preference for self-direction or use it within the non-curriculum activities such as the student union? Do conventional courses in effect persuade people that education is not about respect, identity commitment, value, and transformation?

The student focus grid (Figure 21.2)—without the descriptive labels of respect, identity, and so forth—is a very useful tool to help students explore their own motivation. Post-graduate students in another institution were able to plot their own general disposition, and very few placed themselves in the external quarter.

It would be an interesting exercise to see how students generally in the university might rate themselves. There may be many who are internally referenced but who have learned to associate education with external reference behaviour. They must either endure it or not bother at all.

There is one further important observation to make about the internal/external dimension. As the students moved through their programmes, whether internally or externally referenced, they had no option but to take responsibility for some of their work, particularly the preparation of material for their own assessment. Students who were already internally referenced became more confident in themselves; those who were externally referenced discovered they could also be internally referenced. The transformers demonstrate this tendency most dramatically, but it applies to most of the students in the sample. The requirement that students should take responsibility gives students the experience of taking responsibility. There is a net movement towards the internally referenced.

The drift to an internal focus of reference through their independent studies programmes can be seen in the experiences of those former independent study students who move into conventionally taught courses.

Fiona (a builder of commitment), for instance, said of her teachers' certificate course that students "weren't allowed any self-expression or control"; she enlisted the help of a neighbouring university in organising a questionnaire to help her course to cater "for the needs of the students." Delia, a prover, found her university post-graduate diploma programme in psychology "atrocious"; she could learn it better herself. Doreen, a transformer, found her post-graduate professional conversion course "frustrating . . . a straitjacket . . . work that I had already done to a greater depth. I arranged my own alternative." Jim, a transformer, describes his experiences on a Certificate for Qualification in Social Work (CQSW) course as follows:

It was a very structured course. I told them "There's no way I'm going to stick through lectures" and the tutor said "If you are prepared to take the risk, what we will do is we will give you an extension from lectures for a whole term. If at the end of that term all your essay marks are O.K., you do it in any way you want." I got A's and B's in all of them.

More interesting and significant is the experience of those who were originally strongly externally referenced on joining the diploma course. Moira, as a taker, was one of those who said on entry onto the programme "I would have preferred a set course." She was pleased to have transferred to "a normal course at last" for her subsequent education. However, the culture of student control that she had previously resisted had obviously rubbed off on her because she soon discovered that "lectures . . . were not the most efficient use of our time" and that she "would have chosen a more varied reading list" than the one given to her by her tutors. She then realised that it was a matter of her "extracting the value of what I am doing, for my needs, and what I need to learn." She got a first-class honours degree. Sally, an earner, found that her fellow MA students in a major university, faced with establishing the independence necessary for the production of a dissertation, were "sort of worried because they wanted help . . . I knew what I had to do and just got on with it. . . . I know it's because of the independent study."

A further indication of the development of internal reference comes from comparing students' current self-perceptions and their self-perceptions prior to applying to the programme. Figure 21.4 shows how they feel their level of independence and how their commitment to what they are doing have changed as a result of their independent study.

In the self-perception grid, every one of the first 24 students interviewed reported feeling more independent as a result of their independent study. Some of them, mainly the transformers, report a dramatic increase in both independence and commitment. Others, mainly the earners of respect, report increases in independence but little growth in commitment.

One student actually experienced a decrease in her commitment to artwork as a direct result of her independent study. Her tutor ignored her need to build her own commitment and imposed on her a programme designed to get her a qualification. Pushing her from an internal reference into the mould of the external reference reduced her commitment. Giving

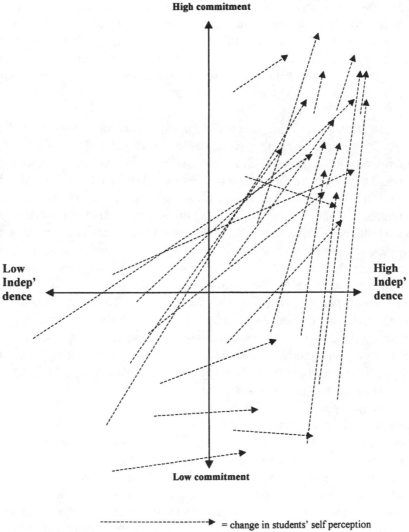

Figure 21.4 Student Self Perceptions Pre And Post Independent Study

the externally referenced students experience of internal reference increases their independence and, in many cases, also increases their commitment.

The Development of Independent Capability

A dominant characteristic of former independent study students, hinted at in these brief cameos, is their strong belief in their own power to perform.

Kenny is a director of a city company specialising in headhunting for accountants. His course was in underwater technology. He puts his success down to his insight that his job is not about accounting. It is about understanding the needs of individual people and organisations and being able to bring them together. Delia runs a refuge and rescue service for alcoholics. She has to secure funds, premises, and support from unsympathetic councils, and she has to train staff. She uses an adaptation of the Diploma in Higher Education planning activity as an effective means of getting clients to get a grip on themselves. Denny was denied entry to business studies courses so he designed his own. He now runs four separate businesses and is planning a major new investment. The Diploma in Higher Education gave him the "nerve" to give it a go. There are successful teachers and community workers, most of whom have or are securing promotion or positions of responsibility. One has recently made himself unemployed, and the one whose experiences in art were unsatisfactory describes herself as working as a housewife. All the others are in paid or fee-earning activity.

Confidence in the power to take effective action seems to be a general outcome of independent study as shown by this selection of comments about their overall gain from their experience:

> *I don't think that anything is beyond me.*
> *I have the confidence to do almost anything, to try almost anything.*
> *I can cope with most things that people can throw at me now.*
> *It's like finding a muscle you haven't used.*
> *I know I can do it whatever it is . . . I think my personal power is now much higher.*
> *I feel autonomous, much more confident in my own ability.*
> *My level of confidence is based on fact, not myth. . . . Am much more in control.*
> *I've got the confidence to actually do it as well.*
> *I know now that when I make decisions I will actually carry them through and that I CAN carry them through.*
> *I now know that I can really do it.*
> *Confidence to do almost anything, to try almost anything.*
> *A feeling of being able to get up and do something.*
> *You can do what you want to do and not follow the sheep.*
> *I know I can do it now.*
> *I previously would not have had the nerve to do what I am doing.*

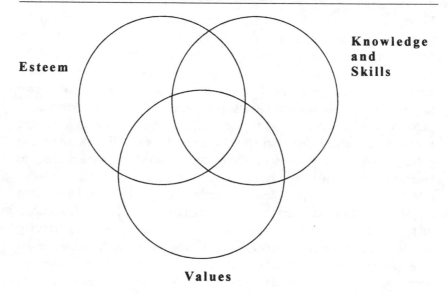

Figure 21.5 Three Components of Personal Power To Perform Components of Capability

Each of above statements represents students' own reflections on the overall value of their independent study experience. Closer analysis of students' fuller explanations of their confidence in their "power to perform" reveals three separate and interrelated components (Figure 21.5).

First, they have confidence in themselves as people; they have greatly enhanced *self-esteem* as illustrated by these statements by different students:

> *It has given me a lot more confidence to talk to people at different levels.*
> *I'm more self-assured and confident.*
> *I feel more able to instigate things . . . with people in authority.*
> *Independent study gives you a certain feeling of self-worth.*
> *I'm a lot more secure in myself . . . I have a higher opinion of myself.*
> *It gives students formal acknowledgement of where they are.*
> *I can now say no.*
> *I can now look other people in the eye . . . I feel much better about myself.*
> *(Independent study is) a means of helping people to value themselves.*
> *I have the ability to criticise myself.*

I do not feel threatened if I don't know something.
(I am) no longer feeling embarrassed about everything I did . . .
Definitely self-esteem has come out of it.

Second, the students have confidence in their *judgements and values*: That is, they have confidence in their ability to make judgements, have opinions and to be decisive. Some more extracts from a range of students illustrate the point:

I certainly express my opinions more freely.
I have a lot more confidence in my own ability and judgement.
It has allowed me to make my own decisions.
I am much clearer in what I want and what I don't want.
I am more ready to take a decision.
It built up my confidence in . . . trusting my judgement about things.
I am quite prepared to argue, whereas before I would get all timid.
I'm now much more confident to back my judgement and take things on.
As a person you feel you're independent, you're a free agent, you can decide for yourself.
I've learned how to cope with dilemmas.
I've got an opinion about world affairs.
Now I question a lot.
I have the ability to criticise myself—and I decide things for myself.

The third component of their personal power is confidence in the soundness and relevance of their *skills and knowledge,* and in their *ability to acquire new skills and knowledge when appropriate.* Here is a selection of the many statements students have made about their confidence in their ability to continue to learn through their own initiative:

It gave me the skills to acquire the information that I need at any given time for anything.
If I don't know something I know I can find it out.
(I can) decide priorities of what to learn and to pick out information.
Anything I want to know now I can teach myself.
I am more confident about finding things out for myself.
I enjoyed studying—I don't ever want to stop.
I enjoy working with others because that is one of the ways in which I learn.

Table 21.1 Independent And Dependent Capability

	Dependent Capability	Independent Capability
Knowledge and Skills	Received	Learned
	Tested by others	Self-monitored
	Relevance determined by others	Relevance negotiated by self
	Fragmented	Integrated
	Prescribed application	Adaptable and extendable
Esteem	Labels, status uniforms	Proved self-worth
	Recognised qualification	Confidence in own ability
	Failure = threat	Failure = opportunity
		Trust in intuition
Value	Priorities set by others	Can set own priorities
	Avoids judgements	Trust in own judgement

All of these statements about esteem, values, skills, and knowledge have a distinct internal flavour about them. Collectively, they describe students who have an *independent capability*. They therefore chime with the earlier proposition that independent study promotes students' internal focus of reference. It seems appropriate, therefore, to speculate about what these three components might look like if they had an external focus of reference. Or, to put it another way, how does *independent capability* differ from *dependent capability*?

Table 21.1 is one attempt to define the difference.

Though they may be highly skilled and knowledgeable, the *dependently capable* are likely to have acquired their expertise through instruction, training, and supervised practice, mastering known procedures or solutions that deal with predictable situations or problems. In totally new situations, where the context is unfamiliar or when entirely new problems appear, they will need re-training or strong guidance. They derive their esteem from their formal status, their certificated expertise, and the authority of those they represent. They aim to eliminate error by using tried and tested techniques; any failure is seen as a threat to their expertise. When unfamiliar situations or problems arise and judgements are needed, the dependently capable will seek guidance from superiors and will expect priorities to be set by those in authority.

At the other extreme, the *independently capable* are confident in their expertise and in their understanding of its internal interconnectedness. It has been learned, not given. Having been responsible for its acquisition, they know they can adapt or extend it when necessary. They have confidence in their own worth, both as individuals and as experts in their own right. With an inner confidence in themselves, one that is not dependent upon how others perceive them, they see error or failure as opportunity for learning, not as a threat. They trust their intuition. When faced with unfamiliar situations, they are prepared to back their own judgements, even to take risks, in order to explore new ideas. They know they can learn from the experience.

The importance of being able to distinguish between dependent and independent capability can be shown below (Figure 21.6).

The capability required for Position Y is one that is able to use readily accessible information to service the needs of familiar situations having predictable problems. Such situations may even require a high degree of skill and considerable specialist knowledge, but once such skills and knowledge have been acquired their application is relatively straightforward.

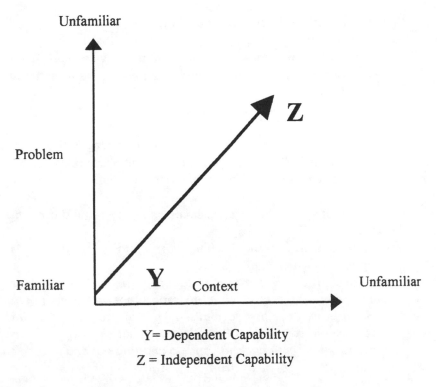

Y= Dependent Capability

Z = Independent Capability

Figure 21.6 Dependent And Independent Capability

As one moves away from the predictability ends of the problem/context axes there is a greater need for a more flexible and responsive capability, where one is able to make judgements, acquire new skills and knowledge, use the skills of others, and take calculated risks. There is a greater need for confidence in one's personal power to perform. The closer one is to Position Z, the greater the need for an independent capability.

The evidence from the students who completed their higher education by independent study suggests that their confidence in their own power to perform—that is, in their independent capability—derives directly from their experience of taking responsibility for their own development, for their own life change, for the satisfaction of deeply relevant personal needs, and for the acquisition of relevant skills and knowledge by their own efforts. They achieved all of these within the unfamiliar and demanding context of higher education. In short, they proved they could take it on.

The students themselves explain how independent study is relevant to the development of their confidence in their power to perform:

> *It's the fact that you know that you did it.*
> *I think the fact that you are actually required to input so much and rely on your own resources so much actually gives you much greater confidence about independence and ability to actually fend for yourself.*
> *It works because you have to cope with it.*

Evidence of how independent study helps with learning is shown by the freedom students feel to make and learn from mistakes and the experience it gives of being responsible for their own learning:

> *It gave a great space to make mistakes again, to rebuild a confidence.*
> *The opportunity to fail—that's where learning takes place . . . it is acceptable to learn from mistakes.*
> *(What makes it work?)—the person taking responsibility for their own learning—it places much more importance on learning than teaching. It was the first formalised kind of programme I had done where it was really valid to learn in that way.*
> *You have to get off your backside and go and find out and it wasn't that difficult . . . You learn from it . . . You don't get supervision, you get help.*

These comments on learning from mistakes present an interesting challenge. Being at ease with risking getting something wrong on the grounds that such experience is the basis of learning is an essential feature of survival in position Z. It would be interesting to discover the extent to which higher education programmes actually deny students opportunities to learn from mistakes. How many courses present their students with tightly defined content, prescriptive reading lists, carefully planned notes, and lectures directly focused on the questions known to be in the examination paper? How many work on the proposition that students must be protected at all cost from the risk of failure, and must be nurtured every step of the way? Is there more concern for lecturers' "pass-rates" than for the education of students?

The kind of experiences described in this study are not the experiences of therapy, as some critics have suggested. They are experiences of personal development through education, tested within what is normally seen to be the business of higher education, namely the pursuit of excellence. None of the students' primary needs can be met to the satisfaction of the students themselves without rigorous scrutiny of their own achievements. Respect is best earned, for instance, when the students themselves know they have achieved at least the levels achieved by other graduates, not at some compensatory level. Value, identity, and commitment are best tested against the rigours of the field itself, the reactions of clients, the recognition of acknowledged experts, or even the publication of their work. Qualifications have to be tradable on the open market. The most productive environment for independent study is one that combines mutual support with rigour and high aspiration.

Some Implications for Higher Education

Any society in which progress and change are common features requires its people to be independently capable. It should be a distinctive role of higher education to prepare people with real capacity for managing and coping with change and uncertainty. The speed of technological, economic, and social change means our jobs and circumstances change more frequently and less predictably than before. The explosion in the expansion of specialist knowledge (which is doubling every eight years by one estimate), puts a premium on giving people confidence in their own ability to learn and shows how futile it is to try to sustain the formal-transmission-of-knowledge-model of higher education. Major employers now recognise the importance of these personal qualities of independent capability in their graduate recruitment. They also know they do not find them in the normal round of graduate recruitment. One of the world's largest business companies no longer seeks to recruit graduates of business studies programmes to its higher positions because they find them lacking in flexibility, openness, and the ability to continue learning for themselves.

At a series of seminars at the RSA organised in 1988 for chairs of leading companies, vice-chancellors and polytechnic directors, the overwhelming consensus was that the time was now right for higher education to find more ways of helping more students develop the qualities of independent capability.

Agreeing that graduates should be independently capable is one thing. Knowing how to help them develop such qualities is another. Many institutions are attempting to meet the need by "bolt-on" activities on the assumption that the skills and qualities of personal capability can be achieved as extras, using traditional teacher-student relationships. Students, it is argued by advocates of this approach, can be helped to cope with problems by being given problems to cope with—as exercises. Students can be helped to learn how to learn by being given instruction in learning methods. Values clarification can be pursued within the context of teacher-organised seminars.

The problem with this approach is that it assumes that possession of skills is in itself enough. It misses entirely the point about the development of people's confidence in their power to perform their skills in different situations. Only when the full importance of the need to foster students' internally focused power to perform is acknowledged is it appreciated that students need to have real experience of exercising such power as part of their course. Moreover, there is much educational research elsewhere that suggests that directly involving students in their mainstream courses actually enhances their level of understanding of key concepts and raises the general quality of their work.

When one adds the opportunity independent study gives for students to address their own deep personal needs, to develop their personal independence and commitment, and to acquire publicly recognised qualifications, what emerges is an impressive amount of "value added." Furthermore, 9 out of 10 of the students lacked normal entry requirements, and they represented a very wide variety of personal circumstances.

The sum effect of the experience of independent study reported by former students lends support for an otherwise fading slogan that is not normally applied to education: The medium is the message. Confidence in one's capability is developed through having to be capable on one's course.

The student experiences on which I have reported have one clear implication for the increasing numbers of teachers who wish to help students to develop their specialist expertise, their personal potential, and their capability is simply this: find as many different ways as you can to give more students more opportunities to have more responsibility for their own learning.

References

RSA. (1980). *Capability Manifesto*. London, UK: Royal Society for Arts.

Stephenson, J., & Yorke, M. (1998). *Capability and Quality in Higher Education*. London, UK: Kogan Page.

Taylor, M. (1986). Learning for self-direction in the classroom: The pattern of a transition process. *Journal of Studies in Higher Education, 11* (1), 55–72.

Weaver, T. (1994). Knowledge alone gets you nowhere. *Capability, 1*, 1–6.

PART VI

BARRIERS TO FACILITATING THE GROWTH OF COMPETENCE

In our preface to the last Part of our book we indicated that the barriers to the introduction of competence-based education included a lack of clarity about what was to be achieved and how it was to be achieved. This will become more evident from David O'Reilly's chapter in this Part. But a further problem becomes apparent as soon as one does try to articulate high-level competency goals. *Some people are strongly—bitterly—opposed to them, not only for themselves, but also for others.* As we will see in the longer of the two chapters in this section, this is only the beginning.

Chapter 22

Competence and Incompetence in an Institutional Context[1]

Dave O'Reilly

In an earlier paper (O'Reilly, 1993), I reflected on the various tensions which had led to the reorganisation of Independent Study at the University (then Polytechnic) of East London (UEL) and I speculated on the role that learning contracts might yet play in Higher Education at UEL and elsewhere. I would now like to up-date the story of Independent Study at UEL, but, more importantly, to focus on four issues which I hope will be of more general interest. These are:

- the contextual determination of competence and incompetence;
- the disciplining of Independent Study and its consequences;
- an ecological metaphor of learning as sustainable development;
- movement towards a theorisation of competence *and* incompetence.

I should also say that, for reasons which should become clear in the course of reading, I intend to write this piece in a way which challenges to some extent the conventional academic style of impersonality, objectivity and rigor.

The Institutional Situation of Independent Study

In the earlier paper (O'Reilly, 1993), I emphasised that Independent Study had been from its inception in the early 1970s a political project, charged with developing an innovative form of pedagogy which would distinguish the newly-established Polytechnic[2] from the traditional University culture of Higher Education. A key feature was the use of learning contracts, by which a student could negotiate a whole programme of study suited to individual needs, abilities and aspirations. This was intended to make the institution directly responsive to the needs of students, particularly students from the local communities in East London, which were (and are) characterised by some of the lowest take-up rates of Higher Education in the UK.

It was anticipated that this form of open, negotiated learning would not be readily accepted by academics wedded to well-defined disciplines. The institutional strategy, therefore, was to create a central unit, the School for Independent Study (SIS), staffed by lecturers on temporary secondment from the Faculties, to start up the programme, ensure its transfer into the Faculties and then to wither away. Contrary to this plan, by the late 1980s, SIS was not only still alive and kicking, but had become a significant chunk of the Polytechnic, with as many students enrolled on Independent Study programmes as on the taught courses of the smaller Faculties. The tensions anticipated from the start had by now ramified and multiplied: they included (O'Reilly, 1993):

- a failure to secure ownership of Independent Study by the Faculties;
- suspicion of separatist tendencies in SIS, exacerbated by its relative isolation in a satellite building;
- methods and terminology in Independent Study not well understood across the University;
- a proliferation of conflicting models of learning within SIS;
- the pressures on teaching and administrative systems of opening access to the University for large numbers of non-traditional students;
- jealousy of Independent Study's success;
- an overload of innovation at SIS;
- growing pressure on resources and quality assurance across the University.

The list could go on—it was a complex situation. One thing I would emphasise is that by the late 1980s there was no great debate across the University about competency-based learning and Independent Study, as there had been in the 1970s. Though problem-based learning and associated competency models were still important in SIS philosophy and practice, they were no longer pre-eminent, but had to compete with models from person-centred learning, experiential learning and positions defined by sociological theory (Robbins, 1988). It would be difficult to identify a common philosophy holding together SIS staff, many of whom worked full-time in the School, while it was becoming increasingly difficult to find specialist tutors from the Faculties, as even the most sympathetic colleagues came under pressure to take on heavier workloads within their subject base. Nevertheless, the issue of competence was fundamentally what was at stake.

Independent Study had commenced with an experimental Diploma in Higher Education (DipHe), equivalent to the first two years of a full-time Honours Degree. The DipHe was followed rapidly by a full Degree, the BA/BSc(Hons) by Independent Study, and later by the MA/MSc by Independent Study. On each programme, independent learners were supported by a combination of central tutors and tutor groups in SIS and specialist supervisors based in Faculties. A fatal result of continued growth in student numbers with diminishing access to the pool of specialist supervision was that SIS staff took on the specialist role for a large proportion of students on the DipHe programme, though much less so on the BA/BSc and MA/MSc. This was wide open to the criticism that SIS tutors were taking on supervision in areas where they were not competent. Had the DipHe students been successful in their studies, then arguments that a student-centred approach to facilitating learning was more important than subject expertise might have cut some ice, but the DipHe had a high non-completion rate and a worryingly long tail around the pass/fail borderline.

In themselves, these were not insuperable problems. Indeed, viewed as a test-bed for mass Higher Education, fuelled by the Polytechnic's need to compensate for shortfalls in recruitment elsewhere, the DipHe and other programmes did well not only to last over 20 years, but also to establish a national and international reputation for good practice (CNAA, 1992; Stephenson, 1989).[3] In comparison, there were less visible areas of the Polytechnic with high non-completion rates and other problems. Why then was it SIS that suffered such a dramatic and sudden reversal of fortune?

From "Competence" to "Incompetence": The Importance of Context

In the run-up to a crucial visit of Her Majesty's Inspectors (HMI) (then the main "quality control" group in Education in the UK) in 1991, SIS was actually considering making a claim for excellence. With over 700 students enrolled on Independent Study programmes at undergraduate and postgraduate levels, new course initiatives in the pipeline, rapidly growing franchising of programmes to colleges of Further and Higher Education, consistently good reports from external examiners on the BA/BSc and MA/MSc, and continuing national and international interest in methods pioneered at SIS, this was not quite so crazy as it might seem in hindsight. Perhaps SIS staff had become somewhat inured to criticism from within the institution; perhaps some of us had an inflated sense of our importance at the cutting edge of innovation in Higher Education. What we were less aware of was a rapidly changing political climate in the Polytechnic and, I suspect, in the bodies regulating it—CNAA (the Council for National Academic Awards), HEFCE (the Higher Education Funding Council for England and Wales) and HEQC (the Higher Education Quality Council).

The inspection of Independent Study was part of an institutional inspection of the Polytechnic by Her Majesty's Inspectors (HMI), which resulted in a report highly critical of institutional procedures, particularly for quality assurance (HMI, 1991a). The severity of the report further undermined the already unsteady position of the Rector, who, as it happened, had been one of the first Chief External Examiners for the BA/BSc by Independent Study and was very much the protector and champion of SIS in the institution[4]. Beset as he now was with defending his own position, his protective power waned just as institutional anxieties about quality assurance (and a real fear of being closed down) focused around the impending separate report on the inspection of Independent Study (HMI, 1991b).

Such was the pitch of anxiety that the then Head of Independent Study had found it impossible to prepare for the HMI visit as she would have wished. From the start, it was unlikely that messages going to HMI from the institution were consistent with a claim for excellence by SIS. The first meeting of SIS staff and the HMI team was, as I recall, a dour affair marked by mutual suspicion, which took place in one of our better teaching rooms—that is to say, a room long in need of redecoration and recarpeting.[5] As the inspection proceeded, the impression gained by SIS staff was that the inspectors were looking for evidence of competence in terms of discipline-based teaching and conventional classroom practice. If this was so, they were bound to be thrown by the apparently anarchic culture of SIS, where each student had a unique programme of study, where interdisciplinarity (shading into non-disciplinarity) was the norm, and where individual lecturers had been given considerable freedom to evolve their own styles of working with tutor groups. With the best will in the world it would have been a struggle to find common ground between fundamentally different paradigms of competent education. Given the poisonous political climate in the Polytechnic, the adverse report of HMI (HMI, 1991b) led inexorably to the disciplining of Independent Study.

The Disciplining of Independent Study

The French philosopher, Michel Foucault, has explored the twin meanings of "discipline" in his studies of the development of academic disciplines (Foucault, 1974) and of the constant interplay of knowledge and power (Foucault, 1980). For Foucault, power and knowledge are inseparable: he refers to the imbrication of power with knowledge and he uses the compound term power/knowledge to convey this sense of intimate overlaying. From this perspective, the growth of disciplines and academic discourses is always a political process—just as I have argued that the history of Independent Study must be seen as fundamentally political. This is not an abstract consideration: in fact, Foucault's notion of power/knowledge is very concrete, active and engaged—in many ways, I would suggest very close to notions of knowledge and action in discourses about competence and capability.[6]

In the previous section I have argued that what counted as competence was determined partly by the power of the Rector and external bodies, such as CNAA, which had long supported SIS, and, when they waned, by other powers in the University and by HMI. In this section I would like to explore the force of disciplines in the changes to which Independent Study was subjected.

It has been argued that universities are a keystone of the Enlightenment project (Finger, 1990) and that disciplines are the main pillars of the University (Usher and Edwards, 1994). By Enlightenment project we might understand the endeavour, originating with the Scientific Revolution of the 17th century, to secure social and material progress through the power of reason and mastery over nature, epitomised in science and technology respectively. Though the modern scientific disciplines are relatively new, they had by the late 19th century established the norm for what Schön (1983) calls the technical-rational-expert and the role model of a discipline based on solid empirical foundations and elaborated by sound methodology, to which all other would-be disciplines must aspire.

As I have mentioned, a very distinctive feature of Independent Study was its outsider character with regard to disciplines. For some of the founders of Independent Study, the very term meant independent of established curricula or syllabi. While this did not directly reject the value of academic disciplines, it did imply that, if the curricular structures with their carefully prescribed ladders of progression, which many academics thought absolutely necessary for training in their discipline, were possibly dispensable, then the identification of the academically legitimate with the disciplined was also questionable.

There is no doubt that in many quarters this was a deeply held reservation about Independent Study as practised at UEL at undergraduate level. It explains why the MA/MSc was always more readily accepted than the DipHe or the BA/BSc, as it could be assumed that a graduate entering a Masters programme would have a thorough grounding in the discipline. It also helps to explain why independent study programmes operating within a discipline framework, such as the BA by Independent Study in Applied Social Sciences at Crewe and Alsager Faculty of Manchester Metropolitan University, have perhaps fared better in the political stakes (Cuthbert, 1995).[7] Not too surprisingly, the solution proposed at Polytechnic of East London (PEL) to "the problem of Independent Study" was to devolve it to the Faculties—in effect, to discipline it.

So persuasive was this strategy to the institution that it was deemed safe to put the four Principal Lecturers from SIS, who might possibly have been associated with the problem, into key positions in managing the devolved operation. Delivery of the programmes was also largely dependent on ex-SIS staff, in many cases thoroughly demoralised, redeployed unwillingly to a new department and feeling very much the lepers of the institution. For students too it was a deeply traumatic experience, throwing into doubt not only the value of their eventual qualification, but also, for a while, even the continued existence of the programmes.

In these circumstances, it becomes very hard to know what is competence any more. As one of the four Principal Lecturers, who became Head of the Central Coordinating Unit for Independent Study, I inherited much of the anxiety about Independent Study, manifested in constant management surveillance and a relentless series of reviews that diverted much-needed energy from the rebuilding of the shattered programmes. External bodies too were demanding reassurances and keeping the whole institution on conditional approval in the wake of the HMI report. From my position it was difficult to discern the attitude of these bodies to Independent Study. Certainly, I can remember no signals of strong support, though there may have been goodwill at work behind the scenes. It must be remembered that these bodies (CNAA, HEFCE, HEQC) were in a state of considerable flux themselves. One sometimes has the sense, perhaps mistaken, that some of the manoeuvres of powerful individuals from these bodies were part of a wider political game, in which the whole Polytechnic, let alone Independent Study, was a rather battered pawn.

To cut a long story short, Independent Study never did take root at undergraduate level in the Faculties. From over 600 students in 1990 it dwindled to near zero in 1997, as the few remaining students completed their studies. Despite pockets of genuine goodwill and the outstanding efforts of individual staff, the Faculties were as always stony ground for Independent Study—they didn't own it, they didn't really understand it, they were convinced it was resource expensive and now they associated it all too vividly with institutional ignominy. Even in Social Sciences, where the Dean gave his personal backing to the largest of the devolved units, recruitment has dwindled and is no longer viable, overwhelmed maybe by the further structural changes of modularisation and semesterisation which followed hard on the heels of devolution.

Independent Study continues at Masters level at UEL. Aspects of independent study, such as learning contracts and critical reviews, have been introduced into many other courses, supported by the Enterprise in Higher Education initiative. Ironically, these same elements of action plans and critical review have resurfaced as key elements of the University's QILT (Quality in Learning and Teaching) initiative for continuous quality improvement across all areas (Laycock, 1995). Yet the undergraduate programmes are like a bubble that has burst—a change so startling that I feel a need to reach beyond causal explanations, a need to find a metaphor to comprehend what has happened.

Seeking a Metaphor: Rainforest Learning?

In the previous section I have argued that the non-disciplinary, learning process orientation of Independent Study was too much at odds with the content-based disciplines of the University ever to take root in its original form in the Faculties. Elsewhere (O'Reilly, 1992), I have elaborated on this theme as the impossibility of a postmodernist course in a modernist institution—that is, the impossibility of sustaining a radically student-centred approach, responsive to individual needs and differences in an increasingly fragmented society, in an educational environment of disciplines still (desperately) seeking scientific rigour and universal truth. That it was sustained for so long may be because its duration coincided with the emergence of what Beck (1986) has called the "Risk Society", in which individuals are put under pressure to take responsibility for their personal biographies and career paths precisely at the moment when social and technological risks become both globalised and intensified, apparently far beyond the competence or capability of any individual to control them or of education to empower people in this brave new world (Jansen & Van der Veen, 1991).

To the more rigorously-minded, "postmodernism" and "Risk Society" may be little more than metaphors, so I might as well go all the way in creating a metaphor for the (to me) special case of Independent Study. The metaphor chosen is not unrelated to some standard metaphors of education, as the cultivation of minds, like the cultivation of tender young plants (though we might bear in mind an altogether grander and darker metaphor, that of the Tree of Knowledge of Good and Evil). In sympathy with the HMI who visited SIS in its advanced stage of androgogical excess, the metaphor I grasp is (not the nettle but) the jungle, or, to be more politically correct, the rainforest.

To make sense of this, let us return to the conventional metaphor of cultivation. Disciplines are the modern farming methods of the university, cultivating reasonably standard ideas in reasonably standard minds under controlled conditions, feeding their well-disciplined rows of students with measured amounts of intellectual nutrient and using powerful poisons to keep out weeds and pests. In contrast to this, Independent Study was a jungle: no rows, no signs of discipline, no very obvious administration of intellectual nutrient, a flagrant tolerance of weeds. All very confusing for a farmer—and not a little frightening.

A rainforest ecology is characterised by tremendous biodiversity, such that a small area of jungle may contain several hundred species, many unique to that biological community, yet all interdependent in a delicate and easily disrupted ecological balance. Rainforests are distinguished not only by the sheer quantity of life they support but by the diversity of that life, the number of different species of plants and animals. Temperate countries are poor by comparison. Great Britain, for example, is twice the size of the Malay Peninsula. Yet it has only 1,430 plant species to the peninsula's 7,900. A high proportion of animals and plants in tropical rainforests are endemic to one area—that is, they live nowhere else.

In the words of Alfred Wallace:

> If the traveller notices a particular species and wishes to find more like it, he may often turn his eyes in vain in every direction. Trees of varied forms, dimensions and colours are around him, but he rarely sees any of them repeated. Time after time he goes towards a tree which looks like the one he seeks, but a closer examination proves it to be distinct. He may at length, perhaps, meet with a second specimen half a mile off or he may fail altogether, till on another occasion he stumbles on one by accident (Caufield, 1985, pp. 59–62).

To me, this is a remarkably apt description of the Independent Study learning community at Holbrook Annexe, where each of the several hundred students had a unique programme of study, subtly supported by the complex life of the community. All too late, science is beginning to appreciate the intricate order of the rainforest, too late to stop its wholesale destruction, not only in the name of greed and need, but also of fear—fear (to take a psychoanalytical turn) of the jungle, the spider and the serpent. The rainforest serves as a metaphor for the heart of darkness within ourselves, that we fear more than anything: its destruction assuages our fears in the short term, but only at the cost of a terrible impoverishment.

So, Independent Study as rainforest education—a fanciful metaphor? In some ways, of course; but in others, I think not. It leads me to struggle with the whole notion of education as enlightenment, the inexorable illumination of dark places. It leads me to wonder whether the unmitigated pursuit of knowledge, or of competence, can only lead to disaster, and whether the pursuit of competence must always be balanced with a healthy regard for the importance of incompetence in all our words and deeds.

Competence/Incompetence:
Towards a Balanced Theorisation

I would like to suggest that many of the current discourses of competence are deeply rooted in Enlightenment ideals and positivistic notions of progress. I have in mind the Enlightenment ideal of conscious, rational mastery over our destinies. I have in mind the positivistic notion of progress as the accumulation of ever more powerful scientific theories. In wider intellectual terms, these positions are defended most cogently by Habermas (1984) and typified by his notion of "the ideal speech act" (which I take as a peculiarly esoteric form of ordinary competence). In discourses of competence more generally, they surface as models of professional development centred on the accumulation of more and more competencies at ever-increasing levels of sophistication, until one attains mastery, or wizardry, or even wisdom—depending on the management guru one follows.

To some extent, these positivistic tendencies towards unlimited personal growth are ameliorated in models which emphasise cycles of learning (Kolb, 1984), though even here expansionist tendencies may be overlaid on the rather static cycle. Within limits, I have no quarrel with this—indeed, the capability spiral (Stephenson & Laycock, 1993) unpacks the different dimensions of the learning contract cycle. What does concern me, however, in discourses of competence generally, is the invisibility of incompetencies, which are present only by implication, through their gradual eradication or as the *unmentionable other*.[8]

A very important consequence of this splitting off and rejection of our incompetencies is the institutionalisation of unrealistic norms of competence (for instance, in the medical profession), which puts tremendous pressure on individuals to hide their mistakes, rather than to share and learn from them, and to collude in hiding the mistakes of colleagues. Indeed, a significant element of professional practice may be directed towards hiding incompetence, or to reconstructing incompetence as a higher form of competence.

In terms of the metaphor of enlightenment, it seems to me that, at the extreme, the achievement of total enlightenment would be a terrible dystopia, a world of all light and no shadow, all day and no night, a nightmare of total surveillance in which the individual is increasingly answerable for self-enlightenment and responsible for self-surveillance. I doubt if any of us wants that. My argument is that, to avoid it, we need to incorporate incompetence into our models of professional development.

My own way of making sense of this can be conveyed in another variant of the learning cycle, though this time a simplification of Kolb's model rather than an elaboration. The hermeneutic cycle envisages learning as a process of making meaning by moving between different positions.[9] For example, in this paper, as I have endeavoured to make sense of the events at UEL, I have moved between positions which are relatively more subjective and more objective; between individual and institutional perspectives; between past and present; between personal passion and impersonal analysis. Perhaps to some readers this has made for a disconcerting read. What I have done deliberately (though fairly mildly) is to move beyond the academic paradigm which allows only the objective, impersonal and analytic polarities of Cartesian dualisms to be expressed in academic writing, to include the other polarities as of unquestionably equal importance. I would emphasise here that this is not to see these polarities as somehow fixed and essential, but to see them as relative positions that we may move between, if we wish and if we are able. It is in the moving between that the possibilities of new perspectives reside and the possibility of learning (of new formations of power/knowledge) is to be found.

No doubt in my hermeneutic wanderings I have also moved between being right and being wrong, between clarifying and confusing, between competence and incompetence, between knowing and not knowing. Yet how are these to be judged? If my model holds water, then we need to embrace not knowing in order to know. As Brew (1993, p. 97) has observed:

> Wisdom may come through experience, but it does not come through an accumulation of experience. Unlearning is about being prepared to throw out what one has learned and begin afresh. I'm inclined to say that it is the process of learning that is important; that there is only the journey, never the destination. However, I think what I am referring to is the process of unlearning: the attempt to access our inner knowings; the coming face to face, again and again, with our ignorance, with our not-knowing. The highest point of knowing is not knowing. Herein lies the paradox of learning from experience.

Likewise we need to embrace incompetence in order to be competent.

Summary

I have used a case study, of the fall of Independent Study at UEL, to argue that judgements of competence and incompetence may be crucially dependent on the institutional context in which they are made. I have used Foucault's notion of power/knowledge to analyse the tensions in the HMI inspection of Independent Study and its subsequent disciplining. Then I moved to a different position, attempting to understand the underlying dynamics through metaphor. Finally, and very sketchily, I have tried to bring the analytical and metaphorical together in the hermeneutic cycle as a model of learning in which incompetence is just as important as competence in our cycles of learning and development.

The model of knowledge as always partial, always situated and always contested has been developed particularly in postmodernist and feminist analyses (Nicholson, 1990). That the underpinning notion of knowledge as power/knowledge is akin to notions of competence or capability and that the two discourses might learn from each other is a more novel proposition, but one that I hope will be worth exploration rather than outright rejection. In turning the spotlight on incompetence, I think I should also say that an underlying concern I have in writing this paper has been to focus our thoughts on the limits of knowledge and competence, their dark side and the balance to be sought between perfection and imperfection in sustainable careers, learning organisations and communities of practice.[10] My lasting hope for Independent Study is that it proves to be thoroughly biodegradable and infinitely recyclable.

Notes

1. This paper was first presented to the *Expert Seminar on Conceptualisation of Competence, Capability and the Learning Society* organised by Higher Education for Capability, York, UK, June 1996.

2. North East London Polytechnic was renamed the Polytechnic of East London in 1991, and became the University of East London in 1993 with the ending of the binary divide between Polytechnics and Universities in the UK.

3. SIS played a significant role in establishing two conference series: ICEL, the International Conference on Experiential Learning, which has convened in London 1987, Sydney 1989, Pondicherry 1992, Washington DC 1995, and Cape Town 1996, and the LML (Learner Managed Learning) Series, London 1990, Silecia 1991, and Holland 1992 (see Graves, 1995 for a collection of papers from LML-1 and LML-2). The Independent Study experience has also been claimed from some unlikely quarters as a foundation for rethinking the whole of Higher Education (Ainley, 1994) or simply the whole of education (Southgate, 1988).

4. Ironically, and sadly, many students of that time continue to believe that the Rector was the great enemy of SIS, such was the "us and them" mentality that then prevailed. For a statement of the Rector's position see Fowler (1993).

5. For the next HMI visit to Holbrook, to Women's Studies in 1992, this one room was miraculously refurbished just prior to the visit.

6. A less reified wording of power/knowledge could be, for example, empowerment/learning. Because learning transactions are always contested, disempowerment may be as frequent a feature of teaching situations. Equally, unlearning may be as important to empowerment as learning (cf. Brew, 1993).

7. It would be interesting to place the history set out here in the wider context of independent study initiatives in the UK, from Percy and Ramsden's (1980) comparison of the first two programmes in Higher Education in the UK, at NELP and Lancaster University, to Knight's survey of the field in the mid-1990s (Knight, 1994). See also Funnel and Goddard (1996) for an account of a modularised, cross-institutional Independent Study programme at Suffolk College.

8. For example, Michael Eraut's comprehensive critique of theories of professional knowledge and competence (Eraut, 1994) has no listing for "incompetence" in the index, nor can I spot the word in any of the titles in the book's bibliography of over 200 references.

9. Compare Rowan's (1981) account of the hermeneutic cycle in relation to "new paradigm research".

10. An earlier paper explores a similar theme (O'Reilly, 1989).

References

Ainley, P. (1994). *Degrees of Difference: Higher Education in the 1990s.* London: Lawrence & Wishart.

Beck, U. (1986; transl. 1992). *Risk Society: Towards a New Modernity* London: Sage.

Brew, A. (1993). Unlearning through experience. In D. Boud, R. Cohen, & D. Walker (Eds.), *Using Experience for Learning.* Bucks: Open University Press/SRHE.

Caufield, C. (1985). *In the Rainforest.* London: Picador.

CNAA (1992). *Case studies in student-centred learning.* CNAA Project Report 36. London: Council for National Academic Awards.

Cuthbert, C. (1995). Project planning and the promotion of self-regulated learning: from theory to practice. *Studies in Higher Education, 20* (3), 267–277.

Eraut, M. (1994). *Developing Professional Knowledge and Competence.* Brighton: Falmer Press.

Finger, M. (1990). The subject-person of adult education in the crisis of modernity. *Studies in Continuing Education, 12* (1), 24–30.

Foucault, M. (1969: transl. 1974). *The Archaeology of Knowledge.* London: Tavistock.

Foucault, M. (1975; transl. 1979). *Discipline and Punish: The Birth of the Prison.* Harmondsworth: Penguin Books.

Foucault, M. (1980). *Power/Knowledge; Selected Interviews and Other Writings.* Brighton: Harvester Press.

Fowler, G. (1993). Learner managed learning: An androgogic policy for higher education? In N. Graves (Ed.), *Learner Managed Learning: Practice, Theory and Politics.* Leeds: Higher Education for Capability.

Funnell, P., & Goddard, S. (1996). Learning from experience: An individually-negotiated learning route. In J. Tait, & P. Knight (Eds.), *The Management of Independent Learning.* London: Kogan Page.

Graves, N. (Ed.). (1995). *Learner Managed Learning: Practice, Theory and Politics.* Leeds: Higher Education for Capability.

Habermas, J. (1984). *The Theory of Communicative Action. Vol 1 Reason and the Rationalisation of Society.* London: Heinemann.

HMI (1991a). *Polytechnic of East London: Aspects of Provision, Autumn Term 1990—A Report by HMI* (106/91/HE). London: Department of Education and Science.

HMI (1991b). *Polytechnic of East London: School for Independent Study, 19–23 November 1990 – A Report by HMI* (113/91/HE). London: Department of Education and Science

Jansen, T., & Van der Veen, R. (1991). Reflexive modernity, self-reflective biographies: Adult education in the light of the risk society. *International Journal of Lifelong Education, 11* (4), 273–286.

Knight, P. (1994). Independent Study—moving from the margins or to the margins? Paper to the *First International Symposium in Independent Study and Flexible Learning,* Maddingley Hall, Cambridge.

Kolb, D. A. (1984). *Experiential Learning: Experience as the Source of Learning and Development.* Englewood Cliffs, NJ: Prentice Hall.

Laycock, M. (1995). Quality improvement. In *Learning and Teaching (QILT): A Whole Institutional Approach to Quality Enhancement.* UCoSDA Briefing Paper. London: UCoSDA.

Nicholson, L. J. (Ed.) (1990). *Feminism/Postmodernism.* London: Routledge.

O'Reilly, D. (1989). On being an educational phantasy engineer: Incoherence, the individual and independent study. In S. Weil & I. McGill, *Making Sense of Experiential Learning: Diversity in Theory and Practice.* Bucks: Open University Press/SRHE.

O'Reilly, D. (1992). Negotiated learning/negotiated knowledge: independent study and institutional change—A postmodern course in a modernist institution? In D. Wildemeersch & T. Jansen (Eds.), *Experiential Learning, Education and Social Change: The Postmodern Challenge.* Nijmegen: Keulen Communicatie.

O'Reilly, D. (1993). Negotiating in an institutional context. In J. Stephenson & M. Laycock, *Using Learning Contracts in Higher Education.* London: Kogan Page.

Percy, K., & Ramsden, P. (1980). *Independent Study: Two examples from English higher education*. Research into Higher Education Monographs. Guildford, Surrey: Society for Research into Higher Education.

Robbins, D. (1988). *The Rise of Independent Study: The Politics and the Philosophy of an Educational Innovation, 1970–87*. Bucks: Open University Press/SRHE.

Rowan, J. (1981). On making sense. In P. Reason, & J. Rowan (Eds.) *Human Inquiry: A Sourcebook of New Paradigm Research*. Chichester: Wiley.

Schön, D. A. (1983). *The Reflective Practitioner: How Professionals Think in Action*. New York: Basic Books.

Southgate, J. (1988). Changing childhood. *Science for People, 68*, 9–11.

Stephenson, J. (1989). The experience of independent study at North East London Polytechnic. In D. Boud (Ed.), *Developing Student Autonomy in Learning* (2nd Edition). London: Kogan Page.

Stephenson, J., & Laycock, M. (1993). *Using Learning Contracts in Higher Education*. London: Kogan Page.

Usher, R., & Edwards, R. (1994). *Postmodernism and Education*. London: Routledge.

Chapter 23

Some Barriers to the Introduction of Competency-Based Education

John Raven

As we have seen, there is no doubt that higher education, like education more generally, *should* be primarily concerned with nurturing general transferable high-level skills or competencies. Further evidence supporting this claim comes from the work of:

- Roizen and Jepson[1]—who showed that employers are primarily concerned to recruit graduates who possess initiative, the ability to get on with others, problem-solving ability, and the ability to build up their own understanding of their organisations and society and thereafter play an active part in them.
- Flanagan[2]—who showed that it was such competencies that people were most likely to say their education should have helped them to develop and that, where they had been developed (usually through involvement in committee work related to extracurricular activities), it was these developments that represented the most important benefits of their education.
- Marris[3]—who conducted a remarkable comparative study of a number of universities and colleges in Britain, eventually coming to the conclusion that the universities need to distinguish three roles: the transmission of up-to-date specialist knowledge through short, packaged, modules; the development of general high-level competencies; and the provision of courses which enable people to pursue topics that are of particular interest to them—primarily for leisure purposes.

- Winter, McClelland, and Stewart[4]—who showed that the most important benefits of higher education were only available to those who attended ivy league colleges and that these benefits consisted of the development of high-level competencies. These high-level competencies were developed through working with individual members of staff in demanding research activities. Importantly, the main benefits of having developed them were reaped by the community at large rather than as income for the individuals concerned. (Marris reached similar conclusions by comparing the experience of students at Cambridge with those at a number of other institutions in the United Kingdom.)

Actually, it is not necessary to cite any such evidence to come to the conclusion that the main role of institutions of higher education in promoting student development and understanding *must* be to nurture generic high-level competencies (and not to communicate specialist knowledge), because it follows from the simple observation that employers select bankers from chemists, managers from arts graduates, accountants from geologists, diplomats from physicists, and so on. Fewer than 60% of graduates find employment in their discipline of study.[5]

Yet, despite this evidence of the importance of such qualities, few schools or colleges do much to nurture them.[6] And, despite the allocation of huge amounts of time and money to the task, most of those who have tried to create educational programmes that do devote time to trying to nurture them have either given up themselves or had their programmes closed down by others—or the programmes have lapsed when they retired.[7] This has proved to be true of even well-funded, theoretically-based, programmes such as those of Argyris and Schön.

The fact that most schools do not do much to nurture the wider aspects of competence is perhaps more remarkable than the failure of colleges to do so, since the notion that they *should* do so has been promulgated—with the aid of considerable investment in curriculum development programmes—for more than a century. In the last decade or so in Britain, the heavily funded Technical and Vocational Education Initiative (TVEI) was also meant to be centrally concerned with the development of problem-solving ability, the ability to communicate, the ability to work with others, and the competencies which make for enterprise, but it generally failed to implement the necessary activities.

Why do such programmes so often fail to get off the ground in the first place, fail to work, or fizzle out?

Schön attributes the failure of his attempt to reform management education at the Massachusetts Institute of Technology to the hegemony of
the technico-rational model of competence and the way lecturers can gain
prestige and advancement only by working within disciplinary structures.
But there was also the problem that no one really knows what managerial
competence involves or how to recognise it in the workplace. Schön's
students therefore knew only too well that they would in future be promoted not for displaying managerial competence but for doing what they
are required to do in traditional colleges: that is, for parading the "right,
bright" ideas in front of superiors. Eraut[8] has noted the same thing in
teaching. In the course of in-service education, teachers learn to say the
right things to advance themselves in their careers—that is, they learn
"policy-speak" so as to be able to tailor their utterances to currently fashionable policy debates and thus make a good impression on career
gatekeepers. This does not help them to do a better job in their classrooms. In any case, there is very little understanding of the meaning of
competence in the classroom, let alone about how to assess performance
against appropriate criteria. The whole notion is problematic. No one
knows what good teaching consists of. And the problem only becomes
worse when one realises, first, that the teacher's job is to nurture a wide
variety of *alternative* high-level competencies in different pupils or students (for how is one to evaluate a teacher's ability to nurture a *variety* of
competences that cannot be specified beforehand?) and that to do so
they have to intervene in the host of societal systems processes which,
while external to schools, nevertheless overwhelmingly determine what
can be done within schools. Inability and unwillingness to tackle these
external constraints thus lies at the heart of teachers' incompetence. As
we have seen, Boyatzis, et al.,[9] like Schön, found that it was the *students*
who were most resistant to change—mainly because there was no way of
getting credit for having developed the desired competencies in a form
that would count when the time came to get a job.

Because of the documentation available, experience at the School of
Independent Studies at the North East London Polytechnic is particularly
revealing. With the benefit of hindsight, it would appear that the main
problems encountered by the School included the fact that, while there
was indeed a specific orientation toward competency-based education,
ways of thinking about competence and the implications for the role to be
played by members of staff were never clearly articulated. Instead, the
programme was presented as being concerned with non-traditional students who, it was argued, possessed competencies that higher education

had traditionally overlooked; the programme would stem academic drift and introduce individualised forms of "learning."[10] Very quickly, therefore, the School was asked to demonstrate that it was a quality programme equivalent to a traditional degree.[11] Since the accepted way of doing this involves demonstrating that one's *entry* qualifications are high, this resulted in the School being pressurised to bring its admission requirements more into line with those of other departments. In the event, however, the School's willingness to admit "otherwise qualified" students was accepted—but for quite other reasons that, in the end, contributed to its undoing: the Polytechnic as a whole discovered that the School's argument enabled it to admit more students and thus obtain per capita funding from government without having to make any great investment in the infrastructure required to support independent studies. Then there was the problem of specifying outcomes. Although a remarkably innovative procedure for breaking the hold which traditional degree examinations have over course content had been carefully thought through and—incredibly—negotiated with the Council for National Academic Awards, it is not clear that the discussion was really conducted in terms of high-level competencies. Although there was an almost unique—and absolutely essential—emphasis on time being set aside for students to think through their needs and to plan individualised programmes of work, it is not clear that those concerned were provided with a conceptual framework to help them to think in terms of multiple talents and the processes needed for their development. (Make no mistake about it, however, these two components—change in certification and personal counselling are *crucial* to the success of competency-based education.) In the end—so far as can be judged from the writings of Robbins[12] (who, remarkably, remained with the School from its conception to dissolution without apparently ever developing any insight into what it was all about)—the staff eventually lost sight of the School's original competency-oriented objectives, drifting into vague humanistic educational programmes (of the "they will have learned something from the exercise" variety[13]) on the one hand and individualised subject-competency-oriented programmes of study on the other. This led Robbins to recommend that the School return to a discipline-based focus and this, in the end, was exactly what happened as a result of a review by Her Majesty's Inspectors of Schools (HMI's). In a sense, this can be viewed as yet another triumph for the processes that have elsewhere perpetuated discipline-based study. But there is a gloss: HMI's main criticism was not of independent studies or competency-based education. It was that the Polytechnic as a whole had not supported the School of Independent

Studies with the infrastructure which would have been required to make independent studies work. Instead, the Polytechnic had seen Independent Studies as a means of increasing student numbers—and therefore cash flow—at minimum cost.[14]

In the remainder of this chapter, the—often surprising—barriers to work in this area that have come to light in the course of our research will be summarised.

Lack of Understanding of the Nature and Development of High-Level Competencies

One major problem, already highlighted in this book, is that, despite the advocacy of work in this area, there is little formal, explicit understanding of the nature of qualities such as those that have been mentioned, how they are to be fostered, or how their development is to be monitored for formative or summative purposes.[15] It may be thought that this is sufficient to explain the lack of progress.[16] Unfortunately, as the experience of Schön and others has shown, this is far from the case.

The Problem is Not a Lack of Time, Money, Resources, or Staff Training

Before moving on to discuss the less obvious barriers, it is important to appreciate that the significant barriers to educational reform do not include a lack of time, money, resources, traditional support staff, staff training, or accepted forms of staff development.

In the United Kingdom, numerous attempts, each costing millions of pounds, have been made to reform the educational system. These have included the introduction of comprehensive schools and mixed-ability teaching (both of which were, in part, designed to stimulate the invention of ways of identifying and fostering more of the talents of more of the pupils and to focus attention on ways of cultivating talents which are, in many ways, more important than those that pass for academic ability in most schools), some of the curriculum development projects of the 1960s and 1970s (e.g., Nuffield Science and The Schools Council Integrated Science and Humanities Projects) that were intended to foster a wider range of competencies, and the introduction of profiles and records of achievement (which were intended to enable pupils to get recognition for a wider range of talents and thus legitimise more broadly based programmes).[17] None of these "initiatives" met with notable success. They are now being joined by the (equally well funded) TVEI (the programmes for which, as actually implemented on the ground, rarely even address the wider competence objectives [i.e., the development of initiative, the ability to communicate, the ability to work with others, and the qualities that make for enterprise] laid down in the TVEI *Guidelines*), the Manpower Services Commission's (MSC) Higher Education Initiative (intended to foster similar qualities), the Scottish Consultative Council on the Curriculum's guidelines for Secondary Education, and the attempts to improve education by specifying curriculum content, testing pupils and teachers, devolving power to school boards, and offering parents and pupils a choice of school in the context of published performance data.[18]

Progressive education has a still longer history of well-funded and resourced attempts to tackle the problems which confront the educational system. These include the efforts of Dewey,[19] Aikin,[20] Caswell,[21] and the Newton School System.[22] Dewey had one adult to every four pupils in his experimental school. Billions of dollars and endless teacher and support time, as well as professional assistance from university staff, were poured into seven U.S. school systems. Yet, in all these experiments, only about 5% of the teachers ended up doing what it was hoped they would do.[23]

Lack of resources and time for conventional development work are, therefore, not among the main barriers to the introduction of effective education.

The other contributory factors that have emerged in the course of our work will be discussed under nine headings.

(1) The absence of tools to help teachers and lecturers to manage multiple, individualised, competency-oriented programmes of education.

Running competency-oriented educational programmes is a creative and inventive, but difficult and frustrating, job. As indicated in an earlier chapter, teachers or lecturers have to find out what each student cares about and is good at, invent a personalised developmental programme which will enable the student to practice (and thereby develop) some of the wide range of competencies that it is possible for them to develop and which are needed in society, monitor the student's reactions to those experiences, and take corrective action when necessary. When there are 30 or more students in a class, this is an almost superhuman task. We have found that those teachers who do manage it have painstakingly—and often at considerable personal cost—developed the necessary sensitivities, monitoring strategies, and competencies over many (perhaps 20) years.[24]

If more teachers and lecturers are to do what these outstanding teachers appear to do "instinctively," it will be necessary for them to have some tools that will help them to undertake the activities mentioned above explicitly. Those tools will have to enable them to identify each student's motives or values, initiate personalised developmental programmes for each student, and familiarise them (the staff) with the concepts they need to think about multiple talents and their development[25].

(2) The absence of the means of giving students, teachers, and lecturers credit in the certification and placement process for their achievements in these areas.

The next problem is the absence of appropriate summative assessment procedures. To understand the importance of this, we must first note that most students and parents now know that the main benefit offered by the "educational" system is not education at all. It is the award of certificates that will buy entry to courses of further and higher education and thence entry to protected occupations—that is, occupations which afford access to a disproportionate share of the good things in life.[26] Students therefore face a dilemma when they are offered programmes that are genuinely developmental but which do not lead to tradable certificates.[27]

Teachers and lecturers have a similar problem. They would be jeopardising their students' life chances if they offered them programmes that nurtured important high-level competencies but, by taking time away from the syllabi on that they will be tested, simultaneously reduced their chances of obtaining high grades. Perhaps just as important, since teachers' and lecturers' reputations depend on their students' grades, they would be jeopardising their own career prospects as well.

It is for these reasons that it is what is assessed in the certification and placement process—and not the educational aspirations of parents, pupils, teachers, lecturers, curriculum councils, ministers of education, or anyone else—that primarily determines what happens in educational institutions.[28] Teachers and lecturers would generally prefer not to recognise this sociological reality and address the dilemmas it poses.[29] Many of them come into teaching because they want to help people and do a worthwhile job in the community.[30] They resent—and are demeaned by—the child-minding and social allocation roles that society thrusts upon them. Rather than think about how the sociological imperative that educational institutions allocate position and status might be grasped and satisfied in a way which would push them in the direction in that they wish to go, they want someone else (such as employers) to perform these tasks and leave them free to get on with education. Unfortunately Dore's[31] data shows that this is sociologically naïve. Teachers' and lecturers' behaviour continues to be determined by what is assessed in the certification and placement process, regardless of who does the assessing.

Actually, ways of assessing high-level competencies are needed not only for certification purposes. They are also needed if lecturers, teachers, and students are to be able to monitor progress toward important goals and obtain the feedback they need to improve their performance—and, indeed, if they are to know that they have accomplished anything worthwhile in the time they have devoted to the activity. Means of assessing such qualities are equally badly needed for use in evaluation studies and accountability exercises. If no such measures are available, the educational system's failure to achieve its main goals will continue to be unknown on the "factual" register that largely determines the educational policy-making agenda. So long as it is known only "intuitively"—in the way it is currently known to parents, teachers, students, and employers—it does not figure in the discussions which determine educational policy. Proposals to improve education will continue to focus on the easily measurable (but relatively trivial) and miss the important (witness the way the philosophy of educational improvement through testing has swept the world).

The growth of the "profiling," "reports of personal experience," and "statements" movements is, of course, fuelled by a recognition of at least some of these facts.[32] These movements are, unfortunately, nevertheless about to demonstrate, yet again, the truth of my earlier proposition that the problem is not one of money, resources, and goodwill. They, like the great educational reforms that have preceded them, will fail because they do not sufficiently recognise either (a) that both (i) changed educational processes and (ii) the development of a new psychometric model are prerequisites to obtaining meaningful assessments of such qualities, or (b) the dilemmas (which will be discussed below) which are involved in assessing competencies that are, as we have seen, *by nature* permeated by values.[33]

(3) The conflict between the procedures that are required to foster high-level competencies and the widely held view that "teaching" means "telling."

The activities which are required to promote the development of high-level competencies are best indicated by the term "facilitating growth."[34] Yet, overlooking the fact that fostering the abilities required to read, write, and count involves advancing skills or competencies, most people believe that teaching is about "telling"—transmitting *information* from teachers and lecturers to students. Schön[35] has thrown the problem into sharp relief by arguing that while the culturally dominant claims of the technical-rational model of competence has driven the concept of professional competence into a corner, discipline-based studies are unable to help people to develop the competencies they will need to deal with the unique, uncertain, changing, and messy situations that they will later encounter. Such programmes therefore output graduates who are no more competent than they were when they started. He found that the claims of the dominant belief system (perhaps combined, although he does not say so, with the widespread recognition that advancement, both in the educational system and outside, is achieved not by possessing and displaying any kind of useful competence but by demonstrating familiarity and facility with the "in" words and jargon desired by those above one) were so deep-rooted that change was virtually impossible: Despite attempting to do so for 15 years, he and Argyris together were unable to introduce the types of programmes that they had observed in architecture, music, and psychoanalysis into other—even nominally "applied"—areas such as management education.

This equation of education with "telling" on the one hand and knowing the "right" things to say on the other has resulted in a vicious cycle: Teaching as a profession recruits a disproportionate number of people who want to be the centre of attention and the source of wisdom, and these are exactly the sort of people that many pupils and students think they want as "teachers."[36] Those who have the skills and sensitivities which are required to facilitate growth tend not to become teachers or lecturers in the first place—and are, then, often rejected by pupils and students if they do find their way into teaching. The conflict between the satisfactions that most teachers and lecturers want from teaching and those available to those who facilitate development—even in language laboratories—results in many teachers and lecturers finding such activities so distressing that they corrupt them back into telling.

Nuttgens[37] has developed the same argument for pupils and students. In the educational system we promote and advance those who are least willing and able to do anything useful (and squeeze out those who are willing and able) precisely because these are the ones who can most clearly see through the system and realise that what is presented as useful is of little value other than as a means of securing personal advancement. The students who remain are those who are least capable of making their own observations and least interested in developing, and least able to develop, competencies which are useful for anything other than securing personal advancement. Not only does this make change in the educational system increasingly difficult as one moves to higher levels, those who remain are set on tracks which lead to influential positions in society. They continue to earn promotion in the world of work in the same way, scorning management development programmes that would actually help them to do their jobs more effectively but would not provide them with words to show off to their superiors. McClelland[38] independently documented this process several years ago: Those people on whom our society is most dependent for innovation—that is, those who have a high need for achievement—are typically dropouts from school.

What these observations show is that there is a serious conflict between the role required of teachers and lecturers if they are to facilitate the development of competence and:

i)   the accurate observation of parents, pupils, and students that the "educational" system is not mainly about developing competence but about legitimising the rationing of privilege and teaching people how to buy personal advancement by ingratiating themselves with their superiors, and

ii) the satisfactions that teachers and lecturers want from their jobs.

If progress is to occur, it will be necessary to get this conflict out into the open and ensure that it is addressed.

If more emphasis is to be placed on facilitating the growth of competence, it will also be necessary to challenge another assumption that derives even more directly from the technical-rational model of competence. This is that "learning" can be chopped up into 40-minute "periods" or 40-hour "modules." While there is no doubt about the need to create a greater variety of short, specialist, up-to-date, knowledge-based modules to support individualised, competency-oriented, educational programmes, it is crucial to recognise that high-level competencies mainly develop whilst people are involved in difficult and demanding activities which occupy an extended period of time but that, in the end, lead to something worthwhile (thus enabling those concerned to experience the benefits and satisfactions which come from having engaged in such difficult and demanding activities and thus reinforcing the tendency to engage in them). What this means is that it is essential to organise modularised material around the ongoing developmental process—and not to try to organise competency-oriented educational programmes around, or through, modules.[39]

(4) The problems that stem from the transformational nature of the educational activities which are required to foster high-level competencies.

To promote the development of high-level competencies one starts by studying students' motives and incipient talents. One then tries to invent individualised developmental experiences that will test one's initial hypotheses about incipient interests and talents and the processes which will lead them to flower.[40] One cannot know the outcome of this process in advance. One may end up doing things that are quite different to those one initially envisaged. Unexpected talents surface and develop. In this way students are *transformed*.[41] All of this is fine from an educational point of view. But it conflicts with widely held beliefs about the ways in which public money should be spent. It is generally believed that one should not take risks with such money and that contractors (teachers, lecturers, or researchers) should be able to specify in advance what the outcome of the expenditure will be. Funding an *adventure* that may (or may not) transform people or existing understandings is viewed as not merely risky; it is viewed as illegitimate. The solution to this problem has to do not only with legitimising venturesome activity in the public sector. It also involves finding ways of identifying the sorts of people (whether teachers, lecturers, or researchers) who are able to capitalise on what they stumble across in the course of an adventure—that is, people who are able to recognise the value of something they have come upon "by chance" and turn it to advantage. To do this, it will be necessary to develop staff appraisal tools that will make it possible to identify, recognise, reward, and encourage among teachers and lecturers the very competencies that we have been concerned with in this book.

(5) The dilemmas associated with catering for diversity.

We have seen that high-level competencies can only be nurtured when people are doing things they care about and that this means tailoring developmental tasks to students' personal values, priorities, and motives. It is sometimes impossible for one group of students to pursue goals which they care about in the same class group in which other students undertake tasks *they* care about. For example, one cannot, in the same classroom, meet the needs of those pupils who want to develop toughness and strength and those who wish to develop the sensitivities required to learn how to set their minds to the dreamy state required to notice the fleeting feelings on the fringe of consciousness that form the germ of nearly all creative new insights and slowly bring them to the centre of attention so that they become articulate and communicable.

This need for variety and choice conflicts with the widely accepted emphasis on equality and uniformity in public provision (The British National Curriculum has gone over the top on this). It is therefore essential to make explicit, and possibly challenge, the reasons for this distaste for variety in the public domain. One of its causes is the experience-based belief that such variety leads to a *hierarchy* of options—running from those which are of high quality to those that are poor—rather than to alternatives which are very different from each other, but all of which are of high quality. When the quality of provision varies only from good to bad, the more informed, articulate, and powerful get the best deal.

It was to counteract this tendency that education was brought into the public domain in the first place. If the stultifying effects of the emphasis on equality in public provision are to be reduced, it will therefore be necessary to introduce much more effective quality control mechanisms to both (1) document the personal and social consequences of each of a number of demonstrably different options and (2) assure the public that each option is of high quality.

Another objection to providing variety and choice in public education is the fear that it will lead to the ossification, even exacerbation, of class differences in the social structure. Fortunately, the available evidence does not support these fears. In the first place, a wide variety of different patterns of competence is required in modern society. Even a single occupational group requires people who want do very different things and who possess different patterns of competence. For example, Taylor and his colleagues[42] have shown that there are 20 different types of outstanding physician and 12 different types of outstandingly creative scientist. Second, no one person could possibly develop all the concerns and patterns of competence we have identified in the course of our work.[43] Third, students have very different preoccupations, concerns, and talents: they want very different things from their education and very different satisfactions from their work.[44] Fourth, this variation is more closely related to the occupational destinations pupils are bound for than to their social origins—indeed, there is wide variation between the values and aspirations of pupils who come from similar backgrounds.[45] Fifth, there is, in our society, a great deal more intergenerational social mobility—both upward and downward—than people believe. Thus Hope[46] found that there is as much social mobility in Scotland as there is in the United States, and Payne[47] showed both that 72% of adults in Scotland were upwardly or downwardly mobile by at least one category and that 20% of Class 1 occupants originated in Class 7. The picture is therefore a great deal more complex than has often been thought, and it points very strongly toward the need to respect, and build on, the variance in students' values, priorities, and patterns of competence instead of "inculcating middle-class values into working-class children." The spectre of teachers perpetuating socio-economic divisions and creating a caste society if they treat different students in different ways therefore does not seem to be well founded.

(6) Value conflicts.
A host of serious problems flow from the fact that high-level competencies are heavily value-laden and involve social and political beliefs.[48]

The first is that any teacher or lecturer who attempts to foster high-level competencies is invariably confronted by parents and pupils who do not value either (1) the competencies (such as the tendency to ask questions or the ability to find information for oneself) which the teacher hopes to foster or (2) the activities the teacher hopes to initiate to allow pupils to practice, and thereby develop, such competencies. (A teacher might, for example, plan to foster a range of high-level competencies by encouraging a class to try to stop a factory polluting a local river—an activity that would almost certainly generate immediate resistance from some parents).[49]

There are several reasons why this problem cannot be resolved simply by offering the public a variety of programmes which are tailored to different values and which aim to foster alternative talents. Among them are:

a) As we have noted, the idea that teachers and lecturers should treat different students in different ways conflicts with the current emphasis on equality in public provision.

b) Even parents who are basically in favour of educational institutions nurturing high-level competencies are faced by the dilemma that working at such activities will take time away from subject- and grade-oriented activity. However, a related problem is that, while many parents want their children to enjoy the economic and social benefits that are associated with high-status managerial jobs, they do not want them to do some of the things that it would be necessary for them to do in order to develop the competencies required to perform those jobs effectively. For example, managerial ability involves the ability to ask pertinent questions, yet many parents do not want their children to ask questions—particularly if it would mean that they themselves would have to justify their commands. Another important competence is the ability to venture into the unknown, yet many parents cannot tolerate the anxiety which arises when their children undertake tasks which are on the verge of their capabilities.[50] Worse still, many parents (and teachers) know that they themselves lack the competencies which are required to manage independent, adventurous, children who take initiative, think for themselves, and guide their behaviour by reference to personalised reason-based moral codes.

c) Many parents not only do not, on balance, want educational institutions to foster high-level qualities in their own children, they do not want them to foster them in other people's children either: If they did, those other children would do better in life than their own. This is one reason why so many people oppose private schools even when they would not send their own children to them even if they could. Private schools can, and often do, inculcate important values and political beliefs—and foster important value-based competencies. But any state school that attempted to do the same would be engulfed in a political furore.

It follows from the observations we have made that while, in the end, the solution to the problems posed by the value-laden nature of important competencies will have to be found by offering students and parents a variety of demonstrably different educational programmes, the provision of variety is not sufficient in itself. It will also be necessary to, at the same time, surface and challenge many social and civic beliefs and resolve some of the dilemmas that have been identified.

To resolve those dilemmas it will be necessary to:

i) Systematically generate a range of educational programmes that will appeal to people with very different concerns and incipient talents and which will lead them to develop very different concerns and patterns of competence.

ii) Accumulate much better research data on the consequences of each of the alternatives for the students concerned and for the societies in which they live. (Such data should include information on the consequences of each option for (a) the patterns of life satisfaction and competence the students develop at the time, (b) the career options open to the students in the future, (c) the patterns of life satisfaction and frustration that those concerned are likely to experience [in the context of alternative changes in society], and (d) societal change itself.)

iii) Develop the tools and structures that are needed to (a) assure the public that the options, although distinctly different, are all of high quality, and (b) administer that variety equitably.

It follows from these observations that if the public is to be offered a variety of options which have very different consequences and be invited to choose between them, we will need to run our society very differently. Among other things, the public service will have to (1) invent, and provide in each community, a variety of options, and (2) collect, and provide people with, the information they need to make meaningful choices between those options.

The second of these implies that the public service will need to feed information *outward* to the public, rather than upward through a bureaucratic hierarchy to elected representatives who take decisions *for* the public. This will mean that the main decision-makers will be the public, not elected representatives.

The task of supervising the information collected and disseminated at each level will require much greater public and media involvement. If this is to happen we will need a much more transparent public bureaucracy, changed roles for elected representatives, and changed citizenship activities. Put another way, we will need to develop new, network-based, participative (rather than representative) forms of democracy to monitor and influence the public service.

It appears, therefore, that (1) fundamental research directed toward the solution of these practical problems, (2) a wide range of development activities, and (3) programmes of adult civic education to promote the evolution of new means of managing society are unexpected prerequisites to effective education. It follows that one of the first steps to be undertaken by institutions of education is, somewhat surprisingly, to change the beliefs they lead their students to adopt about the procedures that are required to promote social development.

A second problem posed by the value-laden nature of competence is that fostering important competencies means influencing students' values and political, economic, and civic beliefs. This raises the spectre of brainwashing. Once again, the dilemmas this poses are most likely to be resolved by finding ways of making what is going on more visible, by providing markedly different options, and by providing better information on the long-term personal and social consequences of each of the alternatives.

But a still more thorny issue must be addressed. We have argued not only that all important competencies are value-based but also that the effective operation of both our educational system and our staff guidance, placement, and development systems is dependent on the *assessment* of these value-laden qualities. The spectre of explicitly assessing value-based motivational dispositions for these purposes throws the moral questions associated with educators working in this area into sharp relief.

There are a number of things to be said about this issue. The first is, obviously, that unless these questions are addressed, we will continue to squander vast resources on demoralised teaching staff, indifferent students whose aim is not to learn anything worthwhile but to beat the system, and a dysfunctional "educational" system which offers little more than a means of legitimising the allocation of privilege on the basis of qualities that are in reality unrelated to occupational or social performance. The second is that failure to address the issue only drives it underground: People will still try to assess these qualities—but continue to do so by selecting students from private schools or seeking assessments over the telephone—in the course of which those concerned will get information based on chance (and highly unreliable) observations and interpretations of students' behaviour, and without those students having any opportunity for redress. The third is that failure to address these issues means that, as a society, we will continue to promote a disproportionate number of the *wrong* people—that is, highly self-interested people who destroy their organisations in the quest for personal advancement or people whose only competence is the ability to earn prestige and advancement by demonstrating a facility with words that have little connection with current economic and social realities—into senior management positions in society.[51] Once again, therefore, the way forward seems to involve programmes of adult civic education designed to lead people to think through these issues.

Throughout this section we have noted the importance of adult civic education. We may now note that the success of any such activity will be critically dependent on better information about the personal and social consequences which follow from people possessing alternative competencies and beliefs—consequences which will vary with the social and organisational structure in which they live and work. Not only is little research of this kind available, there is both little recognition of the need for it and a widespread belief that it would be too difficult to carry out. To make the problem still more intractable, these misunderstandings and oversights are part of a more general climate in which social research is not viewed (by most social scientists as well as most public servants, politicians, and members of the public) as relevant to the solution of important and pressing problems but, like the educational system itself, mainly as a route to personal advancement.

(7) The barriers posed by the latent functions of the educational system.

By now we have seen that the educational system (a) nurtures the tendency to work out which behaviour one's superiors will favour and then to do whatever is necessary to secure one's preferment regardless of the consequences for one's organisation or society,[52] (b) breeds that kind of facility with words that enables people to create a good impression by using fashionable phrases, (c) advances those who are best able to do these things, (d) squeezes out those who are most anxious to act in the long-term interests of society and those who are best able to invent new ways of thinking about and doing things, (e) selects those who are, because of personal ambition or naïveté, most willing and able to undertake the fraudulent "work" of modern society, and (f) operates to perpetuate an inequitable society by legitimising the way in which privilege is rationed instead of fostering and promoting those best able to identify and introduce changes in the way society is organised. We have also seen how educational programmes which foster the ability to enquire into the workings of society become the targets of systematic campaigns to destroy them and tend, in any case, to be choked off by the reactions of the system of that they are part. These processes make it very difficult to change what happens.

It is time now to introduce further observations about the functioning of the educational system. The first of these is that the way in which it works mirrors the way modern societies work. To substantiate this claim we must first recall from our introductory chapter on the learning society that, despite its rhetoric, the main things manufactured by the marketplace are: (1) useless jobs, and (2) discriminations which compel participation in the make-work activities of which modern society is largely composed. There we saw how the insurance industry manufactures endless jobs and magnifies differences between the rich and the moderately rich in such a way as to induce all to invest in private insurance. The educational system works in much the same way: It creates activities that occupy a lot of time of a lot of people—not only of pupils and students but also of teachers, lecturers, administrators, researchers, publishers, librarians, editors, and test agencies; it manufactures discriminations—both in schools and in lifetime earnings—between individuals whose competence differs only slightly and obscures differences in ability and contribution to society that are of vital importance; it makes use of norm-referenced assessments which require more people to spend more time in the system to attain the ever-higher educational qualifications deemed "necessary" to enter the same occupational position and creates a situation in which the "incompetent and ignorant" must by definition forever remain with us (and thus in need of "education," denigration, ostracism, and "motivation by low income"). The processes we are describing are purely sociological, but they clearly contribute to the difficulties involved in introducing change.

We have also seen how the job definitions laid down for teachers, the denigration of those whose pupils do not perform "well" in norm-referenced assessments as "lazy and incompetent," and the (norm-referenced) accountability procedures set up to check on them force teachers to concentrate on low-level goals, neglect any attempt to intervene in the wider social constraints that prevent them working effectively, and thus behave in ways which are both incompetent and unethical: They do not do the things they would need to do to run any educational programme worth the name; they applaud the gullible and self-interested among their pupils; they ignore, and fail to develop, most of the motives and talents of most pupils; they join in the chorus that denigrates many pupils as stupid and incompetent; and they participate in the process of assigning such pupils to a social scrap heap in which they are treated in demeaning and degrading ways. Clearly, in failing to nurture their pupils' talents—talents which are vital if society is to get out of the mess it is in—such teachers are behaving incompetently (albeit that competence would require them to get outside their classrooms to influence the constraints that force them to behave in this way). But their behaviour is also unethical. This is true both in the sense that they unjustifiably assign large numbers of individual pupils to a demeaning lifestyle and in the sense that they fail to nurture talents which it is vital for our students to possess if they are to transform our society in such a way that the human species will *have* a future— never mind a *desirable* future.

But these are not the only ways in which the educational system seems socially functional in the short term but dysfunctional in the longer term: The system also operates as if it were designed to lay the blame for the ills of society at the door of the uneducated and those who are least able to do anything about social problems instead of at the door of the leaders and managers of society. In the same way, the "devolution of management and control" procedures currently being widely advocated for the educational system throughout the world seem designed to lay the blame for the ills of the educational system on teachers and parents rather than on the administrators and politicians who could do something about them: Teachers and parents are in no position to do anything about the social constraints on what schools and teachers can do, to fundamentally alter the tests that are inflicted on schools, to influence the textbooks that get written, or to generate the understandings and tools which are required to run alternative educational programmes.

In a similar vein, by arguing that the educational system is there to nurture the qualities required to promote something called "economic growth" (but which does not deliver high quality of life) through competitiveness and then arguing that such competitiveness demands the low-level competencies which figure in the most widely disseminated lists of "necessary" "competencies," employers have been able to deflect attention away from the fact that the capitalist system has not been delivering a high quality of life but rather has been destroying the environment in such a way as to ensure the absence of a future, away from what employers have *not* done to promote climates of innovation and genuine efficiency, and away from work which promotes the long-term public interest. By highlighting the costs of schooling and of "looking after the unemployed," employers have been able to deflect attention away from the fact that it is they who have evaded payment of the most significant tax contributions, they who have created unemployment to drive down wages and conditions of work and compel participation in an inhumane and socially destructive system, they who have acted in the most socially destructive—and unethical—ways, they who have conspired to eliminate enquiry-oriented education, they who have failed to develop and utilise the talents of their employees, and they who now wish to foist the costs of upgrading the skills of employees onto an educational system to which they have failed to make a financial contribution.

The educational system emphasises "respect for authority" while leaving those with "authority" with the right to define who will be counted among their members. It presents "science" as concerned with "knowing what is right"—that is, what authority (those in positions of power with an interest to protect) approves of—rather than a process of enquiry. As the work of Robinson[53] and others has shown, those in authority—from Mrs. Thatcher to the National Association of Manufacturers in the United States—correctly recognise that enquiring scientific minds threaten vested interests. By creating a training and assessment system that focuses on low-level "competencies" specified by authorities and assessed by means determined by authority, the educational system creates conditions in which people must accept the dictates of authority if they wish to avoid demeaning lifestyles in which their quality of life is determined by whatever indignities those same authorities choose to heap upon them. More directly, it both teaches that authorities have the *right* to decide what one will learn and what one will do, assess one, and generally push one around and gives that same authority the power to decide what knowledge— actually low-level useless knowledge—will count, thus creating a self-perpetuating structure. It creates a culture of acceptance and dependence. It prevents those concerned from developing the motivation and the competencies required to enquire into the workings of their society and get control over their destinies. The competency movement seems to have been hijacked to perform precisely these functions. Not surprisingly, those responsible for it vehemently deny that it is necessary to problematise, and enquire into, the nature of competence. But there is something else of interest there. Something of an unholy alliance seems to have grown up between those in authority in the system and "postmodernist" sociologists who argue that enquiry into the workings of the system is futile. One may therefore be forgiven for suspecting that support for the postmodernist position may be coming from precisely the same group of people as used their might to bring about the replacement of all classical economists in U.S. ivy league and land-grant universities by neo-classicists in order to discredit the observations that the classical economists had made and introduce the obscuranticisms of the neo-classicists.

Perhaps the most insidious aspect of the educational system is that it nurtures the tendency to accept things that are not what they seem to be and promotes those who are most willing to quote the conventional wisdom despite its lack of reference to reality. Those who are unwilling to notice that things are not as they are said to be are, in the short term, ideally suited to jobs in insurance, the World Bank, "aid" agencies, welfare agencies, the public service, the food industry, and politics and government. The most pervasive, but least remarked, feature of modern society is that *nothing* is what it seems to be—and everything is, in fact, usually the opposite of what it seems to be.[54] The tendency of the educational system to disseminate false consciousness and promote those most inclined to engage in "double-talk" makes it extremely difficult to conduct any rational discussion of wider social processes.

Although it is tempting to see some kind of conspiracy in the parallelism between what happens in the educational system and the wider society and in the educational system's tendency to introduce false consciousness into discussions of social processes when these threaten the short-term interests of those with more power in society, it is not necessary to make that assumption. The educational system has grown on the basis of myths. These include "if we all get more education we will all get good jobs" and "more education will make for economic and social development."[55] It has also grown as a result of the less mythical fact that, whatever doubts there may be about the educational benefits of the system, persisting in the educational system confers a greater likelihood of obtaining a good job. Despite these observations, Robinson's discovery that there *was* a very effective conspiracy to discredit the work of Harold Rugg is disconcerting.[56] Precisely because Rugg's books were *effective* in fostering in pupils the tendency and ability to think critically about the workings of society, the National Association of Manufacturers mounted a deliberate campaign to discredit both Rugg and his books—a campaign from which he never recovered. The documents which Robinson has reviewed show beyond reasonable doubt that this involved numerous accusations which were known to be false and deliberate lies to congressional committees of inquiry. It is hard to credit that work as innocuous as Rugg's—directed toward what is widely agreed to be one of the main goals of education—could have produced such concerted, sustained, dirty tricks. Robinson's (and Bellini's[57]) work leads one to take more seriously the claims of those, such as Chomsky,[58] who are inclined toward conspiracy theories. Their suspicions are supported by the available information on the way in which the Schools Council Integrated Science and Humanities projects were closed down and deprived of resources as soon as it became obvious that they were centrally concerned with encouraging pupils to make their own observations about how society worked (and, in the first case, deploy scientific methodology to check those observations).[59] They are also supported by observations about how a series of specific university departments—such as the Centre for Human Ecology in Edinburgh—have been closed when it became clear that their students were not only becoming embarrassingly good at asking questions but also at using what they did know to press effectively for change. They are also confirmed by the way in which the Conservative government in the United Kingdom, having inveighed against the "Questioning Students of the 1960s" and asserted the need for "people to learn their place," set about introducing changes into the universities that had the effect of eliminating most of the time available to staff for unfettered enquiry, insisting that most research be funded from commercial sources, and controlling the content of all publications based on research carried out with the aid of government grants[60].

If these observations are correct, it is obvious that it would be extremely difficult to do such things as introduce any form of multiple-talent education designed to develop and credential at least some of the talents of all of our children—because this would undermine the educational system's role in manufacturing and legitimising discriminations of a kind which compel participation in institutional arrangements which give meaning to life in modern society.

That this hypothesis is not so far-fetched as it may at first sight appear to be can be seen by reflecting on what happened to attempts to reform examinations in England and Wales. For 20 years committees of the Schools Council for Curriculum and Examinations debated the desirability of establishing a common system of examinations without coming to a conclusion. Then a Minister for Education established a new committee—The Waddell Committee—with a specific remit to come to a conclusion. The committee observed that pupils had a wide variety of talents that could only be fostered through very different types of educational programme. It noted that workplaces and society required a wide variety of people who possessed very different talents. It therefore concluded that there was a need for a wide variety of educational programmes which would foster very different competencies and in the course of which pupils would cover very different syllabi. This led it to the conclusion that it would be necessary to retain a wide variety of examining boards which would each promote a wide variety of courses covering different content, aim at different goals, and be assessed using different forms, or "modes," of assessment. Only the latter would make it possible for pupils to get credit for having developed high-level competencies such as initiative and leadership. Then it did something that was, at first sight, inexplicable. In one sentence embedded in a long paragraph it said "the results will be expressed on a single scale of seven points in the subject area." This, of course, negated all the steps—based on all the educational and occupational observations it had made—that it planned to take to promote and cater for diversity. How does one express assessments of "leadership" on a single scale which also measures knowledge of 17th-century history? If one asks oneself what could have caused such an action, one can only conclude that the sociological need for a single and unarguable criterion to legitimise the allocation of position and status—and with it a whole social system for rationing privilege—had overridden all human, educational, and occupational considerations.

What all this means is that if education is to be brought back into "educational" institutions, those concerned (including teachers and lecturers) will *as part of their professional duties deriving from their remit to achieve educational goals* have to take active steps to influence the way society is organised.

(8) Dysfunctional beliefs about the role of the public servant.

We have seen that competency-oriented education requires teachers and lecturers to pay attention to the needs of individual students and to invent individualised developmental programmes that will lead them to blossom. It also requires them to get together with other teachers and lecturers to invent better ways of meeting students' needs, to find ways of influencing the tests which are available from test publishers (so that tests cease to direct their attention toward low-level goals and away from high-level goals), and to influence the beliefs which parents and others hold about education itself and about how the public service should operate. Unfortunately, teachers, like other public servants, are not generally expected to be inventors and activists of this sort. They are viewed as functionaries who should do the bidding of elected representatives. To solve this problem we not only need to rethink our beliefs about how the public service should operate and to create structures (à la Kanter[61]) that promote innovation, we also need to apply new criteria to judge the effectiveness of public servants and to develop new tools to use in staff appraisal, so that teachers and lecturers can get credit for engaging in the difficult, demanding, frustrating, and time-consuming activities that are required if they are to do their jobs more effectively.

Several things follow from this brief discussion. What we are saying is that teachers and lecturers, like other public servants, should be expected to orient themselves more toward the needs of their clients than toward the directives of elected representatives. They should be held accountable for making good, discretionary, and forward-looking decisions about what is in the best interests of their clients rather than for following the directives of their superiors. They cannot be held accountable for following prescriptions, because the requisite activities need to vary so much from one teacher or lecturer to another and from student to student. If these observations are correct, it follows that new procedures are required to hold teachers and lecturers accountable to the public for high-quality performance. Yet the issue is not merely one of criteria and tools of staff appraisal because, having once admitted the need for initiative and diversity, it is obvious that the chain of accountability cannot be purely hierarchical to distant elected representatives. Toffler,[62] Schön,[63] Ferguson,[64] Howard,[65] and I[66] have all argued that the structures that are needed to manage modern society effectively involve replacing representative democracy by new, network-based, participative forms of democracy which would be much more dependent on the involvement of local citizens, place greater reliance on formal evaluation procedures, and make greater use of (Information Technology-based) networks to exchange information.

This discussion also indicates a need to move beliefs about how innovation is to occur away from faith in centre-specified (committee-specified) innovations to the creation of climates which breed innovation at all levels. How such climates are to be created will be discussed under the next heading.

(9) The absence of an innovative educational system.

In the course of this and earlier chapters, we have seen that the attempt to deal with the conspicuous problems of the educational system by trying to prescribe what students will learn and then find out whether they have learnt it using centrally prescribed tests of the traditional type is misguided. We have seen that the barriers to effective education are deep-seated and non-obvious, that what people need to learn to do varies markedly from one person to another, that the available tests are unable to reflect the high-level competencies which students need to develop, and that our hierarchical management system has been unable to eliminate even grossly incompetent teachers and lecturers, never mind create a ferment of innovation. Pervasive innovation in every nook and cranny of the educational system is required. There is no way in which any central authority can lay down what teachers and lecturers will do, never mind prescribe what individual students should learn. Instead, the task of a central authority is to create a structure and set of expectations that will (1) lead to increasing clarity about the goals that are to be achieved and the procedures which are to be used to reach them, (2) encourage all concerned to assess whether they are achieving their goals effectively, (3) encourage them to identify the barriers to success, and (4) lead them to vigorously set about trying to do something about those barriers.

It is clear from these observations that one of the barriers to the evolution and diffusion of educational innovations has to do with the fact that the educational system operates in the context of a set of beliefs to the effect that it is the job of publicly elected representatives and senior management to establish the goals of the educational system and the procedures to be used to reach them—with its corollary that the job of teachers or lecturers is to carry out the activities prescribed by such authorities. These beliefs and expectations discourage teachers and lecturers from studying the needs of their students and trying to invent better ways of meeting them. Unfortunately, these beliefs are only part of a much wider problem: In Britain, since innovation is thought to be the prerogative of management, the educational system does not have a management structure—and a climate of beliefs and expectations—which stimulates and facilitates innovation. We have already seen that the stimulation of innovation involves creating within the educational system what Kanter has called "parallel organisation" activity focusing on innovation. What we are now saying is that we also need to replace our hierarchical management structures—our structures of bureaucracy and democracy—by network-based management structures. These will be discussed shortly. Here it is sufficient to note that the failure to create an innovative educational system is not only dysfunctional in itself—it also has the greatest knock-on effect on society as a whole because teachers and lecturers powerfully communicate to their students their own beliefs about what it is important to attend to and how things should be done.[67]

We may conclude by noting that what has been said implies that the areas in which research and innovation are *most* badly needed in our society do *not* have to do with finding better ways of producing goods of one kind or another but with finding better ways of running society itself.

Summary and Integration

Our next step must be to note that these barriers do not operate independently. We have therefore attempted, following the procedures described by Morgan,[68] to map the connections. The outcome is presented in Diagram 23.1.

What we now see is that:

1. What happens is determined by a *system*, or *network*, of hidden social forces which drive the system.[69]
2. Any attempt to change any one part without considering the system as a whole will be negated by the rest of the system.
3. Pervasive, *systems-oriented*, change is required. But that change, although systemwide, cannot be centrally mandated because too many new things need to be done.
4. What happens is not determined by the wishes of parents, teachers, ministers of education or anyone else but, both directly and indirectly, by the sociological functions the system performs for society. One needs to take these sociological forces seriously and ask how they can be harnessed in the way that marine engineers harness the wind: They won't go away.
5. The effects of these sociological forces are reinforced by inappropriate beliefs about society and how it is to be managed. The educational system *teaches* these beliefs, and what can be done to improve it is very much constrained by them.

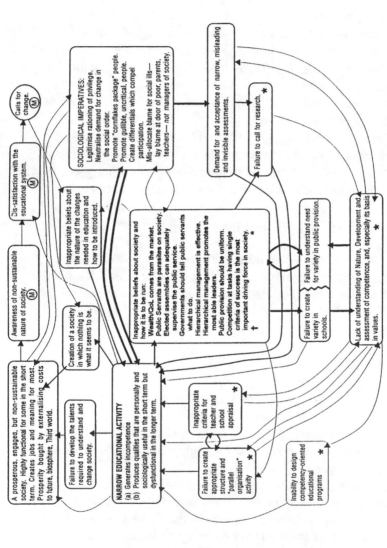

* Intervention in these cells would help change the nature of the qualities nurtured and rewarded in the system. Motives which should be harnessed to do this are marked Ⓜ.

† These need to be replaced by acceptance of the need to make managed economies work—to find ways of giving effect to information concerning the public long term interest, the need to explicitly create variety and information on the personal and social consequences of the options, and to find ways of holding public servants accountable for, and getting them to act in, the long term public interest. This means systematic, broadly-based, evaluation and participative democracy.

Diagram 23.1 Feedback loops driving down the quality of education.

6. Points (2), (4), and (5), individually and collectively, (a) drive common sense attempts to reform the system ever more narrowly, and ineffectively, around the triangle at the top left of the Diagram and (b) divert attention from the necessary developments that are listed in the bottom part of the diagram.

7. The *causes* of the symptoms (and thus the appropriate place to start reform) are far removed from those symptoms.

8. The most important developments have to do with (a) finding better ways of conceptualising and identifying the sociological forces we have discussed, and (b) clarifying how they are to be harnessed—that is, articulating the societal management arrangements required to do so. (Note that both of these call for both classic academic activity to generate fundamental developments in theory and for what might be called "social engineering." Remember [i] that sailing boats could not sail into the wind prior to Newton and [ii] that, once the principles had been articulated, marine engineers were able to do a great deal to find better ways of harnessing the wind to do useful work for mankind instead of allowing it to drive our ships against the rocks.) The most important developments that are needed if the problems are to be tackled are therefore anything but obvious and have to do with the management of social research and development. "Common sense" alone will not work.

9. The fundamental need is to create a system of innovation and learning in which everyone's observations are used to experiment with curricula which will make it possible to cater for diversity and nurture multiple talents, with assessment systems which will help teachers to implement multiple individualised developmental programmes and give pupils credit for the outcomes, and in promoting the development of new forms of democracy and public management. Note that this conclusion is precisely the opposite of that which guides current government policy and informs widely held beliefs about how public management—and hierarchical management more generally—should work. But such work needs to be guided by awareness of the need to use these experiments to better understand and find ways of influencing hidden systems processes and by concepts of comprehensive evaluation which are in stark contrast to the assumptions of the reductionist science that permeate modern society.

In more detail, the diagram shows that:

A. The narrow educational activities that dominate schools are produced by (a) a series of sociological imperatives (e.g., that schools assist in legitimising the rationing of privilege); (b) inappropriate beliefs about the nature of the changes that are needed in education itself, the management of the educational system, and the management of society; (c) failure to initiate research which would yield useful insights into such things as the nature of competence and how it is to be fostered and how to manage the educational system to nurture high-level generic competencies; (d) the absence of (i) systematically generated variety in, and choice between, educational programmes which have demonstrably different consequences and (ii) information about the consequences of each of these alternatives; (e) failure to introduce "parallel organisation activity" to produce innovation within schools; and (f) inadequate dissemination of the results of research into the nature, development, and assessment of generic high-level competencies, and, especially, the implications of the values basis of competence.

B. This narrow educational process has a series of knock-on effects that finally contribute to its own perpetuation. The competencies and beliefs that are nurtured and inculcated in educational institutions reinforce a social order which offers major benefits to "able" people who do what is required of them without questioning that order; it creates endless work that gives meaning to people's lives (but does not enhance the general quality of life); it creates wealth at the expense of the biosphere, future generations, and the Third World; and it protects its citizens from a knowledge of the basis of their wealth. The educational system helps to teach a host of incorrect beliefs which collectively result in nothing being what it is popularly or authoritatively said to be. This double-talk makes it extremely difficult to conduct any rational discussion of the changes needed in society. The sociological imperative that educational institutions help to legitimise the rationing of privilege helps to create a demand for, and encourages acceptance of, narrow, invisible, and mislabelled assessments. Those predisposed to acquire these "qualifications" are not inclined to see the need for, or to commission, genuine enquiry-oriented research or notice other talents in their fellows. Teachers who discover the hidden competencies of their "less able" students experience acute distress. The lack of understanding of the nature of competence leads to a failure to underline the need for a variety of value-based educational programmes and thus to the perpetuation of narrow educational activity.

C. The main motives for change are widespread awareness that there is something seriously wrong with the educational system and, more specifically, awareness that it fails miserably in its manifest task of identifying, nurturing, recognising, and utilising most people's motives and talents. The most commonly proposed solutions to this problem, based as they are on other misunderstandings, are, however, inappropriate. Another motive for change is that there is increasing recognition that we have created a non-sustainable society and that basic change in the way society is run is essential.

D. There are a number of points at which it should be possible to intervene in the feedback loops to create an upward spiral. These involve: (a) promoting wider recognition that one cannot get value for human effort in modern society unless we introduce better means of monitoring and evaluating the long-term effects of what we are doing and better ways of giving effect to information on such effects. This points to the need to change the way we run society, to the need to introduce more, and more appropriate, social research and evaluation activity, and to the need to find ways of holding public servants and politicians accountable for seeking out and acting on information in an innovative way in the long-term public interest; (b) introducing the "parallel organisation" activities that are required to promote innovation within educational institutions; (c) establishing a greater variety of distinctively different, value-based, educational programmes and providing information on the short- and long-term, personal and social, consequences of each; (d) creating public debate about the forms of supervision—the nature of the democracy—needed to ensure that public servants seek out and act on information in an innovative way in the public interest; and (e) disseminating what is already known about the nature, development, and assessment of competence and its implications.

The Way Forward

The points at which one could fruitfully intervene to begin to promote the necessary developments and understandings are shown in Diagram 23.2 Dissemination of what is already known about:

- The nature of competence and the ways in that the development of its components are to be assessed,

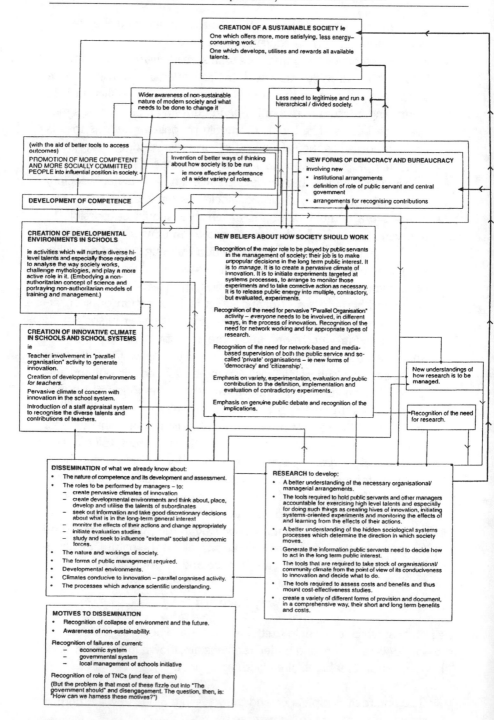

CREATION OF A SUSTAINABLE SOCIETY ie
One which offers more, more satisfying, less energy–consuming work.
One which develops, utilises and rewards all available talents.

Wider awareness of non-sustainable nature of modern society and what needs to be done to change it

Less need to legitimise and run a hierarchical / divided society.

(with the aid of better tools to access outcomes)
PROMOTION OF MORE COMPETENT AND MORE SOCIALLY COMMITTED PEOPLE into influential position in society.

Invention of better ways of thinking about how society is to be run
– ie more effective performance of a wider variety of roles.

NEW FORMS OF DEMOCRACY AND BUREAUCRACY
involving new
• institutional arrangements
• definition of role of public servant and central government
• arrangements for recognising contributions

DEVELOPMENT OF COMPETENCE

CREATION OF DEVELOPMENTAL ENVIRONMENTS IN SCHOOLS

ie activities which will nurture diverse hi-level talents and especially those required to analyse the way society works, challenge mythologies, and play a more active role in it. (Embodying a non-authoritarian concept of science and portraying non-authoritarian models of training and management.)

NEW BELIEFS ABOUT HOW SOCIETY SHOULD WORK

Recognition of the major role to be played by public servants in the management of society: their job is to make unpopular decisions in the long term public interest. It is to manage. It is to create a pervasive climate of innovation. It is to initiate experiments targeted at systems processes, to arrange to monitor those experiments and to take corrective action as necessary. It is to release public energy into multiple, contractory, but evaluated, experiments.

Recognition of the need for pervasive "Parallel Organisation" activity – everyone needs to be involved, in different ways, in the process of innovation. Recognition of the need for network working and for appropriate types of research.

Recognition of the need for network-based and media-based supervision of both the public service and so-called 'private' organisations – ie new forms of 'democracy' and 'citizenship'.

Emphasis on variety, experimentation, evaluation and public contribution to the definition, implementation and evaluation of contradictory experiments.

Emphasis on genuine public debate and recognition of the implications.

CREATION OF INNOVATIVE CLIMATE IN SCHOOLS AND SCHOOL SYSTEMS

ie
Teacher involvement in "parallel organisation" activity to generate innovation.

Creation of developmental environments for teachers.

Pervasive climate of concern with innovation in the school system.

Introduction of a staff appraisal system to recognise the diverse talents and contributions of teachers.

New understandings of how research is to be managed.

Recognition of the need for research.

DISSEMINATION of what we already know about:
• The nature of competence and its development and assessment.
• The roles to be performed by managers – to:
  – create pervasive climates of innovation
  – create developmental environments and think about, place, develop and utilise the talents of subordinates
  – seek out information and take good discretionary decisions about what is in the long-term general interest
  – monitor the effects of their actions and change appropriately
  – initiate evaluation studies
  – study and seek to influence "external" social and economic forces.
• The nature and workings of society.
• The forms of public management required.
• Developmental environments.
• Climates conducive to innovation – parallel organised activity.
• The processes which advance scientific understanding.

RESEARCH to develop:
• A better understanding of the necessary organisational/managerial arrangements.
• The tools required to hold public servants and other managers accountable for exercising high level talents and especially for doing such things as creating hives of innovation, initiating systems-oriented experiments and monitoring the effects of and learning from the effects of their actions.
• A better understanding of the hidden sociological systems processes which determine the direction in which society moves.
• Generate the information public servants need to decide how to act in the long term public interest.
• The tools that are required to take stock of organisational/community climate from the point of view of its conduciveness to innovation and decide what to do.
• The tools required to assess costs and benefits and thus mount cost-effectiveness studies.
• create a variety of different forms of provision and document, in a comprehensive way, their short and long term benefits and costs.

MOTIVES TO DISSEMINATION
• Recognition of collapse of environment and the future.
• Awareness of non-sustainability.

Recognition of failures of current:
  – economic system
  – governmental system
  – local management of schools initiative

Recognition of role of TNCs (and fear of them)
(But the problem is that most of these fizzle out into "The government should" and disengagement. The question, then, is: "How can we harness these motives?")

Diagram 23.2 New Societal Management Arrangements

- The roles to be performed by effective managers, particularly public servants, and
- The nature and workings of society, could impact:
- The climate for innovation in educational institutions;
- The quality of the developmental environments available to students;
- The level and diversity of talents that are nurtured and credentialed;
- The level of awareness about the non-sustainable nature of modern society and the developments needed to change it; and
- The extent to which the developments needed to run modern society more effectively are recognised.

These developments would be mutually supportive. What is more, the developments in education would flow round to reinforce changes in society and these, in turn, would facilitate—rather than inhibit—developments in the educational system.

The key developments that are needed are new forms of democracy and bureaucracy. But to get these we need changed beliefs about the topics covered in the central boxes in Diagrams 23.1 and 23.2. Changed beliefs in these areas—spelt out in *The New Wealth of Nations*—would lead directly to both new forms of bureaucracy and democracy and to the implementation of the research needed to develop the understandings and tools that are needed to run the educational system—and society more generally—effectively.

The heaviest feedback loops are those on the right-hand side of the diagram, and it is on producing the developments indicated by the contents of the boxes that precede them that attention needs to focus.

Most people could contribute in one way or another to intervention at these "leverage points": Everyone can do something to help to promote a wider debate in the media. Everyone can strive to influence local educational systems. Most people could form, or contribute to, groups to put pressure on politicians. They could press to have recruitment into teaching based on the ability to facilitate growth rather than on qualifications which primarily index the willingness to regurgitate what "authorities" want to hear. They could try to persuade employers to change their selection criteria. They could campaign to get test agencies to invest in the research and development required to broaden the range of their products. They could take legal action against test agencies for damaging people's lives and careers and society at large. They could press for social change so that there is less need for educational institutions to manufacture discriminations that compel participation in the useless activities of which modern society is so largely composed.

The most important single change they could try to bring into being would, however, involve getting national and local governments to change the philosophy which informs their current thinking about how the system is to be managed. The need, both within the educational system and outside it, is to create a climate which facilitates development, rather than one in which it is assumed that those in authority should prescribe the activities to be carried out by public servants, teachers, and lecturers and then check up to find out whether those instructions have been obeyed. The new arrangements would include a network-based structure to supervise the public service, tools to run the educational system (and the public service in general) more effectively, and a support structure to conduct the necessary research.

Technological change is also extremely important. Teachers and lecturers teach, and students work, toward the goals that are *assessed*. Teachers, lecturers, and administrators do those things for which they will be credited in staff appraisal systems, and teachers and lecturers attend only to those educational processes they can monitor. Teachers and lecturers need tools to help them administer individualised, competency-oriented, developmental programmes. Such tools would help them to identify and harness students' motives, create individualised programmes, monitor the results, and record the outcomes. The availability of easy-to-use tools in these areas would transform education, regardless of whether or not steps were taken to overcome the other barriers to effective education that have been identified in this book.

However, the most difficult, but vitally important, task facing national, regional, and local government is to initiate the developments needed to create a society in which there would be no need for educational institutions to perform their latent sociological functions. Ironically, the development and dissemination of the understandings needed to divert the educational system away from these functions, and toward the real goals of education, is unmistakably a task for the educational system itself. Unfortunately, as we have seen, Robinson has shown that even a relatively innocuous attempt to address this agenda threatened vested interests to such an extent that a concerted campaign was established to crush the activity.[70] There is no reason to suppose that future activity in this area would not meet with a similar response. There are, however, a number of new features in the situation which might lead to a different outcome: (1) we can now anticipate, and prepare for, the reaction of those who have a major interest in the perpetuation of the system, (2) there is now much more widespread dissatisfaction with the educational system, (3) there is now a much wider awareness that the way our society is organised will have to change dramatically, and (4) it is now clear that major social reform is essential to even the relatively short-term interest of those who are most likely to resist change.[71]

It should now be apparent that one of the reasons why the reform of education has proved to be so difficult is that it involves the reform of government and society.

It follows from the observations made in this chapter that if we are to translate our social and educational values into effect, we will need, above all, to analyse the workings of our society with a view toward identifying leverage points at which it would be possible for us to intervene for the common good. To do this, each of us could do worse than begin by asking ourselves, as individuals: "What are my social and educational values?" "What prevents me from translating those values into effect?" "What can *I* do to influence the current situation?"[72]

Implications for the Organisation of Research[73]

This book has three main objectives: first, to problematise the concept of "competence" and highlight the high-level competencies that are required if the planet is to *have* a future in anything approaching its present form; second, to disseminate what is already known about the nature, development, and assessment of competence; and, third, to identify the barriers to change and the most important developments that are required if we are to move forward.

I have shown that the barriers to the introduction of educational programmes which would achieve the wider goals of general education—goals which have been stressed in report after report for more than a century—are deep-seated and non-obvious. However, what it is most important for anyone concerned with either the process of policy improvement or with policy research to note is that it has only been possible to clarify the nature of the qualities which are to be fostered, the strategies to be deployed to foster them, and the barriers to implementing educational programmes that would foster them in the course of skirmishes conducted in "spare time" on the sidelines of projects that were funded for other reasons—or which were, indeed, not funded at all. The research that was needed did not fit easily into the dominant framework of beliefs about how research should be organised, conducted, and funded. This will continue to be true in the future: The work that is required to overcome the barriers, for example, involves action which is *integrated with* a great deal of fundamental theoretical research—often into topics which have not, in the past, been viewed as amenable to research. Neither the fundamental research nor the requisite action can be fitted into the current framework of beliefs about how either research or innovative action should be funded or conducted.

If work of the kind we have carried out in the past and need to carry out in the future is to be undertaken, it will be necessary to clarify and promote a set of beliefs about the nature of science, the research process, and the institutional framework needed to carry it out that is markedly at variance with the set which is most widely held by public servants and academics at the present time. If we are to do this, we will first have to become a great deal clearer about what we want to say and then embark on a programme of adult education which will lead to resolution of the dilemmas that have, in the past, prevented policymakers from overtly supporting research of the kind which led to the conclusions and developments summarised above.

The barriers to public funding of the requisite research and development in the past have included:

(1)   mistaken beliefs about the *nature* of outcomes that it is most important to aim for in, or satisfy from, a research project. The most useful outcomes of research typically consist of *insights developed in the course of the research* and *not* the previously formulated hypotheses "tested" within—or precise questions answered from—it.[74]

(2)   the apparently "political" nature of many of the issues, questions, and processes that needed to be understood if the presenting problem was to be solved. These issues were not thought to be appropriate topics for scientific research in the first place, and our conclusions were branded as political statements rather than accepted as scientific findings when we arrived at them. (This problem has dogged the physical and biological sciences in the past—witness Galileo—but is now popularly associated primarily with the social sciences. What it really indicates is that the research is challenging previously unquestioned views of the world itself.)[75]

(3)   the time-scales involved: The "research programme" which led to many of the insights summarised above has been intermittently sustained for more than 40 years.

(4)   the non-obvious nature of many of the real causes of the presenting problem. One consequence of the distance between the symptoms (e.g., disenchantment of pupils) and their causes (e.g., beliefs of adults about how their society works and should work)—and

thus remedial action—is that researchers who tackle them are accused of not having answered the questions they were asked to answer. Time after time we have found that issues we explored because they *seemed* somehow relevant—but which we were not asked to explore and the exploration of which even we ourselves would at the time have been hard-pressed to link to the presenting problem—have, in retrospect, turned out to be *central* to understanding the reasons for, and finding ways of solving, that problem. Unfortunately, they were often still far outside the perceived sphere of influence of those who commissioned the research—an observation that again contributes to our understanding of the problem because it tells us that the problem is in part due to the way society is organised and points to the need for new societal management structures and mechanisms.

While influencing widely held beliefs about the initiation, conduct, content, and management of social research would require a major campaign, it may be possible to tackle one subset of inappropriate beliefs more easily. Many of the fundamental new insights into the nature, development, and assessment of competence which were briefly mentioned above emerged in the course of attempting to grapple with "applied" problems.[76] Likewise, the *need* for much of the fundamental research highlighted in this chapter emerged from an attempt to grapple with those same applied problems. To develop the tools which are required to orchestrate competency-oriented educational programmes, we need new theory. Yet the very idea that the requisite tools *might* be produced is dependent on already having developed a feel for the kind of theory on which they might be based. Understanding this close, cumulative, and cyclical relationship between research and action is of crucial importance. The fundamental research that is required to generate the necessary new understandings and tools can only be carried out in the context of action. One cannot, for example, test out a new theory about how high-level competencies might be assessed in contexts in which the relevant competencies are not exercised and developed—that is, in traditional educational programmes. But one cannot change educational processes in any important way without (1) a better understanding of pedagogic processes and (2) the means of giving students and lecturers credit for new kinds of achievements. But one cannot give students credit for these achievements without the tools that it would be the central objective of the exercise to develop. Not only is this a catch-22 situation, the teachers, lecturers, and researchers concerned need to have both the time required for, and the ability to tolerate, the frustrations involved in innovative work[77] and the time and the personal qualities required to gain the confidence of students, parents, and prospective employers.

The idea that fundamental research can usually be undertaken only in an action context will appear to many to be a contradiction in terms. But that is not the end of the confusion, because the need to do something about an applied problem is also the best stimulus to recognising the need for fundamental research. These two observations imply that the concept of a university as an institution that is not heavily involved in innovative action is misguided.

Unfortunately, it is not only the universities as they are currently organised that are unable to undertake the necessary research effectively. Policy research institutes, as currently envisaged and operated, are equally unsuited to the task. This is partly due to the assumptions on which contract research is based and the arrangements which are made for its execution. But it is also partly due to a desire to discourage policy evaluation units from engaging in either fundamental research or controversial—especially politically relevant—research.

This is not the place to embark on a discussion of the institutional framework—the relationships to be established between researchers and the users of research, the career structures which are required, the criteria to be applied to researchers' work, and the climate of expectations that are required if important social research is to be carried out effectively.[78] What it *is* appropriate to do is to encourage those who have persisted thus far to review this information and do what they can to ensure that it is taken on board by the university lecturers and college staff who currently disseminate inappropriate beliefs to students—students who will, in future, become the administrators, politicians, and citizens who control the organisation and funding of social research.[79]

Notes

1. Roizen & Jepson, 1985.

2. Flanagan, 1978.

3. Marris, 1964.

4. Winter, McClelland, & Stewart, 1981.

5. Roizen & Jepson, 1985; Association of Graduate Careers Advisory Services, 1992.

6. Raven, 1994; HMI, 1980; Fraley, 1981; Winter, McClelland, & Stewart, 1981.

7. Schön, 1987; Fraley, 1981. The School of Independent Studies was disbanded after a review by HMI in 1994.

8. Eraut, 1994.

9. Boyatzis, et al., 1995.

10. Cross, 1988.

11. Adams, Robbins, & Stephenson, 1981.

12. Robbins, 1988.

13. It could have been argued that the development of the competence to plan one's own life and gain control of one's destiny was a super-ordinate competence which took precedence over the development of more specific and specifiable competencies, but, so far as I know, this was never argued, and the development of this competency was never considered in the assessment and validation process.

14. See Raven (1991) for a more detailed account of the work and problems of the School.

15. Schön's (1983, 1987) work confirms how little is known about how such qualities are to be fostered.

    However, I am often told that the relevant understandings are widely available in the voluminous writings on Progressive Education. Unfortunately, this is incorrect.

    The chaotic activities perpetrated in the name of Progressive Education are well illustrated in the work of Barth (1972), Aikin (1942), Rathbone (1971), Rugg (1926), Rugg and Schumaker (1928), Wright (1950, 1958), ORACLE, Leith (1981) and Bennett (1976). Cremin (1961), Fraley (1981) and Ravitch (1974) have provided useful summaries of the Progressive Education movement in America.

    By and large, "Progressive Education" has involved little more than a reaction *against* a single-valued concept of human quality and excellence—that is, against the equation of "ability" with "the ability to do well at school." Many teachers and other observers have noted that this "ability" does not correlate highly with performance at non-school tasks. Indeed, they have noted that, as part of a socio-logical system for allocating position and status, this way of thinking tends to lead, on the one hand, to the *wrong* (i.e., purely self-interested) people being placed in influential positions in society, and, on the other, to many people who do contribute in very worthwhile ways to society not getting the respect and financial rewards they deserve. The problem has been that this reaction against a dysfunctional system did not lead to a better one—but only to such things as teachers addressing themselves mainly to pupils of "average" ability and even, in some cases, to pouring scorn on those who sought to do "well" at traditional school tasks—and thus to the cult of uniformity and mediocrity. Few sought to implement "talents unlimited" (Taylor 1974, 1985) types of educational programme.

Several writers have tried to add new goals without seeking to basically change teachers' focus. Thus Dewey (1899, 1910, 1916) seems to have been preoccu-pied with, on the one hand, fostering the skills of the research scientist (the ability to conceptualise, analyse and experiment), and, on the other, with creating "demo-cratic" classrooms. His writing does not encourage teachers to make use of mul-tiple-talent concepts of ability (by, for example, encouraging them to think about the wide range of alternative talents which schools might foster). Still less does it encourage them to foster different competencies in different children. Kilpatrick (1918) indicates that, in translating a plan into a reality, pupils should practise purposing, planning, executing and judging. These are high-level competencies, but Kilpatrick does not analyse them and present them in a way that would en-courage teachers to reflect on what it means to, e.g., plan and execute, or on the prerequisites to getting pupils to practise (and thereby develop) the qualities which are necessary if one is to make good plans or judgements.

Perhaps the largest group of Progressive Educators—the "child-centred" teach-ers who have suggested that the child should be left to do his or her own thing and thereby learn "instinctively" what it is important for him or her to learn—have been opposed to the very idea of stating objectives, believing that these should emerge from an evolving situation. However, they have nowhere discussed how teachers are to recognise, or facilitate the development of, children's unique talents.

The "bible" of the Progressive Education movement (the 1926 Handbook of the NSSE) nowhere identifies the competencies that are to be fostered, how they are to be fostered, or how they are to be assessed for either formative or summative purposes.

It is true that French et al. (1957), Stratemeyer et al. (1947), Caswell and Campbell (1935), Tyler (1936), and the Education Policies Commission (1938) have attempted to identify goals. Unfortunately they have muddled together goals at a wide variety of levels, the frameworks are not multiple-talent, and the goals are only weakly linked to the recommended curriculum processes.

The extent to which the Progressive Education Movement has been discredited can be inferred from the paucity of references to it in the 13-volume *Interna-tional Encyclopaedia of Education* (Husen & Postlethwaite, 1985). Here there is not a *single* reference to multiple-talent or competency oriented versions of Progressive Education.

16.   See Raven (1977a, 1984a&b, 1988a) and Raven, Johnstone, & Varley (1985) for our contributions to resolving these difficulties.

17. See Hargreaves (1988) for a discussion of these movements.

18. I have discussed the inadequacy of the latter measures, as introduced by the government, as a mechanism for school improvement in Raven (1989a).

19. Dewey, 1902.

20. Aikin, 1942.

21. Caswell, 1942.

22. Whiting, 1972.

23. Fraley, 1981.

24. Raven, Johnstone, & Varley, 1985.

25. The development and provision of such tools is not as unrealistic as may at first sight appear because the computers that are required to run programmes designed to elicit the relevant information from pupils and suggest appropriate individualised experiences to both pupils and teachers are now widely available. Nevertheless the development of the necessary tools does remain dependent on the wider adoption and refinement of the framework for thinking about the nature and development of competence which has emerged in the course of our work and is summarised in Raven (1984a).

26. Raven, 1977a.

27. Raven, 1977a, 1980a&b. Under the circumstances, the wonder is that any school pupils are willing to enrol in genuinely developmental activities. But, they are. However, as Schön noted, and as is widely reported, it becomes increasingly difficult to persuade students further up in the educational system to devote time to such activities. They know too well that advancement, whether in the educational system or outside, is not achieved by demonstrating occupational (let alone personal or civic) competence but by discerning and saying the right things to the right people (Sternberg, 1986, has included a knowledge of what to do to secure promotion in the academic world as one of his varieties of "intelligence" [Thus, incidentally, confounding values, problem-solving ability, and acquired information]).

28. Raven, 1977a; Dore, 1976; Broadfoot, 1979.

29. Raven, 1977a&b.

30. Morton-Williams et al., 1966.

31. Dore, 1976.

32. See Broadfoot, 1979, 1983, 1986; Stansbury, 1976, 1980; Burgess & Adams, 1980, 1986.

33. No one will, of course, announce that these movements have failed—any more than they announced that the Great Educational Reforms which have preceded them for the last 40 years have failed. They will simply be replaced by yet another well-intentioned but ill-researched "initiative" that will be promoted equally loudly as the solution to the educational system's problems.

34.   Raven, 1980a; Raven, Johnstone, & Varley, 1985.

35.   Schön, 1983, 1987. Schön does not, however, perhaps himself sufficiently acknowledge the sociological functions of the "educational" system or ask how to come to terms with them. Nor does he give his students sufficient credit for having correctly assessed the way the educational system works and discerned the sociological rather than educational functions it performs.

36.   Morton-Williams et al., 1966.

37.   Nuttgens, 1988.

38.   McClelland, 1961.

39.   Note that this comment applies with equal force to the competence areas that are currently embedded within the curriculum—the 3Rs. It is easy to see that—as is spelt out in Raven (1989b)—the teaching of reading and the ability to communicate is seriously hampered by teachers' failure to relate what they are doing to children's interests and pre-occupations. This is less obvious in the case of mathematics, but the comment actually applies with even greater force.

40.   Raven, 1980a; Raven, Johnstone, & Varley, 1985.

41.   Bachman et al., 1978; Jackson, 1986.

42.   Price et al., 1971; Taylor & Barron, 1963.

43.   Raven, 1984a.

44.   Raven, 1977a.

45.   Raven, 1977a; Sigel, 1985; Pellegrini et al., 1985; Burns et al., 1984; Miller et al., 1985, 1986.

46.   Hope, 1985.

47.   Payne et al., 1979.

48.   See Raven (1984a) for the evidence that high-level competencies are value-laden and involve social and political beliefs. See Raven (1980a&b) for a discussion of the importance of coming to terms with values.

49.   See Raven (1989a) for a fuller discussion of this issue.

50.   See Raven, 1980a&b.

51.   See Raven, 1984a; Hope, 1985; Nuttgens, 1988.

52.   Hogan (1990) has noted that the available evidence suggests that about half of those managers who appear to be competent, confident, intelligent, poised, and skilled in human relations either: i. destroy the careers of competent subordinates in order to minimise challenge and competition, ii. destroy the developmental potential of their sections (i.e., get rid of the time and the personnel required for the "parallel organisation activity" which is required for innovation and to provide

for the future) in order to seem able to reduce costs and appear "efficient," or iii. refuse to take important decisions that affect the future of the organisation because these would result in their becoming unpopular and thus jeopardise their future.

53. Robinson, 1983.

54. I have the impression that more people in the UK than the US have observed that the educational system is not what it seems to be and generalised this observation to other aspects of society and chosen to resist. In the US more students have simply accepted the mythology, and, as a result, failed to question market mythology, religious mythology, and democratic mythology.

55. Actually, having more people involved in the useless tasks of education, insurance, defence, transportation, etc. *constitutes* economic development. Thus growth of education does not *lead* to GNP; educational employment is *part of* GNP.

56. Robinson, 1983.

57. Bellini, 1980.

58. Chomsky, 1987.

59. The director of SCISP was run out of the country.

60. See Raven, 1986, 1995 for a fuller discussion of these issues.

61. Kanter, 1985.

62. Toffler, 1980.

63. Schön, 1971/1973.

64. Ferguson, 1980.

65. Howard, 1980, 1982a&b.

66. Raven, 1983, 1984a, 1988b, 1989a.

67. The downtrodden and rather ineffectual images which teachers have of themselves are documented in Raven (1977a) and the fact that these are communicated to pupils is documented by Raven and Varley (1984).

68. Morgan, 1986.

69. In fact, further reflection on the nature of this network of forces suggests that it is disconcertingly coherent—and this in turn suggests that it may have a single organising principle.

    We have seen that schools are increasingly required to operate as if there was only one type of ability which people possess to a greater or lesser extent. That is, they are required to organise themselves as if a single-factor model of ability accounted for most of the variance in human abilities (although this variance is sometimes expressed as three 'types' of ability—namely 'academic', 'technical' and 'manual'). Yet both common observation and the material reviewed earlier in this book clearly shows that people possess a wide variety of different talents. The single-factor model of ability that informs schools' practice mirrors, and feeds into, myths about the efficiency and inevitability of hierarchical organisation in which "the more able rise to the top." In this way, a system is created in which the gullible, the devious, the manipulative, and those most concerned with their own advancement rise to the top without their particular "talents" being noted.

This monocultural concept of mind is paralleled by the monocultures of mind that are selected and promoted in reductionist, authoritarian, science: it is not acceptable to think in ways which do not accord with the received wisdom. Worse, as Vandana Shiva (1998) in particular has noted, these monocultures of mind in science embrace and support the perspectives of reductionist science. In the quest for "accuracy"—expressed, for example, as a quest for objectivity and comparability in the assessments made in schools—it is typically only acceptable to conduct "scientific" studies in terms of one 'variable' at a time. In this way, any dawning realisation that it is vital to look at *all* the potential outcomes of a "scientifically-based" practice—such as an agricultural, educational, or economic intervention—is rendered "unrealistic and absurd," worse, "unthinkable," literally "unimaginable." How *could* one examine, simultaneously, *all* the short- and long-term, personal, ecological, and societal outcomes of an experimental variation? How *could* one examine *all* the short- and long-term effects on all plants, animals, and the biosphere of applying a particular pesticide? That is to say, how *could* one treat the examination of effects as a *cultural* question? How, in short, could one enact *comprehensive* evaluation, holistic science? The proposal is clearly preposterous. But such work is "absurd" and "unrealistic" *precisely **because*** reductionist science embraces a monoculture of mind in which the encouragement of alternative ways of thinking through public discussion with people who are not steeped in the "relevant" traditions of the "science" is deemed illegitimate.

But into exactly what do these monocultures in education, in agriculture, in economics, indeed in culture itself, feed?

They feed into:

- Hierarchical structures of dominance: hierarchical structures in which men dominate women, in which Western "scientific" cultures dominate and exterminate traditional cultures of knowledge such as those possessed by traditional farmers and Dowist scientists. They feed into cultures in which people who are most concerned to dominate over others rule over those who would behave in more culturally appropriate (i.e., sustainable) ways offering higher quality of life to all. They feed into legitimising dominance mythology in which it is argued that evolution (and therefore the current direction of society) is associated with the "survival of the fittest" (instead of the "survival of the fitting") and in which mankind is therefore viewed as having both a divine and a scientific duty to dominate over ("hold dominion over") all other species of plants and animals.
- They feed into the worldwide elimination of cultural diversity through economic imperialism and the subterfuge (GATT, MAI) of domineering and destructive business arrangements.
- They feed, through the hegemony of—that is, the preoccupation with—the economic determinism that is embedded in market theory (once again expressed

in terms of single-variable concepts of wealth and the reduction of diversity to single-variable expressions of costs and "quality" [thereby rendering invisible other costs and potential criteria of wealth, development, and well-being]) into the hegemony of materialism—viz into a monocultural concept of what makes for the good life. Then, by counting only those variables that can be commoditised and reduced to financial terms, they lead into calculations of efficiency which exclude consideration of most important inputs and outcomes.

- They feed into the worldwide acceptance of a "1984 culture" in which nothing is what it seems or is said to be—and is usually its opposite. Examples include the worldwide political correctness of applauding the "celebration of diversity" in schools and the promotion of "Multiculturalsm"—but actually implementing policies that either eliminate the very thing being discussed or in such a way as to individualise it and thus destroy any genuinely *cultural* (i.e., group connectedness) components having the potential for growth and, in this way, promote its opposite—that is, a global *monoculture.*

- They feed into the worldwide portrayal, through the media, of a monocultural (materialistic) image of the good life that presents the most destructive and unsatisfying culture the world has ever known (namely mainstream American society) as hugely desirable. This effect is largely achieved through the reductionist process we have mentioned by eliminating portrayal of—or, paradoxically, seeming to applaud (as in fictional portrayals of police brutality in the course of eradicating crime)—negative features. This arises through the hegemony of cultural concerns which make it very difficult to discuss, and certainly almost impossible to organise a programme of scientific studies to develop measures of, that culture's less desirable features. People who articulate these wider concerns are somehow made to appear "crazy" and "outlandish."

It would seem from these reflections that the forces that are driving us at an ever increasing rate toward our own destruction as a species are, like the wind that drives our sailing boats against the rocks, simultaneously turbulent and coherent. Unless we come to better understand them we are doomed.

If I am right, the emergence of hierarchy, the mythology promoting the supposed efficiency of hierarchy, the mythology of the efficiency and effectiveness of the marketplace, the obscurantism of economic theory which renders invisible non-materialistic components of wealth, the emergence of capitalism, the antics of elites and capitalists and capitalist governments, and, paradoxically, the writings of Marx that attribute all ills to capitalism, are all *expressions* of a single underlying process. They are all symptoms, not causes. It is not plotting capitalists or elites who perpetuate the system: the elites, the views they express, and the actions they take are all somehow chosen and selected because of the functions they play in a deeper and hidden system.

What are the forces that drive these interlinked processes? How are we to intervene in them? If they are symptoms rather than causes of the problem, how far can we get by advocating comprehensiveness in science, seeking to encourage the funding of mavericks in the scientific process, by making explicit other criteria of wealth, by changing our societal and institutional organisational arrangements, by insisting on the right to experiment along different lines and to determine the criteria against which those experiments are to be evaluated? If these are not appropriate strategies, what else to do? How, other than experimenting with these tools on the basis of what we know, are we to gain insights into the processes we have not so far observed?

70.   Robinson, 1983.

71.   We are committed to producing another book that will spell these out in greater detail.

72.   Jack Whitehead suggested these questions.

73.   The *topics* requiring research and development—including the development of such things as tools to help teachers to orchestrate numerous individualised competency-oriented educational programmes and those required to hold public servants accountable for exercising high-level competencies are listed in a later chapter of my *New Wealth of Nations*. However, since that book was written it has become clear (as was argued in Note 69 above) that there is perhaps more of a coherence in these disparate social forces than was apparent when the relevant chapter in *The New Wealth of Nations* was written. In this book we have encountered the enormous pressures pushing teachers and others toward singe-factor concepts of ability in schools and looked at the way these feed into concepts of "ability" in "hierarchy" that in turn legitimise "authority": We have also seen the need to insist on *comprehensive* evaluations of educational programmes and individual people—to document *all* the personal and social, short- and long-term, consequences of any course of action. This challenges reductionist science and the way in which science is organised—for how is one to move toward anything approaching *comprehensiveness* without allowing mavericks to obtain the resources they need to substantiate their position? It therefore emerges that reductionist science itself represents one of the central problems. Finding ways of organising research in such a way as to be able to invest in the generation of multiple perspectives on "unresearchable" topics turns out to be fundamental. Furthermore, as emphasised in Note 69, one of the most vital research topics is to develop a better understanding of the hidden social forces which drive the constellation of mutually reinforcing processes depicted in Diagram 23.1.

74.   See Donnison, 1972; Nisbet & Broadfoot, 1980; Raven, 1985.

75.   See Raven (1984b) for a discussion of the dilemmas that our work posed for our sponsors.

76.   See Raven (1984a) for more detail.

77.   See Raven (1982b, 1984c) for discussions of the problems created by current beliefs and expectations.

78.   Donnison (1972), Cherns (1970) and I (Raven, 1975, 1982a&b, 1985, 1987a, 1995) have discussed some these questions.

    What emerges is that, at an absolute minimum, we need to press for the establishment of a number of policy-research units. Unless the universities change dramatically in character (and not in the direction in which our present governments would have them change), these units should not even be university-based because the criteria to be applied to the researchers' work are so very different to those appropriate in academe. Academic time scales are also inappropriate. Teams of researchers need to be able to devote their full time to the work and they need to be provided with an assured career structure that does not require them to conform either to traditional bureaucratic or academic criteria. While researchers need sufficient contact with policy makers to become thoroughly familiar with the problems which need to be tackled, they also need considerable scope to determine the way in that they will tackle them and to follow up on new issues which come to light. There also needs to be some mechanism whereby people who are "peripheral" to main stream decision making can initiate studies and ensure that they are carried out from their own perspective. Thus, instead of being employed on short term contracts to solve problems posed by administrators, and instead of being accountable to administrators, researchers need to have secure employment and to be accountable to a Director who is him or herself accountable for creating a climate of innovation and dedication concerned with developing new understandings and ideas and tools to be used to run the public service more effectively.

Because the 'string and sealing-wax' grants provided by the SSRC/ESRC have led many to adopt quite inappropriate expectations, it is important to underline the scale of funding that should be envisaged. Ironically, more appropriate standards for funding are to be found in within-civil-service research units. It is not uncommon to find £250,000 being devoted to projects with very limited objectives. The extent of the underfunding of policy research can also be judged from the fact that two years *losses* of the British Steel Corporation would have funded the Scottish Council for Research in Education since Stonehenge was built. Yet far more of our national resources are devoted to—even misapplied in—education than steel.

It is also important to emphasise the need to challenge the grossly inefficient US contract research model, where, owing to widely held views about what constitutes good research, and acceptance of "sponsors" right to redirect research as those who control the purse strings change, it is not uncommon to find that several million dollars have been spent on evaluation programmes which neither advance understanding nor improve the programmes one iota.

79. Of course, the potential value of this exercise will be subverted if it is viewed by those involved, not as a means of accomplishing anything useful but as an opportunity to bandy about the "correct" phrases (in this case "usefulness"!) in order to secure personal advancement. As Nuttgens (1988) has observed, and as our research (Raven, 1984a) has confirmed, one of our central problems in the UK stems from our interest in saying a lot that amounts to nothing in order to look good and secure advancement. This is combined with a disinterest in finding new things to do, better ways of thinking about things, or better ways of doing them. This process results in the interesting statistic that out of every 1,000 articles published in American Educational Research Association journals only 20 contain any new empirical data—and only 2 contain substantive amounts of data. The so-called "knowledge explosion" is, therefore, an explosion of non-knowledge. These observations suggest that our first step might best be, not to establish a working party, but to undertake a collective value-clarification and

prioritisation exercise. As Rothschild (1982) observed, we will, in the end, destroy the very foundation on which our existence depends if we continue to mount trivial "academic" researches, the results of which contribute to our personal advancement but do not help society to tackle the huge and pressing problems that beset it. It is precisely for this reason that the Universities have found themselves beset by cries for "accountability" . . . even though the criterion which is proposed will only exacerbate the problem. But whose fault is it that we are unable to offer alternative, and more appropriate, criteria for use in staff appraisal and accountability exercises?

References

Adams, E. A., Robbins, D., & Stephenson, J. (1981). *Validity and Validation in Higher Education. Research Papers 1–4 and Summary Report.* London: North East London Polytechnic, School of Independent Studies.

Aikin, W. M. (1942). *The Story of the Eight-Year Study. Adventure in American Education. Volume I.* New York: Harper Bros.

Association of Graduate Careers Advisory Services. (1992). *What Do Graduates Do?* Cambridge, England: Hobson's Publishing.

Atkins, M. J., Beattie, J., & Dockrell, W. B. (1993). *Assessment Issues in Higher Education.* Newcastle upon Tyne: School of Education, University of Newcastle upon Tyne.

Bachman, J. G., O'Malley, P. M., & Johnston, J. (1978). *Adolescence to Adulthood: Change and Stability in the Lives of Young Men.* Ann Arbor, Michigan: The Institute for Social Research.

Barth, R. S. (1972). *Open Education and the American School.* New York: Agathon Press.

Bellini, J. (1980). *Rule Britannia: A Progress Report for Domesday 1986.* London: Jonathan Cape.

Bennett, N. (1976). *Teaching Styles and Pupil Progress.* London: Open Books.

Boyatzis, R. E., Cowen, S. S., Kolb, D. A., et al. (1995). *Innovation in Professional Education: Steps on a Journey from Teaching to Learning.* San Francisco, CA: Jossey-Bass.

Broadfoot, P. (1979). *Assessment, Schools and Society.* London: Methuen.

Broadfoot, P. (1983). Evaluation and the Social Order. *Journal of the International Association of Applied Psychology, 32,* 307–327.

Broadfoot, P. (Ed.). (1986). *Profiles and Records of Achievement.* London: Holt, Rinehart and Winston.

Burgess, T., & Adams, E. (1980). *Outcomes of Education.* London: MacMillan Education.

Burgess, T., & Adams, E. (1986). *Records of Achievement at 16.* Windsor: NFER-NELSON.

Burgess, T., & Pratt, J. (1970). *Polytechnics in Pakistan.* London: North East London Polytechnic.

Burns, A., Homel, R., & Goodnow, J. (1984). Conditions of life and parental values. *Australian Journal of Psychology, 36*, 219–237.

Caswell, H. L. (1942). *Education in the Elementary School.* New York: American Book Co.

Caswell, H. L., & Campbell, D. S. (1935). *Curriculum Development.* New York: American Book Co.

Centre for Educational Sociology. (1977). *Collaborative Research Dictionary.* Edinburgh: University of Edinburgh.

Cherns, A. B. (1970). Relations between research institutions and users of research. *International Social Science Journal, XXII,* 226–242.

Chomsky, N. (1987). *The Chomsky Reader.* London: Serpent's Tail.

Cremin, L. A. (1961). *The Transformation of the School.* New York: Knopf.

Cross, H. (1988). Innovation in higher education: The School for Independent Study. *New Era in Education, 69* (3), 80–84.

Dewey, J. (1899). *The School and Society.* Chicago: University of Chicago Press.

Dewey, J. (1902). *The Child and the Curriculum.* Chicago: University of Chicago Press.

Dewey, J. (1910). *How We Think.* New York: D. C. Heath.

Dewey, J. (1916). *Democracy and Education.* New York: MacMillan.

Donnison, D. (1972). Research for policy. *Minerva, X,* 519–537.

Dore, R. (1976). *The Diploma Disease.* London: Allen and Unwin.

Education Policies Commission. (1938). *The Purposes of Education in American Democracy.* Washington, DC: National Education Association.

Eraut, M. (1994). *Developing Professional Knowledge and Competence.* London, England: Falmer Press.

Ferguson, M. (1980). *The Aquarian Conspiracy: Personal and Social Transformation in the 1980s.* London: Paladin.

Flanagan, J. C. (1978). *Perspectives on Improving Education from a Study of 10,000 30-Year-Olds.* New York: Praeger Publishers.

Fraley, A. (1981). *Schooling and Innovation: The Rhetoric and the Reality.* New York: Tyler Gibson.

French, W. et al. (1957). *Behavioural Goals of General Education in High School.* New York: Russell Sage Foundation.

Galton, M., & Simon, B. (1980). *Progress and Performance in the Primary Classroom.* London: Routledge and Kegan Paul.

Galton, M., Simon, B., & Croll, P. (1980). *Inside the Primary Classroom.* London: Routledge and Kegan Paul.

Goodlad, J. (1983). *A Place Called School.* New York: McGraw-Hill.

Goodlad, J., Klein, M. F., and Associates. (1970). *Behind the Classroom Door.* Worthington, OH: Charles A. Jones Publishing Co.

Hargreaves, A. (1988). The crisis of motivation and assessment. In A. Hargreaves and D. Reynolds (Eds.), *Educational Policy: Controversies and Critiques.* Lewes: Falmer Press.

HMI (Her Majesty's Inspectors). (1978). *Primary Education in England: A Survey by Her Majesty's Inspectors of Schools.* London: Department of Education and Science: HMSO.

HMI. (Scotland) (1980). *Learning and Teaching in Primary 4 and Primary 7.* Edinburgh: HMSO.

Hogan, R. (1990). Unmasking incompetent managers. *Insight,* 21 May, 42–44.

Hope, K. (1985). *As Others See Us: Schooling and Social Mobility in Scotland and the United States.* New York: Cambridge University Press.

Howard, E. (1980). *Some Ideas on Improving School Climate.* Denver: Colorado Department of Education.

Howard, E. (1982a). *Instrument to Assess the Educational Quality of Your School.* Denver: Colorado Department of Education.

Howard, E. (1982b). Involving students in school climate improvement. *New Designs for Youth Development*. Tucson: Associations for Youth Development Inc.

Husen, T., & Postlethwaite, N. (Eds.). (1985). *International Encyclopaedia of Education*. London: Pergamon.

Jackson, P. W (1986). *The Practice of Teaching*. New York: Teachers College Press.

Kanter, R. M. (1985). *The Change Masters: Corporate Entrepreneurs at Work*. Hemel Hempstead: Unwin Paperbacks.

Kilpatrick, W. H. (1918). The Project Method. *Teachers College Record, 19*, 319–335.

Leith, S. (1981). Project work: An enigma. In B. Simon and J. Willcocks, *Research and Practice in the Primary Classroom*. London: Routledge and Kegan Paul.

Marris, P. (1964). *The Experience of Higher Education*. London: Routledge and Kegan Paul.

McClelland, D. C. (1961). *The Achieving Society*. New York: Van Nostrand.

Miller, K. A., Kohn, M. L., & Schooler, C. (1985). Educational self-direction and the cognitive functioning of students. *Social Forces, 63*, 923–944.

Miller, K. A., Kohn, M. L., & Schooler, C. (1986). Educational self-direction and personality. *American Sociological Review, 51*, 372–390.

Morgan, G. (1986). *Images of Organization*. Beverly Hills, CA: Sage.

Morton-Williams, R., Finch, S., & Poll, C. (1966). *Undergraduates Attitudes to School Teaching as a Career*. London: Government Social Survey Department.

National Society for the Study of Education. (1926). *Twenty-Sixth Year Book: The Foundation and Techniques of Curriculum Making*. Bloomfield, IL: Public School Publishing Co.

Nisbet, J., & Broadfoot, P. (1980). *The Impact of Research on Policy and Practice in Education*. Aberdeen: University Press.

NSSE (1926). See Rugg (1926)

Nuttgens, P. (1988). *What Should We Teach and How Should We Teach It?* Aldershot: Wildwood House.

ORACLE *See* Galton & Simon (1980), Galton, Simon & Croll (1980), Simon & Willcocks (1981).

Payne, G., Ford, G., & Ulas, M. (1979). *Education and Social Mobility: Some Social and Theoretical Developments.* Organisation of Sociologists in Polytechnics. Paper No. 8.

Pellegrini, A. D., Brody, G. H., & Sigel, I. E. (1985). Parents book-reading habits with their children. *Journal of Educational Psychology, 77,* 332–340.

Price, P. B., Taylor, C. W., & Nelson, D. E. (1971). *Measurement and Predictors of Physician Performance: Two Decades of Intermittently Sustained Research.* Salt Lake City: University of Utah, Department of Psychology.

Rathbone, C. H. (Ed.). (1971). *Open Education: The Informal Classroom.* New York: Citation Press.

Raven, J. (1975). Social research in modern society: i: The role of social research; ii: The institutional structures and management styles required to execute policy-relevant social research. *Administration, 23,* 225–246 and 247–268.

Raven, J. (1977a). *Education, Values and Society: The Objectives of Education and the Nature and Development of Competence.* Oxford: Oxford Psychologists Press.

Raven, J. (1977b). School rejection and its amelioration. *Educational Research, 20,* 3–9.

Raven, J. (1980a). The most important problem in education is to come to terms with values. *Oxford Review of Education, 7,* 253–272.

Raven, J. (1980b). *Parents, Teachers and Children: An Evaluation of an Educational Home Visiting Programme.* Edinburgh: Scottish Council for Research in Education.

Raven, J. (1982a). Public policy in a changed society. *Higher Education Review, 14,* 80–89.

Raven, J. (1982b). What's in a name? Some problems in the evaluation of pilot projects. *Scottish Educational Review, 14,* 15–22.

Raven, J. (1983). Towards new concepts and institutions in modern society. *Universities Quarterly, 37*, 100–118.

Raven, J. (1984a/1997). *Competence in Modern Society: Its Identification, Development and Release.* Unionville, NY: Royal Fireworks Press (1997); Oxford, England: Oxford Psychologists Press (1984).

Raven, J. (1984b). A public servant's dilemma. In W. B. Dockrell (Ed.), *An Attitude of Mind.* Edinburgh: Scottish Council for Research in Education.

Raven, J. (1984c). Some barriers to educational innovation from outside the school system. *Teachers College Record, 85*, 431–443.

Raven, J. (1985). The institutional framework required for, and process of, educational evaluation: some lessons from three case studies. In B. Searle (Ed.), *Evaluation in World Bank Education Projects: Lessons from Three Case Studies.* Washington, DC: The World Bank, Education and Training Department, Report EDT5, 141–170.

Raven, J. (1986). Fostering competence. In T. Burgess (Ed.), *Education for Capability.* London: NFER-Nelson.

Raven, J. (1987a). Policy research. *New Horizons, 28*, 31–48.

Raven, J. (1987b). Values, diversity and cognitive development. *Teachers College Record, 89*, 21–38.

Raven, J. (1988a). The assessment of competencies. In H. D. Black and W. B. Dockrell (Eds.), *New Developments in Educational Assessment: British Journal of Educational Psychology, Monograph Series No.3*, 98–126.

Raven, J. (1988b). Choice in a modern economy: New concepts of democracy and bureaucracy. In S. Maital (Ed.), *Applied Behavioural Economics.* Brighton, England: Wheatsheaf.

Raven, J. (1989a). Equity in diversity: The problems posed by values— and their resolution. In F. Macleod (Ed.), *Families and Schools: Issues in Accountability and Parent Power.* Brighton, England: Falmer Press.

Raven, J. (1989b). Parents, education and schooling. In C. Desforges (Ed.), *British Journal of Educational Psychology, Monograph Series No. 4, Special Issue on Early Childhood Education*, 47–67.

Raven, J. (1991). Reforming higher education. Review of *The Rise of Independent Study* by D. Robbins. *Higher Education Review*, Spring, 71–77.

Raven, J. (1994). *Managing Education for Effective Schooling: The Most Important Problem is to Come to Terms with Values.* Unionville, NY: Trillium Press; Oxford, England: Oxford Psychologists Press.

Raven, J. (1995). *The New Wealth of Nations: A New Enquiry into the Nature and Origins of the Wealth of Nations and the Societal Learning Arrangements Needed for a Sustainable Society.* Unionville, NY: Royal Fireworks Press; Sudbury, Suffolk: Bloomfield Books.

Raven, J. (1997). Educational research, ethics and the BPS. Starter paper and peer reviews by P. Mortimore, J. Demetre, R. Stainthope, Y. Reynolds, & G. Lindsay. *Education Section Review, 21* (2), 3–26.

Raven, J., Johnstone, J., & Varley, T. (1985). *Opening the Primary Classroom.* Edinburgh: Scottish Council for Research in Education.

Raven, J., & Varley, T. (1984). Some classrooms and their effects: A study of the feasibility of measuring some of the broader outcomes of education. *Collected Original Resources in Education, 8*, No.1, F4 G6.

Ravitch, D. (1974). *The Great Schools Wars.* New York: Basic Books.

Robbins, D. (1988). *The Rise of Independent Study.* Milton Keynes: Open University Press.

Robinson, D. W. (1983). *Patriotism and Economic Control: The Censure of Harold Rugg.* D. Ed. Dissertation, Rutgers University, New Jersey. Also available in University Microfilms International, Ann Arbor, Michigan (1984).

Roizen, J., & Jepson, M. (1985). *Degrees for Jobs: Employer Expectations of Higher Education.* Guildford: SRHE and NFER-Nelson.

Rothschild, Lord. (1982). *An Enquiry into the Social Science Research Council.* London: HMSO.

Royal Society of Arts (1980). *Capability Manifesto.* London: Royal Society of Arts.

Rugg, H. (1926). In: *National Society for the Study of Education: 26th Yearbook*. Bloomington, IL: Public School Publishing Co.

Rugg, H., & Shumaker, A. (1928). *The Child-Centered School*. Yonkers: George Harrap.

Schön, D. (1971/1973). *Beyond the Stable State*. London: Penguin.

Schön, D. (1983). *The Reflective Practitioner*. New York: Basic Books.

Schön, D. (1987). *Educating the Reflective Practitioner*. San Francisco: Jossey-Bass.

Sigel, I. E. (1985). A conceptual analysis of beliefs. In I. E. Sigel (Ed.), *Parental Belief Systems: The Psychological Consequences for Children*. Hillsdale, NJ: Erlbaum.

Shiva, V. (1998). *Biopiracy: The Plunder of Nature and Knowledge*. London: Green Books.

Simon, B., & Willcocks, J. (Eds.). (1981). *Research and Practice in the Primary Classroom*. London: Routledge and Kegan Paul.

Stansbury, D. (1976). *Record of Personal Experience, Qualities and Qualifications*. (plus Tutor's Handbook.) South Brent: RPE Publications.

Stansbury, D. (1980). The record of personal experience. In T. Burgess and E. Adams, *Outcomes of Education*. Basingstoke: MacMillan Education.

Sternberg, R. J. (1986). *Intelligence Applied*. New York: Harcourt, Brace, Jovanovitch.

Stratemeyer, F. B., Forkner, H. L., McKim, M. C., & Passow, A. H. (1947). *Developing a Curriculum for Modern Living*. New York: Teachers College; Columbia University Press.

Taylor, C. W. (1974). Developing effectively functioning people. In B. C. Lloyd, J. B. Seghini, & G. Stevenson, *Igniting Creative Potential*. Utah: Jordan School District.

Taylor, C. W. (1985). Cultivating multiple creative talents in students. *Journal for the Educationally Gifted, VIII* (3), 187–198.

Taylor, C. W., & Barron, F. (Eds.). (1963). *Scientific Creativity*. New York: Wiley.

Toffler, A. (1980). *The Third Wave.* New York: Bantam Books.

Tyler, R. W. (1936). Defining and measuring the objectives of progressive education. *Educational Research Bulletin, XV,* 67f.

Whiting, D. (Ed.). (1972). *Blowing on a Candle: The Flavour of Change.* Newton, MA: Newton Public Schools.

Winter, D. G., McClelland, D. C., & Stewart, A. J. (1981). *A New Case for the Liberal Arts.* San Francisco: Jossey Bass.

Wright, G. C. (1950). *Core Curriculum in Public High Schools: An Enquiry into Practices, 1949.* Office of Education Bulletin No.5. Washington, DC: Federal Security Agency.

Wright, G. S. (1958). *Block-Time Classes and the Core Program in the Junior High School.* Bulletin 1958, No.6. U.S. Dept. Health, Education and Welfare. Washington, DC: US Government Printing Office.

PART VII

THE ASSESSMENT OF COMPETENCE

We have seen that major barriers to the introduction and implementation of high-level competence-based education stem from the absence of appropriate means *assessing* components of capability. Teachers teach and students work toward what is assessed, and both tend to neglect wider educational objectives. Without better measures of high-level competencies neither students nor teachers can get credit for their work. Nor can the contributions that people make to society be recognised or detractors passed over. Without better measures, attempts to generate meaningful evaluations of either individuals or educational programmes are doomed; such evaluations will continue to produce misleading—and unethical—data because they will focus on that which it is easy to assess and neglect that which is most important. The following chapters offer an important stimulus to rethinking in this area.

Chapter 24

The Problems Posed for the Assessment of Competence by the Espoused Goals of Higher Education

W. Bryan Dockrell

"Universities are no longer just knowledge factories. They give young people confidence and competence. There is more attention to people and less to subjects" (Sir Graham Hills, *The Observer*, June 1992).

If what is to be assessed and how it is assessed should relate to the purposes of higher education, confidence and competence, and people and not subjects, then a fundamental issue for universities is that the assessments we make of students' mastery of subject matter is largely irrelevant.

There are actually two strands to this argument that will be elaborated in this chapter. The first is that the subjects studied are largely irrelevant to students' future careers. The second is that we make claims for higher education that are broader than simple mastery of a discipline.

What Do Employers Want?

Occupation is one indicator of what outcomes of study are important. In 1990, over 40% of graduates in history from British universities and nearly 40% of graduates in physics went into marketing, management services, or financial work (Association of Graduate Careers Advisory Services, 1992). Much more important for employers than the specific body of knowledge and understanding and sets of skills that students have acquired are the general transferable skills that higher education is expected to develop and academics are expected to report on (Roizen & Jepson,

1985; Combes, 1991). It is not surprising that in many universities, departments have revamped their degree courses to put greater emphasis on communication skills, teamwork, organising, and problem-solving, with the consequent requirement that these very different competencies be assessed. Learning is not context free, but the assumption of employers is that broader competencies are acquired. There is evidence that indeed they can be developed and can be assessed. Perhaps the most thorough study of this broader impact of higher education is that of McClelland and his colleagues (Winter, McClelland, & Stewart, 1981).

A statement by the (former) Committee of Directors of Polytechnic (CDP) divides higher education programmes into: "1) direct vocational preparation, 2) basic professional preparation, 3) 'general education'" (CDP, 1991). Students with some degrees (e.g., civil engineering, electrical and electronic engineering, computing, business/management studies, and art and design) go overwhelmingly into degree-related occupations though, even here, a significant proportion still enter management and financial services. How even these degrees fit into the CDP groups is not clear. Are they "direct vocational preparation" or "basic professional preparation" or neither? It is by no means obvious that they provide the specific competencies for the particular job. What they have to offer employers may be a combination of some specific, subject-derived competencies; underpinning knowledge and skills; generic, subject-derived, competencies and skills that are relevant to a range of related occupations; and personal qualities (or, conceivably, none of the above).

On the other hand, the (British) Association of Graduate Careers Advisory Services reports that graduates from physics, the biological sciences, and foreign languages enter almost as wide a range of jobs as do graduates from English, history, and the social sciences. Substantial numbers of both go into management and financial work. Only 10% of historians are in further academic study (not all presumably in history) and only 7% are in teacher training. In these cases it is presumably generic transferable skills of a more general kind that are not derived from the study of the particular subject and personal qualities that are relevant.

What are these generic skills and personal qualities and how do they relate to and how are they derived from higher education?

Some Stated Goals of Higher Education

The varied purposes of higher education may be gathered under the following four headings.

General Education

The medieval universities may have originated in Bologna and Paris as training colleges for lawyers and theologians, but the development of the "trained mind" has long been the justification of higher education. Newman asserted 150 years ago that a university education "educates the intellect to reason well in all matters, to reach out towards truth, and to grasp it" (Newman, 1853, paragraph 126). Fifty years ago it was claimed for Oxford Greats that its aim was "to continue to the limits the training of its students' minds in accuracy, power and independence." It was concerned with "precision, penetration and consistency," "a readiness to examine convention and to think out problems to the end" (Last, 1935, pp. 32–33). The extent to which a university education in the 19th or early 20th century actually achieved these exalted aims is open to question, but the mythology remains very powerful.

The concern with higher education as a liberal education has been a feature of higher education in the United States more than in Britain, as at the University of Chicago half a century ago. However, much more attention was given there to the assessment of the intended outcomes.

If we accept this purpose, the question is: How do we observe, assess, and report the achievement by individual students of these outcomes, especially if we agree with Allen (1988) about the multifarious goals of higher education? How do we assess and report on a student's "willingness to question orthodoxy and to consider new ideas," their "sense of social responsibility," their "motivation towards accomplishment" and so on? And how do we evaluate our own success in developing them in our students?

Knowledge Creation/Dissemination

Higher education must provide the future generation of scholars. In a small elite system this purpose was important, if not dominant. If universities were about producing knowledge, then the production of scholars was of pre-eminent importance. In a system of mass higher education, however, should not the education of the mass of students who are going to play a productive role in society determine the teaching and the assessment and the requirements of the tiny minority who are to become the researchers and scholars of the next generation be of lesser importance? Identifying the needs of this smaller group is important, but should we allow those needs to distort the whole pattern of assessment and instruction? In the past, the identification of the students most likely to contribute to the development of the subject has been a major task of the university assessment system. Who will take on where we leave off? Indeed the commonest justification of the Honours Degree system is that it identifies the future scholars. However important the preparation of the next generation of scholars, as enrolment in higher education widens it becomes increasingly less significant, at least at the undergraduate level.

Specific Vocational/Professional Preparation

In the last 20 years in the UK, universities have accepted an increasing number of degree courses preparing people for initial qualifications to practise a profession. Consequently, a substantial proportion of both the undergraduate and post-graduate university enrolment is in these programmes. However, it has been asserted that the way in which they are designed and assessed has more to do with power-sharing between higher education and the professional bodies than with any model of how professional expertise develops (Eraut, 1992). The major criticisms are the way that patterns of study and placement separate "theory" and "practice" and (the misguided belief) that professional action consists simply of applying the former to the latter.

General Preparation for Employment

There have been numerous attempts to define the "core skills," "generic competencies," and "personal qualities" that higher education helps to develop. They include obvious skills in writing and speaking, both in the mother tongue and in other languages; in numeracy; and in the use of communications technology. They also contain other intellectual skills such as the ability to reflect on and learn from practical experiences; the ability to assimilate large quantities of information quickly and to analyse issues from several perspectives; the ability to solve problems and make decisions; evaluation of risks and consequences; and an understanding of the nature of change and the preparedness to adapt appropriately. There are also social skills such as working effectively in groups or teams and personal qualities, including drive, self-motivation, self-assessment, time management, ability to work without close supervision, leadership potential, enterprise, and initiative (Brown, 1991).

Some Statements from the "Disciplines"

The following statements, drawn from Hartog (1937), provide a picture from across UK universities within subjects and across subjects within universities.

Arts

"Quality and breadth of thought"

Literae humaniores is concerned with "powers of reasoning," "precision, penetration and consistency," "a readiness to examine convention and to think out problems to the end," "to make men relatively immune from the risks that are run by such as trust to beliefs, uncritically accepted from others."

> Thus it may be said in brief that the aim of Greats is, first, to continue to the limits the training of its students' minds in accuracy, power, and independence, and, secondly, to direct their thoughts to subjects on which reflexion will give them some firmly established and coherent view of life, together with insight into the nature of man's relations to his fellows and the methods by which progress in human affairs has been achieved (p. 33).

A combination here of generic transferable skills and personal qualities which has produced "men who in the most varied walks of life whether as statesmen or ecclesiastics, as lawyers or administrators, in the public service or in commerce, industry and the professions, whether at home or abroad—have shown themselves peculiarly qualified for positions in which initiative must be taken and responsibility borne" (p. 30).

Modern Greats takes much the same line. "Both (classical and modern greats) are designed as the study of a civilisation as a whole" (p. 104).

> Economic theory provides a splendid training in subtle and accurate reasoning and clarity of expression. But by its side philosophy, equally austere and exacting makes the student aware of the limited scope and validity of the claims of deductive reasoning to be found in economics. And the historical studies . . . make him aware of the flux and change in those fundamental conditions which the economic theorist has perforce to assume static (p. 104).
>
> It thus produces "men qualified to take to take a wider view" (p. 105).

The London B.A.(General) degree was designed in the same way. "It was thus divorced from the narrowly vocational purpose . . . namely the provision of specialists teachers in secondary schools, whom the specialised Honours Degree attempts to equip with such completeness as is possible in the time for their life's work, both in knowledge of facts and in the techniques of study" (p. 59). The general degree "is therefore less interested in the amassing of facts, or the technicalities of method, than in quality and breadth of thought, in disinterested and philosophic grasp. Such are its ideals. Its crown should be a Prime Minister rather than a Permanent Secretary" (p. 59).

History at Cambridge "provides . . . a general outlook and a general method of approach." "It includes many students who are not, never will be, and do not want to be, historians." It provides "a sufficiently good general training (within a particular field) to be generally useful" (pp. 48–49).

In no case is it assumed that specific competencies are provided, still less that they provide direct preparation for any particular occupations. All four make the same claim for generic transferable competencies and personal qualities.

Science

"Trained minds and, what counts for much,
personality and presence."

Science degrees are more likely to assume that their content and methods will be relevant to future careers. Physics was thought to prepare students predominantly (but not exclusively) for life as a physicist, as a researcher, in industry, or as a teacher. At Leeds it is expressed explicitly. "Every graduate shall primarily have the knowledge and grip of his subject". Though narrowness of outlook and intellectual shortsightedness should, so far as possible, be corrected in the specialist student" (p. 86). Students were encouraged to attend lectures on a different subject. They included "Music, Economics, Botany, Electrical Engineering, Philosophy and Medieval History." The question of competence is addressed. In "answer to the question 'What can your students do?'" the reply is:

> in factory, workshop or laboratory, a good Honours Physics graduate, particularly if he has had a further period of research training, should be able to attack with ultimate success most problems of a technical nature which come his way. If he is not familiar with details of technique, his training . . . will have brought out his powers of initiative and self-reliance, in addition to having placed the tools of his profession at his elbow (p. 86).

These are subject-derived generic competencies, underpinning knowledge and skills and personal qualities that are relevant across a range of related occupations. There is no claim to provide the specific competencies required for particular occupations. Those who do not pursue careers in physics are "men with good general scientific knowledge, trained minds and, what counts for much, personality and presence. These men, while not engaged primarily in using their scientific knowledge, will doubtless in their executive or administrative posts play a more useful part on account of it" (p. 89). So physics, at least at Leeds, provides generic transferable competencies.

Physics at Manchester placed its emphasises on the systematic observation of personal qualities. "Employers want to know about a man's keenness, pertinacity, vitality and power of working companionably with his colleagues" (p. 83). Observations are kept in a dossier that "is largely based on contact in the practical classes . . . It is as important to make this judgement accurate as it is to conduct the degree examination fairly" (p. 83). The personal qualities are revealed in the practical class and by inference are developed in them.

Engineering/Architecture
"Versatility and balance of mind"

Mechanical Sciences at Cambridge have an entirely different justification.

> As a result of the broad nature of the training provided, it is not claimed that Cambridge moulds its students into fully-fledged engineers, but, on the other hand, it is claimed that Cambridge-trained men acquire a working knowledge of the fundamentals underlying all branches of engineering—structural, mechanical and electrical. They are not, it is true, specialists in any one direction, but they possess a versatility and balance of mind which enables them to strike out with equal facility along any line which they may subsequently be called upon to pursue. The Cambridge view is that premature specialisation cramps the imagination and is destructive to the length and breadth of mental vision. It is held that in a university course of engineering, instruction should primarily concentrate on teaching those essentials which, if not acquired at this stage, will never be acquired. Technicalities which will automatically be picked up in a student's subsequent career are useful as stimulating interest, but apart from this they are of secondary importance. The view is taken that education does not consist of the memorisation of a number of facts and formulae, useful as these may be when leavened with intelligence; at its best it should aim at something much deeper and more lasting, for the good of education is the power of reasoning and the habit of mind that remains when all efforts of memorisation have faded into oblivion (p. 76).

"The practical experience which is necessary for every engineer in addition to the theoretical knowledge is in most cases obtained subsequent to graduation in the course of an apprenticeship" (p. 79). It is exclusively a matter of generic, professionally relevant, subject-derived general competencies and not a matter of underpinning knowledge and skills ("the memorisation of facts and formulae"). The specific job-related competencies are to be acquired later. It is the classical defence of the paraprofessional higher education programme in that the subject of study is relevant but in general, not specific, ways.

The Liverpool architecture degree talks in terms of specific knowledge and skills. Students will have "assimilated the basic technical knowledge . . . established methods of specification and estimating . . . (and) the ability . . . to design, the capacity to carry out research to solve the problems presented by contemporary architectural programmes and to make explicit their solutions in adequate project and working drawings" (p. 145). However, it also includes personal qualities "training, which . . . included periods of group study will also have prepared him for systematic teamwork" and generic skills "he will have achieved a certain measure of all-round competence in planning, in construction and design generally" (p. 145). The first two or three sound like very specific job-related competencies. The later ones are more generic and less occupationally specific.

Business/Economics
"Capacity to learn, think and write"

The justification of the Manchester B.A. (Commerce) and B.A. (Admininstration) is in much the same terms. "The possession of a degree in commerce or administration is not, in itself, a proof of competence in business or public service. What it does signify is some acquaintance with economic and administrative problems, some capacity to learn, think and write and some power, not only to fill a post efficiently, but also to see the place of this in the social order" (p. 130). As with engineering, the competencies that are generic and job related are derived from the specific studies. What's more, it works. "At present several hundreds of men and women holding degrees of the faculty are in commercial or public life. There is evidence from employers that graduates learn more quickly and are fitted for promotion after a shorter practical training than those who have received no university education. Perhaps, however, the most telling evidence of the value of the work of the Faculty is that, throughout the recent trade depression, there was no unemployment among its graduates" (p. 131). These professional degrees are preprofessional. Their justification is in terms of generic competencies that are job-related and subject derived, underpinning knowledge and skills, and personal qualities. Can we assume other generic transferable skills that are not subject derived?

Economics at Cambridge wants its cake and ha'penny too:

The Tripos was instituted . . . in order to give encouragement to a form of liberal education which has already a high place in many of the leading universities of the Old and New World, and at the same time to make special provision for students who are proposing to devote their lives to the professional study of Economics, and for those who are looking forward to a career in the higher branches of business or in public life (p. 116).

What is more "It is indeed true that a man is likely to be more efficient in business who has braced his mind to hard work in subjects that have no connection with it, than if he has occupied himself with an enervating form of technical instruction, however directly that may bear on his after work" (p. 116). That is, the merit of economics as a subject of study is that it has no relevance to the higher branches of business or public life. It is both an argument for generic transferable skills and an argument against "technical instruction." (The notion that economics has nothing more to offer to business than it has to national government has its appeal, but not perhaps to economics graduates.)

Medicine
"More than a test of utilisable knowledge and skill"

Some professional degrees do speak in terms of specific job-related competencies. In medicine at London "a few examiners . . . maintain that the only purpose is to test the candidate's utilisable skills" (p. 69). However, "the practice of medicine brings the practitioner into situations in which errors of commission, as well as of omission, may have results that are dangerous to life, and so an examination that determines the qualification to practice must be more than a test of utilisable knowledge and skill. it must also be a test to determine that the candidate has sufficient knowledge and understanding of the subject to avoid actions that may have serious results to the individual and to the community (p. 73). Higher education provides not only professional competence but also subject-derived underpinning knowledge and skills.

Edinburgh was less sure about the underpinning knowledge. "The purpose of the final examination, as an obvious safeguard to the public, is clearly defined." However, "no general practitioner requires for practical purposes all the actual knowledge which may be necessary to pass (the) examinations. In the long run the purpose of such tests must be to enforce a standard of training in the basic and medical sciences which will . . . provide an adequate scientific foundation for the further study and practice of medicine" (p. 63) and furthermore, "some students who have difficulties with the . . . examinations . . . ultimately prove to be quite capable doctors" (p. 68). In which case does the subject-derived knowledge underpin practice or not?

It is possible to derive from (or impose on) all this a picture of a wide range of outcomes from higher education? First, there are aspirations predominantly to provide specific subject-derived competencies, if we use the term broadly, together with some underpinning knowledge and skills and personal qualities, and in the case of architecture there are aspirations to provide at least generic subject-derived transferable skills.

Implications

It follows from what I have said about both employers' expectations and the statements that many of those involved in higher education have made about their purposes that the claim that higher education is about "knowledge and understanding" is spurious. It is not what employers want. It is not what graduates do. Nor is it what is actually claimed.

What then should we assess? Should it be the general outcomes or the vehicle used as a means to achieving those outcomes?

Cognitive Science as a Possible Model

Do we need a general model for the impact of education? Cognitive science offers one: "The cognitive science framework assumes that the operation of the mind consists of interactions among three components; an architecture of cognition, mental representations, and processes that manipulate these representations" (McShane, Dockrell, & Wells, 1992, p. 252).

The "architecture of cognition" specifies the fixed modular structures that provide the basis for learning and set constraints. "The architecture of the cognitive system is the innate and invariant structure by means of which the content of experience is processed and stored by an organism" (p. 252). It is not modifiable, at least not in young adults, except negatively by trauma.

"Propositions, schemes, mental models and images are examples of some of the representational structures" (p. 253). These are the knowledge that is provided by the specific disciplines.

"Theories of processing are concerned with how mental representations can be manipulated subject to the limitations imposed by the architecture. The later stages, in what are often called central processes are implicated, are concerned with processes of inference, planning and problem solving" (p. 253).

What we acquire competence in (and presumably are taught) are different representational structures (propositions, schemes, mental models, and images) and processes (of inference, planning, and problem-solving). Different subjects may provide different structures and processes, not just different objects of study. They may offer not just different bodies of knowledge but different ways of thinking.

Those programmes that are specifically and narrowly vocational are concerned with bodies of knowledge and specific skills and perhaps (and perhaps not) with developing "representational structures" and "processes" and applying them to specified situations, building specific neural networks. Preprofessional degrees are concerned primarily with "structures" and "processes" as they relate to a specific occupation and with applying them across a wider range of contexts. A liberal education is, presumably, concerned with "structures" and "processes" per se that have a wide relevance. How do we assess them?

References

Allen, M. (1988). *The Goals of Universities*. Milton Keynes, UK: Open University Press.

Association of Graduate Careers Advisory Services. (1992). *What Do Graduates Do?* Cambridge: Hobson's Publishing.

Brown, G. A. (1991). Assessing Enterprise Learning. Sheffield: Employment Department.

Combes, J. E. (1991). Education and training tomorrow: Higher education seen from the point of view of the company. In *The Role of Higher Education in Society: Quality and Pertinence*. Paris: UNESCO.

Committee of Directors of Polytechnics. (1991). *A Report to the Committee*. Unpublished Mss.

Dockrell, W. B. (1991). Higher education: What procedures for evaluation? In *Planning and Management for Excellence and Efficiency of Higher Education*. Caracas: UNESCO/CRESALC.

Eurat, M. (1992). Developing the professional knowledge base. In R. A. Barnett (Ed.*), Learning to Effect*. London: Society for Research in Higher Education.

Hartog, P. (Ed.). (1937). *The Purposes of Examinations*. London: Evans Brothers.

Last , H. (1935). Literae Humaniores (Greats), University of Oxford. In. Sir Phillip Hartog (Ed.), *The Purposes of Examinations*. London: Evans Bros.

McShane, J., Dockrell, J., & Wells, A. (1992). Psychology and cognitive science. *The Psychologist 5* (6), 252–255.

Newman, J. H. (1852/1929). *The Idea of a University Defined and Illustrated*. London: Longmans (First published 1852).

Roizen, J., & Jepson, M. (1985). *Degrees for Jobs*. Guildford: SHRE and NFER-Nelson.

Winter, D. G., McClelland, D. C., & Stewart, A. J. (1981). *A New Case for the Liberal Arts*. San Francisco: Jossey-Bass.

Chapter 25

Competence-Based Assessment

Alison Wolf

Editorial Introduction

In this chapter, Wolf illustrates the self-defeating nature of attempts to generate atomistic specifications of vocational competence and then to use these as a basis for decontextualised "objective" assessments. Her chapter stands as a marker for her even more outstanding book with the same title. In that book, Alison documents the way in which the attempt to move away from traditional knowledge-based "educational" programmes and replace them by courses in which students learned how to *do* things they would later need to be able to do—and testify to the outcomes in these competency-based terms—got corrupted back into the very thing that it had been hoped to move away from (i.e., assessments of pre-scribed cognitive content) precisely because there were no appropriate means of assessing these other outcomes.

* * * * *

The idea of competence has, in the UK, become almost inextricably linked with a particular assessment philosophy promoted by the National Council for Vocational Qualifications (NCVQ, now merged into the Qualifications and Curriculum Authority), and, to a rather lesser extent, by the Scottish Vocational Education Council (SCOTVEC, also now part of a unitary body, the Scottish Qualifications Authority—SQA). These organisations have regarded assessment as an extremely powerful weapon, capable on its own of guaranteeing quality, promoting a truly "competence-based" approach to training and learning, and increasing the skills levels of the population. While they are certainly right about the powerful effect of assessment on practice, their own approach has, unfortunately, had results quite at odds with the ideals of those first responsible for promoting a competence-based approach. Competence-based assessment as it has been understood in the UK is not, in fact, the only possible way of assessing people's competence or capability; but it is important to understand why it has had not merely disappointing but actively pernicious effects, and how, therefore, they might be avoided.

The ideas behind the type of competence-based assessment practised and preached in the UK are essentially American in origin. The literature on competence-based assessment, which appeared in Britain in the 1980s, is packed with direct echoes of U.S. literature of 10 years before. What is dramatically different between the two countries and periods is that government policy in the UK ensured the general adoption of competence-based approaches by tying them to central government funding. In the United States, localised experimental work had little or no long-term effects, so that American advocates of the approach are now rediscovering it, in part through the British programme.

The following definition is an American one. Yet it summarises all the major features of competence-based assessment as currently advocated in the UK:

> Competence-based assessment is a form of assessment that is derived from a specification of a set of outcomes; that so clearly states both the outcomes—general and specific—that assessors, students and interested third parties can all make reasonably objective judgements with respect to student achievement or nonachievement of these outcomes; and that certifies student progress on the basis of demonstrated achievement of these outcomes. Assessments are not tied to time served in formal educational settings.[1]

The three components of competence-based assessment which are especially important, and that the definition above encapsulates are:

1. the emphasis on outcomes; specifically, multiple outcomes, each distinctive and separately considered.
2. the belief that these outcomes can and should be specified to the point where they are clear and "transparent". Assessors, assessees, and "third parties" should be able to understand what is being assessed and what should be achieved.
3. the decoupling of assessment from particular institutions or learning programmes.

These characteristics define the practice of competence-based assessment. However, the emphasis on outcomes and "transparency" is not peculiar to the competence-based context. It is also a defining characteristic of a rather broader theory of measurement, that of "criterion referencing." Criterion referencing is similarly concerned with clearly specified outcomes and with assessments that address these outcomes separately rather than dealing with "pass marks" or "norms." It too has been a very influential approach in recent years (for example within the English National Curriculum), and it too hails conceptually from the United States. Nonetheless, competence-based and criterion-referenced assessment are not synonymous. The former involves an idea of competence that is essentially non-academic. In practice, as noted in the same American text from as that from which our first definition was derived,

> It tends . . . to derive from an analysis of a prospective or actual role in modern society and . . . attempts to certify student progress on the basis of demonstrated performance in some or all aspects of that role.

In other words, it is vocational in the broadest sense and is bound up with the idea of "real-life" performance. Indeed, in its early days in the United States, "performance-based" assessment (and education) were the terms used more often than "competence."

Competence-based assessment became important in England following the 1986 governmental Review of Vocational Qualifications. This led directly to the creation of the National Council for Vocational Qualifications, with a remit to establish a National Vocational Qualifications (NVQ) system of approved vocational awards. The review argued that "assessments carried out by many bodies do not adequately test or record the competences required in employment," that "assessment methods tend to be biased towards the testing either of knowledge or of skill rather than of competence," and that there are "many barriers to access arising from attendance and entry requirements."

These were well-founded concerns, and it is interesting to find in the early documents how broad a conception of "competence" prevailed. Unfortunately, however, a number of influential figures also believed that it was possible to find a simple, all-embracing, way of identifying and translating this conception into practice. This had enormous appeal to politicians and the added advantage of excluding entirely any need for consultation with or input from the despised education sector.

The strategy was to create "lead industry bodies"[2] that represent a given sector of industry or employment and give them full responsibility for drawing up detailed standards of occupational competence. These standards, in turn, were to be used, unamended and unchanged, as not merely the *basis* for, but the sole effective *definition* of, vocational awards. No qualification will be recognised as an "NVQ" unless based on the standards issued by the lead industry body concerned, which meant, in effect, that parts of the standards become a qualification, with a certain amount of "topping and tailing" to explain recording and verification procedures.

As national qualifications, NVQs each cover a particular area of work at a specific level of achievement. They are based on the fundamental assumption that, for each industry, there exists a single identifiable model of what "competent" performance entails. The idea that, for each role, there exists such an agreed-upon notion of competence, which can be elicited and command consensus, is fundamental to any assessment system of this type. It is also an heroic—and a questionable—assumption.

The structure of an NVQ is modular or "unit-based." These units are defined as groups of "elements of competence and associated performance criteria which form a discrete activity or sub-area of competence which has meaning and independent value in the area of employment to which the NVQ relates."[3] An element of competence is a description of something that a person who works in a given occupational area should be able to do. It reflects an action, behaviour, or outcome that has "real meaning" in the occupational sector to which it relates. For example:

> *create, maintain and enhance effective working relationships* is an
>   example of a management competence, while
> *inform customers about products and services on request* is taken
>   from a list of financial services competences.

Both share two compulsory qualities. They involve an active verb and an object—that is, they are performance-based—and they are not tied in any way to particular training programmes.

As expressed, both these examples are obviously very general statements indeed. Each could apply to a huge number of contexts—and to performance of very variable quality. However, the key aspect of NCVQ-approved standards is that they go into far greater detail than this. Lead bodies are expected to define very precisely the nature of what is expected, with the first level of detail corresponding to highly specified *performance*

Figure 25.1 Sample Performance Criteria from an NVQ Element: Financial Services (Building Societies)—Level 2* Element title: "Set up new customer accounts"

Performance Criteria:
- Internal/external documents are complete, accurate and legible and delivered to the next stage in the process schedule
- All signatures/authorisations are obtained to schedule and actioned promptly
- Correspondence to customer is accurate and complete—all necessary documents enclosed—and despatched promptly
- Correspondence to other branches of society and other organisations/professional agencies is accurate and complete—all necessary documents enclosed—and despatched promptly
- Cash transactions and financial documents are processed correctly and treated confidentially
- Computer inputs/outputs are accurate and complete
- On completing the setting up, the account is filed in the correct location
- Indicators of contingencies/problems are referred to an appropriate authority

*Provided as an exemplar in the *Guide to National Vocational Qualifications* (NCVQ, 1991).

criteria. These are the statements by which an assessor judges whether an individual can perform the workplace activity at the standard required. In effect, the performance criteria state explicit measures of outcomes. Figure 25.1 provides an example of an element of competence with its performance criteria.

To be accredited with a competence, a candidate must demonstrate successfully that he or she has met *every one* of these criteria. This is because competence-based assessment, as interpreted by the National Council for Vocational Qualifications, requires *one-to-one correspondence with outcome-based standards.* This must be comprehensive: Evidence must be collected of a candidate's having met every single performance criterion. Failure to do this, it is argued, removes an essential characteristic of the system—the fact that we know exactly what someone who has been assessed can do.

It is important to emphasise this objective, because it lies at the heart of the particular interpretation of competence-based assessment that we have experienced over the last decade. A competency-based system will, it has been argued, be far superior to traditional forms because it is so transparent, and because it delivers exactly what is described. And it can *be* delivered because performance criteria are so clearly defined that the assessor can describe a candidate as having unambiguously achieved (or "not yet achieved") them. The requirement is thus for a one-to-one relationship between criteria and competence, and between assessment and criteria.

It is for this reason that the process of NVQ accreditation does not involve any formal discussion of curriculum (except insofar as it is implicit in the standards) or approval of learning programmes. *The assumption is that use of the standards will ensure the latter's quality.*

We have noted the *assumption* that assessment will be unproblematic because it simply involves comparing behaviour with the transparent "benchmark" of the performance criteria. The reality, unfortunately, is somewhat different. As a result, the short history of NVQs has also been one in which the quest for clarity has produced an ever more complex and complicated "methodology."

The second part of the paper discusses the technical reasons for this. Here we simply illustrate it by an example. The criteria in Figure 25.2 are intended to apply to a playgroup assistant or registered childminder. Yet, as they stand, they could equally well apply to a child psychiatrist or specialised speech therapist. How does the assessor know what the "standard" actually is?

This lack of clarity became noticeable fairly early on—well before large numbers of NVQs were actually assessed or delivered. The response was

Figure 25.2 Performance Criteria from an NVQ Element: Childcare and Education—Level 2 Element title: "Help children to recognise and deal with their feelings"

Performance Criteria:

4.3.1   Children are encouraged to express their feelings in words and actions and through play in the safety of a secure and accepting environment.

4.3.2   Methods and activities used to explore feelings are appropriate to children's level of development and enable them to begin to recognise, name, and deal with their own and others' feelings in socially acceptable ways.

4.3.3   Emotional outbursts and negative reactions from children are dealt with in a calm and reassuring manner whilst ensuring the safety of the child concerned and minimising the disruption to other children.

4.3.4   Learning opportunities that arise in the daily routine are used to help children develop their understanding of feelings and social relationships.

4.3.5   Opportunities to help children extend their vocabulary of words relating to feelings are developed where possible.

4.3.6   Any concern over the recognition and expression of feeling in individual children is shared with parents, colleagues, or other professionals as appropriate to the situation.

4.3.7   Ways of expressing and dealing with feelings are demonstrated by the candidate in appropriate situations.

to institute a new notion, that of the "range statement." These quickly became a compulsory addition to all standards. Range statements officially "describe the limits within which performance to the identified standards is expected, if the individual is to be deemed competent." In other words, they contextualise the performance criteria, and hopefully make clear whether it is a psychiatrist or a childminder who is in question. They impose further assessment requirements because competence must be fully assessed "across the range." They also greatly increase the length of the documentation—sometimes taking up as much space as the performance criteria themselves.

The implications for assessment of this burgeoning detail were horrendous. Suppose one takes, as an example, the elements concerned with finance from the Level 2 NVQ concerned with "business administration." These comprise about one-seventh of the NVQ as a whole, and incorporate, directly and unamended, the underlying standards.

These elements include 63 different performance criteria. Of these, only a few occur naturally together and so allow of integrated assessment. For example, a candidate must demonstrate that he or she can calculate gross pay and voluntary deductions, must complete returns, must identify discrepancies, and must deal with queries. On top of that, all these criteria must be assessed with respect to each component part of the "range statement."

The "range statement'—a different one for *each* of the 12 competences in this one unit—is equally important. In our example, we find that, in addition to dealing with income tax, National Insurance and pensions, bonuses, overtime, and a whole range of records, candidates must demonstrate that they can deal with attachment of statutory sick pay, maternity pay, and holiday pay. (One wonders what the accountants would think.) Faced with these demands and with the requirement to demonstrate paperwork on all required outcome measures, an atomised, tick-list system is almost bound to result.

In spite of the level of detail created by range statements, they were rapidly followed by another compulsory addition to standards: "specifications of underpinning knowledge and understanding." These came in response to a growing concern that NVQs were far too narrow—and also backward looking: something that was in fact virtually guaranteed by requiring lead bodies to focus entirely on analysis of current jobs.

The original architects of NVQs assumed that knowledge requirements would be clearly understood by trainers and assessors on the basis of the criteria for competence and delivered in an integrated fashion. When critics argued—convincingly—that "underpinning knowledge" was in fact being neglected, a new development programme brought together practitioners to make the assumed consensus explicit. In the event, workshops that tried to "extract" or "induce" knowledge requirements from standards demonstrated quite quickly that the knowledge extracted was not at all standard but was subject to very different interpretations.

Nonetheless, formal "knowledge lists" followed, codifying at least an interpretation of what the standards required and creating further detailed assessment requirements. Finally, the "transparency" of assessment requirements came into question in its turn. Just as "range" and "knowledge statements" have been added to standards, so too have assessment requirements. Industry bodies are now expected to add lists of "assessment specifications" to the standards that examining and awarding bodies use.

Yet another level of detail and centralisation was thus added. The resulting standards and qualification have become huge and unwieldy documents. The apparently economical notion of "competence" has become exhaustively defined and constrained. In the process it becomes increasingly undeliverable and increasingly unattractive to employers as a basis for either their own training programmes or as a way of certifying employees. It also becomes increasingly questionable as a suitable approach for a world of rapid technological change and fluid job boundaries.

The early American experiments on which the English programme drew similarly ended with huge volumes of unmanageable paperwork and over-detailed prescription. The contrast between the apparent simplicity and broadness of "competence" as a concept and the restrictive and rigid reality is remarkable. Yet the tendency is inherent in the idea of completely transparent, unambiguous "outcomes" as an operational idea. It becomes inevitable if one attempts to measure competence precisely and use it as a basis for national (or international) certification and accreditation.

What all this detail has failed to do, however, is to realise the claim made for "competence-based assessment": to make everything clear and unambiguous, so that "consumers" know exactly what an award-holder can do. In spite of the baleful effects of detailed documentation on the type of skills and abilities being assessed, and in spite of the atomised check-lists, assessors' interpretations—and measurement practice—have continued to differ. The next section explains why this must inevitably be the case if one relies on paper-based outcome definitions.

The Limitations of "Specified Outcomes"

There are general theoretical reasons why attempts to specify outcomes so clearly that anyone can assess them reliably are doomed to failure. Suppose, for example, that one was interested in something highly specific and abstract—far less context-dependent than the average workplace competency, and so, presumably, easier to define. A very specific mathematics skill is a good example—say the ability to multiply whole numbers.

In the United States, where "criterion-referenced" tests have been most developed, the definitions of items to be used to test such skills have become extremely precise—there must be so many items, of such-and-such difficulty, with so many questions involving one digit (e.g., 3 x 2), so many involving two digits (e.g., 12 x 20), and so on. And yet, having constructed such a test, can one really say, with absolute confidence, that "these students can multiply double-digit numbers"? How many errors are they allowed? Would they have done as well on a different set of questions? Does 11 x 11 count as the "same" as 99 x 99?

Many of the performance criteria in competence-based qualifications are almost as narrow as the examples furnished by academic criterion-referenced tests. We have already referred above to the "level II" NVQ in business administration. (This is one of the larger NVQs in terms of entries, since it is well suited to accrediting specific office skills.) It is from this that the example in Figure 25.1 is drawn. The "range statement" for this competence informs one that:

> The Competence includes paper-based filing systems covering the retrieval of information from alphabetical and numerical filing systems, involving indexing systems and lateral and vertical filing methods. It requires competence in booking in and out procedures and the tracing of missing or overdue files.

The assessment guidance adds that, if assessed outside the workplace, students must demonstrate competence by dealing consecutively with a minimum of 20 items to be extracted, on a minimum of three separate occasions. A completely different set of documents must be provided for each simulated assessment.

Yet all these additional requirements simply occasion new queries. Suppose there was a slight overlap in the documents used for assessment. Does that invalidate the assessment? Does it matter if the documents are extracted from a system containing 20 files rather than 2,000? How many of them have to come from files for which document movements are actually recorded? What sort of indexing system counts? And so on.

However "precise" one becomes when one goes down this route, there is always a call for yet more definition. This is exactly the UK experience with NVQs. Performance criteria might mean all sorts of things—so we added range. Range can be interpreted in all sorts of ways—we added more lists. At the end of this process, and in all good faith, people can still be ascribing "competence" to very different behaviour.

The original claim was that "individual performance . . . is judged against explicit standards . . . and (therefore) individuals know exactly what they are aiming to achieve."[4] Assessment was seen to require far less in the way of complex judgement than the opaque criteria employed by traditional school-based or higher education.

In fact, nothing could be further from the truth. The inherent variability of the contexts in which competence is tested and displayed means that assessors have to make constant, major decisions about how to take account of that context when judging whether an observed piece of evidence "fits" a defined criterion. In other words, they operate with a complex, internalised, and holistic model—not a simple set of descriptors lifted from a printed set of performance indicators.[5]

The Limitations of Assessor Judgement

If written definitions cannot provide the required clarity, the alternative is to rely on a pre-existing consensus and understanding on the part of the assessors. The whole of competence-based assessment starts from an assumption that there exist "standards of competence" for an industry or role and that these standards can be articulated through written documents. The documents do not create the standards: they articulate and clarify them for professionals. The latter understand them because of their prior knowledge and implicit understanding of what "competence" in their own context means. Thus the developers of "standards of competence" will explain that one goes on defining "as long as it is necessary. You stop when everyone understands."

We have argued that standards cannot begin to provide item specifications so tight that anyone could use them to construct reliable and consistent assessments. But does this, in fact, matter? Or can a shared occupational culture make the requirements unambiguous so that the endless spiral of specification which, we argued, was always attendant on criterion-referencing is broken by the existence of shared expertise?

It must be said that there has been very little independent evaluation of whether UK standards are implemented in any comparable or consistent way—and, indeed, that it would be rather difficult to do this at all clearly. By nature, those using them in workplaces will be dealing with very different contexts, so it is not clear how one would measure "sameness" precisely. Nonetheless, one must seriously question whether it is likely even in principle that a combination of definitions and prior consensus will produce any very uniform behaviour and also *whether the assumption of pre-existing "standards" and shared understanding is reasonable at all*. One of the exemplars offered by NCVQ in its guidance comes from publishing and states that *costs are minimised through forward purchase of optimum quantities and timing in relation to schedule requirements*. Is it really likely that, industry-wide, there will be consensus on whether this has been achieved, what would be involved, or how one would recognise it?

Certainly such evidence as exists is not terribly encouraging. Black and his colleagues at the Scottish Council for Research in Education (SCRE) studied in detail the way in which a number of colleges were delivering apparently quite specific stock control modules within the Scottish National Certificate, which also embodies competence-based approaches. All the departments were experienced and had close ties with local industry, and the colleges themselves assumed that the stock control modules would be quite easy to deliver to a common standard. In fact, however, both content and standards deviated greatly within the group.[6]

In research at the Institute of Education,[7] we asked experienced college tutors and workplace supervisors to devise exercises based on very detailed specifications. In spite of the shared occupational culture of the individuals concerned, the assessment items they produced, following these specifications, proved to be very different in content. We also looked at the level of difficulty at which the assessors ascribed mastery by asking them to administer and make judgements using a more standardised "anchor test" at the same time as they used their own. The standard at which they ascribed "competence" on this common exercise turned out to be markedly different, implying that the underlying standard being applied to the different, and therefore not directly comparable, exercises of their own was also highly variable. Comparable results were obtained with tourist guide examiners operating out of different regional offices, even though they had mostly done their own training together and operated an external examiner system that created some cross-region links.[8] And a large study of NVQ assessors at work, conducted by the University of

Sussex, revealed that a very high proportion related their judgements not simply to the NVQ requirements but to other standards as well, including a variety of pre-existing standards in their own workplace or industry. Many also stated that they made assessment decisions that were not strictly in line with the standards.[9]

Discussions of competence-based assessment often imply that assessor judgement is only a minor issue because the assessment criteria are so minutely and clearly specified that one is well down towards the more mechanistic end of the spectrum. Nothing could be further from the truth. Workplaces vary hugely: thus, any assessment process is complex, incremental, and, above all, judgmental. *It has to be because the actual performance which one observes—directly, or in the form of artifacts—is intrinsically variable*: One person's playing of a piano piece, one person's operations plan, is by definition not exactly the same as another's, and cannot be fitted mechanistically to either a written list of criteria or to an exemplar.

The current approach to competence-based assessment has led us down a cul-de-sac. This is partly the result of over-ambitiousness regarding what can, or should, be achieved in the way of national uniformity and central control over content and standards; partly because of a failure to understand either the nature of human judgement; and partly because "occupational standards" have been concerned, in practice, not with competence and capability but with the precise task analysis of current jobs. However, it is important to realise that this was one, not "the," definition of what assessing competence can involve and that a more enlightened model may have a benign rather than a malign effect on practice.

Notes

1. Adapted from Grant et al. (1979).

2. The "lead industry bodies" have now been reconstituted, with additional responsibilities, as "National Training Organisations."

3. NCVQ (1991).

4. Fletcher (1991).

5. See e.g. Christie & Forrest (1981); Cresswell (1987); Wolf (1995).

6. Black et al. (1989).

7. Wolf & Silver (1986).

8. Wolf (1995).

9. Eraut, Steadman, Trill, & Porkes (1966).

References

Black, H. et al. (1989). *The Quality of Assessments.* Edinburgh: Scottish Council for Research in Education.

Christie, T., & Forrest, G. (1981). *Defining Public Examination Standards.* London: Macmillan.

Cresswell, M. (1987). Describing Examination Performance. *Educational Studies, 13* (3) 247–265.

Eraut, M., Steadman, S., Trill, J., & Porkes, J. (1966). *The Assessment of NVQs.* Research Report No. 4. Sussex: University of Sussex Institute of Education.

Fletcher, S. (1991). *NVQs, Standards and Competence.* London: Kogan Page.

Grant, G., Elbow, P., Ewens, T., Gamson, Z., Kohli, W., Neumann, W., Olesen, V., & Riesman, D. (1979). *On Competence: A Critical Analysis of Competence-Based Reforms in Higher Education.* San Francisco: Jossey-Bass.

NCVQ (National Council for Vocational Qualifications). (1991). *Guide to National Vocational Qualifications.* London: NCVQ.

Wolf, A. (1995). *Competence-Based Assessment.* Buckingham: Open University Press.

Wolf, A., & Silver, R. (1986). *Work-Based Learning.* Sheffield: Employment Department.

Chapter 26

Assessing the Self-managing Learner: A Contradiction in Terms?

Stan Lester

Summary

Although the ethos of the self-managing learner is becoming more widely accepted in higher education, it is frequently undermined by inconsistent approaches to assessment. If educational programmes are to support genuinely self-managed learning, there is a need to move away from content- or outcome-based assessment systems to a recognition that evaluation of content and outcome are the responsibility of the learner.

Once these implications are recognised any external assessment becomes problematic, although an acceptable solution may be achievable through basing assessment on activities or processes of learning such as enquiring, creating, reflecting and evaluating.

Introduction

Within higher education, traditional approaches to teaching and learning have tended to emphasise the content-based dimension represented by subject-matter, theories and bodies of knowledge, at the expense of developing capability in overarching processes such as enquiry, reflection, creative synthesis and self-managed learning. Although institutions often espouse these latter as desirable if not fundamental aims (Allen, 1988),

This chapter, which was previously published as Chapter 9 in D. O'Reilly, L. Cunningham, & S. Lester (Eds.), *Developing the Capable Practitioner*, Kogan Page, London (1999). It is © Kogan Page and is reprinted here by kind permission of the publisher.

the reality can be a focus which develops them in a limited and haphazard way and encourages a relatively narrow kind of academic competence (Barnett, 1994). The recent introduction of approaches based on functional approaches to competence offers little more in this respect, as knowledge-based content simply becomes replaced or supplemented by content in the form of competence standards, dominating the learning process through their focus on predefined objectives and outcomes (Lester, 1995a).

In contrast, the majority of learning which occurs in daily life is not driven by a syllabus or competence framework, but identified and managed by people in accordance with their own objectives. This form of learning may not always lead to outcomes which would be recognised for accreditation, but particularly when the learner's objective is a compelling one it is usually extremely effective.

The importance of intrinsic motivation of this type for educational settings has long been recognised, for instance by Lindeman (1926) and Dewey (1938) among others. In higher education it has gained ground through structures such as negotiated learning contracts and design credit accumulation awards, and through approaches to development which respect learners' self-direction and ability to manage their learning actively. The latter include for instance reflective practice (Schön, 1983, 1987), action learning (Revans, 1980) and action research (Carr & Kemmis, 1986), which now underpin a considerable number of programmes and have gained academic credibility as well as demonstrating their relevance to practice. There are convincing rationales for their use, both from the perspective of learning effectiveness (see for instance Knowles, 1990; Evans, 1992) and socioeconomic considerations (e.g., Ackoff, 1974; Reich, 1991).

However, a significant problem which can occur when introducing these approaches in higher education environments is that they become accepted at a surface level, but fail to become deeply embedded. Operationally, reflection/action and self-managed approaches can remain as methods within a traditional programme methodology, working at what Cunningham (1994) terms a tactical level as opposed to a strategic one. Conceptually, and more insidiously, they can be embraced as methodologies but without any real acceptance into the academic culture of their underlying epistemologies and values. In both situations learners receive conflicting messages—explicitly in the first where there are indications as to where self-managed learning is permissible and where it is not, and implicitly in the second, where a surface-level message is contradicted by a deeper one.

Assessment

One of the most revealing indicators of underlying academic theory-in-use is assessment practice. Assessment also tends to have a disproportionate influence on learners because of the perceived value of certification, so the values implicit in how assessment is carried out can easily undermine espoused philosophies of learning. This point is illustrated by the following examples, from programmes claiming to be based in reflective practitioner and action learning approaches respectively.

The first concerns a student on a full-time vocationally-oriented degree, who was completing an account of his work placement. He had developed an innovative approach to the project he was involved in, discussed its relative merits and its relationship to relevant contextual issues, and thought through quite carefully how it would work in practice. However, he was having a lengthy and unproductive argument about it with a tutor, who disagreed with the logic behind it and suggested it was inadequately referenced. The student was twice referred to books which backed the tutor's point of view, and despite including a well-argued critique of these the account was eventually given a mediocre pass accompanied by comments about needing to relate practice to theory.

The second involves an experienced manager and business owner following a postgraduate management programme. The programme explicitly aimed to develop practice, but for reasons of external prestige and apparent validity clung to a system of written examinations to supplement action learning projects and a learning portfolio. After the first year he commented that there appeared to be two types of knowledge about management, the practical knowledge which he learned (through various means) out of necessity to run his business, and the type of knowledge which the exams tested, which sounded good but didn't actually work.

These scenarios illustrate two not very useful lessons. One is that while it's acceptable to think about what you are doing, experiment, and develop your own theories, the results are practical, situational, and subjective rather than real knowledge. The first student was being trapped in a double-bind in which the tutor had tacitly accorded his own theories an objective status without making his standpoint clear. The student was developing personal knowledge and using it effectively, but his tutor was demanding that it conformed or at least had a clear relationship with more 'objective' knowledge. The converse lesson is that while theory is good for passing courses, it doesn't help get things done in the real world. The manager was beginning to see around the schizoid nature of the assessment system, but at the same time learning to bracket the 'formal' theory rather than critically engaging with it to develop his own models. In both cases, the result is divergence between the theories students think of as valid for qualifications and those that they actually use to guide their action.

More generally, the principle which is being applied is that of a set of orthodox or 'accepted' theories (those of the expert community, whether they are authors, teachers, or standard-setters) being held up as correct or at least as a necessary starting-point, while others (particularly those of the learners) need either to conform or to be argued convincingly in terms of the orthodox theories if they are to be taken seriously. The principle applies equally whether the theories are expressed in academic terms or are theories of practice articulated as behavioural objectives or competence statements. In all cases, the problem is that the learner is presented with an external definition of what is right or acceptable, in a way which encourages referential or atomistic learning (cf. Ramsden, 1986) and discourages critical thinking, creativity and self-managed learning.

The Challenge of Self-managed Learning

Moving beyond this normative or discourse-based approach to assessment is a key prerequisite to enabling educational programmes to support genuinely self-managed learning. It is also problematic, as while the epistemologies which underpin self-managed approaches are gaining acceptance from the viewpoint of learning practice, they pose a fundamental challenge to much current assessment practice and in some respects to the idea of external assessment per se.

For instance, Schön describes a constructionist (sic) epistemology of practice in which "our perceptions, appreciations, and beliefs are rooted in worlds of our own making which we come to accept as reality" (1987, p. 36), and where learners are involved in "worldmaking" as much as taking the world for granted. Not dissimilarly, Cunningham (1990) advocates a Post-Modern (sic) ethos which acknowledges there are no right and wrong answers to be found 'out there', but emphasises a reflexive approach which requires value-judgement and wisdom. The idea of 'worldmaking' is also reflected in the work of Korzybski (1958), Bateson (1971), and Bandler and Grinder (1975), who identify the difference between the 'territory' or external reality, which we cannot know directly, and our personal maps of it.

The implication is not only that *"there is a necessary difference between the world and any particular model or representation of (it)"*, but that "*the models of the world that each of us creates will themselves be different*" (pp. 7–8).

From an assessment viewpoint, these ideas suggest that to assess learning by reference to what it is expected will be learned is doing no more than imposing one interpretation or model of the world on another. This is perhaps acceptable in a pragmatic sense when learning is framed as a process of acquisition and accumulation, but it is completely inadequate for learning which is purposive, self-managed, critical or creative. If the learner is recognised as a map-maker or participant in 'worldmaking' rather than as just a map-reader and interpreter, it is contradictory to expect him or her to work within and be assessed against logics, theories and discourses of others' making: the results will at best be a form of gameplaying and deception where espoused theories are set up at divergence with theories-in-use, and at worst a chronic disability with regard to independent and creative thinking, learning and action.

Validating Personal Theory

The dilemma, then, is that recognising the learner as a self-managing worldmaker or mapmaker contradicts the notion of assessment at least as commonly practised. This perspective or epistemology of personal knowledge generates particular challenges for assessment, as it starts from the position that knowledge and theory are constructed by the individual in the process of mapmaking or worldmaking. Not only does this make any direct assessment of knowledge and theory nonsensical, it suggests that because individual knowledge and practice is unique, it is also intrinsically valid through the fact of its being known and done. (This is not the same as its being useful, something which I will revisit shortly.) Whereas from a normative or discourse-based stance there are reference-points from which to judge understanding or performance—the map is either assumed to be the territory, or the best representation of it—from a personal knowledge perspective these are revealed as no more than subjective maps, even if for many purposes successful ones.

To offer theories, curricula or competence frameworks or similar maps as guidelines which might be treated as matters for reflection and enquiry is completely congruent with self-managed learning (see, for instance, Lester, 1995b), but to insist through assessment that they are followed or used as a basis for judging validity is not. According these maps a pseudo-objective validity also dictates an orientation towards the past, as it points to working rationally from a pre-existing base rather than working intuitively and imaginatively as well as rationally towards a future direction or outcome.

A self-managed, personal knowledge perspective frees learners from the constraints of having to work from a starting-point of conventional thought, and enables them to focus—critically and creatively—on the future. However, at first sight it also leaves the door open to a solipsistic latitude in which the learner can self-validate any outcome without rigour or creativity. On the other hand, as soon as validation is asked for, it is tempting to fall into the trap of holding up one model of the world as superior to another, or at least providing justification based on already familiar (or accessible, e.g. published) theory.

Introducing rigour and validation to personal theory is nevertheless achievable through the idea of 'fitness for purpose'. In practice, we tend to review our ideas in terms of their effectiveness in leading towards a purpose, or set of purposes, which we have defined; we are responsible for deciding whether, in our own terms, our ideas are sensible or not, even if part of the validation process involves consulting written material, entering into a dialogue, or gaining an expert opinion. This test of fitness for purpose is an everyday, practical one, as well as being essential to any form of effective self-managed learning or reflective practice. It is equally applicable to practical outcomes and more purely theoretical ones (developing understandings of . . .), and because the purpose is internally defined, it respects the learner's map or world-view and remains congruent with it. Because it is purposive rather than based on precedent (cf. Schutz, 1970), it is also future-oriented and allows room for lateral and creative approaches as well as more incremental and rational ones.

The limitation of fitness for purpose is that it operates within the boundaries set by the purpose itself, and so is totally dependent on how well the latter has been framed or constructed. In practical terms, this can often translate to blinkered thinking, 'firefighting', or pursuing aims regardless of their wider consequences, as well as offering scope for unethical, unjust or criminal behaviour. While critical, lateral and creative thinking can all be employed within these bounds, learning is ultimately limited because the whole learning system is controlled by the purpose and how it has been framed; fitness for purpose is essentially a single-loop test of validity which in itself has no ethical, moral or spiritual dimension, but can be as narrowly pragmatic or instrumental as the learner wants it to be.

To move beyond this limitation points to considering the fitness *of* the purpose, or how well it has been framed in terms of wider contexts and issues. Fitness of purpose represents a double- or multiple-loop test of validity, as it asks the learner to consider the congruence of his or her objectives in broader contexts and question the assumptions on which they are based: effectively, move out of the logic or frame or reference in which the purpose is based, and question its congruence in a wider context. Clearly this can be a process of many loops or levels as the learner considers successively bigger pictures and wider perspectives, and identifies and questions assumptions embedded in both the purpose itself and the theories and actions associated with it. Fitness of purpose is still based within a personal knowledge epistemology, as it avoids imposing external definitions of congruence and asks the learner to consider assumptions reflexively, making judgements of value and exercising wisdom. However, it has moved from within-frame, single-loop thinking to a without-frame, double- or multiple-loop approach which is unbounded by predefined frameworks and where learning is ultimately unlimited. It respects the learner's map of the world, but enables the map to be extended and redrawn, including in previously unexplored dimensions.

Extending fitness of purpose conceptually leads into the idea of systemic wisdom, and to a state of systemic congruence in which wisdom becomes holistic and intuitive as something akin to Bateson's Learning III or perhaps IV is attained (Bateson, 1971). However, for the purposes of assessment it is likely that fitness of purpose is adequate at the level of anything currently deemed to be assessable, and it is sufficient to be aware that there are levels of learning which go beyond consciously uncovering and questioning assumptions and developing contextual congruence, and which also transcend the limitations of language and perhaps conscious thought.

Assessment Revisited

Although the model outlined above—personal knowledge, fitness for purpose and fitness of purpose—provides a framework for testing and questioning personal models and maps, it does not directly solve the issue of assessing the self-managing learner. It is essentially a self-assessment model which is intrinsic to self-managed learning, incorporating both a pragmatic, practical perspective and one of higher-level, critical thinking. However, it is not a model for external assessment, for its integrity and effectiveness depends on the learner managing the process; the presence of an assessor deciding for the learner how well a theory serves its purpose or what assumptions are being made defeats the object of self-critical evaluation and undermines the value of the learning process.

Assessing the self-managing learner does then appear to be a contradiction in terms. The learner has no intrinsic need for assessment, for part of the process of learning involves gathering feedback, reviewing it, and acting on it in a reflexive cycle of enquiry and action. Feedback and advice may be offered actively to learners, but there is a difference between feedback as a statement of observation or personal opinion provided as a resource for the learner to use according to his or her own judgement, and assessment which assumes to make some form of external judgement. Assessment is in itself problematic, and it has been argued that assessment commonly views people *"through a filter of assumptions denying much of their potential, dignity and creativity"* (Daley, 1971, p. xiii), something which is hardly consistent with the concept of self-managed learning.

Despite this, the perceived need for external assessment and validation is unlikely to disappear even with a wider appreciation of self-managed learning; there are still reasons for assessment which are broadly (if not unproblematically) seen as educationally and socially desirable. Traditionally, these have included:

- motivating learners to cover or consolidate a syllabus or set of standards
- identifying further learning needs
- validating a level of knowledge, understanding, or competence expected for a qualification or "licence to practice"
- selecting for further education/training or employment
- providing feedback to learners about their progress
- providing feedback about the effectiveness of a teaching, training, or learning process.

(cf. Atkins, Beattie, & Dockrell, 1993, pp. 6–7).

Of these, most can be achieved by other means; the only one which is particularly problematic is qualifications, and current trends suggest that assessment issues will increase in intensity as on the one hand there is growing pressure from governments and to some extent employers both for qualifications and for explicitly rigorous assessment processes, and on the other there is an increasing need for self-managing learners who are adept at going outside conventional boundaries.

Overcoming this conflict depends on assessment methodologies which uphold the *"potential, dignity and creativity"* of the learner, and ensure that learning is supported which goes "outside the box", rather than being constrained within perspectives and logics of others' making. These methodologies will not be found at the level of attempting to assess knowledge and understanding, or theories of practice about what constitutes competent work performance, but will need to enable learners themselves to develop and test personal theory and practice through the model discussed or something akin to it. In effect, assessment needs to move from assessment of 'content' or conformance to an expected outcome (vertical assessment, Lester, 1995a), to assessment of the learner's processes in developing and evaluating their personal models, maps and theories-in-use (horizontal assessment, Lester, 1995a).

A methodology for 'horizontal' assessment might consider the learner's actions in enquiring, creating (whether in a creative or process-based sense), reflecting and evaluating. Within this, personal knowledge, fitness for purpose and fitness of purpose provide a series of levels which can be used in defining criteria, so that while at a basic level the processes of enquiring, creating and reflecting may relate to fairly self-contained and purposive personal referencing, at higher levels they will involve greater exploration of underlying assumptions and location in contexts and contexts of contexts.

Within this type of assessment there needs to be room for negotiation, as the assessment system will still be the product of a map or world-view, even if at a more overarching and less restrictive level than with a content or outcome-based model. Basing assessment on a small number of principles rather than on rules or criteria will assist this flexibility, as well as assisting learners to move beyond closed paradigms of thought. For instance, there are many methods of enquiring, based in different methodologies and epistemologies and emphasising different directions of thought, and equally, creating can be an imaginative leap in which the result just seems to materialise, a planned journey from current state to planned state, or a creative process using a mixture of logic and imagination.

Conclusion

If self-managed learning is to be assessed, it requires an approach to assessment which respects the learner's model of the world while providing a framework for testing it from within and encouraging further critical and creative development. In the model I have proposed, the focus of assessment moves from a 'vertical' or content-based dimension where what has been learned is compared with a model of what it is expected will have been learned (whether this is a syllabus, outcome or set of standards), to a 'horizontal' or process-based dimension, where value is attached to development from unvalidated personal theory through fitness for purpose towards systemic wisdom. For the individual learner, there is now an infinite horizon rather than the invisible ceiling of my first student's double-bind, and the lessons become ones of freedom, responsibility, and wisdom.

A model of this type has several advantages. It respects the uniqueness and individuality of knowledge and action, while requiring that theories and actions are challenged and developed in a wider context than that of the individual's personal outcomes. It respects creative right- and whole-brain thinking and learning (Sperry, 1969) as well as the logical, left-brain processes which typically dominate assessment outside of the creative arts. And finally, it encourages testing against current contexts and future needs, rather than dictating historic models and discourses as starting-points. Although it is still necessarily the product of a particular perspective and therefore not unproblematic, it is more consistent with supporting the learner to be self-managing: confident as an explorer and a creator of theory and action, contextually aware, and developing towards systemic wisdom.

References

Ackoff, R. L. (1974). *Redesigning the Future: A Systems Approach to Societal Problems.* New York: John Wiley.

Allen, M. (1988). *The Goals of Universities.* Buckingham: Society for Research in Higher Education/Open University Press.

Atkins, M. J., Beattie, J., & Dockrell, W. B. (1993). *Assessment Issues in Higher Education.* Sheffield: Department of Employment.

Bandler, R., & Grinder, J. (1975). *The Structure of Magic I.* Palo Alto: Science & Behavior Books.

Barnett, R. (1994). *The Limits of Competence: Knowledge, Higher Education and Society.* London: Routledge.

Bateson, G. (1971). *Steps to an Ecology of Mind.* New Jersey: Jason Aronson.

Carr, W. & Kemmis, S. (1986). *Becoming Critical: Education, Knowledge and Action Research.* Lewes: Falmer Press.

Cunningham, I. (1990). Beyond modernity: is postmodernism relevant to management development? *Management Education and Development, 21* (3), 207–218.

Cunningham, I. (1994). *The Wisdom of Strategic Learning: The Self-Managed Learning Solution.* Maidenhead: McGraw-Hill.

Daley, A. (1971). *Assessment of Lives: Personality Evaluation in a Bureaucratic Society.* London: Jossey Bass.

Dewey, J. (1938). *Experience and Education.* New York: Macmillan.

Evans, N. (1992). *Experiential Learning: Assessment and Accreditation.* London: Routledge.

Knowles, M. (1990). *The Adult Learner: A Neglected Species* (4th edition). Houston: Gulf Publishing.

Korzybski, A. (1958). *Science and Sanity* (4th edition). Lakeville, CT: International Non-Aristotelian Publishing Company.

Lester, S. (1995a). Professional pathways: A case for measurements in more than one dimension. *Assessment and Evaluation in Higher Education, 20* (3), 37–49.

Lester, S. (1995b). Beyond knowledge and competence: Towards a framework for professional education. *Capability, 1* (3), 44–52.

Lindeman, E. C. (1926). *The Meaning of Adult Education*. New York: New Republic.

Ramsden, P. (1986). Students and quality. In G. C. Moodie (Ed.), *Standards and Criteria in Higher Education*. Guildford, Surrey: Society for Research in Higher Education/NFER-Nelson.

Reich, R. B. (1991). *The Work of Nations*. London: Simon & Schuster.

Revans, R. W. (1980). *Action Learning: New Techniques for Management*. London: Blond & Briggs.

Schön, D. A. (1983). *The Reflective Practitioner: How Professionals Think In Action*. New York: Basic Books.

Schön, D. A. (1987). *Educating the Reflective Practitioner*. London: Jossey-Bass.

Schutz, A. (1970). In H. R. Wagner (Ed.), *On phenomenology and Social Relations*. Chicago: Chicago University Press.

Sperry, R. W. (1969). A modified concept of consciousness. *Psychological Review, 76*, 532–536.

Chapter 27

Where Do We Stand on Assessing Competencies?

David C. McClelland

Typically psychologists interested in discovering what personality traits are associated with executive leadership have first selected a self-report questionnaire which has been carefully worked over in the psychometric tradition so that it is known to be reliable and, often, to yield factorially pure scales. For example, in an early study, two such personality tests were employed in an attempt to predict long-term managerial success within the American Telephone and Telegraph Corporation (AT&T) (Bray, Campbell, & Grant, 1974). The hope was that when such psychometrically sound tools were "applied" to a problem of this sort, some of the characteristics measured by the tests would predict who got ahead.

The tests assessed a wide variety of characteristics, such as self-reported needs for achievement, for dominance, and for order, as well as traits of ascendancy, masculinity, self-confidence, and lack of nervousness. Yet, none of these—or the 13 other such personality measures—predicted who would be promoted to middle management eight years later. So much for the hope that standardized self-report personality tests would pick out those more likely to do well in business.

The competency approach starts the other way round. It begins with the problem and works back to discovering what human characteristics

---

contribute to solving it. For example, we were once asked to develop competency tests that would screen in human service workers (HSWs) who could perform successfully on the job (McClelland, 1994). The existing test—the General Aptitude Test Battery (GATB)—that was being used for this purpose was screening out a number of middle-aged, mostly African-American, women with about a sixth-grade education who had shown they could perform very well as HSWs. Furthermore, it had never been shown that the GATB was significantly correlated with outstanding performance on the job. We first established criterion groups of existing HSWs who had been nominated as "outstanding" or "typical" by supervisors. Then we spent some time in the field observing what HSWs did on the job and discovered that a lot of their time was spent getting information under trying conditions from disadvantaged clients so that they could recommend appropriate types of assistance.

So we designed a test that measured the listening/judging competencies they had to show in the field. It was called "the scenarios test" and consisted of actual interviews of clients tape-recorded in the field together with a still photograph of the client. The testees listened to the tapes that were not always easy to understand because of background noise and the use of "street talk" and answered factual questions about what they had heard, wrote out what they would recommend in the case (scored against expert judgement), answered questions as to what the attitudes of the clients were on various issues (checked against what the clients actually said), and so forth (McClelland, 1994, p. 68). In short, rather than using an existing test that examined aptitudes of unknown relationship to performance as a HSW, we designed a new test of the competencies our job analysis had shown to be needed in the field. And, not surprisingly, it proved to be valid—that is, the "outstanding" HSWs scored much higher on it than the "typical" HSWs.

When it came to assessing managerial competencies, it proved impractical to make on-the-job observations, and in any case we were interested in what executives were thinking as well as in what we could see them doing. So we employed an intensive interviewing technique—the Behavioral Event Interview, or BEI—which was designed to discover just what executives were thinking and doing as they went about their work.

Once again, we asked a number of knowledgeable people in the organization to nominate executives in a certain category whom they considered truly outstanding. When people were independently named by several nominators, we put them in the "outstanding" category and then chose a matched group of people doing the same kind of work who were not nominated by anybody to represent "typical" performers. From comparing and contrasting the way outstanding and typical executives described how they went about their work, we were able to develop coding systems for transcripts of the interviews that identified the competencies shown more often by the outstanding than by the typical executives. Scoring systems were developed for competencies as varied as achievement orientation, self-control, initiative, team leadership, analytical thinking, interpersonal understanding, and so forth (see Boyatzis, 1982).

The method of obtaining and scoring interviews was expensive and laborious, particularly as we had to develop coding systems that were explicit enough to obtain high coding reliability. We never gave up hope of developing competency tests, although, for a variety of reasons, much of our work focused more on using the measures obtained from the behavior event interviews than on developing competency tests.

One reason for this was that the competency models that were created to predict outstanding performance in a given job led directly to training those who selected new hires for a job in BEI interviewing techniques so that they could more easily spot those who showed the competencies that were needed.

Several studies have shown that this approach has led to selecting more successful salespeople than a more conventional selection procedure still used in other parts of the same company. For example, of 33 salespeople hired by L'Oreal using the BEI method, only 15 percent had to be separated compared to 41 percent of the 41 people hired by the traditional method. The BEI hires also achieved their quotas more often and showed a greater average increase in per-quarter sales. Nine of them were promoted (or became candidates for promotion); none of the 41 hired by the old method were promoted or became candidates for promotion. The costs of building such a competency model are clearly more than offset by bottom-line advantages in increased sales and decreased turnover costs.

Another use of such a competency model is to give people feedback from their BEIs about how they scored on various competencies compared to the scores of those who were outstanding executives in the company. They can compare their real level of expressing a competency with the ideal level as shown by more successful managers. When there are discrepancies it motivates improvement. In addition, the scoring definitions for various competencies (which contain concrete real-life examples of more competent behavior) can be taught to those involved and in this way provide specific information on the patterns of thinking, feeling, and behaving that are required. Such guidance has a powerful effect on behavior and performance.

Detailed information of this sort has also provided a basis for career counseling and for explaining why a person should or should not be promoted.

This is not to say that using the BEI as a method for measuring competencies is not without drawbacks. One problem with the BEI approach is that each competency study using this method tends to discover a set of competencies that appear unique to that particular job in that company in that organization. Actually, much of the problem stems not so much in the fact that generic competencies for a particular job really differ, but from the fact that organizational cultures tend to develop their own language for communicating ideas. Thus those conceptualizing the differences in the interviews of the outstanding and typical performers tend to use terminology specific to the culture of that organization. For example, what is "achievement orientation" in one company has to be called "drive for results" in another company to communicate the finding so it will be widely understood, although what is coded may be identical in the two cases. One would like to think that a fairly standard set of competencies would be critical for success in a variety of, say, sales jobs. Can one generalize at all across so many unique competency studies?

As an answer to this problem, Hay McBer has developed a standard dictionary of frequently encountered competencies for coding BEIs that are routinely applied in new studies, along with the search for new competencies unique to the new situation. If a client needs to re-label one of the standard competencies to communicate its meaning widely, that makes good sense, but we file the data under the generic name of the competency in the dictionary.

Finally, a serious problem with the BEI approach is that predictions of success in the future are made on the basis of competencies discovered in a single study of outstanding and typical performers at a particular moment in time. It is perfectly proper to derive a set of competencies from comparing BEIs of one set of outstanding and typical cases, but those competencies may capitalize on chance differences between the cases in this particular comparison. So one should check the ability of the competencies that were associated with better performance in the first set of cases to predict who will be outstanding in a second set of cases before one can be comfortable in using the competencies, let us say, for selecting or promoting people. Unfortunately, such cross-validation is expensive. Fortunately, it has become less of a problem as more of the competencies are part of a standard dictionary (like the one Hay McBer has developed) and as more studies are carried out to employ the standard codes. In effect, there are cross-validations to be found in the database. It would be possible to say to Company X that several key competencies of a sales model developed for that company, for example, have also been found to differentiate between more and less successful salespeople in some other studies of salespeople.

There is also the danger that the characteristics, which have been associated with success in the past or at the moment of the first study, may not predict success in the future when the company may be in a changed situation. One aspect of this question has to do with changes in the operating situation that companies know is going to take place. For example, most of them realize that executives are going to have to know how to manage diversity in the future, but they would not expect such a competency to show up as characteristic of better performers at the present time. So we have developed a coding system for this competency because it has shown up in a number of interviews but we, and the companies that use it, expect it to be associated with better performance only sometime down the road.

Another aspect of this question has to do with whether the competency model built on present differences in performance will actually predict better bottom-line performance next year. It is quite possible that some competencies associated with better performance now may be the *result* of better performance, not the cause of it. For example, self-confidence is a competency often found to be more often present in BEIs of better performers, but perhaps that is because they have been performing better in the year before the BEI is carried out. That's why they have been nominated as outstanding. The crucial test is whether that competency *predicts* better performance in the year or years after it is measured.

So what solid evidence is there that competency measures derived in this way from BEIs actually predict successful performance under the demanding conditions just described? Fortunately, Hay McBer has developed a close enough relationship with a large global multinational food and beverage business to be able to get the kind of performance data we need to check out the ability of the competency model we developed to predict success in a number of groups of executives in the company. In fact, the company was as interested as we were to determine the answer to the question Was the competency model working? We have permission to report the findings in this important study as long as we do not mention the specific competencies that we found to be related to executive success.

The competency model was derived in the usual way by comparing BEIs obtained in 1992 from groups of executives at a fairly high level in the company who had either been nominated as outstanding or not. Based on the original sample interviewed, approximately 18 competencies were viewed as important, most of them because they showed up significantly more often in the group nominated as outstanding compared to the rest of the executives in the sample. However, some competencies such as "multicultural sensitivity" were added, not because they distinguished between the two groups, but because the company thought they were competencies that everyone should show. In short, they are what has been called "threshold competencies" (Boyatzis, 1982).

Next, we obtained a 1993 performance measure for those in the original group of executives and in a new larger group whose competencies had also been assessed through BEIs. The main hard measure of performance in this company is the extent to which the goals set for an executive's annual operating plan are achieved. The goals include bottom-line profitability in the unit managed and also other objectives to be implemented. The individual executive bonus received is proportional to the extent that the annual operating plan for that person was achieved in the past year. We took these bonus figures and adjusted them for the overall success of the division in which an executive worked. That is, achieving 90 percent of the annual target might be the highest anyone achieved in one division due to poor market conditions; whereas in another division a number of people might have surpassed the target. In effect, we ranked achievement against plan within divisions.

Then we considered outstanding performers who were in the top third for adjusted bonus received and who had no actual negative rating for performance from any qualified judge in the company. They were compared with those who fell in the bottom two-thirds of the ranking order for bonus received. Some of the managers who had been nominated as outstanding in 1992 actually fell in the bottom two-thirds category for bonus received for 1993 and vice versa. This underlined our caution that past performance does not always predict future performance.

Next, we sought to determine which competencies that differentiated those nominated as outstanding in 1992 from the rest would best predict actual performance in 1993, as measured by the bonus received. In this instance, we determined the median frequency for each competency for all the executives in the sample (we could have used the mean scale score also) and gave a person credit for having the competency if he or she scored above that median. Then we compared the percentage of those who were top performers in 1993 who scored above the median frequency on each competency with the percentage of those who performed in the bottom two-thirds in 1993 and who scored above the median on each frequency. We found that significantly more of the top than the other performers in 1993 scored high on 11 out of the original 18 competencies we had identified for the company's management competency model.

One would normally determine what combination of these competencies would best pick out the top performers in 1993 using a linear multiple-regression model. For theoretical reasons, we took a different approach. Weights for various competencies in a regression model are calculated to be optimal for the particular set of subjects and scores obtained, but they are unlikely to be the same in applications of the regression equation to different set of subjects. Furthermore, we believed that the competencies could be grouped into those relating to individual effort or initiative on the one hand and organizational know-how on the other and that a top performer should possess at least one competency in each of these categories.

Requiring one of a set of related competencies gives greater generality to the model because it allows for alternative manifestations of a basic individual or group competency. So, as Table 27.1 demonstrates, we created a formula that required possession of at least one of three individual and at least one of three organizational competencies from the set of 11 competencies that differentiated outstanding from typical performers in 1993.

As Table 27.1 demonstrates, the formula was not only very successful in picking out the top performers in 1993 for the original sample, which is not surprising since the model was based on the BEIs from these people. All of those (100%) judged highly qualified by the competency formula based on BEIs obtained in 1992 actually were top performers in 1993. Only a few of those not so judged by the formula were in the top performing group in 1993. The competency formula also did very well in categorizing who would be the above-average and below-average performers by the 1993 bonus measure in a second U.S. group of executives. Thirty-two out of 43 cases, or 74%, were correctly predicted to be either outstanding or typical performers in 1993. What is more, the formula worked very well in picking those who had been nominated as outstanding both in Asia and Europe.

Table 27.1 Predicting Executive Success from a Competency Index

Predicting Executive Success *Within the US* from a Competency Index
(Based on Behavioral Event Interviewing Scoring)
Actual Performance
(Assessed According to 1993 Individual Incentive Bonus)

Score on the Competency Index	Initial Sample[1] N (=100%)	% in top third on performance index	New Sample N (=100%)	% in top third on performance index
Higher[2]	12	100	17	65
Lower	17	24	26	19
Tetrachoric r	.93*		.66*	
Percent correctly classified	25/29, or 86%		32/43, or 74%	

Predicting Executive Success *Outside the US* from the same Competency Index
(Based on Behavioral Event Interviewing Scoring)
Actual Performance (Assessed from Nominations)[3]

Score on the Competency Index	European N (=100%)	% judged as outstanding	Asian N (=100%)	% judged as outstanding	Combined N (=100%)	% judged as outstanding
Higher[2]	11	82	7	86	18	83
lower	8	13	9	11	17	12
Tetrachoric r					.90**	
Percent correctly classified	16/19, or 84%		14/16, or 88%		30/35, or 86%	

* p<.05
** p<.01

1. The initial sample consisted of people nominated as outstanding or typical in 1992 and the competency index was derived from the competencies that differentiated significantly between the outstanding and typical performers in this group. However, in this table top performance in the US samples was considered being in the top third of bonus performers corrected for division in the following year, 1993.
2. In the United States in 1993, outstanding performers differed from typical performers by scoring above the median frequency on at least one of three personal initiative competencies, at least one of three organizational competencies, and at least four other competencies from the set which differentiated them from typical performers. The same competency index was used in the studies conducted outside the US, except that for a few competencies the median frequencies had to be raised to fit the data. It was additionally required for both samples that the person score above the median frequency on at least one of three additional competencies associated with better performance overseas. Thus, to be classified as belonging to the higher scoring group according to this competency index a person had to score above the median frequency on at least six competencies in the United States and seven competencies overseas, drawn from the specified groups of competencies.
3. In the overseas samples, the measure of performance was nomination as an outstanding performer for 1993.

I cannot overemphasize the importance of recognizing that there are alternative combinations of characteristics that lead to success in a particular job. Too many consultants and companies operate on the assumption that what we need to discover is the *one best* set of competencies that leads to success. We are acting like cookie-cutters. We are trying to find the best competency mould so that we can pick or shape individuals to fit that mould. Yet everyone who has been in a business for any length of time has observed instances in which the same job has been performed very well by two people who appear to have quite different characteristics. The fact is that often various combinations of competencies lead to success.

Despite its successes, the BEI procedure has some important limitations for measuring competencies. It justifies its high cost when high-level executives are being chosen, but it cannot be used to assess competencies in large pools of applicants. If rating scales are cheap but suspect without BEIs to back them up, and if BEIs are expensive and time-consuming to carry out, how are we to deal with a problem like screening for competencies the many thousands of people who apply to the Foreign Service every year? This brings me back to the original purpose of carrying out BEIs. It was to define competencies in behaviorally specific ways so that tests of those behaviors could be devised and used to screen large numbers of applicants.

Although several competency tests that initially looked promising have been developed with a view toward dealing with this problem, none has been cultivated to the point where one could have faith in using it. Why is this so? I believe that the main reason is that there is no organization devoted to developing, validating, and promoting such tests. I was present in the early days when the Educational Testing Service (ETS) was established in response to a felt need among colleges to have some way of screening applicants for academic aptitude.

Various scholastic aptitude tests existed and were in use here and there, but there was no central organization with responsibility for developing and standardizing such tests until ETS was created as a non-profit organization with grants from various foundations. As we all know, ETS has developed into the major player in the testing movement—in fact, too major a player in my opinion, as it has led people to use the aptitude tests it has developed for all sorts of purposes for which they are not appropriate.

So what we need is a similar non-profit institution set up to develop, standardize, and promote the use of competency tests. In this case

I believe the appropriate institutions that should be pushing for this development are not the liberal arts colleges but the professional schools—the business schools, the divinity schools, the nursing schools, the medical schools, the law schools, and so forth. For it is increasingly being recognized that all the professions require more than just certain kinds of knowledge for successful practice. To function successfully, professionals—such as business executives—need certain competencies. The schools that educate them should screen for some of these competencies and devote themselves to developing others, as the Weatherhead School for Business Administration at Case Western Reserve University has done under the leadership of Dr. Richard Boyatzis. (I have come to believe that it is probably not appropriate for busy, competitive, for-profit enterprises to engage in the kind of careful research needed to develop sound tests of this sort with wide applicability.)

References

Boyatzis, R. E. (1982). *The Competent Manager.* New York: Wiley.

Bray, D. W., Campbell, R. J., & Grant, D. L. (1974). *Formative Years in Business: A Long-Term AT&T Study of Managerial Lives.* New York: Wiley.

McClelland, D. C. (1994). The knowledge-testing educational complex strikes back. *American Psychologist, 49,* 6–9.

Chapter 28

The Assessment of Competence

John Raven

In previous chapters, I have shown that new forms of assessment are required so that:

1. Lecturers can manage individualised competency-oriented educational programmes. If high-level competencies are to be developed, students must be able to practise doing the things they need to do while undertaking activities they care about. If they are to be able to do this, lecturers must be able to help each student to identify his or her concerns, interests, and patterns of competence and monitor his or her reactions to his or her experiences.

2. Students can identify their own distinctive talents, monitor their progress as they develop them, and get credit for their accomplishments. New forms of assessment are also required to enable people to get credit for the talents they have developed at work and in the community, for this is where people obtain their most important developmental experience and information. Only in this way will it be possible to break the stranglehold that educational institutions currently have on job-entry qualifications.

3. Lecturers can get credit for their accomplishments in accountability exercises and evaluation studies. They, like the other public servants they really are, need to be able to get credit for doing such things as paying attention to their clients' needs and inventing better ways of meeting them.

4. Evaluators can design studies which will enable administrators to find out how to improve educational programmes and policies.

5. It becomes possible to implement a more effective manpower policy based on more sensible guidance, placement, and development

    procedures and selection policies that are better at getting the right people into, and excluding the wrong people from, important positions.

6. It becomes possible to encourage and recognise diversity and thus break the conceptual stranglehold currently held by single-factor concepts of ability, monocultures of mind, reductionist science, and authoritarian social control more generally.

In this chapter I will first suggest a basis on which an alternative measurement paradigm might be built. Later I will describe the ways in which this paradigm has already been operationalised and ways in which its implementation could be improved.

The place to begin to build an alternative *measurement* paradigm must be with the question What is competence? This has been discussed in earlier chapters and at greater length in my *Competence in Modern Society*. The discussion that follows will be limited to issues that are essential as a basis on which to build an alternative assessment paradigm and will pass over other aspects of the topic, important though they are in themselves.

We will begin by taking an example—one that we have mentioned before—namely "initiative". As we have seen, initiative is a quality which it is vital for educators to foster. It is seen as essential to both competitive capitalism and successful socialism. What *is* initiative?

To take a successful initiative, people have to be self-motivated. Self-starting people must be persistent and devote a great deal of time, thought, and effort to the activity in which they are engaged. They need to initiate innovative action, monitor the effects of that action, and learn from those effects more about the problem they are trying to tackle; the social, political, and environmental context in which it is situated; and what is effective and ineffective about the strategies they are using. To succeed, they must anticipate obstacles in the future and invent ways of circumventing or overcoming them. They will need to build up their own, unique, store of *specialist* knowledge. They will have to get help from others. More often than not, it will be necessary to establish coalitions with others to gain control over social and political forces that would otherwise deflect them from their goals.

Perhaps the crucial point to be emphasised in attempting to clarify the nature of competence is that no one is going to do any of these things unless they care about the activity they are undertaking. Values are, therefore, central.[1] In practice it turns out that what is valued may be a particular *outcome* (such as stopping a factory polluting a river) or it may be a particular *style of behaviour* (such as finding better ways of doing things or getting people to work together effectively).

What has been said has major implications for psychological and educational measurement. It means that one must know someone's values, preoccupations, or intentions before one attempts to assess his or her abilities. The exercise of important abilities demands time, energy, and effort. As a result, people will only display them when they are undertaking activities that are important to them. It does not make sense to attempt to assess abilities (including, as we saw in previous chapters, such things as "cognitive ability") except in relation to valued goals.

These observations are in sharp conflict with many traditional canons of psychometry. I have argued that one cannot assess abilities independently of values. This means that it is essential to adopt a two-stage approach when assessing competence. We must first find out which types of behaviour someone values, and then, and *only* then, assess his or her ability to bring to bear a wide variety of potentially important cognitive, affective, and conative components of competence to undertake the activity effectively.

It is important to emphasise that the widely held view that one can use one set of measures to assess values and another set of measures, independently, to assess knowledge, skills, abilities or competencies, simply does not make sense. The latter will only be developed and displayed when the situation in which the individual finds him or herself triggers or releases the former. Furthermore, since people often cannot tell one what their distinctive preoccupations and concerns are (since they do not know what other people's are) one of the best ways of finding out what people care about is to ask: "In the course of pursuing what kinds of activity does this person display multiple and high-level talents?"

Our example—initiative—also highlights another way in which the assumptions on which the dominant measurement paradigms in psychology and education are based fail to engage with important aspects of competence. Conventional psychometric theory places great stress on internal consistency or factorial purity. Scores derived from tests composed of items which do not correlate with each other are said to be meaningless. Yet it would seem from our example that this assertion is not correct. People's initiatives are more likely to be successful the *more* independent and different components of competence they bring to bear to achieve their goals effectively. For example, they are more likely to be successful if they re-conceptualise the problem, obtain the help of others, persist over a long period of time, and so on. Yet their inclination and ability to do any one of these things in pursuit of their goals is unlikely to be closely related to their inclination and ability to do others. Furthermore, if they do any one of them particularly well that will, to some extent, compensate for their failure to do others.

It follows from the observations made in the last paragraph that, if we are to assess such qualities as initiative, instead of trying to develop measurement tools which are as internally consistent as possible, we need to try to develop *indices* made up of items which are as little correlated with each other as possible.[2] This is actually not so heretical as at first sight it appears, because it is standard practice to make use of multiple regression equations which involve summing over maximally independent variables in order to obtain the best predictions of behaviour.

The insights we have developed so far may be summarised as follows: If we are to find ways of assessing important human traits it will be necessary to abandon our desire to develop value-free, internally consistent measures. Instead, we will need to develop value-based, maximally-internally-heterogeneous *indices* which do justice to the psychological complexity of these qualities.

Cognitions of Institutional Structures

This is an appropriate point to introduce one more disturbing insight which has emerged in the course of our work: value-based cognitions of social processes are central to competent behaviour and need to be documented in any meaningful assessments of competence.

Behaviour is very much determined by such things as people's beliefs about how things *should* be done and who should relate to whom about what. It is very much influenced by their perceptions of roles—by what they think it is appropriate for someone in their position to do, by what they think other people expect them to do, and by how they think other people will react to their behaviour. It is determined by their understanding of what is meant by terms such as "management," "participation," "majority decision-taking," "managerial responsibility," "wealth," and "democracy." The disturbing conclusion is that if we are to assess competence in any meaningful way, it will be necessary to assess such beliefs.

Because this conclusion raises the spectre of social control and brainwashing, it is necessary to reinforce it by reminding the reader that, as I showed in an earlier chapter, we initially came to this conclusion from exactly the opposite starting point: When we compared more with less competent farmers, teachers, bus drivers, blacksmiths, managers, and military officers we found that, in each case, it was what the more effective people did to influence the social context in which they worked—viz. other people's expectations, the legal (regulatory) context, the economic context, and so on—that was most important. Put the other way round, the most important source of incompetent occupational behaviour in modern society is the inability and unwillingness to do something about the wider social, institutional, and political constraints arising from outside one's job—because it is these factors that overwhelmingly determine what one *can* do within it.

The Need to Describe the Situation in Which an Individual Finds Himself or Herself as an Integral Part of the Assessment

Although the way in which people define the situation in which they find themselves has a marked effect on their behaviour, that context has other direct and indirect effects. It influences their behaviour directly through the constraints it places on what they can do, and it influences it indirectly through the concepts, understandings, and competencies that people are able to practise and develop.

It therefore emerges that, if one wishes to assess competence, it is necessary to assess both the perceived and the actual institutional context in which it occurs. As we saw earlier, it is either meaningless or wildly prejudicial to say that people lack the ability to do something that they have never had the opportunity to practise doing. That is why a "back to basics" approach reinforces a "single-factor" model of ability. The only way out of the dilemma is to make assessment of the context part of the assessment of the individual.

Identification of Values and Cognitions

Although satisfactory measures of competence must be value-based and include the wider social and civic perceptions and understandings just mentioned, one unfortunately cannot discover these simply by asking people to identify the behaviours they value and their beliefs about how society works and their role in it. Because they do not know much about the values, preoccupations, and thoughtways of others, they cannot perceive, still less identify, the ways in which they themselves are distinctive. That is why it is impossible for students who have come through one type of educational programme to tell one how the issues on which they will in future tend to focus, and their ways of approaching those problems, differ from those of others who have come through other programmes.

Not only are people unable to perceive and identify their own distinctive values and beliefs, they are also often unable to identify important *shared* value-based social cognitions because they are common to all members of their cultural group.

Recapitulation and Restatement

In the course of these remarks I have introduced some ideas that my colleagues and I have taken many years to stumble upon and make explicit—and that contrast sharply with many traditional assumptions in psychology and education. For this reason, many people have found it helpful for me to re-present the same ideas in different way. I will now do this, making use of a three-dimensional diagram proposed by Ron Johnson, shown in Figure 28.1.

Johnson argues that behaviour is the result of three sets of variables: skills and abilities, motivation, and the situation in which people find themselves. For our purposes we can substitute "components of competence" for "skills and abilities" and "values" for "motivation." So far, so good. But I have also argued that:

1. Components of competence will only be developed and displayed whilst those concerned are undertaking tasks they care about. They cannot be abstracted in the way suggested by the diagram and assessed independently of motivation. Motivation is *an integral part* of competence.
2. Effective performance—the resultant—is much more dependent on the number of independent and substitutable competencies that are brought to bear in a wide variety of situations in order to reach a goal than it is on the level of competence or ability displayed in relation to any one of them in a particular situation. It is the total number of competencies that individuals display in many situations over a long period of time in order to reach their valued goals that we need to assess, not their level of ability in relation to any one of them. Any *overall* index of a person's "ability" or "motivation" is virtually meaningless.
3. The situation in which an individual is placed influences the values which are aroused and the competencies which are practised and developed directly—quite apart from its influence on the behaviour

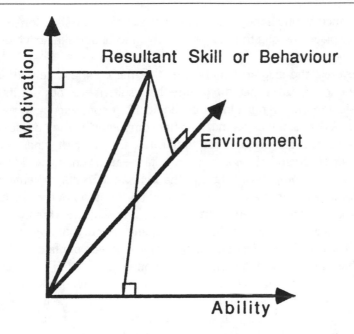

Figure 28.1 Johnson's Model

that emerges at the end—when a person with a particular pattern of motivation and abilities is placed in a particular situation. Not only do environments have the power to transform people, people actively select themselves into, and attend and respond to different features of, particular environments. Johnson's diagram does not recognise this. It gives the impression that a change in some feature of the environment will lead to an increase (or decrease) in the quality or frequency of a particular behaviour and that the motivation and ability of the actor will remain the same.

Despite these limitations, Johnson's diagram is useful because it emphasises (1) that it is important to assess all three sets of variables, (2) that behaviour is a product of all three sets of variables, (3) that the components of competence can only be assessed in relation to a task the individual cares about, (4) that behaviour is influenced by people's perceptions of the situation in which they find themselves, their understandings of the way the organisation works, and the reactions they expect from others, and (5) that people will only display the levels of competence of which they are capable if they define the situation in which they are placed as one that will enable them to undertake activities they care about.

Above all, the diagram emphasises that the competence with which people perform tasks they are given—the resultant—cannot, on its own, be treated as a meaningful index of their current competence to perform those tasks, let alone as an index of the competencies they possess.

The diagram can also be used to illustrate the fact that other people's ratings of observed behaviour—the resultant—are even less valid indices of the ratee's competence than is the behaviour itself, for what raters perceive depends on their own values and priorities, what they take to be the demands of the task and situation, and their subjective ability to manage the ratee—who has values, priorities, and talents that may well differ from their own. Many lecturers (and managers) lack confidence in their own ability to manage independent, thoughtful, questioning students. This makes them unwilling to create situations in which such qualities could be developed and displayed. And it has a marked effect on the interpretation they place on such behaviour when it occurs.

Having said that, it is important to note that it is only the (already "contaminated") "resultant" behaviour, further contaminated by their own values and abilities, that any observer can see with the unaided eye. The only way round this difficulty involves, on the one hand, getting inside the ratee's head, and, on the other, making the values, priorities, assumptions, and competencies of the rater as explicit as possible.

A Formal Model of Competence, Motivation, and Behaviour and Its Assessment

We return now to the task of elaborating our model of competence and the way in which its components are to be assessed. We have seen that it is inappropriate to try to assess the self-motivated competencies that make for effective behaviour except in relation to activities which the person concerned cares about. We have also seen that there are many components of competence, that many of them are relatively independent of each other, and that these competencies are cumulative and substitutable.

This way of thinking about competence may be made more concrete by reference to Grid 1.

On it, some of the types of behaviour which people value have been listed across the top. These behaviours have been grouped into the three clusters (achievement, affiliation, and power) identified by McClelland in

Examples of Potentially Valued Styles of Behaviour

Examples of components of effective behaviour	Achievement				Affiliation				Power		
	Doing things which have not been done before.	Inventing things.	Doing things more efficiently than they have been done before.	Developing new formal scientific theories.	Providing support and facilitation for someone concerned with achievement.	Establishing warm, convivial relationships with others.	Ensuring that a group works together without conflict.	Establishing effective group discussion procedures.	Ensuring that group members share their knowledge so that good decisions can be taken.	Articulating group goals and releasing the energies of others in pursuit of them.	Setting up domino-like chains of influence to get people to do as one wishes without having to contact them directly.

Cognitive

Thinking (by opening one's mind to experience, dreaming, and using other sub-conscious process) about what is to be achieved and how it is to be achieved.

Anticipating obstacles to achievement and taking steps to avoid them.

Analysing the effects of one's actions to discover what they have to tell one about the nature of the situation one is dealing with.

Making one's value conflicts explicit and trying to resolve them.

Consequence anticipated:
Personal: e.g. "I know there will be difficulties, but I know from my previous experience that I can find ways round them."
Personal normative beliefs: e.g. "I would have to be more devious and manipulative than I would like to be to do that."
Social normative beliefs: e.g. "My friends would approve if I did that": "It would not be appropriate for someone in my position to do that."

Affective

Turning one's emotions into the task:
Admitting and harnessing feelings of delight and frustration: using the unpleasantness of tasks one needs to complete as an incentive to get on with them rather than as an excuse to avoid them.

Anticipating the delights of success and the misery of failure.

Using one's feelings to initiate action, monitor its effects, and change one's behaviour.

Conative

Putting in extra effort to reduce the likelihood of failure.

Persisting over a long period, alternatively striving and relaxing.

Habits and experience

Confidence, based on experience, that one can adventure into the unknown and overcome difficulties, (This involves knowledge that one will be able to do it plus a stockpile of relevant habits).

A range of appropriate routineised, but flexibly contingent behaviours, each triggered by cues which one may not be able to articulate and which may be imperceptible to others.

Experience of the satisfactions which have come from having accomplished similar tasks in the past.

Grid 1 A Model of Competence

1958 and confirmed empirically in our own previous work.[3] Down the side are listed a number of components of competence which, if present, are likely to result in the activity being successful. These components of competence include cognitive activities such as making plans and thinking about obstacles to goal achievement, affective activities such as enjoying the activity or wishing that a necessary but distasteful task was completed, and conative activities such as exercising will, being determined, and persisting. However, also listed are a number of other factors which contribute to successful performance—such as having the support of others and believing that one's behaviour is consistent with both one's own and others' views of what it is appropriate for someone in one's position to do.[4]

The importance of separating these value and efficacy components in assessment can be re-emphasised by taking another example. An individual who values success at football may show a great deal of initiative in relation to football, be very sensitive to feedback from the environment, seek the help of others to improve performance, monitor, and continuously improve his or her style, seek out new techniques and ideas, be sensitive to minor cues that suggest ways to improve, be sensitive to the approval or disapproval of his or her peers, have the willpower to persist in the face of difficulty, and be able and willing to persuade local politicians to provide a pitch or field. Nevertheless, if the ability of this same person to engage in these complex, cognitive, affective, social, and conative activities is assessed in relation to performance at mathematics—a goal which, for the sake of argument, we may assume this individual does not value—then one might erroneously conclude that he or she is unable (and not just unmotivated) to engage in the activities that have been mentioned. Teachers, psychologists, and managers have, in the past, too frequently been guilty of drawing such erroneous conclusions.

Attention should be drawn to the fact that, while this model is readily comprehended as a model designed to help us to understand and assess motivation—the styles of behaviour someone values and his or her ability to pursue those goals effectively—it is, in reality, a model of competence.

Descriptive Statements and Profiles

In principle, Grid 1 can be used to identify the behaviours that people value and the components of competence they tend to display in pursuit of them. For any one person, an assessor could, after having made relevant observations, enter ticks in the appropriate cells under the behaviours the person values. By adding up the ticks in any one column, the assessor can obtain an index of how likely it is that the person concerned will undertake that kind of behaviour effectively. By summing the scores obtained in adjacent columns under each of the overall headings, scores which indicate the probability that a person will reach achievement, affiliation, and power goals can be obtained.

This yields a profile which is directly comparable with those published by McClelland, and which he (in the present context, misleadingly) refers to as profiles of motivation.

It is important to note, however, that because, as has been indicated, the Grid should be considerably extended, the procedure would become cumbersome if it were applied whole-heartedly. A way round this problem will be suggested shortly.

Heterogeneous Indices or Internally Consistent Factor Scores?

Not only must values be assessed as an integral part of the assessment of competence, the components of competence we have identified cannot be meaningfully analysed or identified in factorial or dimensional terms. The scores obtained by summing down the columns in Grid 1 are, quite obviously, not unidimensional. Indeed, the more independent and hetero-geneous the competencies that are composited, the better—provided, of course, each relates to goal achievement. At this point many readers will (as a result of their training in the dominant internal-consistency, factor-analytic, measurement paradigm) be thinking "Such scores are not mean-ingful!" It is therefore important to note that, while the factor analysts' claim that such heterogeneity shows that the scores which are obtained are not unidimensional is correct, the assumed corollary—that they are not meaningful—does not necessarily follow. No one would argue that multiple regression coefficients are meaningless simply because they are calculated by summing across as many maximally independent predictors of performance as possible.

Overall Indices Versus Detailed Descriptive Statements

In practice, an account of the types of behaviour which a person values and the competencies they display in the course of carrying out those activities provides much more useful information than a single total score. Such a description is radically different from a profile of scores across a series of factorially independent dimensions. The assumptions behind a factorial profile are that behaviour is best described and understood in terms of people's relative scores on a small number of dimensions. The assumption behind the model developed here is that behaviour is best to be understood by identifying people's values, compulsions, perceptions, and expectations and the components of competence they tend to dis-play spontaneously in pursuit of their valued goals.

"Atomic" Versus "Variable" Models

The difference between factorial profiles and descriptive statements can be illustrated by using examples from physics and chemistry. Physicists have shown that the behaviour of a projectile is best described by some such equation as:

$$s = ut + \tfrac{1}{2}ft^2$$

(The distance travelled at a particular time is determined by the initial velocity multiplied by the time elapsed plus half the acceleration multiplied by the square of the elapsed time.)

The factor analysts' model is analogous. For example, it may assert that the degree of leadership which will be displayed is a function of the person's scores on variables such as extroversion and intelligence.

Unlike physicists, chemists have found a very different type of equation to be most useful in their work. They argue that substances and the environments in which they are placed are best described by listing the elements of which they are composed and the relationship between these elements. The descriptors (elements) are drawn from a large set known to all chemists. The elements that are not present do not need to be listed. The behaviour of the substance in a particular environment is then described by equations that make it possible to describe transformations as well as monotonic combination:

$$Cu + 2H_2SO_4 = CuSO_4 + 2H_2O + SO_2$$

(Copper plus sulphuric acid yields copper sulphate, water, and sulphur dioxide.)

It is being argued here that human beings might best be described and understood by adopting a model that has more in common with that used by chemists than that used by physicists. Such a framework would enable us to indicate people's values and the components of competence they show a spontaneous tendency to display in pursuit of them, and together with the relevant and significant features of their environments without restricting us to the small number of variables that characterise factor-analytic models.[5]

We will now push the chemical analogy further. If we were to pursue this model we would find ourselves writing *summary* descriptions of people and the environments in which they live and work. This might take the following form (the symbols that are used are exemplary only and should in no way be taken to suggest that we have developed even a preliminary version of a more complete table of "human elements"):

$$Achs_4Pow_3;Auth_4PartCit_2;NuP_4HostP_3;DP(T)_1$$

Such a statement might be interpreted to mean that the individual concerned showed a spontaneous tendency to display four components of competence in pursuit of achievement goals and three components of competence in pursuit of power goals. Four items that contribute to the set dealing with authoritarian perceptions of society, and only two of the set dealing with participatory citizenship, were endorsed. Four aspects of the environment were supportive of the individual's goals: The manager modelled achievement behaviour but did not delegate, encourage participation, or create developmental tasks for his or her subordinates. There was "hostile press" from other people in the individual's environment. Concern with efficiency and effective leadership were scorned. The task that the individual was set had little developmental potential: It was a routine task that prevented the person concerned from developing perceptions and expectations appropriate to innovation.

If the equation were written in some way that permitted movement, one would conclude that the individual would be likely to become frustrated and lose motivation to engage in achievement and leadership behaviours.

In fact, of course, such summary statements could be filled out in a great deal more detail, and very usefully too. One could identify exactly what type of achievement or power behaviour the individual thought it was important to engage in, one could identify exactly which competencies were brought to bear in pursuit of each interest, one could identify the particular perceptions and expectations that encouraged and prevented the person concerned from engaging in such behaviour, and one could say more about the role models to whom he or she was exposed by managers, colleagues, and subordinates.

The next point to be made is that such *statements* about people can be extended to include statements about their environments. One can identify the way in which the motives and competencies of other people in the environment "engage with" those of the individual and result in emergent—and vitally important—*group* characteristics not possessed by any individual within it or achievable by "summing the parts"; one can identify the way in which the presence or absence of other people and particular working arrangements—which facilitate or inhibit certain types of behaviour—*transform* the individual and result in motives, competencies, and behaviours that would not otherwise be displayed; one can say something about the tasks set and their probable effects on the person's future development and motivation. Such statements enable us to describe (or, more correctly, model) the *transformational* processes that occur in homes, educational institutions, and workplaces.

By insisting that statements about the individual are accompanied by statements about both the situation in which the observations were made and the relevant previous experience of the individual—and thus prior opportunities to learn—we can also overcome the serious challenges to faith in the possibility of "objective" psychological and educational assessment that are typically levelled at work in this area. In previous chapters we have seen that: (1) values are triggered, and competencies thus released or suppressed, by the situations in which people find themselves; (2) people can only have developed high-level competencies if the situations in which they have previously found themselves have tapped their values (or, put the other way round and in a more concrete form, they may be perfectly capable of learning to do something they are currently unable and unwilling to do if they are placed in a situation that engages their values); and (3) people may be able to unleash high-level competencies that they currently do not display if they come to value the task they are being expected to undertake.

Our position is, therefore, that a description of the situations that have in the past tapped people's motives, the competencies they displayed in those situations (and would therefore probably transfer to any new task they might now come to value), and whether the situation in that they currently find themselves (and are now perhaps being observed and assessed) taps their values must form an integral part of any meaningful assessment of their competence.

* * * * *

For the sake of clarity, I will now briefly recapitulate the argument that has just been presented. We first noted that people's areas of competence can be identified by putting ticks in the cells of a two-dimensional grid which has valued behaviours across the top and components of competence down the side. We then noted that the internally heterogeneous summary scores (analogous to multiple regression correlation coefficients) that can be obtained by summing the ticks in adjacent columns of the grid are conceptually identical to McClelland's "motivation" scores. However, we also noted that the original (tick-based) "description" of the behaviours the individual valued and the competencies displayed whilst undertaking those activities was much more revealing than the profile of summary scores. We further noted that since the printed grid was only an illustrative sample drawn from a much larger theoretically definable grid (with the result that putting ticks on the grid would become cumbersome if pursued wholeheartedly), we could achieve the desired effect by writing "chemist-style" descriptive statements about people. These identify the behaviours they "value" and the competencies they display whilst undertaking those activities. We then noted that this very same procedure would enable us to describe the relevant (and only the relevant) features of the environments in which people live and work—and those in which they had previously lived and worked. We would be able to identify different types of group having different emergent properties not derivable from summing the parts. (But we also noted that this would make the identification of the basic characteristics of the individual difficult.) We finally noted that this way of proceeding would enable us to both model the transformational processes that have proved so intractable in developmental psychology and education and to handle the problems that the situational specificity of behaviour pose for conventional (trait-based) concepts of "ability."

* * * * *

One final observation may be made about our research and the nature of the future scenario that would stem from its adoption. The crucial—almost idiosyncratic—feature of what we have been doing has been that we have been mapping and sampling relevant *domains* of competence—including their motivational basis and their cognitive, affective, and conative components. At the present stage in the development of our science, this has been no routine activity. Quite the opposite: It is only possible to carry it out effectively after one has developed a thorough understanding of the area one is dealing with. To pursue such work one needs not so much a new methodology as a climate that emphasises that scientists should devote a considerable amount of time to what is, after all, the crucial phase of any scientific enquiry worth the name—namely developing concepts and understanding. However, as the framework for thinking about and mapping the domains of competence becomes clearer, the task of assessing people will become more like carrying out a chemical analysis than "measuring" their height with a ruler or taking their temperature with a thermometer after the manner of a physicist.

Implementing Generic Competence Assessments

Assessment performs many functions. Teachers and lecturers need it to monitor the effects of their actions. Students need it to find out how well they are doing and improve their performance. Administrators need it to study the effects of individual teachers and lecturers, educational institutions, and groups of such institutions. Summative assessments are required at the point of interface between educational institutions and society so that students can get recognition for the competencies they have developed and thus get an opportunity to use them—and develop them further—in the course of employment.

The preoccupation with traditional tests and the criteria established to assess test "quality" has not only resulted in invalid, unreliable, and dysfunctional tests, it has also resulted in the failure to develop diagnostic and prescriptive tools more suited to such purposes as evaluating and improving educational programmes on the one hand, and to diagnosing and remedying students' learning difficulties (e.g., in reading) and offering individualised programmes of competence-based education geared to each student's interests, values, and talents, on the other. To either assist with reading difficulties or implement competency-oriented education, teachers and lecturers need to be able to obtain information about the motives and potential interests of each student, invent a possibly developmental experience for that student (i.e., one that harnesses the students' motives, builds on the competencies that have already been developed, and addresses the problems the student has in pursuing his or her own goals), monitor the student's reactions to that experience (especially his or her specific difficulties), and take corrective action when necessary.

In addition, authenticating and governing Boards need to be able to assess particular policies and programmes of study: They need to be able to document the distinctive features of the programmes and demonstrate that they have distinctive consequences for those who pass through them. They also need to be able to find out whether individual lecturers are identifying and developing at least some of the talents of each of the students enrolled in their courses. Educational officials, administrators, lecturers, students, and employers need to be able to undertake stock-taking exercises to look at the human resources available. To do these things they must, both individually and collectively, assess the quality of the developmental environments and experiences that are available and their probable consequences. For these purposes there is a need for a set of "mirrors" that enable people, individually or collectively, to take stock of what is happening so that they can, if appropriate, decide to change it.

In the remainder of this chapter I will summarise what we have been able to do, using the model developed above, to fill some of these gaps. In the course of so doing, the methodologies we have employed to operationalise the model will be illustrated. However, if the reader is not to be too disappointed with what is to follow, it is important for him or her to approach the material with realistic expectations. Virtually all the work on which this discussion has been based has been carried out in "spare time," on an unfunded basis, as private skirmishes on the edges of a series of unrelated and non-cumulative projects that were commissioned for reasons having little to do with the central theme of this book. Given the unquestioning acceptance of the dominant paradigm by those who control funds and review research proposals, and given the desire for quick returns and immediate answers among those who commission research and evaluation studies, it has proved impossible to obtain funds for research that would have addressed these issues directly.

In setting appropriate expectations it is also important to say that, precisely because there has been no continuity in funding or projects, there has been no continuity in staffing either. No sooner have those concerned been socialised into (earlier versions) of the way of thinking presented here than they—complete with their hard-won insights and expertise—have had to move on.

In this context, the progress that has been made looks less insignificant. It has proved possible to use the measurement model outlined above without difficulty in programme evaluation. It was used in both our evaluation of the Lothian Region Educational Home Visiting project (which was a Levenstein-like programme of adult education designed to "emphasise the unique and irreplaceable role of the mother in promoting the development of her children"[6]), and in our evaluation of the links established between primary schools and agencies of non-formal education, such as zoos and museums.[7] In both cases, it enabled us to show that, contrary to the received wisdom, adults (whether parents or teachers) had, for better or worse, dramatic effects on both children's and adults' values and on their competence to undertake valued activities effectively. It has also been employed without difficulty when assessing what might loosely be called national and organisational climates and patterns of competence associated with economic and social development and decline.[8]

We have had more difficulty in using it for *individual* assessment purposes. However, even here, one set of procedures (Behavioural Event Interviewing and Records) provides relevant and useful information in an elegant and cost-effective way, and other procedures (based on value-expectancy methodology) have been shown to have considerable potential. In this chapter, methods based on externally generated *statements* will be reviewed first, followed by behavioural event interview methods, and then methods based on value-expectancy-instrumentality theory.

Statements

There are two essential prerequisites to obtaining meaningful external assessments of competence. First: assessors should be thoroughly familiar with the conceptual framework summarised above and developed more fully in *Competence in Modern Society*.[9] Second, they, like good mothers[10] and managers,[11] should both have gone out of their way to pay attention to what their children and subordinates say and do (and to the meanings of their gestures and innuendoes) and thereafter have created situations in which students or subordinates can enthusiastically pursue activities that they care about, growing in confidence and competence in the process. If they have done these things, teachers, lecturers, and managers will, if they are good observers, find it relatively easy to put ticks in the cells of an extended version of Grid 1 to indicate which activities their students or subordinates value and the competencies they display spontaneously whilst pursuing them. An alternative is for assessors simply to list, after the manner of a chemist (or doctor, when writing a prescription), the behaviours that those being assessed value and the competencies they display while pursuing those valued activities. The lists of values and components of competence published in *Competence in Modern Society* may be used as aides-mémoire for this purpose. If this approach is adopted, teachers and managers can also usefully describe the situations in which students and subordinates have worked, using the framework presented for describing classroom and organisational climates (in terms of the motives they tend to arouse and the behaviours they tend to encourage) presented in my *Education, Values and Society* and *Competence in Modern Society*.

It is important to note that whereas most external assessments of people take the form of *ratings* (going from, e.g. "intelligent" to "stupid"), what one gets by following the procedures described above is a series of *statements* about, or descriptions of, people and the environments in which they have been observed. Ratings are made on a small number of scales assumed to be adequate to map the totality of the individual's competence. Statements draw on a vast pool of potential descriptors to make succinct statements about the individual and context.

It will be readily apparent that this procedure requires teachers, lecturers, and managers first to become thoroughly familiar with the ideas summarised above (a task no more difficult than that required of every student who aspires to be a chemist) and then to devote a considerable amount of time to the process of (1) studying students' or subordinates' interests and talents and (2) creating situations in which those talents can be expressed. (If lecturers, teachers, or managers have failed to create appropriate individualised developmental environments, or failed to make their observations in such environments, any statements made about—or ratings made of—high-level competencies will be meaningless.) Because of the time required, the use of rating systems—such as are often found in staff appraisal systems—is not a feasible, or at least a sensible, proposition in many settings. On the other hand, familiarity with (indeed, day-to-day use of) the competency framework is crucial to the development, release, and effective deployment of human resources. It is therefore essential that teachers, lecturers, and managers develop the habit of thinking more carefully about their students' and subordinates' talents and how best they can be developed and deployed. This objective might best be achieved, however, not by pitching them directly into assessing these qualities, but by encouraging them to use the results of the more student-based assessment procedures and climate surveys to be described below.

In the past we have experimented with, indeed advocated the use of, behaviourally anchored rating scales.[12] In essence, this procedure requires raters to agree on, for example, precisely what level of initiative is indicated by a specific behaviour of a particular ratee. At first, the approach appeared to be very promising. However, we encountered serious difficulties when trying to implement the necessary procedures. The reason for this took some time to emerge. Although it was obvious from our earliest trials that behaviour that one teacher would describe as "initiative" would be described by another as "the student trying to ingratiate himself with his teacher," it was not until we had recognised the centrality of values in the assessment of competence that we were able to appreciate that this problem could not be resolved without first finding out what the *student's* values were and then respecting those values, *whatever* they were. Once that was done, we could begin to get some agreement about what was meant by such qualities as "initiative" in relation to the student's own priorities. But, even then, if one wished to assess his or her competence, one had to develop behaviourally anchored scales for *all* the competencies listed in *Competence in Modern Society* in relation to all possible goals. The task became even more cumbersome than putting ticks in an extended version of Grid 1. We backed off.

Behavioural Event Interviews

Behavioural Event Interviews[13]—or their development as collections of personal reports on critical incidents (or records of behavioural events)—

require teachers and lecturers to share more of the responsibility for assessment with students. Students are asked to think of—or keep records of—times when things went particularly well and particularly badly for them; they are asked to report both events that they were particularly pleased about and events that led them to feel frustrated and uncomfortable. They are asked to record what happened, what led up to the situation, and what the outcome was. They are asked to say what they were trying to do or accomplish.

(In this connection care has to be taken to reassure them that it is both appropriate and important to record "unacceptable" goals—such as passing the time as pleasantly as possible in warm friendly conversation—because workplaces and society need people who value such behaviour and do it well.) They are asked to describe their thoughts and feelings while they were engaged in the activity. And they are asked to say what others did, what they did, and how others reacted.

These records can then be scored by the teacher or lecturer, or by an external agency, using a variant of Grid 1. The student's or subordinates' values and the competencies displayed when pursuing them are very apparent to anyone familiar with the conceptual framework developed above. The basic interview or record sheets remain available should those being assessed wish to challenge the overall statements that are made about their values and pattern of competence. When the interviewing and scoring are carried out jointly by student and teacher—and possibly by the students' peers—a wealth of information is available to guide future placement and development. The methodology is elegant and, provided all concerned are prepared to take personal development seriously, it has the potential progressively to initiate both staff and students into ways of thinking about human resources and their development and utilisation that are essential to the future development both of the educational system and society.

Variants of this methodology have been developed independently by Stansbury[14] and by Burgess and Adams.[15] Their work is important for two reasons. On the one hand, it indicates that it is feasible to envisage that such assessments might be much more widely employed in schools and colleges. On the other, it—like the experience at NELP—alerts prospective users to the amount of time that is required if students are to be offered the guidance and counselling that is required as a basis for effective competency-oriented education, which is itself a prerequisite to meaningful assessments of multiple talents.

Adams and Burgess[16] went on to produce what is, in a sense, an even more important variant of their methodology. They encouraged teachers to keep records of occasions on which they felt pleased with what they had done, perhaps occasions on which they had contributed in worthwhile ways to education and the educational system. The teachers were then encouraged, but not obliged, to discuss these records with colleagues with whom they felt comfortable and, in due course, with head teachers and administrators. What then happened was remarkable. It became apparent to all that all teachers—and not just a few—wished to contribute to the effective functioning of schools. Furthermore, they had all done so—*but had done so in very different ways*. Their previously invisible concerns and talents surfaced. Morale improved dramatically. It became apparent that the schools needed a wide variety of people who were concerned to do, and were good at doing, very different things. And a wide variety of talents was available. There was no such thing as a model teacher to which all teachers needed to approximate. The process contributed in a fundamental way to the recognition and utilisation of high-level competencies. It provided virtually the only viable practical solution to the widely acknowledged—but seemingly insoluble—problem of the need to accredit workplace learning. As Wolf[17] shows, most attempts to solve this problem set out to document courses taken or assess formal, low-level, general (as distinct from idiosyncratic and tacit) knowledge acquired. Adams and Burgess's scheme ends up recognising the high-level competencies members of staff have developed. Although widely ignored as "just another staff-appraisal system," their scheme is in fact a development of the greatest importance. It is my belief that its effectiveness would be further improved if the discussions which are involved were to be, at least in part, conducted with the aid of the framework for thinking about competence, its development, and its utilisation outlined here.

The Assessment of Competence Using Value-Expectancy Methods

Value-expectancy methodology is designed to get inside people's heads, assess the (reinterpreted) three dimensions in Johnsons's diagram, and compute the resultant(s). The methodology enables us to assess people's values, their perceptions of relevant features of their environment, what they expect the effects of their actions to be, and how much importance they attach to each of the consequences that are anticipated. The consequences that are examined include those arising from the individual's own competence (or the lack of it) and consequences that follow from other people's reactions to that behaviour. If appropriate, people's confidence in their ability to deal with the reactions they expect from others are also documented. The methodology enables the assessor to combine these bits of information together in order to calculate the strength of the resulting disposition to undertake different kinds of tasks effectively in particular kinds of situation.

It is easiest to introduce the theoretical basis of value-expectancy-instrumentality methodology by reference to the work of Fishbein. In the late 1960s, Fishbein[18] stimulated a paradigm shift in the then-quiescent area of "attitude" measurement by emphasising, and finding an elegant way of handling, something which everyone had always known—but which had not been taken into account in the theories or practice of attitude measurement current at the time (and which is still neglected in the measurement of personality and abilities). This is that behaviour—such as buying biscuits or using contraceptives—is primarily determined by multiple beliefs and feelings that come into play in particular situations rather than by a single underlying "attitude" or by personality variables.[19]

Fishbein made two fundamental contributions to our ability to think about, and handle, these issues. First, he focused attention on something that has been repeatedly emphasised in this book, namely that it is the respondent's attitude toward, or value for, *the behaviour in question*—and not his value for the object of the behaviour—that it is important to assess. One should study the respondent's attitude toward *using* contraceptives, rather than his attitude toward the contraceptives. Second, he found a means of tying together three well-established, empirically based, theoretical viewpoints about behaviour determination in psychology and sociology.

The first of these traditions holds that people will be inclined to engage in an activity if they are relatively certain that the activity will lead to satisfactions which they value. The second holds that they will be more likely to do something if they feel that the behaviour is consistent with their self-images—with their view of the sort of person they want to be. The third viewpoint is that people will be more likely to engage in a behaviour the more certain they are that other people expect them to do so, and the more dependent they are on a favourable reaction from those other people.

There is considerable evidence[20] to support each of these viewpoints taken individually. The predictive validity of measures based on any one of them is typically of the order of .4. The beauty of Fishbein's work was that, for the first time, it enabled us to assess each set of variables more systematically and then tie the three sets of variables together. The method of combining and weighting the component parts is itself supported by a considerable body of empirical research. The effect of these developments is that predictive validities of .8 to .9 are not uncommon.

Before moving on, attention may be drawn to the way in that Fishbein's model parallels that developed above in connection with Grid 1. There, we argued that the capacity to undertake a valued activity effectively was multiply determined and that it was dependent on bringing to bear a number of relatively independent—but substitutable—competencies, each having cognitive, affective, and conative components. It was argued that effective behaviour depends on having an appropriate self-image, on perceiving oneself as having the support of relevant reference groups, and on having an appropriate institutional framework in which to work (i.e., on *shared* beliefs about priorities, relationships, and ways of doing things).

In non-technical language, what the Fishbein version of value-expectancy-instrumentality theory does is ask people what they think the consequences would be if they were to engage in any particular behaviour and then weight those consequences with the importance attached to each. Three domains of possible consequences are systematically studied. These may loosely be called *personal* consequences, *self-image* consequences, and *the reactions of reference groups*.

The *personal* consequences that are studied include such things as "I would enjoy doing this"; "It would take up a great deal of time which I would prefer to devote to other things"; and "I would have a lot less money for other things."

The *self-image* (or, more correctly, personal normative belief) consequences include such things as "No self-respecting person would do this"; "It is my duty to do this"; and "I would be working for the long-term good of mankind if I did this." The *reference group* consequences include "My grandmother would object to my doing this"; "My workmates would encourage me to do this"; and "God will punish me if I do this."

Each of these perceived consequences has to be weighted by the importance attached to (or motivation to comply with) them: What my grandmother thinks won't have much influence on my behaviour if I don't *care* what she thinks.

So, to apply the model fully, we first have to find out how *certain* the people we are assessing are that, if they engaged in the behaviour, each consequence would follow—and then how important each of those consequences is to them. We then multiply the certainty ratings by the probability ratings and sum the resulting products.

To use value-expectancy-instrumentality theory to index the likelihood that people will display selected competencies in the course of undertaking tasks they care about we first identify tasks that they have a "felt need" to carry out by asking them to complete a *Quality of Life* Questionnaire (see Figure 28.2a).

On this questionnaire they are first asked to indicate how *important* various features of the environment are to them and how important they think it is to be able to do various things at work. Thereafter, they are asked to say how *satisfied* they are with each of these same features of the environment and with their opportunity to do each of the things they have said they would like to do. Their responses are then examined in order to identify an item they have rated both important and unsatisfactory.

The *Consequences* Questionnaire is then used to explore their perceptions of the consequences of trying to do something about this unsatisfactory state of affairs. What do they think would happen if they tried to persuade other people to do something about it? What would happen if they tried to do something about it themselves? The consequences that are studied cover the domains identified in Fishbein's model. They include such things as conflict with other values, whether doing it would enable them to be the sort of person they want to be, and their perceptions of how their reference groups would react.

The process may be illustrated by taking an example: supposing we are interested in exploring the consequences that students expect to follow from trying to persuade their fellows to behave more responsibly. The students would first be asked what they thought the *personal* consequences would be. They often think that trying to do this would make them uncomfortable and unhappy, leave less time for other activities they value, and demand abilities that they feel they do not possess. In the absence of these abilities, any attempt on their part to persuade other people to behave responsibly would demand a great deal of effort and would lead others to think that they were getting above themselves, and the whole thing would be a disaster. They would look, in their own eyes and in the eyes of others, very foolish indeed.

After they have been asked what they think the general consequences would be, they are asked what sort of person would do these things and whether they would like to be that kind of person. They sometimes feel

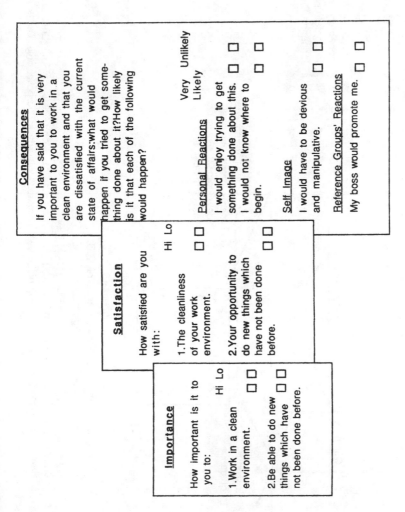

Figure 28.2 The Assessment of the Components of Competence: An illustration from *The Edinburgh Questionnaires*. Part A: The Process. Part B (Flow Chart) will be found on the next page. Note: This is a schematic representation only and does not bear a direct relationship to the Questionnaires.

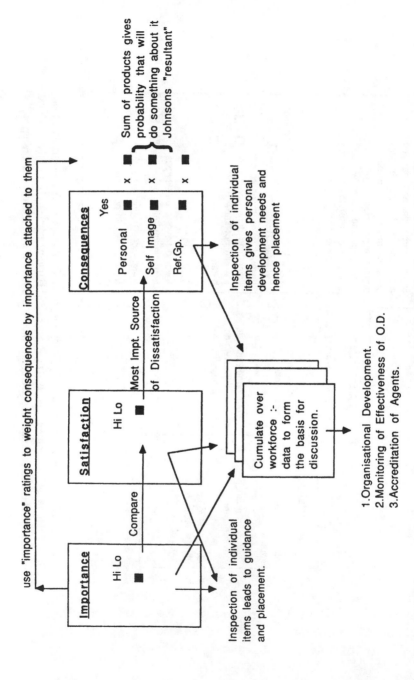

Figure 28.2 (Continued). The Assessment of the Components of Competence: An illustration from *The Edinburgh Questionnaires*. Part B: Flow Chart. The Figure has been prepared for illustrative purposes only: The flows are over-simplified and schematic.

that the sort of person who would try to persuade his fellows to behave more responsibly would be a rather pious, priggish, killjoy and that, to be successful, they would have to be devious and manipulative. They may not themselves wish to be any of these things.

Finally, they are asked how others would react: Would their friends support or reject them? Would their teachers condemn them because they would have exposed their behaviour as self-interested, rather than concerned with the good of all? Would they, like Socrates, be deprived of career opportunities because they had identified themselves as the sort of person who takes moral issues seriously?

If one cumulated these results one would have a clear assessment of the strength of the student's disinclination to engage in the activity (see Figure 28.2b).

But, by going through the process we have described, one obtains a great deal more useful information than this single index. In the case just described, one would have learned a great deal that would be of value in helping one to devise an individualised, generic-competency-oriented, developmental programme to help the student concerned, if he or she so wished, to resolve value conflicts and thus release energy into chosen tasks and to practise and develop competencies required to reach valued goals. The student could, for example, be brought to pay more attention to the probable long-term social consequences of not behaving in a socially responsible way. He or she might be encouraged to meet other people who *had* behaved in a responsible way and had not been punished or forced to behave in ways that were incompatible with being the sort of person they want to be. As a result of getting to know them, the student might learn how to persuade other people more effectively without having to be obnoxious. He or she could be helped to practise the skills required to obtain the co-operation of others.

Classroom Climate Measures

Not only would the information obtained by using the above procedure be of value in making it possible to design an *individual* programme of development for this particular student. The data collected from all students in a group would be of value in enabling the lecturer (or an external accrediting agency) to assess the quality of the lecturer's overall programme of placement and development and his or her ability to release the know-how, goodwill, and enthusiasm of all students—and thereafter to improve his or her performance in both these respects.

Accreditation of Institutions Combined
with Observer Judgements

This is the basis for the final suggestion to be made in this chapter. I have already indicated that this methodology can be used to document the effects of educational programmes and to highlight deficiencies in them. I have argued that such assessments would enable us to place the validation of courses on a sound basis. Let us now back up one step. It is a relatively straightforward matter to determine the presence or absence of classroom processes that are likely to lead to the identification and development of the talents of each student.[21] Having demonstrated that some lecturers had created developmental environments for their students, one could infer that they must have had opportunities to *observe* their students exercising high-level competencies in the course of undertaking tasks they cared about. Under these circumstances, any statements they made about students' values and areas of competence would have a good chance of being meaningful.[22]

The Question of Validity

The validity of value-expectancy-instrumentality measures such as those described has been established in a number of studies. However, this has not been done by computing conventional correlation coefficients but rather, as Messik[23] and House[24] have advocated, by establishing a network of connections between the "measures" and their causes and consequences.

The first study in which the theoretical model outlined here was fully operationalised was in an evaluation of an educational home visiting scheme.[25] The scheme sought to "underline the unique and irreplaceable role of the mother in promoting the educational development of her children." Home visitors, who were all trained teachers, visited the homes of two- to three-year-old children for an hour a week for about nine months. By working with the children in their mother's presence, they sought to portray effective mothering behaviour in such a way as to lead the mothers to do likewise. The evaluation showed that the home visitors had a dramatic effect on the mothers' beliefs and expectations, but very little effect on their behaviour. The only behaviour that changed significantly was that the mothers became more likely to hand their children over to professional carers. This was, of course, exactly the opposite of what was intended. We were able to show that this occurred because, although the mothers now believed that it was both important and effective to do such things as talk to their children and had come to believe that intelligence was more readily influenced than they had previously thought, neither the environmental constraints on their behaviour nor their basic values had changed. As far as environmental constraints were concerned, for example, they still lacked the time needed to do the things they had always believed they should do and now recognised to be even more important than they had imagined. As far as their values were concerned, they would still have preferred their children to be dependent on, rather than independent of, them. Thus, despite the fact that they now believed even more strongly than before that the behaviours that the home visitors modelled were both important and efficacious, they were still prevented from doing them by environmental constraints and value conflicts. They resolved this dilemma by handing their children over to professionals—for whose competence they had developed a great respect. They ended up feeling even more guilty than before about not doing things they already knew they should be doing.

It emerged that, if the programme was to be effective, the home visitors would, among other things, have had to set out to *influence* the mothers' values. They would also have had to help them, as a central objective of the project, to develop the competencies they needed to get more control over their own lives—and especially to influence public provision. This, naturally, posed serious dilemmas for the home visitors. Our interest here is, of course, methodological rather than substantive. The point is that the value-expectancy measures we developed proved to be sensitive to the effects of the educational programme, enabled us to identify what worked and what did not and the reasons why, helped us to understand counterintuitive effects of the intervention, and enabled us to identify the (often unexpected) remedial actions that were necessary.

In another project[26] we used the methodology to study the effects of different types of educational programme on primary school pupils. We found that, contrary to common assertion, different teachers had dramatically different effects on pupils' concerns, on their priorities in education, life, behaviour, and patterns of competence. Thus, some teachers led their pupils to feel that it was important to select tasks that were socially important and to obtain the cooperation of others to carry out those tasks effectively. The pupils learned how to tackle such tasks and how to win others' cooperation. That they had learned to do these things could be demonstrated by examining the consequences they anticipated: One did not need to observe their behaviour. They understood how the local democracy and bureaucracy worked, how to identify leverage points within it, and how to influence it. They knew the strengths of their fellow students. Pupils in other classes did not think it was important to do these things or important to learn how to do them, and (rightly) anticipated disastrous consequences should they try to do them. One of the most striking results of the project was the discovery that, contrary to common assertion, what teachers did reflected (even if it did not match) their priorities,[27] and the patterns of educational activity they created were in turn reflected in their students' values and patterns of competence. Once again, therefore, the methodology enabled us to document teachers' concerns and patterns of competence—and it also enabled us to develop measures of programme outcomes that were sensitive to the effects of the educational programmes pupils were offered. These measures in turn enabled us to pinpoint strengths and deficiencies in the programmes.

The objective of the work reported in *Competence in Modern Society* was to develop a set of tools (*The Edinburgh Questionnaires*) that would be useful in staff guidance placement and development and in organisational development.[28] The work showed, somewhat unexpectedly, that the "British disease" stemmed from a lack of interest in doing such things as finding better ways of doing things, finding new things to do, finding better ways of thinking about things, working at a task that would in the long run benefit the whole organisation or society, or getting people to work together effectively. Surprisingly, the negative consequences that were anticipated should they decide to do any of these things were not a significant deterrent to undertaking these activities. They simply did not think it was important to do them. The methodology worked: The problem was other than what it was assumed to have been. *The Edinburgh Questionnaires* have since been used in Samoa, Tonga, Japan, China, Hong Kong, Singapore, the Philippines, Canada, and the United States.[29] Whereas some people had reacted to the Scottish data by saying "Of course, could it be otherwise?," the cross-cultural data make it transparently obvious that things not only *could* be otherwise but *are* dramatically otherwise (in Japan and Singapore) and have the consequences with which we are all too familiar.

Taking these results together with those obtained with the Taylor-Nelson Monitor[30] one obtains an acutely disturbing picture: The British (with the Dutch) are most likely to support the "new" values—conservation, recycling, quality of life defined in other than materialistic or "economic" terms, community support networks, humanitarian values—but they are unwilling to do the things they would need to do to translate those values into effect. Given the predictable paralysis, it is not surprising that those who espouse the "old" values are able to impose their will on the majority, creating a deeply divided society in the process. Once again, then, use of the methodology we have described has enabled us both to understand how the societies concerned got into the economic situation in which they find themselves and to document what would need to be done if they are to create the new kind of society they want. The methodology has also enabled us to generate data that enable people, as individuals or as groups, to take a look at their beliefs, attitudes, priorities, and expectations in a kind of a mirror and ask themselves whether they like the look of what they see and, in particular, what they think the probable consequences of those beliefs, understandings, and perceptions will be. (If they do not like what they see, they can go on to ask what they could do about it.)

Taken together, these studies suggest that the methodology does have considerable validity in that it enables us to understand, predict, and influence behaviour. It has enabled people to get more control over their lives and own organisations. Additional, convincing, evidence of the validity of value-expectancy methodology, interpreted and applied more narrowly, will be found in Feather.[31]

Addendum: Research in Progress

Although we have not been able to attract the necessary funding, we have, over the past decade, been working on some computerised tools designed to surface people's motives and talents and help them to explore their developmental needs. These tools are also designed to be used by managers in their discussions with their subordinates to help them to think about their talents, how to develop and utilise them, and how to redeploy their diverse workforce in order to harness their creativity, initiative, and know-how in order to create innovative organisations. These tools would also be of value in helping to manage, and document the consequences of, individualised competency-oriented educational programmes in higher education.

We have also been working on a school improvement kit. This will include:

- A *Grid* designed to familiarise teachers with the competency framework briefly discussed above and help them to identify pupils' motives and competencies both as an aid to thinking about how to harness those motives to create individualised developmental programmes and as a basis for recording the high-level talents pupils have developed.

- A *Classroom Climate Questionnaire* designed to familiarise teachers with the outcomes of our research into the nature of developmental environments and help them to take stock of the extent to which they themselves have been able to create such environments, decide how to improve them, and assess the effects of changes made.
- A *School Climate Questionnaire* designed to familiarise all concerned with what we have learned about climates of innovation and take stock of the extent to which a local authority has been able to create a climate of enthusiasm and innovation which effectively harnesses, recognises, and rewards the motives and talents of all members of staff.
- A *School Context Questionnaire* designed to focus attention on key facets of the interfaces between schools and society. These include relationships with other schools and the public service; the interface with employers and higher education; and the interface with parents and others with an interest in education.

Both *The Computerised Edinburgh Questionnaires* and the components of the *School Improvement Kit* are clearly adaptable for use in higher education, and I would welcome contact with anyone interested in doing so.

Notes

1. The term "value" is not quite right—because the behaviours in question often seem to be rather compulsive. People engage in them "despite themselves." This is difficult to reconcile with the term "valued activity," which conjures up an image of a "freely chosen" activity. Yet people do usually agree that these activities are important to them, and it is in this sense that they can truly be said to value them. McClelland has tried to avoid the difficulty by using the term "need." Unfortunately, this has led him to claim that his measures are not measures of values. This is not only untrue, it has also, as I have shown (Raven, 1988), caused endless confusion and unnecessary argument.

2. While it may be thought that the viewpoint developed here might be reconciled with traditional factor-analytic theory by focusing on qualities like "the ability to make one's own observations," a little reflection shows that this is not the case. Our argument is precisely that such qualities cannot be assessed independently of valued goals. They have no *generalised* meaning. Therefore, they cannot be assessed by factorially-pure scales.

3. Raven, Molloy, & Corcoran (1972); Raven (1977).

4. These components of competence are spelt out in more detail in Raven (1977, 1984/1997).

5. It is not, in fact, difficult to reconcile some such model with the facts to that factor-analysts point as a justification for their model. They point out that most human traits are correlated with each other. They go on to argue that it is unnecessary to retain a large number of independent dimensions, or categories. However, many of the correlations are of the order of .2 and most are of the order of .3 to .5. Even the latter leave some 75% of the variance on one trait "unexplained" by the variance on the other. There is, therefore, a *good* chance that someone who is not good at one thing will be good at another. Even factor-analysts point out that this is because the second ability has probably caught the interests of the person concerned and, therefore, been practised and developed. While the factor-analyst's model does, in fact, provide for such possibilities (by including provision for specific factors) these are generally neglected in practice. If we were forced to state our case in factor-analytic terms, we would therefore find ourselves arguing that the important things to record about an individual are his specifics, not his generalities.

6. Raven (1980); McCail (1981).

7. Raven, Johnstone, & Varley (1985).

8. Raven (1984/1997); Graham & Raven (1987).

9. Raven (1984/1997).

10. Raven (1980).

11. Klemp, Munger, & Spencer (1977).

12. Smith & Kendall (1963); for a summary of the procedure as we have used it, see Raven (1977).

13. McClelland (1978); Spencer (1983).

14. Stansbury (1976, 1980).

15. Burgess & Adams (1986).

16. Adams & Burgess (1989).

17. Wolf (1995).

18. Fishbein (1967); Fishbein & Ajzen (1975). However, see also Vroom (1964); Porter & Lawler (1968); Feather (1982); Mitchell (1982).

19. This is the explanation of the still widely-encountered statement that "there is little relationship between attitudes and behaviour." It is true that there is little relationship between behaviour in a particular situation and scores on a single, factorially-pure, attitude or personality scale. But there is a very close relationship between behaviour and "attitudes" (or behaviour tendencies) indexed by identifying and summating the perceptions, beliefs and feelings which come into play in the particular situation using the techniques under discussion here.

20. Reviewed in Raven & Dolphin (1978).

21. Raven (1977); Walberg (1979, 1984, 1985); Howard (1982).

22. This would place the procedure advocated by the Scottish Examination Board (1985) for Social and Vocational Education on a firm basis. For this syllabus, the SEB does not require teachers to assess individual pupils' social and vocational competence. It insists only that they certify that the *course* was likely to lead to these outcomes. This is something we are in a position to validate. From there it would be but a short step to trust the teachers' judgement about individuals.

23. Messick (1989, 1995).

24. House (1991).

25. McCail (1981); Raven (1980). For earlier applications of the partially-developed model see Raven, Molloy, & Corcoran (1972).

26. Raven & Varley (1984).

27. I am talking here at a fairly gross level. Teachers varied a great deal from one to another in their educational objectives. In relation to this variation between teachers, the slippage between one teacher's objectives, and what he or she did, looks less stark than it does when researchers focus on such things as the discrepancy between teachers' reporting that they have conducted an "open-ended" discussion lesson, and external observers' ratings of the "openness" of that discussion. What was striking in our study was how few teachers thought it was important to

have open-ended discussions. Those teachers who did so got on with it, albeit imperfectly. Not surprisingly, the rest conducted no such discussions.

28. Raven (1983, 1984/1997); Raven & Sime (1994).

29. Graham & Raven (1987); Graham, Raven, & Smith (1987).

30. See Nelson (1986).

31. Feather (1982). It is, perhaps, useful to mention that, although the evidence of validity cited here has not been expressed in the form of correlation coefficients, it provides exactly the information that those coefficients seek to provide: namely, evidence that scores based on verbal behaviour relate to other aspects of behaviour and vary with experimental manipulation (cf. Messick, 1989).

References

Adams, E., & Burgess, T. (1989). *Teachers' Own Records*. Windsor, England: NFER-Nelson.

Burgess, T., & Adams, E. (1986). *Records of Achievement at 16*. Windsor, England: NFER-Nelson.

Feather, N. T. (Ed.). (1982). *Expectations and Actions: Expectancy-Value Models in Psychology*. Hillside, NJ: Erlbaum.

Fishbein, M. (Ed.). (1967). *Readings in Attitude Theory and Measurement*. New York: Wiley.

Fishbein, M., & Ajzen, I. (1975). *Belief, Attitude, Intention and Behavior*. Reading, MA: Addison Wesley.

Graham, M. A., & Raven, J. (1987). *International Shifts in the Workplace—Are We Becoming an "Old West" in the Next Century?* Provo: Brigham Young University Dept. of Organizational Behavior.

Graham, M. A., Raven, J., & Smith, P. C. (1987). *Identification of High-Level Competence: Cross-Cultural Analysis between British, American, Asian and Polynesian Labourers*. Unpublished manuscript: Brigham Young University Hawaii Campus, Dept. of Organizational Behavior.

House, E. R. (1991). Realism in research. *Educational Researcher, 20*, 2–9.

Howard, E. (1982). Involving students in school climate improvement. *New Designs for Youth Development*. Tucson: Associations for Youth Development Inc.

Howard, E. (1982). *Successful Practices for Making the Curriculum More Flexible*. Denver: Colorado Department of Education.

Howard, E. (1982). *Instrument to Assess the Educational Quality of Your School*. Denver: Colorado Department of Education.

Klemp, G. O., Munger, M. T., & Spencer, L. M. (1977). *An Analysis of Leadership and Management Competencies of Commissioned and Non-Commissioned Naval Officers in the Pacific and Atlantic Fleets*. Boston: McBer.

McCail, G. (1981). *Mother Start. An Account of an Educational Home Visiting Scheme for Pre-School Children.* Edinburgh: Scottish Council for Research in Education.

McClelland, D. C. (1978). *Guide to Behavioral Event Interviewing.* Boston: McBer.

McClelland, D. C., Baldwin, A. L., Bronfenbrenner, U., & Strodtbeck, F. L. (1958). *Talent and Society.* Princeton, NJ: Van Nostrand.

Messick, S. (1989). Meaning and values in test validation: The science and ethics of assessment. *Educational Researcher, 18* (2), 5–11.

Messick, S. (1995). Validity of psychological assessment. *American Psychologist, 50* (9), 741–749.

Mitchell, T. R. (1982). Expectancy-value models in organisational psychology. In N. T. Feather (Ed.), *Expectations and Actions: Expectancy-Value Models in Psychology* (293–312). Hillside, NJ: Erlbaum.

Nelson, E. H. (1986). *New Values and Attitudes throughout Europe.* Epsom, England: Taylor-Nelson.

Porter, L. W., & Lawler, E. E. (1968). *Managerial Attitudes and Performance.* Homewood IL: Dorsey Press.

Raven, J. (1977). *Education, Values and Society: The Objectives of Education and the Nature and Development of Competence.* Oxford, England: Oxford Psychologists Press.

Raven, J. (1980). *Parents, Teachers and Children: An Evaluation of an Educational Home Visiting Programme.* Edinburgh: Scottish Council for Research in Education. Distributed in North America by the Ontario Institute for Studies in Education, Toronto.

Raven, J. (1983). *The Edinburgh Questionnaires: A Cluster of Questionnaires for use in Organisational Development and in Staff Guidance, Placement and Development.* Oxford, England: Oxford Psychologists Press.

Raven, J. (1984/1997). *Competence in Modern Society: Its Identification, Development and Release.* Unionville, NY: Royal Fireworks Press (1997); Oxford, England: Oxford Psychologists Press (1984).

Raven, J. (1988). Toward measures of high-level competencies: A re-examination of McClelland's distinction between needs and values. *Human Relations, 41,* 281–294.

Raven, J., & Dolphin, T. (1978). *The Consequences of Behaving: The Ability of Irish Organisations to Tap Know-How, Initiative, Leadership and Goodwill.* Edinburgh: Competency Motivation Project.

Raven, J., Johnstone, J., & Varley, T. (1985). *Opening the Primary Classroom.* Edinburgh: Scottish Council for Research in Education.

Raven, J., Molloy, E., & Corcoran, R. (1972). Toward a questionnaire measure of achievement motivation. *Human Relations, 25,* 469–492.

Raven, J., & Sime, J. (1994). *Computerised Edinburgh Questionnaires.* Oxford: Oxford Psychologists Press.

Raven, J., & Varley, T. (1984). Some classrooms and their effects: A study of the feasibility of measuring some of the broader outcomes of education. *Collected Original Resources in Education, 8* (1), F4 G6.

Scottish Examination Board (1985). *Scottish Certificate of Education: Social and Vocational Skills on the Standard Grade. Revised Scheme for Moderation of Internal Syllabuses and Assessment Arrangements.* Edinburgh: HMSO.

Smith, P. C., & Kendall, L. M. (1963). Retranslation of expectations. *Journal of Applied Psychology, 41,* 149–155.

Spencer, L. M. (1983). *Soft Skill Competencies.* Edinburgh: Scottish Council for Research in Education.

Stansbury, D. (1976). *Record of Personal Experience, Qualities and Qualifications* (plus Tutor's Handbook). South Brent: RPE Publications.

Stansbury, D. (1980). The record of personal experience. In T. Burgess and E. Adams, *Outcomes of Education.* Basingstoke: Macmillan Education.

Vroom, V. H. (1964). *Work and Motivation.* New York: John Wiley.

Walberg, H. J. (Ed.). (1979). *Educational Environments and their Effects.* Berkeley, CA: McCutchan.

Walberg, H. J. (1984). Improving the productivity of America's schools. *Educational Leadership, 41* (8), 19–31.

Walberg, H. J. (1984). *National Abilities and Economic Growth*. Chicago: University of Illinois, Office of Evaluation Research.

Walberg, H. J. (1985). Classroom psychological environment. In T. Husen and N. Postlethwaite, *International Encyclopaedia of Education*. London: Pergamon.

Wolf, A. (1995). *Competence-Based Assessment*. Buckingham: Open University Press.

Capability, Competence, and the Learning Society: Lessons from State Failure

Given the urgency, documented in Chapter 1, of developing the capability to introduce and run a sustainable society, the evidence of this book is that we are far, far, away from our goal.

The overwhelming impression must be that our institutions of higher education are falling way short of helping us either to develop the necessary understandings (whether of societal or organisational arrangements or of such things as the nature, development, and assessment of competence) or to foster the relevant competencies in students.

Most of the important developments we have reviewed have come from underfunded academics who have been able to poke about in areas that few others have had either the inclination, the tools, or the abilities to poke into. This is no way to get the understandings and tools we so urgently need. Our academic institutions have clearly failed both to nurture the relevant competencies among students and staff and to provide the organisational arrangements required for such work to be carried out effectively.

Those who run these institutions themselves clearly lack the requisite capabilities both at an individual and at a collective level.

But the issue is wider. For more than half a century, there has been widespread public disquiet about the workings of the educational system (including the universities) and the functioning of the economic system.

With a few notable exceptions, the politicians and public servants charged with doing something about these conspicuous problems have let society down. They have initiated massive bureaucratic re-arrangements that have drained time and energy. But, by and large, they have not initiated the research and development that would have been needed to clarify the nature of the problems (including the systems constraints on tackling them), the competencies required to tackle them, the ways in which those competencies could be nurtured and assessed, or the changes in organisational arrangements needed to develop and release competent behaviour (including the ferment of innovation that is required if we are to tackle the hugely important problems which confront our society).

At one level, these observations provide clear evidence of personal incompetence and incapability. At another level, they show that our societal management arrangements fail to elicit competent behaviour and thus generate incapability. But the second of these observations only underlines the importance of the first: Failure to establish appropriate organisational arrangements stems from individual incompetence and incapability.

It is to be hoped that what has been said in this book will stimulate the developments that are required and stem the tendency—so evident at the conferences organised in connection with its preparation and in many of the papers submitted as potential contributions to it—for people to rush around trying to justify and do what someone in authority had told them to do even though what is being done (as Wolf has more thoroughly documented) has much in common with the very activities that need to be eradicated. The central importance to competence of re-thinking our beliefs about the kinds of activity that merit financial reward in such a way as to focus attention more on personal discretion to participate in a ferment of change and less on compliance with the demands of authority could not be more apparent.

About the Authors

Tony Becher is an Emeritus Professor of Education at the University of Sussex, UK. His book on "Professional Practices" (Transaction Publishers, 1999) is concerned with continuing professional education and other aspects of professional life.

Richard E. Boyatzis is Professor and Department Chair, Department of Organizational Behavior, Weatherhead School of Management, Case Western Reserve University, Cleveland, Ohio, USA. He was previously managing director of McBer & Co.

Ian Cunningham currently chairs Strategic Developments International Ltd. and the Centre for Self Managed Learning. He is Visiting Professor in Organisational Capability at Middlesex University, London.

Lynne Cunningham is a freelance Research and Management Development Consultant, based in London, and working mainly on European partnership projects. She is an Associate of Agora Consultancy Ltd., and has worked with Higher Education for Capability.

Carolyn Desjardins was Executive Director of the National Institute for Leadership Development, Phoenix, AZ, USA. She was heavily involved in leadership development, gender-based team building, and workshops for deans and vice presidents.

W. Bryan Dockrell was formerly Professor of Education in the University of Newcastle, UK, and Director of the Scottish Council for Research in Education.

Sheila Huff, now based in Buffalo, NY, USA, has done extensive training of competency teams in companies, universities, and government agencies both in the United States and elsewhere. In the field of education, her competency research includes presidents and faculty in non-traditional colleges, special education teachers, K–12 school principals, daycare teachers, and student leaders.

Irene Ilott is Head of Research and Development at the College of Occupational Therapists, the professional body representing 23,000 occupational therapy personnel in the UK.

George Klemp is president of Cambria Consulting, a management consulting firm specializing in human resource management and one of the principal developers of job competency assessment technology. He is based in Boston, Massachusetts.

Stan Lester is sole principal of Stan Lester Developments, an independent consultancy and research firm based in Taunton, UK. He is also a visiting academic in the School of Lifelong Learning and Education at Middlesex University, London. His work focuses principally on professional and work-related development and its accreditation.

David McClelland was Professor of Psychology, Harvard University and, with David Berlew, the founder of McBer & Co., a consulting organisation set up to capitalise on his scientific discoveries and promote research and consultancy in the field of motivation and competence.

Dave O'Reilly worked in the School for Independent Study at the University of East London from 1981–91 and was Head of Independent Study from 1991–94. He is currently Head of Research in Educational Development at the University of East London. His interests include experiential, problem-based, and work-based learning and the politics of knowledge.

John Raven is an independent researcher and consultant on the nature, development, assessment and release of competence. He is particularly interested in the personal, organisational, and social consequences of alternative patterns of motivation in different social contexts. He is based in Edinburgh, UK.

Reg Revans, although best known for the variant of Action Learning that he developed at the National Coal Board in Great Britain, has actually been much more concerned with the creation of learning organisations. He has the distinction of being encouraged to resign from his professorship in Manchester University in 1965 for attempting to incorporate workplace-based growth of competence into the Business School programme.

Darlene Russ-Eft is Director of Research Services at AchieveGlobal Inc., one of the world's leading resources for training and consulting. Her office is located in San Jose, CA, USA.

Donald Schön was formerly Ford Professor of Urban Studies and Planning, Massachusetts Institute of Technology, Cambridge, MA, USA.

John Stephenson is head of the International Centre for Learner Managed Learning at Middlesex University, and was previously Director of Higher Education for Capability and Head of the School for Independent Study at the University of East London. He is advisor on computer-based work-based learning for the UK Government's University for Industry project.

Alison Wolf is Executive Director of the International Centre for Research on Assessment and Head of the Mathematical Sciences Group at the Institute of Education, University of London, UK.

Studies in the Postmodern Theory of Education

General Editors
Joe L. Kincheloe & Shirley R. Steinberg

Counterpoints publishes the most compelling and imaginative books being written in education today. Grounded on the theoretical advances in criticalism, feminism, and postmodernism in the last two decades of the twentieth century, Counterpoints engages the meaning of these innovations in various forms of educational expression. Committed to the proposition that theoretical literature should be accessible to a variety of audiences, the series insists that its authors avoid esoteric and jargonistic languages that transform educational scholarship into an elite discourse for the initiated. Scholarly work matters only to the degree it affects consciousness and practice at multiple sites. Counterpoints' editorial policy is based on these principles and the ability of scholars to break new ground, to open new conversations, to go where educators have never gone before.

For additional information about this series or for the submission of manuscripts, please contact:

> Joe L. Kincheloe & Shirley R. Steinberg
> c/o Peter Lang Publishing, Inc.
> 275 Seventh Avenue, 28th floor
> New York, New York 10001

To order other books in this series, please contact our Customer Service Department:

> (800) 770-LANG (within the U.S.)
> (212) 647-7706 (outside the U.S.)
> (212) 647-7707 FAX

Or browse online by series:

> www.peterlangusa.com